The Israeli-Palestinian *Road Map for Peace*

A Critical Analysis

Derick L. Hulme, Jr.

University Press of America,® Inc.
Lanham · Boulder · New York · Toronto · Plymouth, UK

Copyright © 2009 by
University Press of America,® Inc.
4501 Forbes Boulevard
Suite 200
Lanham, Maryland 20706
UPA Acquisitions Department (301) 459-3366

Estover Road
Plymouth PL6 7PY
United Kingdom

All rights reserved
Printed in the United States of America
British Library Cataloging in Publication Information Available

Library of Congress Control Number: 2008934817
ISBN-13: 978-0-7618-4370-2 (paperback : alk. paper)
ISBN-10: 0-7618-4370-1 (paperback : alk. paper)
eISBN-13: 978-0-7618-4371-9
eISBN-10: 0-7618-4371-X

∞™ The paper used in this publication meets the minimum
requirements of American National Standard for Information
Sciences—Permanence of Paper for Printed Library Materials,
ANSI Z39.48—1984

For Charlotte Jude Hulme,
With all my love

TABLE OF CONTENTS

Preface … vii

Acknowledgments … ix

1. Introduction … 1
2. Context—Process … 13
3. Context—Substance … 37
4. Context—Terrorism … 57
5. The *Road Map for Peace* … 91
6. Conclusion … 125

Notes … 137

Selected Bibliography … 193

Index … 221

About the Author … 241

PREFACE

The eruption of the al-Aqsa Intifada in September 2000 left in tatters the *Oslo Accords*, the most promising effort to date to resolve the decades-old Israeli-Palestinian conflict. Seeking to prevent the Palestinian Authority's (PA) complete collapse, forestall Islamist militants' growing power, and address Israelis' security concerns, the Bush administration embraced a "two state solution" as the foundation of a renewed effort to revive the moribund "peace process". Conceived in mid-2002, the *Road Map to a Permanent Two-State Solution to the Israeli-Palestinian Conflict* sought to enlist the good offices of the European Union, Russia, and the United Nations Secretary-General in resolving one of the international community's most longstanding and dangerous disputes. Procedurally focused, the "performance-based" *Road Map* called upon Israel and the PA to undertake parallel measures to reduce violence, strengthen Palestinian governmental institutions, and address pressing humanitarian concerns prior to establishing an independent Palestinian state and securing a final, comprehensive, and lasting peace; the US and its "Quartet" partners were to assist, facilitate, and monitor a process envisioned to be completed by December 2005.

Launched amid cautious optimism, the *Road Map* foundered almost immediately. Neither Israel nor the PA proved willing *and* able to fulfill their respective commitments, while the Quartet remained little more than an impotent bystander to ongoing hostilities. While scholars have noted the unique challenges confronting *conflict resolution* in contrast to *dispute settlement* exercises, the *Road Map*'s failure was both foreseeable *and* preventable. Intractable differences between Israelis and Palestinians about such "final status" issues as Jerusalem, borders, settlements, and refugees were exacerbated by the divergent historical sympathies of Quartet members; the US special relationship with Israel contrasted sharply with Russian, EU, and UN concern about Palestinians continuing lack of statehood. In addition, the *Road Map* confronted significant process oriented disagreements. The non-US Quartet members, resentful of

Preface

Washington's post-1967 dominance of peacemaking efforts, insisted upon the Quartet's leadership of an empowered, multilateral peace process defined by ambitious deadlines, parallel performance requirements, and comprehensive objectives. In contrast, the US embraced a Washington-dominated, bilaterally focused effort sensitive to Israeli concerns about artificial deadlines, an "imposed" peace, and an international conference model of negotiation, and to Jerusalem's emphasis on sequential obligations, incremental negotiations, and "performance" based criteria for progress.

While the *Road Map*'s obvious hurdles were daunting, policymakers' shortcomings doomed *any* prospects for success. Washington's refusal to countenance meaningful input in the initiative's formulation was especially problematic. The Bush administration's effective exclusion of both its Quartet "partners" and the principals themselves from the drafting process mitigated against the development of a shared "ownership stake" in the initiative, while reinforcing widespread resentments concerning US unilateralism and Jerusalem's fears about an imposed settlement. In addition to such an ill-considered approach to the *Road Map*'s development, the failure of Israeli, Palestinian, and US leaders to identify, manage, and exploit the pendular dynamic of terror squandered a fleeting moment of diplomatic opportunity. The mistaken, and widely shared, assumption that terrorism necessarily forecloses negotiations prevented policymakers from recognizing those domestic political and international strategic developments that afforded an all-too-rare possibility for achieving lasting conflict resolution. As ostensibly intractable transnational conflicts proliferate, it is imperative that decisionmakers develop those conceptual skills and perceptual sensitivities requisite for enhancing prospects for achieving longterm peace and security.

Derick L. Hulme, Jr.
Alma, MI
June 2008

ACKNOWLEDGMENTS

I wish to thank the following individuals for their contributions to this book. Svitlana Kobzar, Shabam Mirsaeedi, and Amy Willey provided research assistance, Barbara Tripp, Olivia Hulme, and Charlotte Hulme copyediting support, and archivists at the Nixon Presidential Materials Project and Gerald R. Ford and Jimmy Carter Presidential Libraries invaluable assistance. The editorial staff at University Press of America was unfailingly helpful and generous with their time. Most importantly, I want to thank my lovely family—my wife, Diana, and daughters, Olivia and Charlotte—for their patience and good humor throughout the project.

INTRODUCTION

A confluence of factors, including escalating Israeli-Palestinian violence, the US-led invasion of Iraq, and the Bush administration's post-9/11 "war on terror," prompted the 30 April 2003 release of the *Road Map to a Permanent Two-State Solution to the Israeli-Palestinian Conflict.* Sponsored by the US, the European Union (EU), Russia, and the United Nations (the "Quartet"), it articulated fundamental principles and procedures by which to achieve a full and final resolution of the Israeli-Palestinian conflict. Unfortunately, little progress had been achieved by the *Road Map*'s anticipated completion date of December 2005, highlighting the difficulties of third party efforts to resolve longstanding, existentially-rooted national conflicts.

OVERVIEW

The "performance-based and goal driven" *Road Map*, seeking to "end the occupation that began in 1967" by facilitating the "emergence of an independent, democratic, and viable Palestinian state living side by side in peace and security with Israel and its other neighbors," asserted that a "two state solution . . . will only be achieved through an end to violence and terrorism, when the Palestinian people have a leadership acting decisively against terror and willing and able to build a practicing democracy based on tolerance and liberty, and through Israel's readiness to do what is necessary for a democratic Palestinian state to be established." Its initial phase, entitled, "Ending terror and violence, normalizing Palestinian life, and building Palestinian institutions," called on the Palestinian Authority (PA) to address Israel's pervasive sense of insecurity by ending "violence and terrorism and undertak[ing] visible efforts on the ground to arrest, disrupt, and restrain individuals and groups conducting and planning violent attacks on Israelis anywhere," including deploying its "security apparatus" to pursue "sustained, targeted, and effective operations aimed at confronting all those engaged in terror and dismantlement of terrorist capabilities and infrastructure." Israel likewise was to call "for an immediate end to violence against

Palestinian [sic] everywhere," "progressively resume security cooperation" with the PA, and engage in "no actions undermining trust, including deportations, attacks on civilians[,] confiscation and/or demolition of Palestinian homes and property, . . . [and] destruction of Palestinian institutions and infrastructure."[1]

The *Road Map*'s Phase I also included significant non-security related obligations. Most importantly, Palestinians were to "undertake comprehensive political reform," including creating a draft constitution "based on strong parliamentary democracy and cabinet with empowered prime minister," achieving a "genuine separation of powers, including any necessary Palestinian legal reforms for this purpose," and conducting "free, open, and fair elections" "in the context of open debate and transparent candidate selection/electoral campaign based on a free, multiparty process." In addition to facilitating such efforts, particularly those concerning "election assistance, registration of voters, movement of candidates and voting officials," Israel also was required to take "all necessary steps to help normalize Palestinian life," including "lifting curfews," "easing restrictions on movement of persons and goods," "allowing full, safe, and unfettered access of international and humanitarian personnel," "immediately dismantl[ing] settlement outposts erected since March 2001," and "freez[ing] all settlement activity (including natural growth of settlements)."[2]

The *Road Map*'s Phase II focused on "creating an independent Palestinian state with provisional borders and attributes of sovereignty . . . as a way station to a permanent status settlement," while identifying such "primary goals" as "continued comprehensive security performance and effective security cooperation, continued normalization of Palestinian life and institution-building," "ratification of a democratic Palestinian constitution," "formal establishment of office of prime minister," and "consolidation of political reform." It also advocated pursuing "a comprehensive Middle East peace" defined by Arab restoration of "pre-intifada links to Israel" and "[r]evival of multilateral engagement on issues including regional water resources, environment, economic development, refugees, and arms control issues."[3]

Phase III, seeking a "final and comprehensive permanent status agreement that ends the Israel-Palestinian conflict . . . and fulfills the vision of two states, Israel and sovereign, independent, democratic and viable Palestine, living side-by-side in peace and security," highlighted the need for "consolidation of reform and stabilization of Palestinian institutions," "[c]ontinued sustained and effective security performance, and sustained, effective security cooperation." It also stressed links among "a comprehensive Middle East settlement between Israel and Lebanon and Israel and Syria," Israeli-Palestinian negotiations, and "Arab state acceptance of full normal relations with Israel and security for all the states of the region."[4]

While acknowledging deep divisions between Israelis and Palestinians over security, territory, humanitarian responsibilities, political institutions, and leadership, the *Road Map* identified only the most general principles upon which such issues were to be resolved. Referencing UN Security Council Resolutions 242, 338, and 1397, it advocated a "just, fair, and realistic solution to the refugee issue," supported "a negotiated resolution on the status of Jerusalem that takes into account the political and religious concerns of both sides, and protects the religious interests of Jews, Christians and Muslims worldwide," endorsed establishing a "viable" Palestinian state with borders designed "to enhance maximum territorial contiguity," and called for "further action on settlements" in the context of ending Israel's post-1967 "occupation". Missing, however, were both specific proposals upon which negotiations might be initiated and outlines of a possible "comprehensive permanent status agreement."[5]

Such substantive ambiguity reflected the Quartet members' conviction that, given their own fundamental disagreements about the Israeli-Palestinian conflict, the *Road Map* must remain inherently process oriented. While the *Road Map*'s endorsement of a "two-state solution" reflected recent US acceptance of its Quartet partners' longstanding objective, Bush remained sympathetic to Israeli security concerns, skeptical of Palestinians' commitment to a negotiated settlement, and loathe to attenuate deep-rooted political, diplomatic, economic, military, and intelligence ties with Israel; Russia, the EU, and the UN questioned Israel's commitment to land for peace negotiations, readiness to engage with Palestinian leaders, and willingness to compromise for peace. Such differences contributed to divergent perspectives concerning the *Road Map*'s implementation. While the EU, Russia, and the UN embraced the *Road Map*'s language of "clear phases, timelines, target dates, and benchmarks aiming at progress through reciprocal steps by the two parties," as well as its insistence that the Quartet "assist and facilitate implementation of the plan," "evaluate the parties' performance," provide "consensus judgement" about transitioning between phases, convene two international conferences to promote "Palestinian economic recovery" and progress toward "a final, permanent status resolution," and lend necessary "operational support," the US shared Israeli reservations concerning both the timetable for implementation and Quartet responsibilities. Dismissing its partners' concerns that realization of Israel's Phase I security and terror related objectives absent parallel progress on settlements and normalization measures risked premature Israeli withdrawal from the *Road Map* process, the US was willing to tolerate slippage in the implementation timetable, preferring to achieve critical Phase I objectives rather than proceeding prematurely to Phase III's final, comprehensive peace. Similarly, the US shared little of its colleagues' enthusiasm for expansive interpretations of the Quartet's monitoring, evaluating, supporting, facilitating, and assisting responsibilities, fearing "mission creep" in the direction of a Quartet imposed peace.[6]

OBSTACLES

Objectives

The *Road Map* confronted serious obstacles, including, most significantly, disagreements about the very nature of its objectives. Couched in the rhetoric of negotiated *settlement* and Israeli-Palestinian *conflict*,[7] the *Road Map* blurred fundamental differences both among Quartet members and between Israelis and Palestinians about the basic character of the Israeli-Palestinian relationship. Buchanan's discussion of conflict theory is instructive, noting that although "the terms *disputes* and *conflicts* are used interchangeably, as are *settlement* and *resolution*," "these terms have distinctive meanings. 'Disputes' involve negotiable interests, while 'conflicts' are concerned with issues that are not negotiable, issues that relate to ontological human needs that cannot be compromised. Accordingly, 'settlement' refers to negotiated or arbitrated outcomes of disputes, while 'resolution' refers to outcomes of a conflict situation that must satisfy the inherent needs of all. Hence we have *dispute settlement* and *conflict resolution*."[8] If "conflict resolution [thus] is a fundamentally different exercise from any settlement process," it is imperative to conduct a "thorough analysis of the dynamics of the process . . . [to] reveal whether it is truly a conflict resolution process which results in a just and comprehensive peace or whether it is a conflict management exercise by the powerful to anaesthetize a minor irritant, which occasionally becomes a problem."[9]

While the *Road Map* sanctioned a "two state solution to the Israeli-Palestinian" conflict, Quartet members' embrace of competing "psychologies of victimhood," one espoused by Israelis, the other by Palestinians, prompted the US to emphasize *dispute settlement* while the UN, Russia, and EU focused on *conflict resolution*. Montville's characterization of "victimhood," the "main components" of which "are a history of violent, traumatic aggression and loss; a conviction that the aggression was unjustified by any standard; and an often unuttered fear on the part of the victim group that the aggressor will strike again at some feasible time in the future," highlights the impact of divergent historical understandings on the *Road Map*'s implementation. The assumption by "most Israelis . . . that Gentiles, at best, are indifferent to Israel's survival and, at worst, actively conspire to destroy the state," a perspective that "reflected the deep sense of victimisation Jews had suffered before 1948 and the establishment of Israel and since in the face of Arab hostility," had resonated with successive US administrations, which recognized the myriad threats confronting the Jewish state, including those "from the Arab world, from the *intifada*, from terrorist attacks, from a history of persecution, from being a minority in the region, from international legitimation of the PLO, from the Israeli-Palestinian demographic imbalance, [and] from Arab Israelis joining the *intifada* or demanding more institutional representation and from international acceptance of the Palestinian Authority as an equal member of international fora."[10]

Bush's support of Israel as the "establishment state actor" vis-à-vis the Palestinians as its substate antagonist informed his preoccupation with the *Road Map*'s normalization, rather than redistributive and innovative, features.[11] Focusing on the *Road Map*'s potential for "ending terror and violence, normalizing Palestinian life, and building Palestinian institutions,"[12] and thus on transitioning from an "unmanageable" military/political stage to a "conflict management" or "reduction stage," rather than to a "conflict resolution" or "peace stage," he insisted on Palestinians reforming government structures, curtailing Arafat's power, and abandoning "terrorism" and "violence," while accepting Sharon's reliance upon "economic and military coercive power as the ultimate 'conflict resolvers.'"[13] Such a "normalization first" approach, one that emphasized "'enhanced security for Israel and a durable regional peace', basically meaning the acceptance of Israel into the regional fold under US hegemony, but without too many questions raised about the welfare and rights of the peoples of the region, particularly the Palestinians," undermined prospects both for normalization measures and for the *Road Map*'s more ambitious innovative and redistributive objectives. Israel, as "an established state actor" within "the existing state-centred world order structure," characterized "its ongoing recourse to violence as part of the legitimate security function of the state," and thus claimed "plausible deniability for any of its immoral and violent actions, . . . allowing it to continue virtually without let or hindrance." The PA's leadership, rejecting any effort to "freeze their conflict behaviour without promising them a resolution that will end the Israeli occupation," dismissed the very premise that normalization could occur absent contemporaneous pursuit of innovative and redistributive goals.[14]

Far more sympathetic than Washington to Palestinian disillusionment with US-mediated incremental negotiations dating to the Nixon administration, as well as angst over "unemployment, lack of sovereignty, expropriations of land, emigration, expulsions, closure of the territories, Israeli bureaucratic hassles, Israeli politicians' talk of 'transfer' of Palestinian population, lack or erosion of democracy in both Israel and the occupied territories, IDF [Israeli Defense Force] death squads and corruption," the EU, Russia, and the UN emphasized conflict resolution rather than dispute settlement.[15] They were receptive to Palestinian arguments that Israel, supported by the US, had utilized dispute settlement efforts "to continue their policy of a fait accompli on the ground," consolidating its hold over the Occupied Territories through the "new settlements, the expropriations, the confiscation of land, the keeping of prisoners in the jails."[16] They thus insisted that normalization could be achieved only when coupled with immediate and tangible progress on innovative and redistributive objectives, and demanded that neither Bush nor Sharon use the *Road Map* to reinforce Israel's position as "*primus inter pares* in regional terms."[17]

Substance

Disagreements about the *Road Map*'s objectives were exacerbated by deep-rooted differences concerning the core issues of the Israeli-Palestinian conflict, including borders, Jerusalem, refugees, security, and settlements. The UN, EU, and Russia, sharing Palestinians' perspective on "international legitimacy," insisted on implementing *all* relevant UN General Assembly and Security Council Resolutions. UN Security Council Resolution 242's "land for peace" formula was to be applied to Israeli-Palestinian relations, with Palestinians recognizing Israel's "territorial integrity," "political independence," and "right to live in peace within secure and recognized boundaries free from threats or acts of force" and Israel withdrawing from Gaza and the West Bank to allow for establishment of an independent Palestinian state. Achieving a just settlement of the refugee problem was to be premised upon UN General Assembly Resolution 194's "right of return" principle in which "refugees wishing to return to their homes and live at peace with their neighbours should be permitted to do so" and compensation "paid for the property of those choosing not to return and for loss of or damage to property which, under principles of international law or in equity, should be made good by the Governments or authorities responsible."[18] Israeli settlements in Gaza and the West Bank were criticized as "a serious obstacle to the peace process" and as "illegal under international law," while Jerusalem's deportation of Palestinian civilians and use of "repressive measures" were condemned for contravening the 1949 *Geneva Convention Relative to the Protection of Civilian Persons in Time of War*.[19]

The US, while acknowledging Palestinians' "legitimate rights" and sensitive to refugees' hardships, deviated little from its Israeli ally on most issues related to the Israeli-Palestinian conflict. Although an architect of Resolution 242 and advocate of its "land for peace" approach, Washington, in contrast to the EU, Russia, and the UN, endorsed Israel's position that its withdrawal provisions applied only to *some* of the Occupied Territories, and thus were not intended to establish the 1967 borders as final lines of demarcation.[20] It similarly affirmed Israeli arguments concerning the unacceptability of Resolution 194's unlimited "right of return," need for Jerusalem to "remain undivided" under Israeli sovereignty, and refusal to abandon settlements absent tangible progress on security matters.[21]

Process

Differences over process and procedure, including perhaps most importantly the nature and scope of Quartet responsibilities, further complicated the *Road Map*'s implementation. After turning its full attention to the Middle East following the 1967 War, including cultivating economic, military, and political ties with Israel, the US consistently rejected international pressures to "impose" terms of peace on its newfound ally. Henry Kissinger, Assistant for National Security Affairs, observed in February 1969, "if we pressured Israel we would give encouragement to Arab radicals and Soviet clients, who would see it as a vindication of their intransigence and of their Soviet connection; for the same reason such pressure could also drive Israel to extreme actions, or at least to dig in and concede nothing."[22] Secretary of State George Shultz expressed similar concerns in 1988. Rejecting calls for an international conference "that would have an authoritative role or plenipotentiary powers," he argued, "No sovereign state would agree to attend the kind of conference that would presume to pass judgment on issues of national security"; he insisted that any conference "be specifically enjoined from intruding in the negotiations, imposing solutions, or vetoing what had been agreed bilaterally." While acknowledging the role of third parties in "find[ing] the right inducements to draw the parties off the battlefield and into the negotiating room," Shultz stressed that the *sine qua non* of successful negotiations was "the readiness of the *parties* to exploit opportunities, confront hard choices, and make fair and mutual concessions."[23] Bush likewise emphasized the Quartet's limited role in facilitating "discussions between the parties," rather than its responsibility to devise and implement terms of peace.

In contrast, the EU, the UN, and Russia stressed the Quartet's "active, sustained, and operational support" in "monitoring" progress, "launch[ing] a process . . . leading to a final, permanent status resolution," and determining through "consensus judgment" the timing of the *Road Map*'s implementation.[24] Such activist ambitions were rooted in longstanding desires to transcend Washington's post-1967 dominance of Middle East diplomacy. The EU, having long been thwarted in efforts "to play a special role" in promoting Middle East peace, sought diplomatic influence reflecting its "traditional ties" to the region and commensurate with its growing international stature;[25] increasingly acerbic differences with the Bush administration over Iraq, Iran, North Korea, international trade, and the Kyoto Protocol only reinforced such ambitions. Kofi Annan, United Nations Secretary-General, likewise sought to wrest the Middle East peace process from Washington's proprietary stranglehold, highlighting the UN's critical role in forging multilateral consensus,[26] while President Vladimir Putin's efforts to address post-Soviet Russia's waning power and prestige centered increasingly on assuming leadership responsibilities in resolving the Israeli-Palestinian conflict.

While seeking increased influence vis-à-vis the US through the Quartet's multilateral framework, Russia, the EU, and the UN also emphasized the Quartet's critical role in resolving "the question of Palestine," long perceived to be "the core of the Arab-Israeli conflict,"[27] within the context of overwhelming Israeli military and economic power. Stressing that the *Road Map*'s success depended upon "direct discussions between the parties," the Quartet's non-US members highlighted the importance of a "diplomacy among equals" approach. Moscow's support for such a strategy dated to the post-Yom Kippur War period when it first accorded the Palestine Liberation Organization (PLO) trappings of international legitimacy, including permitting it "to open an office and establish a permanent representative in Moscow," endorsing the Rabat Arab Summit's designation of the PLO as "the sole legitimate representative of the Palestinian people," and supporting the UN's inclusion of the PLO in discussions concerning Palestinian affairs.[28] Subsequent statements by top Soviet officials, including Foreign Minister Andrei Gromyko, Communist Party Chairman Leonid Brezhnev, and President Mikhail Gorbachev emphasized the need to secure "the legitimate rights of the Arab people of Palestine" through "a comprehensive and just settlement,"[29] rejected the US "bid for dominance in the Middle East," stressed Soviet willingness to "work in a constructive spirit" within "the framework of a specially convened international conference" on behalf of "an honest collective search for an all-embracing just and realistic settlement,"[30] argued that the Security Council's permanent members must guarantee any settlement, and insisted "that preparations for an international conference on the Middle East involving *all the sides* concerned should be a focal point for collective efforts to bring about a settlement."[31] Foreign Minister Eduard Shevardnadze, seeking to ensure "that the Palestinian people can realize their right to self-determination," stressed the need "to internationalize the search for a solution," the value of "a multilateral dialogue" in achieving an "all-embracing" settlement, the role of "intermediaries" in "ensur[ing] that the threads of talks and dialogue do not break," and the importance of the Secretary-General establishing a "post of his special representative on the Near East."[32]

The European Union likewise had long emphasized that securing "the legitimate rights of the Palestinians" demanded commitment to multilateral diplomacy.[33] The European Economic Community's [EC] 1980 *Venice Declaration* stressed the EC and UN's role in pursuing a "just solution" to the "Palestinian problem,"[34] while its 1987 *Brussels Declaration* asserted that "an international peace conference to be held under the auspices of the United Nations" would "provide a suitable framework for the necessary negotiations between the parties directly concerned."[35] Subsequent EC meetings reaffirmed the Community's "readiness to participate actively in the search for a negotiated solution" and support for utilizing "the framework of an international peace conference under the auspices of the United Nations, as the appropriate forum for the direct negotiations between the parties concerned," including the PLO.[36]

The UN demonstrated particular sensitivity to the advantages afforded Palestinians by inclusion in multilateral fora. Following the Yom Kippur War, the General Assembly (GA) recognized the PLO as the "sole legitimate representative of the Palestinian people," acknowledged Palestinians' "right to national independence and sovereignty," insisted that Palestinians be "a principal party in the establishment of a just and desirable peace in the Middle East," invited Arafat to speak before the GA and the PLO to participate "in the sessions and the work of the General Assembly in the capacity of observer," and created the "Committee on the Exercise of the Inalienable Rights of the Palestinian People."[37] In subsequent years, it stressed the importance of convening an "International Peace Conference on the Middle East, under the auspices of the United Nations, with the participation of all parties to the conflict, including the Palestine Liberation Organization, on an equal footing, and the five permanent members of the Security Council, based on Security Council Resolutions 242 (1967) and 338 (1973) and the legitimate national rights of the Palestinian people, primarily the right to self-determination."[38] Such a conference was to "constitute a major contribution by the United Nations towards the realization of a just solution to the question of Palestine."[39]

Process oriented differences extended beyond disagreements over the Quartet's role in facilitating peace. Reflecting policies dating to the early 1970s, the US placed far less emphasis than its Quartet partners on quickly achieving the *Road Map*'s ultimate objective, "a final and comprehensive settlement of the Israeli-Palestinian conflict," focusing instead on pursuing its Phase I goals of "ending terror and violence, normalizing Palestinian life, and building Palestinian institutions."[40] Such incrementalism reflected both pragmatic assessments and strategic priorities. Rooted in Kissinger's skepticism about the wisdom and efficacy of comprehensive settlement efforts, Bush adhered to the former Secretary of State's "step-by-step" approach. Premised upon the belief that "neither a lack of direct communication nor unfamiliarity with the enemy has been responsible for the persistent failure to produce an Arab-Zionist (or an Arab-Israeli) accord," and sensitive to Palestinian and Israeli tendencies "to enter the negotiating process for purposes other than actually making concessions to and peace with one another,"[41] Kissinger rejected comprehensive negotiations as likely to isolate the US and Israel, unify the pro-Palestinian Europeans, Japanese, and Soviet Union, and provide a platform for radical Palestinians to torpedo negotiations.[42] Bush echoed Kissinger's concerns, arguing that comprehensive negotiations privileged Palestinians vis-à-vis Israel, enhanced EU, Russian, and UN influence at US expense, empowered radical and extremist elements on both sides, and risked high profile failure.[43] Focused on stabilizing the volatile and strategically significant Middle East, buttressing Israel as a bulwark in the "war on terror," and cultivating Arab moderates, Bush emphasized securing *tangible* improvements in Palestinians' daily lives while ending terror and violence against Israel. While expressing support for a "comprehensive settlement," the Administration demonstrated little sense of urgency about transitioning from Phase I's limited normalization objectives to Phase II's goal of "creating an independent Palestinian state with provisional borders and attributes of sovereignty . . . as a way station to a permanent status settlement."[44] Bush's unwavering support of Sharon's policies—including marginalizing Arafat, conducting aggressive counterterror operations in Gaza and the West Bank, and refusing to implement Israel's Phase I obligations prior to the *complete* cessation of Palestinian violence—testified to the Administration's willingness to accept slippage in the *Road Map*'s implementation in favor of achieving Israel's most pressing security and terror related objectives.

Russian, EU, and UN skepticism concerning Washington's incremental preferences—reflecting concerns that such an approach previously had enhanced US influence, facilitated Israeli control over the Occupied Territories, fractured pan-Arab solidarity, and marginalized Palestinianism—found expression in the *Road Map*'s ambitious timetable. Calling for Phase I to be completed within 31 days and for a "comprehensive settlement" to be reached within 32 months, the *Road Map* abandoned the rhetoric of "peace process" and extended implementation deadlines that had defined Kissinger's "step-by-step" diplomacy, the Camp David *Frameworks*, and the *Oslo Accords* in favor of a commitment to "clear phases, timelines, target dates, and benchmarks" on behalf of rapid "progress through reciprocal steps by the two parties in the political, security, economic, humanitarian, and institution-building fields" leading directly to negotiation of "a final, permanent status resolution." The Quartet's active engagement, coupled with the *Road Map*'s "goal driven" and "performance-based" character, was to provide both Palestinians and Israelis with the confidence necessary to pursue "good faith" implementation of their respective "obligations."[45]

Russian preference for a comprehensive settlement reflected both current realities and historical experience. After having been invited by Nixon and Kissinger to co-chair the post-Yom Kippur War Geneva Conference, the Soviets quickly surmised that it was intended only to provide "a multilateral veneer for subsequent bilateral talks over which the US would exercise a dominant role." Moscow bristled at US efforts "to split the conference into subgroups—Egyptian-Israeli, Syrian-Israeli, and Jordanian-Israeli," as well as at its subsequent mediation of Egyptian-Israeli and Syrian-Israeli disengagement agreements.[46] Frustration at "step-by-step's" marginalization of Soviet regional influence was compounded by concern over its impact on Arab negotiating assets vis-à-vis Israel. Reacting to the 1979 Egyptian-Israeli *Peace Treaty*, Gromyko noted, "The separate deal between Egypt and Israel resolves nothing. It is a means designed to lull the vigilance of peoples. ... We are in favour of a comprehensive and just settlement ... The Soviet Union sides firmly with Arab peoples who resolutely reject deals at the expense of their legitimate interests."[47] Brezhnev, addressing the 26th Congress of the Communist Party in 1981, likewise observed, "In its bid for dominance in the Middle East, the United States has taken the path of the Camp David policy, dividing the Arab world and organizing a separate deal between Israel and Egypt."[48] Moscow's 1984 *Proposals on a Middle East Settlement* returned to the theme of comprehensive negotiations, stressing the need "to find solutions to all aspects of [a] Middle East settlement" and the importance of addressing collectively the "organically interconnected components of [a] settlement."[49] Gorbachev reaffirmed Soviet opposition to "any separate deals," arguing that "they are only holding back and thwarting the search for a genuine settlement"; he called for an international conference, "a normal, effective conference, rather than a front for separate talks," to pursue a comprehensive settlement.[50] Putin, anxious to reestablish Russia's diplomatic *bona fides* following the turmoil of the 1990s, was particularly attracted to the opportunities afforded by the *Road Map*'s commitment to "a comprehensive peace on all tracks, including the Syrian-Israeli and Lebanese-Israeli tracks."[51]

The EU shared Russia's longstanding skepticism toward US dominated incremental negotiations. Supportive of Palestinians' "legitimate rights" and committed to achieving a "comprehensive" settlement through an "international peace conference under the auspices of the United Nations,"[52] the EC had criticized throughout the 1980s the tendency of bilateral agreements such as the Egyptian-Israeli *Peace Treaty* to exacerbate regional "tensions," compromise Palestinian interests, and attenuate Europeans' "traditional ties" to the region; it stressed that "a comprehensive solution to the Israeli-Arab conflict [is] more necessary and pressing than ever."[53] Concerns about US incrementalism were only heightened by *Oslo*'s final collapse in September 2000. While the *Accords*' initial success had generated expectations for a timely conclusion of "permanent status negotiations," its stunning evisceration heightened concerns about expending scarce diplomatic capital on behalf of non-comprehensive objectives. The EU was particularly concerned that US sanctioned incrementalism would sacrifice its primary interests—securing Palestinian national objectives and strengthening Euro-Mediterranean relations—on behalf of the US-Israeli special relationship.

Although the June 1967 War prompted the UN initially to focus on articulating fundamental principles upon which Middle East peace should be premised,[54] it quickly turned its attention to multilateral efforts to secure "a comprehensive, just and lasting solution to the Arab-Israeli conflict."[55] Insisting both that "the question of Palestine is the core of the Arab-Israeli conflict" and that the international community acknowledge Palestinians' "inalienable rights," including those of "self-determination without external interference," "national independence," and "sovereignty,"[56] the General Assembly recognized the PLO as Palestinians' "sole legitimate representative" and demanded that "the Palestinian people [be] a principall party" in negotiating comprehensive peace.[57] Its creation of the Committee on the Exercise of the Inalienable Rights of the Palestinian People provided a forum for ongoing consideration of the Israeli occupation, US diplomatic, economic, and military support of Israel, and Arabs' temptation to pursue "land for peace" negotiations at Palestinian expense.[58] *Oslo*'s implosion, marked by escalating violence, Israeli reoccupation of parts of the Occupied Territories, and collapse of PA administrative and security capabilities, coupled with concern over Bush's post-9/11 unilateralist tendencies and reflexive support of Israel, reinvigorated UN efforts, led by Kofi Annan, on behalf of comprehensive regional peace.[59]

TERRORISM

Terrorism, as defined, perceived, and experienced by Israelis and Palestinians alike, contributed to mutual and deep-rooted feelings of "victimisation" in the decades preceding the *Road Map*'s launch.[60] Israel's forcible displacement of Palestinians during the 1948 and 1967 wars, expropriation and settlement of Palestinian territory following the Yom Kippur War, and policy of collective punishment in response to the two Palestinian intifadas contributed both to Palestinians' "collective sense of threat" vis-à-vis Israel's superior military, economic, and political power and to the type of "painful losses, in lives, in territory, in justice and in legitimacy," that so complicated "traditional methods of diplomatic or political mediation and negotiation."[61] Similarly, Palestinians' post-1967 resort to transnational terrorism, including hostage taking, hijacking, bombing, murder, and, most recently, suicide attacks, reinforced Israelis' outrage and refusal to negotiate with Palestinians absent both the PA's "unconditional public acceptance of Israel's right to exist" and its unequivocal commitment to altering Palestinian political, legal, economic, and institutional realities in support of peace.[62]

However, while terrorism often foreclosed the very possibility of Israeli-Palestinian negotiations, threatening national and international strategic, political, and economic objectives, "compromis[ing] the safety, security, [and] morale of citizens," and provoking "intense public preoccupation with the issue and strong pressures . . . to strike out at the perpetrators," its *pendular dynamic*, or the evolving relationship among "terrorists' actions, decisionmakers' international strategic perspective, and the domestic political environment," afforded episodic opportunities to pursue bilateral and multilateral initiatives in search of peace.[63] Recognizing both that "similar acts of terror will elicit different responses as strategic and political conditions evolve and their relative influence varies," and that changes in terrorists' strategy and tactics may impact strategic interests and domestic political influences, helps explain policymakers' potential to fluctuate between confrontational and conciliatory approaches to terrorism.[64]

Five "distinct phases" may be identified in an actor's "experience with transnational terror that delimit the response options available to policymakers and that define both policy constraints and opportunities."[65] Phase I, characterized by terrorism's strategic and political irrelevance, presents neither significant constraints nor imperatives for decisionmakers; it likewise provides few incentives for negotiated settlement. Although "defined by the emerging political salience of transnational terrorism within the domestic arena," Phase II affords policymakers significant latitude "in determining appropriate responses" as the public, media, interest groups, and legislative actors remain largely "uninformed about terrorist actors and motivations" and engaged only episodically with the issue. Transnational terrorism's Phase III emergence as "a commonplace occurrence directly impacting domestic perceptions of security and wellbeing" generates significant pressures to pursue "punitive, confrontational, and nonconcessionary policies" *and* to deliver *tangible* progress in mitigating fear and anxiety; negotiations present substantial political risks with few obvious benefits.[66] While transnational terrorism's strategic relevance escalates dramatically in Phase IV, creating "imperatives to protect vital national interests," its failure to engage domestic constituencies "affords significant discretion in the choice of response options." Tactical accommodation of terrorist demands and/or efforts to resolve terrorists' core grievances may be pursued far more readily absent the glare of public and media attention that characterizes Phase III. Finally, Phase V is marked by transnational terrorism's development into a "longterm strategic threat with significant domestic political and security ramifications"; such a confluence of "strategic necessity and political imperative demands both visible and successful management of the terrorist threat, effectively circumscribing the range of response options available to policymakers." Tendencies to overemphasize force and discount negotiations are particularly pronounced in Phase III and Phase V's initial periods as demands for immediate results privilege nondiplomatic instruments.[67]

While interphase pendular flux establishes policymakers' initial context of constraints and opportunities, intraphase flux may dramatically alter the decisonmaking calculus. Typically reflecting growing frustration with efforts to address ongoing violence, whether through policies of confrontation or accommodation, such flux liberates leaders to explore previously unavailable options. Whether a product of inter or intraphase flux, fleeting opportunities for negotiation must be recognized and exploited by Israel, the PA, and the US if any hope is to be entertained of avoiding a repeat of the *Road Map*'s failure and of securing a final and peaceful resolution of the Israeli-Palestinian conflict.

CONTEXT—PROCESS

Stressing both a "performance-based" *and* time sensitive approach, Quartet facilitation *and* "direct discussions between the parties," and "parallel" obligations *and* unilateral responsibilities, the *Road Map* reflected deep process oriented rifts between Israel and the US on the one hand and Palestinians, the EU, Russia, and the UN on the other. Particularly serious differences emerged over the nature and extent of Quartet responsibilities, unilateral insistence on preconditions, and incrementalism's role within a "comprehensive" initiative. Such differences, rooted in Kissinger's strategic perspective, were exacerbated by terrorism's debilitating legacy, Israeli and Palestinian political institutions and processes, and the principals' skepticism concerning the decades long "peace process."

KISSINGER'S LEGACY

Recognizing the long shadow cast by Henry Kissinger's post-1973 policies—over Israel, Palestinians, the EU, Russia, UN, and subsequent US administrations alike—is critical to appreciating the *Road Map*'s perspective on process related issues. Committed to cultivating Israel as a linchpin of Middle East stability, enhancing US regional influence, and marginalizing Palestinians, the EU, Russia, and the UN, Kissinger embraced three principles with enduring import for efforts to resolve the Arab-Israeli-Palestinian conflict: US dominance over the "peace process"; no "imposed" peace by third parties; and commitment to "step-by-step" negotiations.

US Dominance

Expectations concerning third party influence over the *Road Map*'s implementation were influenced decisively by Kissinger's successful efforts as US Secretary of State and Assistant for National Security Affairs to minimize Soviet, UN, and European influence over Arab-Israeli-Palestinian relations. Such an approach, embraced by Nixon and Ford in the context of superpower rivalry, Third World dominance of the UN General Assembly, and European subservience to OPEC following the 1973-1974 Arab oil embargo, proved compelling as well for future administrations. The effect of such hegemonic tendencies was three-fold: Israel and the Palestinians developed perceptions about US participation in *any* peace process that colored expectations about the Quartet's role in the *Road Map*'s implementation; the European Union, Russia, and the UN were left woefully unprepared to assume the responsibilities envisioned for Quartet members; and the US was conditioned to view the *Road Map*'s multilateral framework principally as a means of securing "geopolitical arrangements" benefiting itself and its Israeli ally.[1]

Kissinger's emphasis on attenuating Moscow's regional presence reflected in part his belief that "the prerequisite of effective Middle East diplomacy was to reduce the Soviet influence so that progress could not be ascribed to its pressures and moderate governments gained some maneuvering room."[2] Stressing that the "Arabs must recognize that a settlement depends more on cooperation with Washington than with Moscow,"[3] he argued, "the longer the [Arab-Israeli] stalemate continued the more obvious would it become that the Soviet Union had failed to deliver what the Arabs wanted. As time went on, its Arab clients were bound to conclude that friendship with the Soviet Union was not the key to realizing their aims. Sooner or later, if we kept our nerve, this would force a reassessment of even radical Arab policy."[4] Acting to minimize Soviet influence over post-Yom Kippur War diplomacy, he insisted that the Geneva Conference, co-chaired by Washington and Moscow, be little more than a "symbolic" gathering; indeed, the conference was divided into bilateral working groups, making it "impossible for the Soviet Union to use radical Arabs as pawns to block progress at the plenary sessions."[5] Kissinger's success in securing the 1974 Israeli-Egyptian and Israeli-Syrian disengagement agreements and 1975 *Sinai II* accord furthered his efforts to prevent "the coalescence of radical Middle East forces with Soviet strategy" and to reinforce "Sadat's conviction that the United States is the only world power able to bring about a resolution of the Middle East conflict on terms satisfactory to Egypt and the Arabs."[6]

Reagan similarly insisted upon Washington's "special responsibility" in securing peace, arguing, "No other nation is in a position to deal with the key parties to the conflict on the basis of trust and reliability."[7] He embraced Carter's US-mediated Camp David framework as "the only way to proceed,"[8] endorsed "direct, bilateral negotiations between Israel and all of its neighbors," and welcomed a Geneva-inspired international conference which would initiate "a series of bilateral negotiations" and "receive reports from the parties on the status of negotiations," but which would "be specifically enjoined from intruding in the negotiations, imposing solutions, or vetoing what had been agreed bilaterally."[9] He was adamant that such a conference afford neither the Soviet Union, Arab radicals, nor Palestinians a platform by which to espouse "propagandistic and extreme positions."[10]

The Bush-orchestrated 1991 Madrid Conference adhered closely both to Reagan's admonitions and to its Geneva predecessor. Secretary of State James

Baker worked tirelessly to insure that the Conference remain "merely a ceremonial opening to direct bilateral and multilateral negotiations" and to marginalize Moscow's post-Conference diplomatic profile.[11] Clinton similarly asserted Washington's "accustomed third-party role" subsequent to the 1993 *Oslo Accords*, including "throughout the complex follow-up negotiations leading to and beyond the Cairo Agreement of May 1994," the 1994 Israeli-Jordanian *Peace Treaty*, 1995 *Oslo II Agreement*, 1997 *Hebron Accords*, 1998 *Wye River Memorandum*, and 2000 Camp David talks.[12]

Kissinger's refusal to cede diplomatic initiative extended beyond the Soviet Union to the United Nations and key European states. While sharing Nixon's general disdain for the UN—he believed it to be ineffectual, biased against Israel, and dominated by an anti-US coalition of Third World and pro-Soviet states—he particularly feared that UN involvement in Arab-Israeli negotiations would open "the door to a significant Soviet diplomatic role" while generating pressures to "deliver Israeli agreement." Kissinger supported neither UN Special Ambassador Gunnar Jarring's diplomatic efforts nor General Assembly pronouncements on such matters as Palestinians' right to self-determination.[13] Subsequent administrations remained loathe to accord the UN a meaningful role in negotiations, and were especially insistent that the Security Council neither dictate outcomes nor void negotiated agreements among the principals.

Kissinger's longstanding skepticism about EC involvement in Middle East peace efforts was confirmed by Europeans' response to the Arab oil embargo of 1973-1974. Characterizing the EC Foreign Ministers' November 1973 statement declaring the Community's readiness "to do all in their power to contribute to . . . peace" and commitment to negotiate "in the framework of the United Nations" as pandering to Arab oil producers,[14] he observed, "most of our allies were convinced that their oil supplies were better assured by adaptation to Arab political demands than by forming a united front to resist pressures"; he argued that France in particular "would not run the slightest risk of an oil cutoff . . . (and) would participate in no group or policy involving any prospect of confrontation."[15] Such weakness, coupled with the "Year of Europe's" disconcerting failure,[16] devalued the Europeans in Kissinger's eyes as reliable partners in the quest for peace.

Frustrated by its diplomatic marginalization, the EC issued the *Venice Declaration* in 1980. It observed, "the traditional ties and common interests which link Europe to the Middle East oblige them [Member States] to play a special role and now require them to work in a more concrete way toward peace," including establishing "the necessary contacts with all the parties concerned . . . to determine the form which such an initiative on their part could take."[17] Subsequent statements, including the 1987 *Brussels Declaration* and 1989 *Madrid Declaration*, reiterated Members' "particularly important political, historical, geographical, economic, religious, cultural and human links with the countries, and peoples of the Middle East," indicated that "[t]hey cannot therefore adopt a passive attitude towards a region which is so close to them nor remain indifferent to the grave problems besetting it," and argued that "an international peace conference under the auspices of the United Nations" would provide "the appropriate forum for the direct negotiations between the parties concerned."[18] However, confronted by Reagan, Bush, and Clinton's steadfast refusal to cede Washington's dominance over the Middle East peace process, the EC and its successor, the European Union, in practice did little to "impede US diplomacy."[19]

Given such longstanding success in maintaining its decisive influence over Arab-Israeli-Palestinian negotiations, it hardly was surprising that the US dictated the conditions under which the *Road Map* was issued, insisting on the prior satisfaction of demands concerning the restructuring of Palestinian governmental institutions and diminution of Arafat's powers. Having succeeded in launching the *Road Map* on his own terms, Bush rendered largely symbolic the *Road Map*'s multilateral structure, enabling Washington to manage Israeli-Palestinian relations within an internationally sanctioned framework and in a manner conducive to advancing its geostrategic interests concerning Iraq and Saddam Hussein without undue attention to its Quartet "partners" concerns. Israeli and Palestinian reactions to the *Road Map* accordingly were colored by perceptions of US policy and intentions; neither assumed the Quartet's non-US members could or would exert a meaningful counterweight to US influence.

No imposed peace

Kissinger coupled insistence on US dominance over Middle East diplomacy with an absolute refusal to impose terms of peace. He was particularly dismissive of individuals such as J. William Fulbright, chair of the Senate Foreign Relations Committee, who argued, "Because the [Mideast] conflict is a threat to the outside world, it cannot be left solely to the humors of the belligerents. I have never fully understood why some of our statesmen feel it would be a heinous crime for external parties to impose a solution. . . . I think it would be a fine thing—a useful step forward for civilization—if, in the absence of a voluntary settlement by the parties, the United Nations were to impose a peaceful settlement in the Middle East."[20] Kissinger shared Nixon's belief that "only the governments and people involved in the Arab-Israeli conflict can determine whether there will be peace in the Middle East or not. We also know that the age is past where the big powers can—or should—dictate to the smaller nations of the world where their borders should be or how they should live with their neighbors." He stressed that "the primary responsibility for achieving a peaceful settlement in the Middle East rests on the nations there themselves," rejected efforts to "try to impose a peace from the outside," and pledged US support for "peace efforts of the parties in the region themselves."[21] While never wavering in his commitment to "close consultation and close cooperation" with Israel, nor in his belief that *any* attempt to impose peace on Israel "would be rejected" and "could only serve Soviet ends by either demonstrating our impotence or being turned into a showcase of what could be exacted by Moscow's pressure," Kissinger pressured Israel to secure tactical concessions, including agreeing to attend the Geneva Conference, continuing disengagement talks with Syria, and concluding *Sinai II* with Egypt. He argued that such an approach, predicated on "an overall strategy that would be overwhelmingly in Israel's interest," enabled Israeli leaders to make necessary but unpopular concessions under cover of US pressure.[22]

The 1975 US-Israeli *Memorandum of Agreement* effectively institutionalized Kissinger's "no imposed peace" approach. Calling for "coordinated" US-Israeli policy on the timing and composition of a reconvened Geneva Conference, it also committed the US to "oppose and, if necessary, vote against any initiative in the Security Council to alter adversely the terms of reference of the Geneva Peace Conference or to change Resolutions 242 and 338 in ways which are incompatible with their original purpose."[23] Adhering to such a policy, Reagan observed, "The United States has thus far sought to play the role of mediator; we have avoided public comment on the key issues. We have always recognized—and continue to recognize—that only the voluntary agreement of those parties most directly involved in the conflict can provide an enduring solution." While indicating that the US would "put forward our own detailed proposals when we believe they can be helpful," he refrained from proffering a blueprint for the resolution of such critical issues as borders, refugees, Jerusalem, water, and security guarantees, preferring instead to articulate general principles concerning land-for-peace, Palestinian autonomy, and Israeli security.[24] Bush's *Letter of Assurances* to the Palestinians prior to the 1991 Madrid Conference reemphasized that "only direct negotiations based on UN Security Council Resolutions 242 and 338 can produce a real peace. No one can dictate the outcome in advance," and pledged US acceptance of "any outcome agreed by the parties."[25] Clinton shared a commitment to the "US as facilitator" role, resisting pressures to impose peace while committing "Secretary [of State Madeleine] Albright and I and our entire team" to do "everything we possibly can to help the parties" reach agreement.[26]

It was only after the Camp David talks' bitter failure in July 2000 and the al-Aqsa Intifada's eruption several months later that Clinton, shortly before leaving office, advanced the *Clinton Plan* that detailed with unprecedented specificity US positions on such critical issues as territory, security, Jerusalem, and refugees.[27] Although recognizing that the "only path to a just and durable resolution is through negotiation,"[28] Clinton's obvious frustration prompted him to move far beyond the role of third party mediator. In addition to specifying the extent of Israeli withdrawal from the West Bank (94-96 percent) and the need for a 1-3 percent land swap from Israel to the PA as compensation for annexed territory, he provided details concerning security arrangements, including the location of early warning stations, international forces, and Israeli military deployments, formulations for resolving sovereignty over the Western Wall, Haram Temple Mount, and Holy of Holies, and options for addressing the refugee situation.[29] However, while ostensibly portending a greater willingness to impose terms of peace, the *Clinton Plan*, coming in the waning days of a second term administration, had little import. Much as Nixon's disillusionment with the Middle East "peace process" had led to inconsequential ruminations during his final year in office about the need for he and Brezhnev to "step in, determine the proper course of action to a just settlement, and then bring the necessary pressure on our respective friends for a settlement,"[30] Clinton's last minute initiative produced no longterm change in US policy.

Step-by-Step Diplomacy

Kissinger's preoccupation with "reduc[ing] Soviet influence in the Middle East" while protecting Israeli security informed his "step-by-step" approach to negotiations, a strategy which guided US diplomacy for much of the pre-*Road Map* period. Arguing that comprehensive negotiations were likely to enhance Soviet power, encourage Arab radicalism, reinforce Palestinian rejectionism, alienate Israel, and ultimately prove unsuccessful, he highlighted the potential for "step-by-step" diplomacy to afford Israel the opportunity to negotiate bilaterally, and sequentially, with its Arab neighbors, thereby "keeping the political initiative in American hands, . . . preventing the coalescence of radical Arab and Communist pressures, . . . forestalling Soviet mischief, and . . . deferring the most contentious and painful issues until a more propitious moment." He particularly emphasized the need to minimize Palestinians' disruptive influence, observing,

> Once they (the PLO) are in the peace process, they can radicalize all the others. They'll raise all the issues the Israelis can't handle, and no other Arab can raise any other issues once the PLO is raised. . . . Our strategy is to bring the PLO into negotiations at the end, keeping them a step behind Egypt, Syria, and Jordan so that they will be manageable. Otherwise, the PLO will disrupt the negotiations by demanding more than the Arab governments want or can meet. They will have the support of the Soviets. The Israelis will reject the demand, and the negotiations will collapse.[31]

Testifying before Congress in November 1975, Harold Saunders, Deputy Assistant Secretary of State for Near Eastern and South Asian Affairs, observed, "The step-by-step approach to negotiations . . . has been based partly on the understanding that issues in the Arab-Israeli conflict take time to mature. It is obvious that thinking on the Palestinian aspects of the problem must evolve on all sides. As it does, what is not possible today may become possible."[32]

Although Carter initially was skeptical of "step-by-step" and attracted instead to "comprehensive" negotiations "incorporating all parties concerned and all questions,"[33] Sadat's initiation of direct talks with Israel undermined the likelihood that comprehensive negotiations *ever* would be pursued. While insisting that "[a]ny separate peace between Egypt and Israel, or between any Arab confrontation State and Israel, will not bring permanent peace based on justice in the entire region. . . . in the absence of a just solution to the Palestinian problem, never will there be that durable and just peace upon which the entire world insists today," Sadat acknowledged that he had "not consulted, as far as this decision is concerned [to go to Israel], with any of my colleagues and brothers, the Arab Heads of State or the confrontation States";[34] he likewise pursued Egyptian national interests, most importantly return of the Sinai Peninsula, despite Palestinian objections concerning the impact that Egyptian-Israeli accommodation would have on pursuit of their national/territorial ambitions. Seeking to capitalize on the momentum toward peace generated by the Egyptian President, Carter abandoned comprehensive negotiations, embracing instead the Camp David process premised upon Kissinger's "step-by-step" approach, accepting immediate progress toward Egyptian-Israeli peace in exchange for vague promises concerning establishing a self-governing Palestinian authority in the West Bank and Gaza.[35]

The Arab League, PLO, and frontline Arab states recognized the risks posed by the neutralization of Israel's most formidable Arab military and political adversary on the pursuit of political, territorial, and military objectives vis-à-vis the Jewish state. The Arab League responded immediately to Sadat's trip to Israel, noting, "the visit made by President el-Sadat to the Zionist entity . . . constituted a flagrant violation of the principles and objectives of the pan-Arab struggle against the Zionist enemy, a squandering of the rights of the Palestinian Arab people, a departure from the unity of the Arab ranks, . . . and the withdrawing of Arab Egypt from the front of conflict with the Zionist enemy." It decried the establishment of "an alliance between the Zionist enemy and the current Egyptian regime aimed at liquidating the Arab issue and the issue of Palestine, split[ting] the Arab nation and forfeit[ing] its national rights."[36] While the Camp David summit prompted it to declare, "it is impermissible for any side to act unilaterally in solving the Palestinian question in particular and the Arab-Zionist conflict in general," the Egyptian-Israeli *Peace Treaty* elicited calls to withdraw Arab states' ambassadors from Egypt, sever diplomatic and political ties with Cairo, eliminate all economic assistance to any agency of the Egyptian government, and suspend Egypt from the Arab League, Non-Aligned Movement, Islamic Conference, and Organization of African Unity.[37]

Condemning "Sadat's treasonous visit to the Zionist entity," Fatah, the Popular Front for the Liberation of Palestine (PFLP), Popular Democratic Front for the Liberation of Palestine (PDFLP), Sa'iqa, Popular Front for the Liberation of Palestine-General Command (PFLP-GC), Arab Liberation Front (ALF), and Palestine Liberation Front (PLF), called for the PLO, Libya, Algeria, Iraq, Yemen, and Syria to establish a "Steadfastness and Confrontation Front" "to oppose all capitulationist solutions planned by imperialism, Zionism and their Arab tools."[38] The Palestine National Council, noting that "the Camp David Agreements [pose] grave threats to the cause of Palestine and of Arab national liberation," stressed the need for "all Arab and national forces . . . to confront the Sadat conspiracy and to foil the Camp David agreement," while the PLO's Executive Committee "reaffirm[ed] its rejection" of what Arafat termed "the Camp David plot" and "the tripartite alliance—Carter, Begin, al-Sadat."[39] Syrian President Hafez al-Asad, echoing the Steadfastness and Confrontation Front's emphasis on Arab unity and insistence that the Palestinian issue was "the basic concern of all the Arabs and, consequently, no single Arab party may bargain on or undermine this commitment or take any action that would cause damage to the Palestine case and the national rights of the Palestinian people," criticized Sadat for "slander[ing] the Arab nation, to which he has turned his back, forgetting that Egypt is part of this nation," and Camp David for "disengag[ing]

[Egypt] from the Arab nation and mov[ing] [it] closer to usurper and aggressor Israel." He emphasized that Syria did "not make any distinction between one Arab territory and another, while the Camp David partners insist on making a distinction between Egyptian territory and other Arab territories."[40]

Such scathing criticisms of "step-by-step's" "go it alone" approach ultimately constrained neither Israel, the Palestinians, nor individual Arab states from pursuing bilateral negotiations seeking particularized benefits at the expense of multilateral, comprehensive initiatives. Israeli Prime Minister Yitzhak Shamir dismissed any notion that the 1991 Madrid Peace Conference represented a significant deviation from "step-by-step," observing, "We have always believed that only direct bilateral talks can bring peace. We have agreed to precede such talks with this ceremonial conference, but we hope that Arab consent to direct bilateral talks indicates an understanding that there is no other way to peace.... We believe the goal of the bilateral negotiations is to sign peace treaties between Israel and its neighbors and to reach an agreement on interim self-government arrangements with the Palestinian Arabs."[41] Bush similarly told the conferees, "what we envision is a process of direct negotiations proceeding along two tracks: one between Israel and the Arab states, the other between Israel and the Palestinians."[42] The PLO, desperate to ameliorate Intifada-induced hardships for those living in the Occupied Territories and to relieve its post-1991 Gulf War isolation, had little choice but to participate in such a gathering and to pursue subsequent secret, bilateral negotiations that ultimately produced the 1993 *Oslo Accords*.[43]

While noting in early 1994 that achieving "a comprehensive peace between Israel and its Arab neighbors" was one of his "highest foreign policy objectives,"[44] Clinton's tenure was defined by intensive efforts to secure bilateral arrangements involving Israel, the PA, Jordan, and Syria. The *Cairo Agreement, Interim Agreement on the West Bank and Gaza Strip, Hebron Accords, Wye River Memorandum,* and July 2000 Camp David talks sought to implement the 1993 *Declaration of Principles* through a series of US-mediated bilateral negotiations. A similar approach involving Israel and Jordan, and marked by the "personal involvement of the president," resulted in the 1994 Israel-Jordan *Peace Treaty*, the second such treaty between Israel and its Arab neighbors. In addition to establishing "full diplomatic and consular relations," removing "all discriminatory barriers to normal economic relations," and calling for cooperation "in combating terrorism of all kinds," it abjured hostile or discriminatory propaganda, "the threat or use of force," and "organizing, instigating, inciting, assisting, or participating in acts or threats of belligerency, hostility, subversion, or violence against the other party."[45] However reluctantly, Syria likewise abandoned its longstanding opposition to a "separate peace and partial solutions."[46] Recognizing its growing vulnerability in a period defined by Israeli-Jordanian peace, Israeli-PA negotiations, and the collapse of Russia's regional presence, Syria consented to a US-brokered meeting between Israeli Prime Minister Ehud Barak and Syrian Foreign Minister Faruk al-Shara, the goal of which was to initiate "step-by-step" patterned "negotiations which will be concluded with a [Syrian-Israeli] peace agreement."[47] Kissinger's conviction that Egypt, Syria, and Jordan were far more interested in recovering territory than in pursuing either pan-Arab cooperation or Palestinian national/territorial aspirations ultimately was vindicated as Egypt, Jordan, Syria, and the PA, some more readily than others, abandoned both the rhetoric and reality of comprehensive negotiations in favor of bilateral talks aimed at securing individual national objectives.[48]

IMPACT OF TERROR

A defining feature of Israeli-Palestinian relations for decades, terrorism's legacy of violence, disdain for political accommodation, and radicalization/polarization of Palestinian politics exacerbated those deep-rooted procedural differences among Israel, the PA, US, EU, Russia, and the UN that so complicated the *Road Map*'s implementation.

Institutionalize Violence

Although the culture of violence defining Israeli-Palestinian relations at the *Road Map*'s launch dated to events surrounding Israel's creation, the 1967 War and its immediate aftermath marked an unprecedented institutionalization of terror/violence for Palestinians and Israelis alike. The decision by Palestinian guerrilla organizations to embrace "armed struggle" as "the only way to a 'just peace'" had particularly far-reaching consequences, impacting perspectives on direct talks versus third party mediation, insistence on preconditions, and incremental versus comprehensive peacemaking strategies.[49]

Hisham Shirabi, articulating the fedayeen's rationale, observed, "Palestinian resistance envisaged a strategy of attrition based on protracted warfare. It based itself on the premise which held that since force is the basis of Zionist strategy, then the inescapable pre-condition of any settlement should be the invalidation of force as the instrument of achieving a Zionist peace. This could never be accomplished by persuasion, only by force." Lauding violence as the "strategic centrepiece" by which "to draw international attention to the Palestinian cause, pressure Israel on all possible fronts, and foment revolutionary change within Arab states in an effort to liberate Palestine," the PFLP advocated "total war against Israel, Zionism, Arab reaction, and imperialism," including operations "directed at Israeli or Zionist targets both within Israel and abroad, at international airlines servicing Israel, and at US overseas interests."[50] Its September 1970 multiple hijacking, "one of the most dramatic terrorist operations to date," demonstrated transnational terrorism's growing reach and power, while the Black September Organization's (BSO) Munich Olympic kidnapping drama commanded unprecedented international attention while exacerbating Israeli security concerns.[51]

Although the PLO's post-1973 success in achieving Arab recognition as the "sole legitimate representative of the Palestinian people," in establishing unofficial offices, information bureaus, and diplomatic ties with countries in Latin America, Western Europe, Asia, Africa, and the Soviet bloc, and in participating "in the capacity of observer" in the UN General Assembly, International Labour

Organization, and World Health Organization generated pressures to curtail violence,[52] neither Fatah nor the other fedayeen organizations were prepared to abandon the terrorist instrument. Arafat, highlighting the need to forestall by any available means a post-Yom Kippur War rapprochement between Israel and its Arab neighbors, observed,

> after the war, we understood that Kissinger would not relax his pressure on the Israelis until he had forced them to make a token withdrawal from the Sinai ... enough to make Sadat commit himself and Egypt to the negotiating process. ... we realized ... that once Sadat was committed to the negotiating process, the Arab states, all of them, would make peace with Israel as soon as the Israelis were willing to withdraw from the occupied territories. ... We would have been finished. The chance for us Palestinians to be a nation again, even on some small part of our homeland, would have passed. Finished. No more a Palestinian people. End of story.[53]

Ensuing terrorist operations, marked by exceptional brutality, ambition, and creativity, included the PDFLP's murder of Jewish schoolchildren at Ma'alot in an effort to derail Syrian-Israeli disengagement negotiations, the PFLP-GC's killing of 18 Israelis at Kiryat Shmona to advance its "revolutionary struggle" for the "total liberation of Palestine," and the PFLP's kidnapping of OPEC oil ministers and hijacking of an Air France plane to Entebbe, Uganda, to secure the release of imprisoned comrades.[54]

Official pronouncements by the PNC, Fatah, PLO Executive Committee, and PLO Central Committee throughout the late 1970s and 1980s were replete with calls to "continue and escalate the armed struggle," accept "armed popular revolution [as] the sole and inevitable road to the liberation of Palestine," secure by all means "the Palestinian peoples' inalienable national rights," and support the first Intifada as "a new stage of confronting the Zionist-imperialist settlement onslaught."[55] Stressing that there "is no solution for the Palestinian question except through Jihad," the *Covenant* of the Islamic Resistance Movement in the West Bank (Hamas) decried "the Jews' usurpation of Palestine" and called for "instill[ing] the spirit of Jihad in the heart of the nation so that they [the masses] would confront the enemies and join the ranks of the fighters."[56] Although "reiterat[ing]" the PNC's "rejection of terrorism" in a December 1988 speech before the General Assembly,[57] Arafat also endorsed the Intifada, noting that the "rebel's rifle has protected us and precluded our liquidation and the destruction of our national identity."[58] Indicating that "neither Arafat nor anyone else can stop the uprising. The uprising will stop only when practical and tangible steps are taken toward the attainment of its national goals and establishment of its Palestinian state," he praised the "masses of our people, our heroes, [who] are leading the way and holding high the torches of freedom ... so the occupiers will leave and so peace will be established in their free and independent homeland."[59]

Such emphasis on the centrality of violence temporarily receded for PLO affiliated organizations with the conclusion of a series of agreements following the Madrid Conference. Arafat, seeking to finalize the *Oslo Accords*, affirmed that the PLO "recognizes the right of the State of Israel to exist in peace and security," "commits itself to the Middle East peace process, and to a peaceful resolution of the conflict between the two sides," "declares that all outstanding issues relating to permanent status will be resolved through negotiations," "renounces the use of terrorism and other acts of violence," and "assume[s] responsibility over all PLO elements and personnel in order to assure their compliance, prevent violations and discipline violators."[60] The 1994 *Cairo Agreement* committed the PA to securing Gaza and the Jericho Area by establishing "a strong police force," insuring that "no organization or individual . . . manufacture, sell, acquire, possess, import or otherwise introduce . . . firearms, ammunition, weapons, explosives, gunpowder or any related equipment," and taking "all measures necessary in order to prevent acts of terrorism, crime and hostilities directed against [Israel]."[61] Such commitments were reaffirmed in the 1995 *Interim Agreement*, 1997 *Hebron Accords*, and 1998 *Wye River Memorandum*.[62]

However, Ariel Sharon's visit to the al-Aqsa mosque in September 2000 unleashed the fury of the second Intifada, bolstering the appeal of Hamas-type militants while undermining the very legitimacy of PA-Israeli negotiations. Arafat's immediate reversion to pre-*Oslo* rhetoric was telling. Embracing the Intifada's resort to violence in defense of the homeland, he observed,

> innocent blood was shed abundantly on the pure Al-Aqsa land. A new procession of honorable people of this nation was added to the martyrs who defend the holy places and who stand fast on this blessed land and defend its purity with faith and pride. There is no inch of Palestinian territory that has not been saturated with Arab blood that is dear to all of us. The blood that was shed in Al-Aqsa definitely unleashed the wrath in the hearts of our Palestinian masses everywhere in the homeland. The unarmed citizens rose to express their feelings in a legitimate spontaneous *intifada*.[63]

Resort to suicide bombings against Israeli civilians, in violation of the laws of war and of every post-*Oslo* agreement, testified most clearly to a renewed emphasis on violence as Palestinians transitioned in their relationship with Israel from a "conflict management" stage to a "military/political" one defined by frequent and "unmanageable" resort to violence.[64]

Israel's stunning victory in the Six Day War, an apparent vindication of Golda Meir's "choice" to "take the initiative and attack the enemy," confirmed for Israelis the wisdom of relying upon military superiority rather than diplomatic engagement to assure "the security of Israel and the future of the nation."[65] Israel's response to the fedayeen's "war" of the early 1970s reflected such a military emphasis. Reacting to such operations as the Lod airport attack and Munich kidnapping, the newly established Mossad counterterror organization was "charged with assassinating top Palestinian leaders, including Arafat," and with conducting operations throughout Europe and the Middle East against terrorist operatives.[66] The searing experience of the Yom Kippur War—Israeli casualties totaled 2,297 killed and 6,067 wounded—only bolstered policymakers' commitment to maintaining unchallenged regional military superiority.[67] The 1979 Egyptian-Israeli *Peace Treaty*, while effectively neutralizing Israel's most potent military adversary, failed to address security threats posed by the remaining Arab confrontation states, Soviet Union, and PLO. Israeli Defense Minister Ariel Sharon noted that continuing "Arab enmity and confrontation," supported by a "Soviet strategy of expansion in the Middle East and Africa" that armed Arab radicals with "political and military tools," "presents an actual danger to our security" and "potential threat to the existence and integrity of Israel." He warned that the PLO "poses a political threat to the very existence of the State of Israel . . . It constitutes a framework for terrorist organizations operating against Israel, in its territory or in the world at large, with the following purpose: —To undermine the domestic stability in Israel and its security.—To generate international pressure on Israel.—To drag the confrontation states to war against Israel.—To deter Arab countries and moderate Palestinian elements from negotiations with Israel on the basis of Camp David." Confronting such implacable adversaries, Sharon emphasized the need "to maintain a balance of forces and a qualitative and technological edge over any combination of Arab war coalition," the value of preemptive action in preventing "confrontation states or potentially confrontation states from gaining access to nuclear weapons," and the importance of enhancing Israel's "independent capability to develop and produce systems which are vital to ensure our qualitative advantage and our security."[68]

Israel's 1982 "Operation Peace for Galilee," responding to what was characterized as "the ceaseless killing of civilians" on "orders . . . from Beirut," reflected its continuing confidence in the utility of military force. Prime Minister Menachem Begin, although indicating that terrorist "actions were not a threat to the existence of the state" and that Israel was not without "alternative[s]," nonetheless argued, "there is no divine mandate to go to war only if there is no alternative. There is no moral imperative that a nation must, or is entitled to, fight only when its back is to the sea, or the abyss." Noting that nine weeks of military operations had "destroyed the combat potential of 20,000 terrorists," he observed that Lebanon's Palestinian terrorist problem had been "solved" and expressed hope that "with the end of the fighting in Lebanon, we have ahead of us many years of establishing peace treaties and peaceful relations with the various Arab countries."[69]

While such optimism proved ill-founded, Israel's response to Palestinian threats remained reflexively one of force. Its self-proclaimed "iron fist" policy toward the first Intifada deviated little from previous policies.[70] Employing measures characterized by the Unified National Command of the Intifada as "Nazi methods . . . that contravene all international and human laws and norms,"[71] Israeli leaders sought to break the uprising by decapitating its leadership and punishing its followers. Although Prime Minister Yitzhak Rabin acknowledged "the limitations of military power and the possibilities entailed in a political solution,"[72] lamented the high casualties associated with combating the Intifada,[73] and declared that "[e]ven acts of terrorism will not stop the peace convoy," he supported the "all-out war [being waged] against all those continuing the violence and terror" by the IDF, General Security Service (GSS), Israeli police, and border police, and vowed that there would be "no limitation to the activity of these forces against terrorism and violence" beyond "the framework of the law."[74] The al-Aqsa Intifada, marked by escalating civilian casualties, prompted more extensive Israeli resort to extrajudicial killings, house demolitions, and destruction of Palestinian schools, roads, power generation facilities, and other infrastructure-related capabilities.

Restrict Political Options

Frustrated by Arabs' humiliating defeat in 1967 and determined to "awaken" the world's "conscience" to the Palestinians' plight,[75] key Palestinian actors, including the Palestine National Assembly, PFLP, Fatah, PFLP-GC, Sa'iqa, Popular Democratic Front (PDF), and Abu Nidal embraced transnational terrorism as a strategy "to strike at the enemy wherever he may be, and at the nerve centres of his power."[76] While such operations as Lod, Munich, and Khartoum placed "the Palestinian cause before the Arab world and the larger international community in ways that could not be ignored easily" and secured for the PLO an international status "unprecedented for other terrorist or guerrilla organizations,"[77] they promoted among Israeli and US policymakers a "Palestinian-as-terrorist" perspective that militated against *any* negotiations, direct or otherwise. Israel's pre-*Oslo* perspective on the Arafat-led PLO was remarkably consistent, dismissing its potential as a negotiating partner and denying it a role in substantive deliberations. Subsequent to the 1974 Ma'alot killings, both the Cabinet and Knesset declared that the government would "not negotiate with terrorist organizations," while the Likud party characterized the PLO as "no national liberation organization but an organization of assassins" which it would "strive to eliminate."[78] Foreign Minister Yitzhak Shamir ruled out *any* dealings with the PLO in a scathing article in *Foreign Affairs* in early 1982, declaring, "The very act of granting the PLO a status—any status—in the political negotiations would be self-defeating. It would elevate its standing from that of a terrorist organization to that of a recognized aspirant to a totally superfluous political entity. Hence, association of the PLO with any aspect whatsoever of the political process and the prospects of peace are mutually exclusive."[79] Later, as Prime Minister, he denounced Arafat's 1988 speech to the General Assembly as "a deceitful PLO act of momentous proportions . . . aimed at misleading and creating the impression of growing moderation." He noted, "We have no conditions for negotiations or recognition of the PLO. From our point of view, the PLO is not a partner for any peace process. The PLO is a terrorist organization, or a group of terrorist organizations whose goal is to harm Israelis, undermine the existence of the State of Israel, and bring about its destruction." He expressed "hope that for the sake of promoting the chance of peace and ending terror and violence, the United States will never form any official contacts with the PLO, since such a move will encourage extremists and violence and submerge the voices of those who are genuinely interested in promoting coexistence, negotiations, and peace between Israel and its neighbors."[80] Following the Palestine National Council's declaration of Palestinian independence in November 1988, the Israeli government indicated that it would "not negotiate with the PLO" because it had "disqualified itself from participation in the peace process . . . in view of its background and activities, including ongoing acts of terrorism."[81]

Although preliminary backchannel contacts between prominent Palestinians and Israeli officials and academics occurred following the Madrid Conference, it was not until January 1993 that the Knesset repealed legislation forbidding private contacts with the PLO, providing legal sanction for the series of "pre-negotiations" between a small contingent of Israelis and Palestinians that ultimately culminated in Yitzhak Rabin officially recognizing "the PLO as the representative of the Palestinian people" and commencing "negotiations with the PLO within the Middle East peace process."[82] Although loathe "to sit at the negotiating table with . . . those who have wielded knives or pulled the trigger," Rabin observed, "we cannot choose our neighbors and our enemies, including the cruelest of them. We must deal with what we have: the PLO."[83] Buchanan argued that Rabin's negotiation of *Oslo* reflected an admission of "the inevitable, that there would be no meaningful and substantive progress in the Washington talks as long as Arafat and the PLO were not full negoatiating [sic] partners and officially recognized as such."[84] He noted Rabin's fear that failure to address the "radicalization of the *intifada*," growing despair within Gaza, and the PLO's debilitating post-Gulf War weakness risked placing the "danger of death" in the form of Islamic fundamentalism at Israel's "doorstep." Buchanan observed, "From realizing that political compromise with the Palestinians was not possible without dealing with the PLO, it was a short journey [for Rabin] to seeing that by not dealing with the PLO in the immediate future, the rise of absolutist, Islamic fundamentalism would result." He highlighted Rabin's conviction "that Israel had a seven-year 'window of opportunity' to resolve the core [Israeli-Palestinian] conflict and make peace with its neighbours before the Iranian threat," perceived to be Israel's most significant regional concern, "became real."[85]

Although Rabin's successor, Benjamin Netanyahu, adamantly rejected *Oslo*'s premise of negotiating with an Arafat-led PLO, Ehud Barak's election was accompanied by a renewed commitment "to work with the elected Palestinian leadership, under Chairman Yasser Arafat, in partnership and respect."[86] However, the Camp David talks collapse in July 2000 prompted Barak's reversion to pre-*Oslo* rhetoric. Criticizing Arafat for being "afraid to make the historic decisions necessary at this time in order to bring about an end to the conflict," he stressed the "unripeness on the Palestinian side, to achieve a deal, or strike a deal," emphasized Palestinians' need to "deal with their extremist elements," and concluded, "the vision of peace is not dead, but it suffered a heavy blow because of the Palestinian stubbornness."[87] While sharing Barak's belief that "it takes two to tango," Sharon dismissed the very possibility of negotiations with the corrupt, discredited, Arafat-dominated PA, insisting upon new Palestinian leadership and political institutions prior to resuming negotiations.[88]

Nixon, Kissinger, and Ford, sharing Israel's revulsion at Palestinian terror, lay the foundation for the PLO's exclusion from US-sponsored peace talks until the waning days of the Reagan administration. While Nixon rejected "giving in to blackmail demands" or "extortion any place in the world," observing, "The nation that compromises with the terrorists today could well be destroyed by the terrorists tomorrow,"[89] Kissinger stressed that the "international community cannot ignore (terrorist) affronts to civilization; it must not allow them to spread their poison; it has a duty to act vigorously to combat them." He argued that terrorism, "like piracy, must be seen as outside the law. It discredits any political objective that it purports to serve and any nations which encourage it," and declared that "under no circumstances" would he negotiate with the "terrorist" PLO or its constituent organizations.[90]

Ford likewise abhorred transnational terrorism, a phenomenon he attributed to "the work of anarchists and political fanatics." Describing the Munich Olympic killings as "despicable acts of murder and terrorism," he insisted that "the civilized world ostracize any peoples or nation giving sanctuary or refuge to international outlaws of the Black September stripe," observed that any "incident of that kind that involves loss of life enhances my personal sympathy for Israel and the Jewish community," and noted that while such actions had "dramatically" heightened his awareness of Palestinian ambitions,[91] "any extreme radicalism/terrorism by elements of the Palestinian community made it more difficult to arrange any face-to-face negotiations between the Israelis and the Palestinians. Terrorism by any group makes it more difficult for reasonable people to try to resolve questions that are in dispute."[92] Israel's success in shaping "political discourse largely in its favour, treating its ongoing recourse to violence as part of the legitimate security function of the state while stigmatising far lower levels of Palestinian violence (and even non-violent modes of collective resistance) as 'terrorism,'" was critical in persuading Ford to institutionalize the PLO's diplomatic marginalization.[93] Arguing that "Israel cannot be expected to deal with terrorist groups which will not even acknowledge Israel's right to exist,"[94] he negotiated the 1975 US-Israeli *Memorandum of Agreement* that committed the US to continuing "to adhere to its present policy with respect to the Palestine Liberation Organization, whereby it will not recognize or negotiate with the Palestine Liberation Organization so long as the Palestine Liberation Organization does not recognize Israel's right to exist and does not accept Security Council Resolutions 242 and 338."[95]

Although Carter recognized "the legitimate rights of the Palestinian people," called for "a resolution of the Palestinian problem in all its aspects," and indicated that Palestinians must "participate in the determination of their own future,"[96] he accorded Arafat and the PLO no role in the peace process. While the Camp David *Frameworks for Peace* affirmed that "the representatives of the Palestinian people should participate in negotiations on the resolution of the Palestinian problem in all its aspects," they were given no authority to negotiate "the details of a transitional arrangement" leading to Palestinian autonomy in the West Bank and Gaza, including "the modalities for establishing the elected self-governing authority."[97] The Reagan administration similarly asserted that "there should be Palestinian participation at every stage of the negotiating process," while reaffirming Washington's longstanding refusal to "recognize or negotiate with the PLO unless it clearly and publicly recognizes Israel's right to exist and accepts Resolutions 242 and 338."[98] Secretary of State George Shultz's exchange with members of the American Israel Public Affairs Committee was revealing: "Secretary Shultz: What is making peace all about? Well, to me it's really simple. It's sitting down with people who want to make peace, and who are qualified and ready to negotiate. . . . Is the PLO qualified? Audience: No. Secretary Shultz: Hell, no! Let's try that on for size. PLO? Audience: Hell, no! Secretary Shultz: You got it! . . . they don't want peace; they want the destruction of Israel, so they're not qualified. Palestinians? Certainly. They have to be part of peacemaking. There are Palestinians who know that the only answer is through a non-violent and responsible approach to direct negotiations for peace and justice. We have to continue to find them, help them, and support them."[99]

Arafat's December 1988 condemnation of "terrorism in all its forms," "acceptance of resolutions 242 and 338 as a basis for negotiations with Israel," and recognition of "the existence of the Israelis" prompted a significant change in US policy,[100] one which elicited great concern from Israel. Declaring that the US now was "prepared for a substantive dialogue with PLO representatives," Shultz initiated official discussions "about the political and security situation in the region."[101] However, sensitive to Israeli concerns that "any" US-PLO dialogue was "a serious mistake" that "grants further legitimacy to the terrorist organizations," "encourages the violent elements in the field, perpetuates the violence, [and] further entrenches the Arab countries in their intransigence,"[102] Bush accepted Prime Minister Shamir's demands that the PLO "not be a party" to the Madrid Conference and that the Palestinian contingent of a joint Jordanian-Palestinian delegation be "approved by Israel."[103] While Clinton accepted the PA as the Palestinians' legitimate interlocutor and negotiated with Arafat throughout his tenure in office, Camp David's collapse prompted his reevaluation of Palestinians' readiness to pursue a negotiated settlement. Characterizing the PA's complicity in supporting a "culture of violence" and a "culture of incitement" as "inconsistent with the Palestinian leadership's commitment to Oslo's nonviolent path to peace," Clinton particularly indicted Arafat's refusal to reign in extremist elements.[104] The incoming Bush White House likewise expressed deep distrust about Arafat's willingness to act decisively against Palestinian terror and skepticism about the PA's commitment to a negotiated peace. Outraged by escalating suicide attacks against Israeli civilians, Bush was sympathetic to Sharon's argument that Arafat, having given a "green light" to such actions, had forfeited his diplomatic *bona fides* and must be replaced by an empowered Prime Minister committed to combating terrorism at its source.

Radicalize and Polarize Palestinian Politics

Although Arafat's Fatah embraced the centrality of "armed struggle" in pursuing Palestinian objectives, the PFLP's resort to transnational terror in 1968 presented a significant, longterm challenge to PLO efforts to foster the organizational unity and coordination upon which the success of *Road Map*-patterned initiatives ultimately depended. Attempts by Fatah, the PFLP, PFLP-GC, Sa'iqa, and the Palestine Liberation Army (PLA) to forge closer ties by establishing the Unified Command of Palestine Resistance in May 1970 "foundered almost immediately . . . as the PFLP increasingly resorted to terrorism to provoke a direct confrontation with Jordan—one that Fatah and the majority of the PLO sought to avoid." Arafat commented many years later on his inability to control the PFLP, observing, "I begged the leftists to stop their provocations. I told them very frankly they were creating a disaster for our people. But once more they refused me." The PLO's crushing defeat by Jordan's King Hussein in September 1970 created particularly intense pressures on its more moderate factions to adopt the terrorist instrument. Khalad Hassan, a Fatah leader, observed that Fatah's preeminent position within the Palestinian movement would have been jeopardized had it condemned terror following the events of Black September, "We would have lost our credibility as leaders; nobody in the rank and file of our movement would have listened to us; and the terror operations would still have taken place. . . . In the leadership our problem was to find a way to associate ourselves with the grassroots decision to play the terror card, in order to give ourselves the necessary credibility to act, when we judged the time to be right, to control and eventually shut down the terror machine." Ben Bella, a BSO member, likewise noted, "At the time Arafat could not afford to speak against us in public because he knew that what we were doing had the support of the majority in the rank and file of our movement. Our way was the popular way. But in our private meetings he took every opportunity to tell us we were wrong. I remember an occasion when he said to some of us, 'You are crazy to take our fight to Europe.'"[105]

The Yom Kippur War further complicated Fatah's position. Confronted by the risk of Palestinianism being "liquidated" by "the Arab states . . . mak[ing] peace with Israel as soon as the Israelis were willing to withdraw from the occupied territories," and fearful that abandoning terrorism would buttress the Rejection Front's criticism of Fatah's "*istislan* (defeatism) and a willingness to sell out," Arafat continued to engage Fatah in terrorist operations. However, both he and his senior colleagues "also recognized the need to develop a political program perceived as attainable by the Arabs and as hopeful by those living under occupation." A senior official shed light on Fatah's acceptance of a "mini-state formula in which Palestinians would seek sovereignty over Gaza and the West Bank while abandoning, at least for the immediate future, talk of liquidating the 'Zionist entity' in Palestine," observing,

> We have undertaken a careful analysis of the regional and international situation in the light of which we have come to the conclusion that it is imperative, in the overriding interest of the Palestinian people, to accept a compromise. . . . We are not going to be more revolutionary or more uncompromising than the Germans, the Vietnamese and the Koreans, who, like it or not, have allowed the division of their respective countries. Moreover, peace with Israel could reopen the way to gradual evolution leading to the reunification of Palestine which would become one day the homeland of both Jews and Arabs.

Arafat lobbied the PNC to accept a "stage-by-stage" strategy, dismissing as untenable Rejection Front opposition to "a Palestinian mini-state" and insistence on continuing "the revolutionary struggle until the total liberation of Palestine."

As Hani al-Hasan observed, "Our Palestinian people on the occupied West Bank and in Gaza were desperate, and many of them were demanding a political programme which would give the Israelis every possible incentive to withdraw in exchange for peace. So Arafat had to tell them, 'I hear you.'"[106]

George Habash, the PFLP's General Secretary, acknowledged that "two contradictory political lines exist within the PLO . . . One political line says that the only way open for the resistance movement is to enter into the framework of the political solution and to struggle within this framework to achieve whatever is possible. . . . another . . . believes in the continuity of the revolution and in staying away from political settlements." While arguing that "the Palestinian revolution is strained and ends when it becomes a part of the political settlement presently proposed, and the continuity of the revolution is only ensured by resisting and fighting the proposed political settlement plans," he nonetheless shared Arafat's concerns that transnational terror risked alienating "our friends in the world" and decided "to concentrate terror activities against Israel."[107] However, both Wadi Haddad, the PFLP's director of foreign operations, and Abu Nidal, former director of Fatah's Baghdad office, refused to accept any moderation of tactics, conducting high profile transnational terrorist operations against Israeli-related targets and assassinating Fatah leaders and moderate Arabs throughout Europe, Asia, and the Middle East.[108]

Arafat sought unsuccessfully to minimize terrorism's potential to fracture Palestinian resistance efforts by drawing a sharp distinction between terrorists and revolutionaries. Speaking before the General Assembly in November 1974, he stressed the legitimacy of *all* methods of resistance to the Israeli occupation, observing,

> The difference between the revolutionary and the terrorist lies in the reason for which each fights. For whoever stands by a just cause and fights for the freedom and liberation of his land from invaders, settler[s] and colonialists would have been incorrectly called terrorist . . . As to those who fight against just causes, those who wage war to occupy the homelands of others, and to plunder[,] exploit and colonize their peoples—those are the people whose actions should be condemned, who should be called war criminals: for the just cause determines the right to struggle.

Noting the "temerity" of "the Zionist racists and colonialists . . . to describe the just struggle of our people as terror," Arafat decried "Zionist terrorism's" impact on the Palestinian people, emphasizing that the "record of Israeli rulers is replete with acts of terror perpetrated on those of our people who remained under occupation."[109] His November 1985 *Declaration on Terrorism* likewise sought to transcend terrorism's polarizing potential among fedayeen organizations. While proclaiming the PLO's "condemnation of all acts of terrorism, whether they be those in which states become involved or those committed by individuals or groups against the innocent and defenseless, wherever they may be," and commitment to "take all measures to deter violators," Arafat insisted "upon the right of the Palestinian people to resist the Israeli occupation of its land by *all* available means."[110] He similarly distinguished between terrorism and legitimate resistance in an address before the European Parliament. Observing that "[o]ur people, including their leaders, cadres, and citizens, have invariably been the target of organized Israeli state terrorism," he stressed that as "a national liberation movement which took up arms against the oppression and illegitimate terrorism of the occupier, we have invariably, and in the clearest and strongest of terms, denounced terrorism in all its forms and from whatever source—be it by individuals, groups, or states."[111] Speaking before the General Assembly in December 1988, he reiterated the PNC's "rejection of terrorism of all kinds," while highlighting those "UN resolutions endorsing the right of nations to resist foreign occupation, imperialism, and racial discrimination."[112] Fatah likewise emphasized "its strong condemnation of all terrorist Israeli practices," while stressing "the Palestinian people's national inalienable rights and the right of all oppressed peoples under occupation to use *all* forms of struggle for their liberation and national independence."[113]

Arafat's confidence in *Oslo*'s transformative potential enabled the PLO to distance itself more decisively from the terror instrument without fearing for its leadership position in the Palestinian movement. Hopes that the *Accords* would lead rapidly to resolving "final status" issues and to creating a Palestinian state permitted Arafat, despite extremist opposition, to denounce "the use of terrorism and other acts of violence" and to "assume responsibility over all PLO elements and personnel in order to assure their compliance, prevent violations and discipline violators" of the *Accords*.[114] However, the al-Aqsa Intifada fueled explosive growth in popular support for Hamas and its terrorist tactics, prompting Arafat to return to "just cause" criteria for evaluating terrorism in an effort to remain relevant to the Palestinian masses. Declaring that since "the eruption of [the] Al-Aqsa *intifada*, our unarmed people have been facing the broadest collective extermination campaign and barbaric bombardment," he applauded the "legitimate spontaneous *intifada*" and pledged that "[o]ur people of revolutionary struggle . . . [will use] all legitimate means to reach victory."[115]

Such tactical flexibility typified Arafat's approach to terrorism. Periods of Fatah weakness and/or Palestinian vulnerability particularly encouraged resort to the terrorist instrument. While utilizing BSO-type surrogates in the early 1970s reflected Arafat's recognition of Fatah's need to embrace terrorism if it was "to maintain its leadership credentials" following "Black September," Fatah also reserved for itself the right to conduct terrorist operations.[116] Arafat concluded his 1974 address to the General Assembly with a none-too-veiled threat, "Today I have come bearing an olive branch and a freedom-fighter's gun. Do not let the olive branch fall from my hand. Do not let the olive branch fall from my hand. Do not let the olive branch fall from my hand."[117] Following the PLO's crushing defeat by Israel and expulsion from Lebanon in 1982, he observed, "We have learned that armed struggle complements political struggle in all fields. . . . Our decision [to continue our 'struggle'] comes from our people and from the barrel of a gun."[118] Similarly, his support of the "steadfast heroes" of the first Intifada and the "Martyrs" of the second was accompanied by calls to "escalate the war of the sacred stones with utmost vigor and strength" and to respond to the "wave of savage violence that our Palestinian people have been subjected to" with "all legitimate means."[119]

Palestinian weakness also prompted Arafat to pursue accommodation with more radical elements, although always with an eye toward institutionalizing Fatah's dominance of the Palestinian movement. Establishing the Palestine Armed Struggle Command in April 1969 and the Unified Command of Palestine Resistance in May 1970 were early attempts to buttress both Palestinian capabilities vis-à-vis Israel and Fatah's position within Palestinian politics. Similarly, efforts to forge a Steadfastness and Confrontation Front including itself, the PFLP, PDFLP, PFLP-GC, Sa'iqa, ALF, and PLF following Sadat's 1977 visit to Israel reflected Fatah's attempt to outflank radicals in opposing Sadat's perceived sacrifice of Palestinian national/territorial ambitions.[120] Arafat's emphasis during the first Intifada on the PLO Executive Committee's authority and on the need for "[r]evolutionary discipline . . . [to] be practiced to prevent the negative aspects and crush deviations" likewise sought to address both Palestinian weakness and Fatah's vulnerability to the revolutionary appeal of radical Islamist organizations,[121] while the al-Aqsa Intifada prompted similar calls for Palestinian unity when confronting Israel's superior military and economic capabilities.[122]

In contrast, moments of Palestinian strength and Fatah influence provided Arafat both incentive and discretion to reconsider the terrorist option. Having secured unprecedented diplomatic recognition by late 1974,[123] the Arafat-led PLO confronted for the first time the liabilities of unrestrained violence. Recognizing terrorism's potential to undermine a Palestinian movement rapidly developing both the international sympathy and diplomatic presence requisite for inclusion in settlement negotiations, Arafat encouraged Fatah and the PLO to renounce transnational terrorism beyond the borders of Israel and the Occupied Territories.[124] He likewise condemned terrorism before the General Assembly in 1988 and in the 1993 Israeli-PLO *Declaration of Principles*,[125] arguing that conventional diplomacy afforded the increasingly influential Palestinian movement its best hope of securing longstanding objectives while further marginalizing Fatah's radical competitors.

DOMESTIC POLITICAL INSTITUTIONS & PROCESSES

The *Road Map*'s ambitious timetable for securing a comprehensive settlement attributed to Israeli and Palestinian political institutions diplomatic resources that neither possessed. Having neither a strong "presidential" nor a "premiership regime," Israeli politics was beholden to a "coalition system" ill-suited to negotiating and implementing far-reaching agreements.[126] *Oslo*'s fate highlighted the impact of coalition politics on Israeli-Palestinian relations. While Rabin's Labor-dominated government promised "vigorous steps to bring about the termination of the Arab-Israeli conflict," including negotiating with Palestinians on "autonomy" and "self-rule" and working with "Amman, Damascus, [and] Beirut on behalf of peace,"[127] his assassination in November 1995 precipitated a dramatic change in Israeli policies. Rejecting *Oslo*'s commitment to the gradual withdrawal of Israeli forces from Gaza and parts of the West Bank, resolution of final status issues by March 1999, and prompt transfer to Palestinians of authority over education, culture, social welfare, direct taxation, and terrorism,[128] Benjamin Netanyahu, Rabin's successor and leader of the Likud party, significantly impeded *Oslo*'s implementation. Netanyahu's replacement by a Barak-led Labor coalition in mid-1999 prompted yet another policy reversal. Declaring his government's commitment "to work with the elected Palestinian leadership . . . in order to jointly arrive at a fair and agreed settlement for coexistence in freedom, prosperity and good neighborliness in this beloved land where the two peoples will always live," Barak pledged to "honor and implement the agreements which Israel has signed with the Palestinians" and to "accelerate the negotiations with the Palestinians, based on the existing process, with a view toward ending the conflict with a permanent settlement that guarantees the security and vital interests of Israel."[129] Within two years, Barak's crushing defeat by Ariel Sharon precipitated Israel's effective abandonment of *Oslo*. Refusing to countenance *Oslo*'s insistence on negotiating with Arafat and the PA, advancing Palestinian self-rule, and redeploying Israel's military capabilities in the Occupied Territories, Sharon insisted on developing a new approach to Israeli security. While the on-again, off-again, on-again, off-again *Oslo* process reflected to a large degree the personal perspectives of Rabin, Netanyahu, Barak, and Sharon, it also was influenced by coalition partners' demands and Israeli political parties' sensitivity to constituent pressures. Barak, acknowledging the extent to which Israeli-Palestinian negotiations were hostage to domestic politics, vowed, "If there is an agreement, I will submit it, as I promised, to the Israeli people for decision. It is the Israeli people who will decide on the agreement in a referendum."[130]

Although Arafat's Fatah assumed dominance over Palestinian affairs in the late 1960s, Palestinianism as a political movement remained rent by debilitating and largely irreconcilable divisions.[131] Early disagreements centered on the nature and scope of armed struggle,[132] the desirability of establishing a Palestinian "mini-state" in the West Bank and Gaza,[133] and the relationship between fedayeen organizations and Arab states.[134] Conflict between Fatah and Rejection Front members, including the PFLP, PFLP-GC, Palestine Popular Struggle Front (PPSF), Iraqi Ba'ath, and ALF, prompted periodic withdrawals from the PLO itself or from it Executive Committee,[135] criticism of Arafat's pursuit of a "liquidationist settlement," and attacks against Fatah leaders and sympathizers.[136] Arafat's opposition to unrestrained violence and insistence on Palestinianism's secularity elicited stinging criticism by Hamas, the self-proclaimed "Islamic Resistance Movement in the West Bank." Arguing that "[i]nitiatives, proposals and international conferences are all a waste of time and vain endeavors," and that "so-called peaceful solutions . . . are in contradiction to the principles of the Islamic Resistance Movement," Hamas's 1988 *Covenant* observed, "There is no solution for the Palestinian question except through Jihad." It noted that "the land of Palestine is an Islamic Waqf (Trust) consecrated for future Moslem generations until Judgement Day. It, or any part of it, should not be squandered: it, or any part of it, should not be given up." Emphasizing that "the Palestinian problem is a religious problem, and should be dealt with on this basis," the *Covenant* declared, "Resisting and quelling the enemy becomes the individual duty of every Moslem, male or female."[137]

Arafat's 1988 diplomatic offensive, including speeches before the European Parliament and UN General Assembly in which he endorsed Resolutions 242 and 338, recognized Israel's right to exist, and renounced "all forms of terrorism,"[138] paved the way for high level US-Palestinian discussions and for Israeli-Palestinian negotiations leading to the *Oslo Accords*. However, such collaboration with the Jewish "usurp[ers]" prompted scathing criticism both from PLO officials and non-PLO fedayeen organizations.[139] Mahmoud Darwish, in resigning from the PLO's Executive Committee, noted that the PLO, having embarked on "this adventurous decision" fraught with "historic risk," was "finished".[140] Hani al-Hasan, speaking shortly after *Oslo*, likewise observed, "even though I do not belong to the school of rejectionism and fully belong to the school of political settlements[,] . . . settlements are based on balance, whereas the proposed solution is one imposed by Israel as the victor." He concluded, "The PLO which Israel has recognized is one that has submitted to Israeli demands. It is no longer the PLO that embodies the Palestinian people's aspirations to independent statehood after a full Israeli withdrawal from the West Bank and Gaza Strip and upholds the rights of the Palestinian refugees."[141] Such criticism resonated with Palestinian residents of the Occupied Territories, most of whom enjoyed few benefits from *Oslo* and perceived the Arafat-led PA as corrupt, autocratic, and inept. Hamas and its Islamist counterparts' strident militancy provided a stark alternative to the PA, one that attracted increasing support following the al-Aqsa Intifada's outbreak. While Arafat praised the "glorious *intifada*," condemned the "descrat[ing] [of] the Al-Aqsa mosque," and acknowledged the "new, religious, dimension . . . to the Arab-Israeli struggle,"[142] his efforts to identify the PA with resistance to Israeli occupation failed to attract those growing numbers of Palestinians supportive of terrorist violence. PA weakness vis-à-vis Islamist organizations, coupled with Israel's destruction of critical institutional capabilities related to law enforcement, security, social welfare, and the economy, undermined those authoritative Palestinian political institutions requisite for negotiating and implementing the *Road Map*'s two state solution to the Israeli-Palestinian conflict.

THE "PEACE PROCESS"

Finally, the *Road Map*'s promise of rapid progress toward a two state solution struggled to overcome Israeli and Palestinians' deep-rooted skepticism concerning the interminable post-1967 "peace process." Recognizing UNSCR 242's failure to achieve rapid movement toward a "just and lasting peace" in the Middle East,[143] the 1978 *Frameworks for Peace*'s inability to "resolve the Palestinian problem in all its aspects,"[144] and *Oslo*'s post-al-Aqsa demise,[145] the principals were reluctant to commit to the far-reaching concessions upon which the *Road Map* depended. Having yielded precious little of enduring substance over nearly 40 years—the 1979 Egyptian-Israeli and 1994 Jordanian-Israeli peace treaties remained the principal accomplishments—the "peace process'" latest iteration inspired little confidence in the Quartet's ability to transform oft-repeated goals into the diplomatic progress requisite to securing the parties' territorial, security, political, economic, social, and cultural objectives.

CONTEXT—SUBSTANCE

Creating an "independent, democratic, and viable Palestinian state living side by side in peace and security with Israel and its other neighbors" was the centerpiece of the *Road Map*'s goal of reaching "a final, permanent status resolution" of the Israeli-Palestinian conflict by December 2005.[1] Predicated upon resolving such complex, emotionally divisive issues as borders, settlements, refugees, and Jerusalem within the context of Resolution 242's "land-for-peace" formula, the *Road Map* demanded a degree of flexibility anathema to the optimizing bargaining strategies preferred by Israelis and Palestinians alike. Having typically approached negotiations as efforts "to achieve as much as possible" through "unreasonable, combative, and abusive" tactics,[2] the principals had little confidence that *Road Map*-style diplomacy could overcome their profound and wide-ranging substantive differences.

PALESTINIAN STATE

Reflecting Israelis' insistence that Palestinians were only "'Arabs' in the process of being reintegrated into the countries that had welcomed them," Golda Meir, Prime Minister in the late 1960s-early 1970s, denied the very existence of a "Palestinian" people, observing, "It was not as if there was a Palestinian people in Palestine and we came and threw them out and took their country away from them. They did not exist."[3] While subsequently acknowledging Palestinians' national identity, Israeli leaders continued to dismiss the need for an independent Palestinian state, instead endorsing a "Jordanian-Palestinian Arab state east of Israel" that would reflect the close "identity of the Jordanians and the Palestinians."[4] The 1981 *Fundamental Policy Guidelines of Israel as Approved by the Knesset* declared, "The autonomy agreed upon at Camp David means neither sovereignty nor self-determination. The autonomy agreements set down at Camp David are guarantees that under no conditions will a Palestinian State emerge in the territory of Western *Eretz Yisrael*. At the end of the transition period set down in the Camp David agreements, Israel will present its claim, and act to realize its right of sovereignty over Judea, Samaria, and the Gaza District."[5] Foreign Minister Yitzhak Shamir likewise observed in 1982, "the problem is clearly *not* that of a homeland for the Palestinian Arabs. That homeland is Trans-Jordan, or eastern Palestine. There are, however, 1.2 million Palestinian Arabs living in the territories which have been administered by Israel since 1967 in Judea, Samaria and Gaza. Their status and problems were discussed at great length at Camp David. The granting of sovereignty to those areas was ruled out by Israel. A second Palestinian Arab state to the west of the River Jordan is a prescription for anarchy, a threat to both Israel and Jordan, and a likely base for terrorist and Soviet penetration."[6]

Responding to the Palestine National Council's "Declaration of Independence" in November 1988 and to Reagan's subsequent decision to enter into a "substantive dialogue with PLO representatives,"[7] Israeli policymakers reiterated their opposition to "the establishment of an additional Palestinian state in the Gaza District and in the area between Israel and Jordan," noting that such an "independent Palestinian state would pose a threat to Israel's security and to Middle East stability."[8] Shamir, then Prime Minister, argued, "In historic Eretz-Israel two states arose, one Jewish and the other Arab. The two states give full expression to the aspirations of both nations for independence and a homeland of their own. There is neither room for, nor logic, in a second Arab state within Eretz-Israel, and it will never be established."[9] As Buchanan observed, "Shamir insisted that the root cause of the conflict was not territory but the Arab refusal to recognize the legitimacy of the State of Israel; hence he was not prepared to trade territory for peace. All he would offer was peace for peace. Shamir's position was basic and unchangeable. Palestinian autonomy, for a transitional period of five years, was intended to foreclose all other options, not to be the foundation for further negotiations and concessions."[10]

Yitzhak Rabin, both in his 1992 inaugural and subsequent Oslo strategy, similarly rejected establishing a new Palestinian state. Reminding Palestinians in the Occupied Territories, "you have constantly lost ground. For over 44 years you have been deluding yourselves, your leaders have been leading you by the nose with falsehoods and lies. They missed all the opportunities, they rejected all our proposed solutions, and they led you from one disaster to another," he admonished them to "listen to us, if only this time." While acknowledging that "[y]ou will not get all that you want," he pledged "the most fair and realistic offer we can put forth today: autonomy, self-rule, with its advantages and limitations."[11] Palestinians enjoyed no such "fair and realistic" offers from Benjamin Netanyahu, Rabin's successor. Rejecting both a new Palestinian state and *Oslo*'s transitional autonomy arrangements, he scarcely recognized the PA's status as a "self-governing authority." In contrast, Ehud Barak assured Palestinians that the "State of Israel does not wish to control you or your future. We want good neighborly relations with you based on respect and liberty, on broad coordination, on shared interests, and on a separation that will allow you and us to maintain independent identities, development and free choice"; he indicated a willingness to pursue negotiations that "will be heart-rending and difficult because they will involve not only distant maps and locations, but also our beloved homeland."[12] However, any such hint that Israel might accept a Palestinian state in the West Bank and Gaza vanished with the al-Aqsa Intifada and Sharon's defeat of Barak; the new Likud government categorically rejected *any* transfer of Israeli administered territory to Palestinian sovereignty, while moving to wrest *Oslo*-era autonomous powers from the PA.

Palestinians' early perspective on creating an independent state bordering Israel was expressed most clearly in the 1968 *Palestinian National Covenant*. Characterizing Judaism as "not a nationality with an independent existence," Jews as "not one people with an independent personality," and Israel as a "tool of the Zionist movement," it declared, "Palestine with its boundaries that existed at the time of the British mandate is an integral regional unit . . . The Palestinian Arab people possesses the legal right to its homeland, and when the liberation of its homeland is completed it will exercise self-determination solely according to its own will and choice." It thus insisted that the "partitioning of Palestine in 1947 and the establishment of Israel is fundamentally null and void, whatever time has elapsed, because it was contrary to the wish of the people of Palestine and its natural right to its homeland, and contradicts the principles embodied in the Charter of the UN, the first of which is the right of self-determination."[13] The PLO likewise observed that "Israel's right to exist . . . [is] fundamentally and gravely inconsistent with the Arab character of Palestine," while Fatah insisted upon freeing Palestine "from Zionist colonisation in order to recover its national identity" and establish an "independent, democratic State of Palestine, all of whose citizens will enjoy equal rights irrespective of their religion."[14] The Palestine National Assembly categorically rejected "establishing a spurious Palestinian entity in the territory of Palestine occupied since June 5 [1967]," arguing that such an "entity" would "owe its existence to the legitimization and perpetuation of the State of Israel, which is absolutely incompatible with the Palestinian Arab people's right to the whole of Palestine," would "consolidate Zionist aggression against Palestine and the military victories won by Israel in 1948 and 1967," would "be an Israeli colony," and would "lead to the liquidation of the Palestinian cause once and for all to the benefit of Israel." Committed to destroying "the instrument of aggression [Israel]," it declared, "any individual or party, Palestinian Arab or non-Palestinian, who advocates or supports the creation of such a subservient entity is the enemy of the Palestinian Arab people and the Arab nation."[15]

The Yom Kippur War prompted a fundamental reconsideration of such a perspective. While remaining committed to the strategic objective of eliminating the "Zionist entity" from Mandatory Palestine, Fatah, the PDFLP, and Sa'iqa submitted a "working paper" to the PLO's Central Council in early 1974 that advocated establishing "a national authority on any lands that can be wrested from Zionist occupation."[16] Arguing that a "stage-by-stage," "micro-state" approach was a necessary prelude to the eventual extension of Palestinian sovereignty throughout all of Palestine, it criticized "opportunistic currents of thought" promoting such "bombastic slogans" as "The whole of Palestine at once" for failing to recognize the need to "submit a pragmatic programme" to establish a Palestinian national authority.[17] The 12th Palestinian National Council likewise declared in June 1974, "Any liberation step that is achieved constitutes a step for continuing (the efforts) to achieve the PLO strategy for the establishment of the Palestinian democratic state" and for "completing the liberation of all Palestinian soil."[18] Although the PFLP reminded the PLO that "[n]o peace will materialize as long as the Zionist state exists," it, as well as Fatah, the PDFLP, PFLP-GC, Sa'iqa, ALF, and PLF, issued a statement in late 1977 applauding efforts to create "an independent Palestinian national state on any part of the Palestinian Revolution."[19] Both the PLO's Executive Committee and PNC acknowledged in 1979 the acceptability of a "mini-state" approach, affirming Palestinians' "right to an independent state on *any* land Israel evacuates or is liberated."[20]

While maintaining the "inalienable rights of the Palestinian people . . . to self-determination and to the establishment of their independent state in their national homeland,"[21] the PLO's post-1982 policy no longer demanded the ultimate destruction of the "Zionist entity." Speaking in March 1985, Arafat noted the PLO's "progress" following the Lebanese debacle in affirming "the right of all states in the region to exist within safe and internationally recognized borders, including the right of the Palestinian people to self-determination on its land and to establish a Palestinian state."[22] PLO spokesman Bassam Abu-Sharif, commenting in June 1988 on the "prospects of a Palestinian-Israeli settlement," observed, "Palestinians and Israelis are in general agreement on ends and means. Israel's objectives are lasting peace and security. Lasting peace and security are also the objectives of the Palestinian people." Declaring that "all peoples—the Jewish and the Palestinian included—have the right to run their own affairs," he noted that the PLO's *"raison d'etre* is not the undoing of Israel, but the salvation of the Palestinian people and their rights"; he insisted that "the Palestinians would accept—indeed, insist on—international guarantees for the security of all states in the region, including Palestine and Israel."[23] Arafat likewise noted in late 1988, "Our desire for peace is strategic and not a temporary tactic. . . . Our state [recently proclaimed by the PNC] provides salvation for the Palestinians and peace for both the Palestinians and Israelis. The right to self-determination means the existence of the Palestinians and our existence does not destroy the existence of the Israelis."[24] Pledging support for "[a]ll UN resolutions relevant to the Palestine question," including General Assembly Resolution 181 calling for establishing *both* a Jewish and Palestinian state in Palestine,[25] he demanded only that Israel withdraw "from all the Palestinian and Arab territories it occupied in 1967," while promising to void "those articles of the Palestinian Covenant which deny Israel's right to exist."[26] Such an approach guided PA policy throughout the Oslo period.

US opposition to creating a Palestinian state, a dominant feature of its pre-*Road Map* Middle East policy, was rooted in fears expressed repeatedly by Kissinger that "a Palestinian state is likely to have as its objective the destruction of both Jordan and Israel and is likely to have a high potential for disrupting the uneasy equilibrium in the area." Reflecting both Nixon and Ford's perspectives, Kissinger dismissed the "idea of a Palestinian state run by the PLO . . .

(as) not a subject for serious discourse," advocating instead that the West Bank "be returned to Jordan and not be an independent state."[27] Although Carter acknowledged the "legitimate rights of the Palestinian people" and agreed that there "has to be a homeland provided for the Palestinian refugees who have suffered for many, many years,"[28] he, like his predecessors, opposed establishing an independent Palestinian state; the Camp David agreements called only for an "elected self-governing authority in the West Bank and Gaza" capable of providing "full autonomy to the inhabitants."[29]

Embracing "the Camp David framework as the only way to proceed," the 1982 *Reagan Plan* called for "the Palestinian inhabitants of the West Bank and Gaza . . . [to gain] full autonomy over their own affairs."[30] While noting that in "the Middle East context the term self-determination has been identified exclusively with the formation of a Palestinian State," Reagan observed, "We will not support this definition of self-determination." He declared, "as we look to the future of the West Bank and Gaza, it is clear to me that peace cannot be achieved by the formation of an independent Palestinian State in those territories. Nor is it achievable on the basis of Israeli sovereignty or permanent control over the West Bank and Gaza. . . . it is the firm view of the United States that self-government by the Palestinians of the West Bank and Gaza in association with Jordan offers the best chance for a durable, just and lasting peace."[31] The 1987 Intifada did little to alter Administration thinking. While acknowledging that the "continued occupation of the West Bank and Gaza and frustration of Palestinian rights is a dead-end street," and arguing that Palestinians must "achieve rapid control over political and economic decisions that affect their lives," Secretary of State George Shultz observed, "Peace cannot be achieved through the creation of an independent Palestinian state . . . The United States cannot accept 'self-determination' when it is a code-word for an independent Palestinian state or for unilateral determination of the outcome of negotiations."[32]

While indicating that "the fundamental basis of our approach to a Middle East settlement has not changed. . . . we do not support an independent Palestinian state, nor Israeli sovereignty or permanent occupation of the West Bank and Gaza," the George H.W. Bush administration urged Israel to "engage in a serious dialogue with Palestinians that address their legitimate political rights" and to work cooperatively with PLO leaders to "arrive at a mutually acceptable formula for elections" in the Occupied Territories that "can be designed to contribute to a political process of dialogue and negotiation."[33] Secretary of State James Baker promoted a "reasonable middle ground to which a settlement should be directed." Advocating "self-government for Palestinians in the West Bank and Gaza in a manner acceptable to Palestinians, Israel and Jordan," he observed, "Such a formula provides ample scope for Palestinians to achieve their full political rights. It also provides ample protection for Israel's security as well."[34] Preparing for the Madrid Peace Conference, Bush stressed the value of "interim self-government arrangements" during a five year "transitional period" in "break[ing] down the walls of suspicion and mistrust and lay[ing] the basis for sustainable negotiations on the final status of the occupied territories," as well as in helping Palestinians to "achieve rapid control over political, economic, and other decisions that affect their lives" and to "adjust to a new situation in which Palestinians exercise authority in the West Bank and Gaza." While noting that a Palestinian confederation with Jordan was "consistent with longstanding U.S. policies" and was "not excluded as a possible outcome of negotiations," Bush avoided mention of an independent Palestinian state.[35]

Although *Oslo*'s creation of an empowered PA gave expression to decades-long US efforts to establish an interim Palestinian self-governing authority capable of improving Palestinian living conditions and engaging in final status negotiations with Israel, Camp David's collapse in July 2000 and the subsequent eruption of the al-Aqsa Intifada prompted a radical departure in US policy. Asserting the need for a "two-state solution," Clinton announced unprecedented "parameters" for a "comprehensive agreement." He observed, "there can be no genuine resolution to the conflict without a sovereign, viable, Palestinian state that accommodates Israelis' security requirements and the demographic realities. That suggests Palestinian sovereignty over Gaza, the vast majority of the West Bank, the incorporation into Israel of settlement blocks, with the goal of maximizing the number of settlers in Israel while minimizing the land annex for Palestine to be viable must be a geographically contiguous state."[36]

BORDERS

While Palestinians embraced two clearly defined perspectives on Israel's final borders—those who accepted the reality of a Jewish state demanded Israel return to its pre-1967 boundaries, while those opposed to the original UN partition plan called for completely eliminating the "Zionist entity"—Israelis demonstrated no such ambivalence. Foreign Minister Abba Eban articulated in late 1968 what would become Israel's authoritative interpretation of UNSCR 242's perspective on final borders. Arguing that the pre-1967 "ceasefire lines" had contributed to war and instability, and noting 242's recognition of the "right" of "every State in the area . . . to live in peace within secure and recognized boundaries free from threats or acts of force," Eban insisted that 242 was neither self-executing nor definitive concerning the extent of Israeli withdrawal "from territories occupied in the recent conflict." Rather, he emphasized that transforming pre-1967 "demarcation lines" into "secure and recognized boundaries" could occur only through a process of "negotiation and agreement."[37] While refusing to predict the outcome of such a process, he declared, "Three demands which Israel will not waive are a permanent presence at Sharm el-Sheikh, a unified Jerusalem despite concessions to Jordan over the Holy Places, and a Golan Heights for ever out of Syrian hands."[38] Golda Meir likewise observed, "Israel has publicly declared that, by virtue of her right to secure borders, defensible borders, she will not return to the frontiers of 4 June 1967, which make the country a temptation to aggression and which, on various fronts, give decisive advantages to an aggressor. Our position was and still remains that, in the absence of peace, we will continue to maintain the situation as determined at the cease-fire. The cease-fire can be replaced only by secure, recognized and agreed boundaries demarcated in a peace treaty."[39] Foreign Minister Yigal Allon concurred, noting, "The most cursory glance at a map is sufficient to ascertain how little the armistice lines of 1949—lines which were never in the first place recognized as final—could be considered defensible borders." Rejecting withdrawal "to the armistice lines of 1949 that preceded the 1967 war," he stressed the strategic necessity of retaining portions of the Occupied Territories, including "an effective defense line on the Golan Heights."[40]

Shamir was particularly adamant that Israel would "not entertain any notion" of returning to the "defunct pre-1967 armistice lines" nor to "anything approximating them," arguing that such "lines" had "proved to be a prescription for chronic instability and warfare" and that there was "virtually universal agreement" among Israelis "[o]n this point."[41] Speaking as Prime Minister at the opening of the Madrid Peace Conference, he went so far as to question the necessity for *any* territorial concessions. Observing that the "issue is not territory, but our existence," and noting that the conflict "raged well before Israel *acquired* Judea, Samaria, Gaza, and the Golan in a defensive war," he noted, "We are a nation of 4 million. The Arab nations from the Atlantic to the Gulf number 170 million. We control only 28,000 square km. The Arabs possess a land mass of 14 million square km."[42] Although Rabin and Barak subsequently retreated from such an absolutist position—both contemplated partial withdrawal from the Golan, while Barak anticipated making "painful" compromises with the Palestinians—neither envisaged withdrawal to the pre-1967 borders nor proposed final and permanent boundaries, indicating only that the "1967 borders will be amended."[43]

The United States was far more ambivalent regarding final borders than its Israeli friend and ally. President Lyndon Johnson's 1967 *Statement on Principles for Peace* reflected the complexities of US policy, asserting both that "it should be . . . clear that boundaries cannot and should not reflect the weight of conquest" *and* that "a return to the situation of June 4, 1967, will not bring peace."[44] The 1969 *Rogers Plan* similarly emphasized that "any changes in the preexisting lines should not reflect the weight of conquest and should be confined to insubstantial alterations required for mutual security," while indicating that the pre-1967 boundaries "were armistice lines, not final political borders," and that Resolution 242 "neither endorses nor precludes these armistice lines as the definitive political boundaries."[45] Kissinger likewise called upon Israel to agree in principle to a "withdrawal (on all fronts) . . . sufficiently substantial to justify an end to the state of war (or belligerency),"[46] while sympathizing with its tendency to see "in the territories occupied in 1967 an assurance of the security that it had vainly sought throughout its existence."[47] Echoing his Secretary of State, Ford simultaneously criticized Israel's intransigence over borders while acknowledging its "right to seek a defensible frontier which may not correspond identically with the frontiers of 1967."[48]

Carter shared his predecessors' convictions both that a settlement necessitated some Israeli withdrawal from the Occupied Territories *and* that final borders be determined by the parties themselves. Clarifying his campaign position that Israel "withdraw by agreed stages to the June 5, 1967, lines with only such modifications as are mutually accepted," he observed after assuming office, "The Arab countries say that Israel must withdraw to the pre-1967 borderlines, Israel says that they must adjust those lines to some degree to insure their own security. That is a matter to be negotiated between the Arab countries on the one side and Israel on the other."[49] Reagan similarly emphasized that while "the withdrawal provision of Resolution 242 applies to all fronts, including the West Bank and Gaza," Israel had a "right to exist in peace behind secure and defensible borders." Noting that in "the pre-1967 borders, Israel was barely 10 miles wide at its narrowest point. The bulk of Israel's population lived within artillery range of hostile Arab armies. I am not about to ask Israel to live that way again," he observed, "When the border is negotiated between Jordan and Israel, our view on the extent to which Israel should be asked to give up territory will be heavily affected by the extent of true peace and normalization and the security arrangements offered in return."[50] George Shultz likewise noted Israel's obligation "to withdraw—as Resolution 242 says—'from territories occupied in the recent conflict,'" while stressing the need to address the issue of borders "realistically" given Israel's refusal to "negotiate from or return to the lines of partition or to the 1967 borders."[51] Thirty Senators publicly endorsed Administration policy, declaring, "Israel cannot be expected to give up all the territory gained in 1967 or to return to the dangerous and insecure pre-'67 borders. Resolution 242 does not require it to do so. On the other hand, peace negotiations have little chance of success if the Israeli government's position rules out territorial compromise."[52]

The George H.W. Bush administration emphasized Washington's commitment both to ending "the Israeli occupation" and to promoting the principle of "territory for peace." While refusing to proffer suggestions for final borders, Bush and James Baker pledged US assistance in facilitating "direct negotiations based on UN Security Council Resolutions 242 and 338" and readiness to "accept any outcome agreed by the parties."[53] The subsequent *Oslo* process reflected Clinton's similar adherence both to Resolution 242's "land for peace" principle and to the "US as mediator" role in the Israeli-Palestinian context. Only the dramatic eruption of the al-Aqsa Intifada prompted him to abandon such an approach, opting instead to articulate a vision of "secure, recognized borders" both for Israel and a future Palestinian state that actually specified the "criteria" by which the "parties should develop a map," including endorsing Israeli annexation of portions of the West Bank and compensatory "land swaps" from Israel to a Palestinian state.[54]

SETTLEMENTS

Israel's decision following the 1967 War to create irreversible "facts on the ground" prompted over 200,000 Israelis to emigrate to the West Bank and Gaza by 2003, a demographic reality that profoundly impacted the *Road Map*'s prospects for success. Articulating the widespread belief that a "selective settlement policy" was "an integral part" of Israel's "unique defense system," the Labor Party's 1973 *Galili Plan* pledged "intensive action to unify lands for the requirements of existing and planned settlement," promoted "expand[ed] purchases of land and real estate in the occupied areas for the purposes of settlement, development and land exchange," advocated establishing new settlements and reinforcing the existing "network of settlements," and called for increasing settlements' "population by developing trade, industry and tourism."[55] Likud's 1977 platform explicitly linked expanded settlements to Israel's "right to security and peace." While emphasizing the "eternal and indisputable" "right of the Jewish people to the land of Israel," it observed, "Settlement, both urban and rural, in all parts of the Land of Israel is the focal point of the Zionist effort to redeem the country, to maintain vital security areas and serves as a reservoir of strength and inspiration for the renewal of the pioneering spirit. The Likud government will call on the younger generation in Israel and the dispersions to settle and help every group and individual in the task of inhabiting and cultivating the wasteland."[56] Prime Minister Menachem Begin, declaring that Eretz Yisrael was "our land and it belongs to the Jewish nation rightfully," indicated that "Israeli residents will be entitled to purchase land and settle in the areas of Judea, Samaria and Gaza" in an effort, in Buchanan's words, to foreclose any "compromise territorial/political arrangement with the Palestinians."[57]

Reflecting his government's commitment "to strengthen, expand, and develop settlement" as "a right and an integral part of the nation's security,"[58] Defense Minister Ariel Sharon stressed in 1981 the strategic value of "populous and high quality settlement of key border areas in Judea, Samaria, the Gaza District, the Golan Heights, the Galilee and the Negev."[59] Shamir likewise observed, "as Judea and Samaria constitute the heartland of the Jewish people's birth and development as a nation, Israel will not be party to a design that would deny Jews residence in those areas. No less important, the Israeli presence in these areas, both civilian and military, is vital to Israel's defense."[60] Speaking as Prime Minister before the Knesset in 1988, he argued, "There is a wide national consensus on the right of the Jews to live anywhere in Eretz-Israel. This does not contradict peace, nor does it harm the peace process. The Jewish settlements in Judea, Samaria and the Gaza District fulfill an important role in the realm of defense and in preventing the establishment of a PLO state within Eretz-Israel. The very fact that they are in these places contributes to the security and to the safety of movement throughout the country. . . . We will assure the promotion and development of these settlements, and of the settlements on the Golan Heights, and we will expand settlement throughout Eretz-Israel."[61]

Despite previous pledges by top Labor party officials to oppose "the establishment of new settlements," Rabin indicated in 1992 that his new government would "strengthen and build up Jewish settlement along the confrontation lines, due to their security importance, and in metropolitan Jerusalem."[62] He likewise promised that *Oslo* would not compromise longstanding Israeli policy, observing, the "Israeli settlements in Judea, Samaria, and Gaza will remain under Israel's rule without any change whatsoever in their status."[63] Although Barak's government indicated in 1999, "Until the status of the Jewish communities in Judea, Samaria and Gaza is determined, within the framework of the permanent settlement, no new communities will be built," it praised "all forms of settlement as a valued social and national enterprise";[64] Barak promised in 2000 that the "overwhelming majority of the settlers in Judea, Samaria and the Gaza Strip will be in settlement blocs under Israeli sovereignty" under any conceivable final agreement.[65] Sharon's Likud government made no secret of its commitment both to expanding existing settlements and to establishing new ones, devoting significant economic, military, and political resources to their construction, maintenance, and protection, and to insulating them from any multilateral peace initiatives.

Palestinians' initial opposition to Israeli settlement policy reflected concerns that "the settlement mentality and the projects it harbours . . . [threaten] the liquidation of our people's cause as far as the liberation of our homeland is concerned," while risking "the distortion of this cause by proposals for entities and for the establishment of a Palestinian State—in part of the territory of Palestine." Emphasizing the need "to liberate the whole of Palestinian soil," the PNC opposed "the Judaization of parts of the occupied homeland" and advocated "resist[ing] with violence the building of settlements."[66] While Arafat and the PNC's eventual acceptance of a "mini-state objective" transformed the rationale upon which settlements were opposed, Palestinian officials continued to demand "cessation of all settlement activity and land confiscation," "release of lands already confiscated," removal of "settlements which Israel has established in the Palestinian and Arab territories since 1967," and "annulment of all measures of annexation and appropriation."[67] *Oslo* only intensified criticism of Israeli policies. Emphasizing that settlements "cut through geographic and political unity, prevent free movement between the areas of the West Bank and the Strip, and create hotbeds of tension that conflict with the spirit of peace," Arafat highlighted Israeli violations of commitments not to "initiate or take any step that will change the status of the West Bank and the Gaza Strip pending the outcome of the permanent status negotiations," nor to compromise the Occupied Territories' "integrity" "during the interim period."[68] The PNC argued, "Halting settlement in the occupied territories, including Holy Jerusalem, is an indispensable necessity to start the peace process."[69]

Oslo's disintegration highlighted concern over US and Israeli proposals to create West Bank "settlement blocs" under Israeli sovereignty in the context of establishing an independent Palestinian state. Observing that "all of the settlements in the West Bank currently occupy approximately 2 percent of the West Bank," Palestinian negotiators argued that settlement blocs "involving annexation of 4 to 6 percent (not to mention 10 percent) of the land would inevitably damage vital Palestinian interests," "the territorial contiguity of the State of Palestine," "Palestinians' freedom of movement within their own state," "the state's development potential," and Palestinians' "water rights." They declared, "it is impossible to agree to a proposal that punishes Palestinians while rewarding Israel's illegal settlement policies," nor to an approach that "subordinates Palestinian interests in the contiguity of their state and control over their natural resources to Israeli interests regarding the contiguity of settlements."[70]

Pre-*Road Map* US policy toward Israeli settlements was consistently ambivalent, both condemning Israel's transfer of civilians to the Occupied Territories as a violation of international law *and* providing the military, economic, political, and diplomatic support upon which settlements depended. US Ambassador William W. Scranton, speaking before the UN Security Council in March 1976, articulated what he described as the "clear" and "long standing" US perspective that the "substantial resettlement of the Israeli civilian population in occupied territories, including East Jerusalem, is illegal under the [Fourth Geneva] convention and cannot be considered to have prejudged the outcome of future negotiations between the parties on the location of the borders of states of the Middle East. Indeed, the presence of these settlements is seen by my government as an obstacle to the success of the negotiations for a just and final peace between Israel and its neighbors."[71] However, despite rapid settlement expansion, Ford institutionalized the multibillion dollar economic and military aid relationship with Israel initiated by Nixon, arguing that the "time for one-shot transactions has passed"; his fiscal year 1977 security assistance budget provided Israel with $1000 million in military assistance and $780 million in economic aid "to maintain [its] defensive strength and economic health."[72]

Carter's oft-repeated concerns that settlement expansion posed a particularly serious obstacle to Arab-Israeli negotiations—a position expressed passionately during the Camp David process—were shared by Reagan and his top advisors, who declared, "The United States will not support the use of any additional land for the purpose of settlements during the transition period [to Palestinian autonomy]. Indeed, the immediate adoption of a settlement freeze by Israel, more than any other action, could create the confidence needed for wider participation in these talks. Further settlement activity is in no way necessary for the security of Israel and only diminishes the confidence of the Arabs that a final outcome can be freely and fairly negotiated."[73] However, while identifying the "establishment of new Israeli settlements in the occupied territories [as] an obstacle to peace," and noting that the "status of the West Bank and Gaza cannot be determined by unilateral acts of either side, but only through a process of negotiations," Reagan and Shultz departed from previous US policy that settlements were *primae facie* violations of international law, reassuring Israeli officials that support for a "real settlement freeze" was tempered by opposition to the "dismantlement of the existing settlements";[74] agreements such as the 1981 *Memorandum of Understanding on Strategic Cooperation* indicated a willingness to "agree to disagree" about settlements in the context of increasingly supportive bilateral ties.

While the George H.W. Bush administration reiterated Washington's opposition to "new settlements in the West Bank or in East Jerusalem," promised to "conduct that policy as if it's firm, which it is,"[75] declared that "the United States has opposed and will continue to oppose settlement activity in the territories occupied in 1967, which remains an obstacle to peace," and told the American Israel Public Affairs Committee that Israel must "stop settlement activity,"[76] it departed from previous administrations' reliance on empty rhetoric, opting instead to link $10 billion in loan guarantees to Israeli commitments to halt settlement expansion. Scathing criticism of such tactics by the pro-Israeli lobby tempered the approach of the incoming Clinton administration. While declaring that "the settlement enterprise and building bypass roads in the heart of what [Israel] already know[s] will one day be part of a Palestinian state is inconsistent with the Oslo commitment that both sides negotiate a compromise," Clinton neither envisaged dismantling most settlements nor exerted significant economic, political, or financial pressure on Israel to alter its policies. Rather, the *Clinton Plan*, conceding the irreversibility of Israel's "facts on the ground" policy, sanctioned Israeli annexation of sufficient West Bank territory to incorporate 80 percent of settlers within "settlement blocs" in Israel proper.[77]

REFUGEES

Palestinians' insistence throughout the pre-*Road Map* period on resolving the refugee situation according to UN General Assembly Resolution 194's (1948) principles of "right of return" and "just compensation" reflected the ongoing effects of massive dislocations from the wars of 1948 and 1967. Seeking to determine for themselves how best to remedy their circumstances, Palestinians found 194's language particularly appealing: "refugees wishing to return to their homes and live at peace with their neighbours should be permitted to do so at the earliest practicable date . . . compensation should be paid for the property of those choosing not to return and for loss of or damage to property which, under principles of international law or in equity, should be made good by the Governments or authorities responsible."[78] Emphasizing adherence to 194's foundational principles, the PNC insisted in 1974 that the "right of return" was a "foremost" "national right," while Fatah, the PFLP, PDFLP, PFLP-GC, Sa'iqa, ALF, PLF, and PLO issue a *Six-Point Programme* in 1977 demanding "the Palestinian people's rights to return."[79] The PLO and PNC dismissed both UNSCR 242 and the Camp David agreements for ignoring refugees' "inalienable" right "to return to their homes."[80]

Palestinian resistance organizations and executive leadership remained unwavering throughout the 1980s in demanding Resolution 194's "right of return." The PNC declared "its full adherance [sic] to our people's right to return to their homeland," stressed "the inalienable national rights of our Palestinian people, including those of return," emphasized the right to "repatriation" as a "basis for any just political move toward our cause," affirmed the "Palestinian people's national inalienable rights to repatriation," called for "the achievement of our people's right to return," and insisted on "settlement of the question of the Palestinian refugees in accordance with the relevant United Nations resolutions."[81] The PLO's Executive Committee highlighted Palestinians' "inalienable national right" to "repatriation," while the Unified National Command of the Intifada called upon "our masses" to "wrest our people's national legitimate rights to repatriation" from the "new Nazis" occupying Palestinians' homeland.[82] Arafat, speaking before the UN General Assembly in December 1988, focused on 194's insistence on "Palestinians' right to return to their homeland and property from which they were expelled" or to receive compensation should they "not wish to return."[83]

Neither the initiation of direct PLO-US discussions in 1989 nor of PLO-Israeli negotiations in 1991 tempered Palestinians' insistence upon Resolution 194's continuing relevance. Fatah demanded "adherence" to Palestinian's "national inalienable right" to "repatriation,"[84] the PLO's Central Council stressed "our peoples' aims of return,"[85] and Arafat emphasized that the "sacred" right of return was "a right enshrined in international law and reaffirmed by the United Nations in its Resolution 194." While indicating a willingness "to discuss the conditions" by which 194 would be implemented, Arafat reminded Israel that its admittance into the UN was predicated on a commitment to "accept all previous UN resolutions on the Palestine Question, including Resolution 194."[86]

The PA adhered to longstanding Palestinian policy, rejecting the *Clinton Plan* as "reflect[ing] a wholesale adoption of the Israeli position that the implementation of the right of return be subject entirely to Israel's discretion" and as failing "to provide any assurance that refugee rights to restitution and compensation will be fulfilled." Emphasizing that the "essence of the right of return is choice," it insisted that Palestinians "be given the option to choose where they wish to settle, including return to the homes from which they were driven," argued that "[r]ecognition of the right to return and the provision of choice to refugees is a prerequisite for the closure of the conflict," and observed, "There is no historical precedent for a people abandoning their fundamental right to return to their homes whether they were forced to leave or fled in fear. We will not be the first people to do so." While indicating a willingness "to think flexibly and creatively about the mechanisms for implementing the right of return," it stressed that "Resolution 194, long regarded as the basis for a just settlement of the refugee problem, calls for the return of Palestinian refugees to 'their homes,' wherever located not to their 'homeland' or to 'historic Palestine.'"[87]

While not insensitive to refugees' hardships, Israeli leaders never accepted Resolution 194's fundamental premise of choice, arguing that to do so would threaten the very survival of a Jewish Israel. Although stressing their commitment to cooperating "fully" in post-1967 regional efforts "to chart a five-year plan for the solution of the refugee problem in the framework of a lasting peace and the integration of refugees into productive life," neither Prime Minister Levi Eshkol nor Foreign Minister Abba Eban acknowledged 194-type obligations concerning repatriation and compensation.[88] Indeed, throughout the pre-*Oslo* period the government's *Fundamental Policy Guidelines* remained silent on Resolution 194's relationship to a final settlement.[89]

Although the Oslo process marked a radical departure in Israeli-Palestinian relations, it did little to alleviate concerns about Resolution 194's potentially disastrous implications. While Rabin pledged "vigorous steps to bring about the termination of the Arab-Israeli conflict" and urged Palestinians to seize an "opportunity [for peace] which may never recur," he deferred consideration of the explosive refugee issue to future "permanent status negotiations."[90] Barak, unyielding in opposing Resolution 194, argued that identifying a "solution to the problem of refugees *outside* Israeli sovereign territory" was critical to achieving a final settlement; such a posture contributed to persistently "wide gaps" on the refugee issue between Israel and the PA of a "conceptual . . . not just technical nature."[91]

Washington's efforts to resolve the tensions and ambiguities inherent in its concern both for the plight of Palestinian refugees *and* for Israeli sensitivity to Resolution 194 found initial expression in the Nixon administration. While declaring that there could "be no lasting peace without a just settlement of the problem of those Palestinians whom the wars of 1948 and 1967 have made homeless," and emphasizing that a "just settlement must take into account the desires and aspirations of the refugees," Secretary of State William Rogers acknowledged the need to accommodate "the legitimate concerns of the governments in the area."[92] Joseph Sisco, Assistant Secretary of State for Near Eastern and South Asian Affairs, likewise expressed "hope . . . that a just settlement of the refugee problem can be achieved which takes into account the tragic human element,"[93] while recognizing the practical necessity to limit repatriation given Israeli concerns.

While neither Carter, Reagan, nor George H.W. Bush retreated from endorsing Resolution 194's general framework for resolving the refugee issue, they were unprepared to impose its specific demands on Israel. Despite supporting "a homeland . . . for the Palestinian refugees," "resolution of the Palestinian problem in all its aspects," and recognition of "the legitimate rights of the Palestinian people," Carter refused to press Israel on the refugee question; the Camp David *Frameworks*' silence on the issue was particularly telling.[94] Reagan likewise acknowledged "the legitimate rights of the Palestinian people and their just requirements," "the homelessness of the Palestinian people," and "the yearning of the Palestinian people for a just solution of their claims," while failing to press for 194's implementation.[95] Indeed, neither the *Reagan Plan* nor private White House communications with Israeli and Arab leaders detailed strategies for resolving the refugee issue.[96] George H.W. Bush similarly acknowledged Palestinians' "legitimate political rights" without supporting any refugee related measures, including Resolution 194, which could threaten Israel's "security."[97]

Oslo's relegation of the refugee issue to future "permanent status negotiations," coupled with its failure to specify Resolution 194 as the referent for such negotiations, encouraged Clinton to continue the ambiguously noncommittal policies of his predecessors. Expressing support for Palestinians' "legitimate rights" *and* for Israel's "real security," he cautioned both parties to avoid "taking unilateral steps or making unilateral statements that could prejudice the outcome" of negotiations on refugee related questions.[98] However, *Oslo*'s collapse prompted the Administration's public renunciation of 194's bedrock principle, that of Palestinian choice. Arguing that "we need to adopt a formulation on the right of return that will make clear that there is no specific right of return to Israel itself but that does not negate the aspiration of the Palestinian people to return to the area," Clinton stressed that "the guiding principle should be that the Palestinian state should be the focal point for the Palestinians who choose to return to the area without ruling out that Israel will accept some of these refugees." While hoping that the "parties would agree that this [approach] implements Resolution 194," Clinton seriously underestimated Palestinian opposition to retaining discretion only to return to a future State of Palestine, while "rehabilitation in host countries, resettlement in third countries and absorption into Israel [would] depend upon the policies of those countries."[99] Promises to help raise "the money necessary to relocate [refugees] in the most appropriate manner" and to compensate refugees "for their losses" did little to conceal Clinton's abandonment of Resolution 194 as the rhetorical foundation of US policy in deference to Israeli opposition to "any reference to a right of return that would imply a right to immigrate to Israel in defiance of Israel's sovereign policies [on] admission or that would threaten the Jewish character of the state."[100]

JERUSALEM

Israel's occupation of East Jerusalem in 1967 exacerbated the most emotionally divisive issue separating Israelis and Palestinians, sovereignty over the Holy City. Although vowing after the June War not to "exercise unilateral jurisdiction in the Holy Places of Christianity and Islam," Israeli leaders insisted that Israel would "not waive" its demand for "a unified Jerusalem" under Israeli sovereignty.[101] Yigal Allon, speaking in 1976 as Foreign Minister, observed, "Jerusalem, Israel's capital, which was never the capital of any Arab or Muslim State, but was always the capital and center of the Jewish people, cannot return to the absurd situation of being partitioned. The Holy City and adjacent areas essential for its protection and communications must remain a single, undivided unit under Israel's sovereignty." While noting that Jerusalem's "universal status" as "holy to three great religions" demanded "a solution for the religious interests connected with it," he emphasized "a *religious* and not a political solution."[102] The Knesset officially proclaimed Jerusalem, "whole and united," as Israel's capital on 29 July 1980, while promising that the Holy Places would "be protected from desecration and any other offense and from anything likely to prejudice the freedom of access of the members of the different religions to the places sacred to them or their feelings with regard to those places."[103]

Shamir captured Israel's visceral attachment to its self-proclaimed capital, declaring,

> Jerusalem is the eternal capital of our nation and our country. It is engraved in the Bible, on which the exiled in Babylon vowed: If I forget thee, O Jerusalem, let my right hand lose its cunning! Let my tongue cleave to the roof of my mouth, if I do not remember you, if I do not set Jerusalem above my highest joy! Pray for the peace of Jerusalem! These words are a holy tenet for all of us. The Basic Law: Jerusalem, the Capital of Israel, stipulates, in Article One: Jerusalem as a single, united entity, is the capital of Israel. First and foremost, Jerusalem is imprinted in the hearts, in the heart of each one of us!

He told the Knesset, "There are things about which it is unnecessary to speak. They are engraved not only in the pages of books and in history and in law; they are engraved, first of all, on our hearts. The heart of every Jew beats for Jerusalem."[104] Shimon Peres, although leader of the Labor Party and generally critical of Shamir, likewise reminded the Knesset, "There is nothing that unites this house more than Jerusalem. . . . There are no differences of opinion on the issue of Jerusalem. . . . Jerusalem, Israel's capital, within borders decided by the Government of Israel, will remain a united city where Israeli law will prevail, where autonomy will not be imposed—an eternal capital of Israel."[105] The government, reflecting such consensus opinion,[106] insisted that the Holy City was "the eternal capital of Israel, indivisible, entirely under Israeli sovereignty,"[107] denied that "the neighborhoods set up in Jerusalem since the six-day war [be] considered settlements in occupied territory," and prohibited Arab inhabitants of East Jerusalem from participating in proposed "elections of the authorities and representatives of the inhabitants of Judea, Samaria, and Gaza."[108]

Echoing Shamir's insistence at the Madrid Peace Conference that Israeli sovereignty over Jerusalem was nonnegotiable,[109] Rabin's 1992 "Inaugural Address" declared, "This government, just like all its predecessors, believes there are no differences of opinion within this House concerning the eternalness of Jerusalem as the capital of Israel. Jerusalem, whole and united, has been and will remain the capital of the Israeli people under Israeli sovereignty, the place every Jew yearns and dreams of. The government is resolute in its position that Jerusalem is not a negotiable issue." While promising to "uphold the freedom of worship of members of all other faiths in Jerusalem" and "meticulously maintain free access to the holy sites of all faiths and sects," he advocated "build[ing] up Jewish settlement . . . in metropolitan Jerusalem."[110] Indicating that *Oslo* should not be interpreted as signaling any change in policy toward the Holy City, Rabin emphasized that a "[u]nited and unified Jerusalem is not negotiable and will be the capital of the Israeli people under Israel's sovereignty and the subject of every Jew's yearnings and dreams for ever and ever"; he stressed that interim self-governing arrangements would provide Palestinians with "no authority" over Jerusalem's administration.[111]

While the various Israeli-Palestinian agreements of the 1990s recognized Jerusalem as a "permanent status issue" to be resolved through negotiations,[112] Israel demonstrated little flexibility over the sovereignty issue until the July 2000 Camp David talks. Having previously emphasized his commitment to a "united Jerusalem under Israeli sovereignty" and to retaining "Greater Jerusalem" as the "eternal capital of Israel,"[113] Barak unexpectedly indicated the possibility of recognizing Palestinian sovereignty over "certain villages or small cities that had been annexed to Jerusalem just after 1967," albeit within the context of "annexing to Jerusalem cities within the West Bank beyond the 1967 border." Although touching "the most sensitive nerves," Barak emphasized that his proposals would make "Jerusalem wider and stronger than at any time, in any previous time in the history of the city," thereby bolstering "greater Jerusalem, with a solid Jewish majority, for future generations."[114]

Israel's insistence on retaining sovereignty over greater Jerusalem was mirrored by Palestinian demands "to establish a free and independent state with Jerusalem as its capital."[115] Declaring Israel's establishment "null and void," the 1968 *Palestinian National Covenant* asserted Palestinians' "legal right" to their "homeland," defined as "Palestine with its boundaries that existed at the time of the British mandate," and called for the "complete liberation of Palestine," including Jerusalem.[116] The Palestinian National Assembly dismissed the "State of Israel" as "absolutely incompatible with the Palestinian Arab people's right to the whole of Palestine, their homeland," and advocated liberating "the entire territory of Palestine, over which the Palestinian Arab people shall exercise their sovereignty."[117] Indicting efforts by Zionist "terrorists" to deprive Jerusalem "of its Arab (Muslim and Christian) character by evicting its inhabitants and annexing it," Arafat called for "our beloved city of peace" to become the capital of democratic Palestine "where Christian, Jew and Muslim live in justice, equality, fraternity."[118]

The Knesset's proclamation of Jerusalem as Israel's capital and as "the seat of the President of the State, the Knesset, the Government and the Supreme Court" elicited tremendous concern from Palestinians about the future of their "beloved Jerusalem, the throbbing heart of Palestine."[119] The PNC "affirmed that the occupied city of Jerusalem is the capital of Palestine," declared that "the Zionist occupation of Jerusalem [was] a violation of the Palestinian people's rights and a defiance of international laws as well as a provocation of all the believers in the world," and "called on all the world countries and organizations to refuse to carry out anything that will entail an implicit recognition of the Zionist aggression against Jerusalem or its actions therein."[120] Arafat stressed that Palestinians' "firm national rights," including "the establishment of our independent Palestinian state on our national Palestinian soil," with "our fluttering banners . . . raised over holy Jerusalem, capital of our independent Palestine," were "not open to disposal."[121] The PLO's Executive Committee repeatedly demanded an end to "the Zionist occupation of the occupied Arab territories, including Jerusalem," and asserted the "Palestinian people's inalienable national rights, including their right to establish their national, independent state whose capital is Jerusalem."[122]

The PLO's Executive Committee, PNC, Hamas, Unified National Command of the Intifada, and Palestinian leaders from the West Bank and Gaza seized upon the first Intifada's outbreak in December 1987 to reemphasize Jerusalem's importance as the capital of an independent Palestinian state.[123] Noting that the Intifada's "revolutionary irreversible impulse" had delivered the Palestinian people to "a decisive juncture," the PNC proclaimed on 15 November 1988 "the establishment of the State of Palestine on our Palestinian territory with its capital Jerusalem," called upon Israel to withdraw from "Arab Jerusalem," and implored the UN to administer the Holy City "for a limited period in order to protect our people."[124] Arafat lauded the Intifada's "steadfastness," observing, "The state is within a stone's throw, the victory is coming, and our Palestinian flag will be raised, God willing, over Jerusalem, the capital of our city, the first of the two qiplas . . . and the third sacred shrines, the birthplace of the Messiah and the city to where the Prophet Muhammad made his night journey."[125] Prior to the Madrid Peace Conference, the PNC stressed that Jerusalem was "an indivisible part of occupied Palestinian territory," insisted Israel halt settlement construction and fully withdraw from "sacred Jerusalem," and demanded creation of "a Palestinian state with Holy Jerusalem as its capital."[126]

Characterizing Jerusalem as "the heart of our homeland and the cradle of the soul," the Palestinian delegation's opening speech at Madrid criticized Israel's annexation of Arab Jerusalem as "both clearly illegal in the eyes of the world community, and an affront to the peace that this city deserves," noted that Palestinians from Jerusalem had "been barred" from the Conference and "denied a voice and an identity," and declared, "Palestinian Jerusalem, the capital of our homeland and future state, defines Palestinian existence, past, present, and future."[127]

Although *Oslo* permitted Palestinian residents of Jerusalem to participate in elections establishing the Palestinian Authority, it deferred consideration of Jerusalem's final disposition until future "permanent status negotiations."[128] However, its collapse, coupled with the inability of the July 2000 Camp David talks "to bridge the gaps" that were raised "about issues that [had] to do with Jerusalem,"[129] left the situation little changed at the al-Aqsa Intifada's onset. Arafat, recalling his pre-*Oslo* pledge that "[h]istory will not register that the present generation of Palestinians squandered an atom of the soil of its homeland or of Jerusalem," rejected *Clinton Plan* proposals that would "divide Palestinian Jerusalem into a number of unconnected islands separate from each other and from the rest of Palestine," insisting instead on guaranteeing "the contiguity of Palestinian areas within the city as well as the contiguity of Jerusalem with the rest of Palestine."[130] Such insistence on preserving "holy Jerusalem" as the capital of a future Palestinian state defined PA policy for the remainder of the pre-*Road Map* period.

Lyndon Johnson's *Statement on Principles for Peace*, released within weeks of the 1967 War, articulated what would become a basic tenet of US policy, that the Holy City never again be "divided by barbed wire and by machine guns." While noting that Jerusalem was "a critical issue" in any "peace settlement," Johnson refrained from detailing possible solutions, opting instead to encourage "the parties to stretch their imaginations" to reach an agreement.[131] Ambassador to the UN Arthur Goldberg observed, "The United States does not accept or recognize unilateral actions by any states in the area as altering the status of Jerusalem," while his successor, Charles W. Yost, declared, "the part of Jerusalem that came under the control of Israel in the June war, like other areas occupied by Israel, is occupied territory and hence subject to the provisions of international law governing the rights and obligations of an occupying power."[132]

Both Nixon and Ford endorsed Johnson's basic approach, including the need for "the parties concerned" to assume primary responsibility for resolving the issue, the importance of Jerusalem remaining "a unified city within which there would no longer be restrictions on the movement of persons and goods," the necessity for Israel and Jordan both to have "roles . . . in the civic, economic, and religious life of the city," and the demand that all parties refrain from "unilateral actions . . . to decide the final status of the city."[133] Ambassador to the UN William Scranton detailed US policy in a March 1976 statement to the Security Council. Acknowledging that the "deep religious attachment of Moslems and Jews and Christians to the holy places of Jerusalem has added a uniquely volatile element to the tensions that inhere in an occupation situation," he stressed that

> unilateral measures, including expropriation of land or other administrative actions taken by the Government of Israel, cannot be considered other than interim and provisional and cannot affect the present international status nor prejudge the final and permanent status of Jerusalem. The U.S. position could not be clearer. Since 1967 we have restated here, in other forums, and to the Government of Israel that the future of Jerusalem will be determined only through the instruments and processes of negotiation, agreement, and accommodation. Unilateral attempts to predetermine that future have no standing.[134]

Neither Carter, Reagan, nor George H.W. Bush deviated significantly from such an approach, agreeing that "Jerusalem must never again be a divided city," that its "final status should be decided by negotiations," and that settlements in East Jerusalem were an obstacle to negotiations.[135]

Although Clinton likewise stressed that "Jerusalem should be an open and undivided city, with assured freedom of access and worship for all," and rejected "either side taking unilateral steps or making unilateral statements that could prejudice" final status negotiations, his *Clinton Plan* fanned longstanding Israeli fears that "sovereignty over Jerusalem [was] subject to negotiations."[136] Premised upon the belief that Jerusalem "should encompass the internationally recognized capitals of two states, Israel and Palestine," it sought to transcend "symbolic issues of sovereignty" and insure "a way to accord respect to the religious beliefs of both sides" by proposing "Palestinian sovereignty over the Haram and Israeli sovereignty over the Western Wall and shared functional sovereignty over the issue of excavation under the Haram and behind the Wall such that mutual consent would be requested before any excavation could take place." While such an approach—"what is Jewish should be Israeli . . . what is Arab should be Palestinian"—permitted Israel to benefit from prior settlement efforts, it also enabled the PA to claim a modified "Jerusalem" as its future capital.[137]

CONTEXT— TERRORISM

The ability of *Road Map* patterned efforts to pursue "a conflict resolution process which results in a just and comprehensive peace," rather than merely a "conflict management exercise by the powerful to anaesthetize a minor irritant, which occasionally becomes a problem,"[1] depends, according to former Secretary of State George Shultz, not on "a particular procedure" but rather on "the readiness of the parties to exploit opportunities, confront hard choices, and make fair and mutual concessions."[2] Such "readiness" has been particularly elusive given the "existential" nature of the Israeli-Palestinian conflict, one predicated upon "issues that relate to ontological human needs that cannot be compromised," including "claim[s] to the same land, to the same water, to the same air." Both parties' "aggressive manifest conflict processes" have emphasized "physically damaging or destroying the property and high-value symbols of one another; and/or psychologically or physically injuring, destroying, or otherwise forcibly eliminating one another." Resulting losses, "in lives, in territory, in justice and in legitimacy," have contributed to "competing, if not entirely symmetrical, psychologies of victimhood."[3]

TERRORISM: CONSTRAINT AND OPPORTUNITY

While terrorism has played a critical role in institutionalizing violence, hatred, and mistrust between Israelis and Palestinians, it also has contributed to creating episodic moments of diplomatic opportunity likely to reappear in the future. Recognizing that "a state's response to transnational terror is significantly impacted by the relationship among terrorist actions, the international strategic perspective and goals of elite decisionmakers, and key features of the domestic political environment," it follows that "similar acts of terror will elicit different responses as strategic and political conditions evolve and their relative influence varies." Five phases may be identified in "a state's experience with transnational terror that influence the policy options available to decisionmakers and their likely course of action, and that define both the constraints and opportunities perceived by government leaders."[4] Phase I, characterized "by an absence of societal awareness or concern with transnational terrorism and by its irrelevance for the pursuit of policymakers' international objectives," provides government leaders with "significant latitude in pursuing desired policies," yet minimizes the potential "to exploit terror either for domestic political advantage or to realize non-terror related international objectives." In contrast, Phase II is defined by "higher profile terror actions that command growing, if episodic, attention within the domestic arena." Although the "frequency, location, magnitude, and target selection of terrorists" enhance transnational terrorism's political salience and generate growing pressures to do *something* to "appear responsive to the terrorist threat," policymakers retain significant "discretion in determining appropriate responses."[5] As one analyst observed,

> Although terrorism has achieved a measure of political salience, the public remains largely uninformed about terrorist actors and motivations, the media dependent upon government information, and [the legislature] and the interest group community only periodically engaged with the issue. Policymakers have fertile ground upon which to establish their agenda of concerns, as well as to develop the 'definitional boundaries' that distinguish terrorism by the identity of the actor rather than by the methods of action; terrorism 'becomes the activities of persons deemed terrorist' by the government. Manipulation of the labelling process, as well as the 'rally around the flag' effect associated with heightened fear and insecurity, facilitates the pursuit of objectives which may have little relationship to countering terrorism[,] . . . [including] initiatives involving defense spending, foreign aid, intelligence gathering, covert operations, support for international law and international organizations, commitments to friends and allies, and expansion of executive powers.[6]

Phase III, marked by transnational terrorism's transformation into "a commonplace occurrence directly impacting domestic perceptions of security and wellbeing," poses both new challenges *and* opportunities for decisionmakers. As terrorists' identity and objectives become more widely known and understood, policymakers confront "an increasingly vocal, assertive, and knowledgeable public, a vigilant and insistent [legislature] and media, and an active and energized interest group community, none of whom are readily placated by symbolic gestures." However, while the "crystallizing of political sentiment around the need for substantive action" creates significant constraints on elite behavior, "demands for vigorous action, especially when rooted in a crisis atmosphere, provide policymakers with opportunities afforded only by issues with high political salience." Generalized fear and anxiety associated with terrorist threats privilege an "'elitist subsystem' of policymaking that minimizes opportunities for input into the decisionmaking process by the mass public, interest groups, and [the legislature]," while enhancing decisionmaker's ability "to pursue a broad range of non-terror related objectives, both domestic and international, by bolstering approval ratings, squelching media criticism, restraining legislative assertiveness, and limiting interest group effectiveness."[7]

While Phase IV is defined by terrorism's increasingly serious threat to "vital national interests, including the security of friends and allies, the ability to conduct international commerce, and the success of critical diplomatic initiatives," and thus by its enhanced "strategic relevance," its "lack of domestic political salience . . . affords significant latitude in the choice of response options," "ranging from the tactical accommodation of terrorists' demands to the use of military force." Although "threats to international strategic interests necessitate counterterror measures, they also present significant opportunities to pursue non-terror related objectives." Initiatives involving the "negotiation and implementation of multilateral conventions, intelligence sharing, execution of extradition agreements, and application of coercive economic or military policies" may be utilized as "the foundation upon which new bilateral relationships may be developed and ties with friends and allies solidified." Counterterror approaches also may be selected "to convey policymakers' general orientation toward the international arena: reliance upon multilateral negotiations within the framework of organizations such as the UN, NATO, or the Organization of American States emphasizes the value attached to international law, international organizations, and consultative diplomacy; resort to unilateral action reflects a lack of confidence in friends and allies; and the application of overwhelming force demonstrates faith in the utility of the military instrument and a willingness to employ it to protect national interests."[8]

Characterized "by the maturation of transnational terrorism into a phenomenon with direct, significant, and longterm international strategic, as well as domestic political and security, implications," Phase V confronts policymakers with "overwhelming, and often conflicting, pressures to provide both visible and effective management of the terrorist threat"; terrorism no longer can be addressed on an ad hoc, crisis basis, but rather demands the development of "procedures, processes, and institutional capabilities" requisite for providing "appropriate strategic guidance, policy recommendations, and operational resources." While the "convergence of strategic necessity and political imperative . . . circumscrib[es] the range of response options available to policymakers," domestic "perceptions of threat broaden the decisionmaking circle as [the legislature] responds to pressures from constituents, interest groups, and the media to assume greater responsibility for addressing the issue." Although potential "[c]onflicts between strategic evaluations and domestic political pressures present particular challenges, especially for weak leaders in noncrisis situations whose need to subordinate strategic considerations to constituents' demands may be overwhelming"—such circumstances often lead to "misallocation of resources, overemphasis on military measures, and loss of subtlety and nuance in diplomatic relations"—"[a]bsent such conflicting pressures, the pursuit of both terror and non-terror related objectives benefits from a societal commitment to supporting far-reaching anti-terror efforts. Although forced to address terrorism itself as a strategic issue, executive decisionmakers have a unique opportunity to demonstrate effective leadership both at home and abroad by supporting and counseling allies, isolating and punishing adversaries, and forging greater unity among domestic political actors."[9]

HISTORICAL OVERVIEW

The absence of meaningful dialogue between Israelis and Palestinians prior to the early 1990s reflected the particular confluence of terrorist actions, decisionmakers' international strategic perspective, and the domestic political environment within Israel, the Occupied Territories and Palestinian diaspora, and the United States. Assessing the parties' experience with terrorism, including identifying inter and intra-phase transitions, is critical in recognizing both obstacles to diplomatic progress and moments of lost opportunity.

Israel

The PFLP's initiation of transnational terrorist operations against Israeli interests in July 1968 ushered in a period of spectacular *acts de presence*, including the 1970 multiple hijacking operation in Jordan, 1972 Lod airport attack and Munich Olympic hostage seizure, 1974 killings at Kiryat Shmona and Ma'alot, and 1976 hijacking of an Air France plane to Entebbe, Uganda. Israeli analysts devoted increasing attention to the Palestinian fedayeen threat. Harkabi, in a discerning analysis of Fatah, noted its belief that Israel was "an aberrant mistaken phenomenon in our [Palestinians'] nation's history and therefore there is no alternative but to wipe out the existential trace (*Alathar alwujud*) of this artificial phenomenon." He highlighted its "disbelief in the possibility of a political solution," fascination with Franz Fanon's *The Wretched of the Earth* and Algeria's victory over France, and commitment to re-Palestinianize the conflict by utilizing violence to "purify the individuals from venom, . . . redeem the colonized from inferiority complex, . . . [and] return courage to the countryman." He noted Fatah's focus on the "Revolutionary Vanguard's" role in "stimulating" the Palestinian masses' "urge for revenge" and in emphasizing that "the armed struggle and mass consciousness will go side by side, because the armed struggle will make the masses feel their active personality and restore their self confidence." He particularly stressed Fatah's efforts to restore Palestinians "as contestants in the Arab-Israel conflict," "subordinate all other Arab problems to the goal of liberating Palestine," and work cooperatively with Arab states in "the blotting out of the Zionist character of the occupied land."[10]

Harkabi's observations reflected growing Israeli concern about both the human costs and strategic implications of fedayeen terrorism. In early 1969, Israeli sources reported that 281 Israeli civilians and military personnel had died and over 1000 had been injured by terrorism in the year and a half since the Six Day War, figures characterized by Kissinger as "staggering."[11] The brutality of the Lod airport attack, followed shortly thereafter by Munich, Rome airport, Kiryat Shmona, and Ma'alot, generated unprecedented pressures on government leaders to respond to the terrorist threat. Fatah, the PFLP, PFLP-GC, ALF, PPSF, Sa'iqa, and PDF were among those organizations that commanded widespread attention for conducting relentless attacks against Israeli interests within Israel proper, the Occupied Territories, and foreign countries.[12]

While terrorism's domestic political salience increased markedly in the early 1970s, Israeli decisionmakers were ambivalent about its longterm strategic importance. The US embassy in Tel Aviv noted in April 1970 both Defense Minister Moshe Dayan's confidence in Israel's ability "to manage [the] terrorist challenge without real difficulty" and Ambassador Rabin's dismissal of the fedayeen's strategic significance.[13] However, such certitude, a reflection of Israel's smashing success in the 1967 War, the perceived weakness of frontline Arab states, and the dramatic escalation of US military, economic, and diplomatic support following the 1970 Jordanian-Palestinian civil war, withered as fedayeen terror threatened Israel's post-Yom Kippur War objectives. While Israeli efforts to stabilize relations with its Syrian adversary were nearly scuttled by the massacre of Jewish schoolchildren at Ma'alot, it was the unanimous decision by Arab leaders at Rabat in October 1974 to recognize the PLO as the "sole legitimate representative of the Palestinian people," endorse "the Palestinian people's right to return to its homeland and determine its own fate," and support Palestinians' "right to establish [their] own independent national authority under the leadership of the PLO . . . in all liberated Palestinian territory" that highlighted most dramatically terrorism's strategic import.[14] As Prime Minister, Rabin, while "categorically reject[ing]" Rabat, acknowledged its potential "to disrupt any progress towards peace, to encourage the terrorist elements, and to foil any step which might lead to peaceful coexistence with Israel." He expressed particular concern about growing military, political, and economic cooperation between the Arab world and the "organizations [sic] of murderers," and noted that Rabat's "'formula' for the coordination of relations between Jordan, Syria, Egypt and the PLO" may have been "intended to bring about closer military relations between them."[15] Such fears were heightened by the UN General Assembly's overwhelming endorsement of Rabat and by its invitation to the PLO to participate "in the sessions and the work of the General Assembly in the capacity of observer."[16] While Rabin "warn[ed] the Arab leaders against making the mistake of thinking that threats or even the active employment of the weapon of violence or of military force will lead to a political solution," and although he rejected the UN's actions "as incompatible with the very existence of the State of Israel," he acknowledged that "terrorist organizations[']" "successes . . . at the U.N. General Assembly and at Rabat are encouraging them to believe that the targets they had so confidently set themselves are now within reach."[17]

Efforts to address growing public anxiety over Palestinian terror while minimizing terrorism's impact on Israel's international strategic interests included a steadfast refusal to negotiate either with "terrorist organizations" or with Arab states sympathetic to Palestinian efforts to destroy Israel. Rabin, speaking shortly after Rabat, observed, "We shall carefully watch the steps the Arab States will take in the wake of this conference and, in particular, we shall watch the moves of those States with whom we were about to embark on negotiations on stages of progress towards peace. Above all, we shall see whether Egypt is in fact ready for this, or whether she has committed herself to the ban on reaching a separate agreement with Israel. We shall be watching Jordan's moves, too, to see whether she surrenders to Arafat."[18] Such political pronouncements were accompanied by efforts to decapitate fedayeen organizations. The newly created Mossad, charged with "assassinating top Palestinian leaders, including Arafat," conducted a brutal, clandestine war with the fedayeen throughout Europe and the Middle East. Both the Labor and Likud parties also stressed expanding and reinforcing "paramilitary and civilian settlements" to "maintain [those] vital security areas" critical to countering terrorist operations.[19]

Policymakers also explored the potential of palliative measures to undermine terrorists' appeal. Proposals such as the 1973 *Galili Plan* emphasized the "rehabilitation of refugees and economic development in the Gaza Strip," including "[c]hanging the housing situation (establishing places of residence for the refugees near the camps, improving the camps and making the municipalities of neighbouring towns responsible for them); vocational training; improving health and livelihood in trades and industry; [and] encouraging the population to take the initiative in improving their standard of living." A "four-year plan of action" was to be developed for Judea and Samaria to advance the "self-initiative of the inhabitants in the fields of education, religion and services, and in the field of developing democratic forms in social and municipal life," and to facilitate "developing the water services to meet the requirements of the population; developing vocational and higher education; developing electrical communications and transport services; improving streets and roads; developing trade and industry as sources of employment for the inhabitants; [and] helping the refugees' housing situation."[20]

Begin's assumption of power in 1977 coincided with Israel's transition to a Phase III relationship with transnational terrorism. Perceptions about the fedayeen's political and strategic irrelevance that had defined pre-1968 thinking (Phase I) had given way first to growing public awareness of terrorism's episodic impact on the Jewish state (Phase II) and subsequently to general recognition of its ongoing implications for domestic security and wellbeing (Phase III). Israelis, confronting a seemingly endless series of hijackings, kidnappings, and bombings by increasingly well known organizations, demanded that *something* be done to address Palestinian terror. Responding to such pressures, the major political parties sanctioned extrajudicial assassinations of Palestinian leaders, refused to negotiate with the PLO, and stressed the importance of a "powerful and prepared" military in "guarantee[ing] . . . our safety."[21] Although concerned that the PLO was used by Arab countries "as a political and military tool," "serv[ed] the interests of Soviet imperialism," and sought "to liquidate the State of Israel . . . and make the Land of Israel part of the Arab world," Begin and Likud's strategic anxieties were tempered by the Camp David *Frameworks for Peace* and Egyptian-Israeli *Peace Treaty*, the effects of which were to insure that Israel's most formidable adversary not "resort to the threat or the use of force" on behalf of the Palestinian cause; the Egyptian-Israeli *Peace Treaty* specifically enjoined either party "from organizing, instigating, inciting, assisting or participating in acts or threats of belligerency, hostility, subversion or violence against the other Party, anywhere," and promised mutual efforts "to ensure that perpetrators of such acts are brought to justice."[22] Such a Phase III environment afforded neither domestic political opportunity nor international strategic incentive to pursue a negotiated settlement.

Arafat's scathing indictment of Camp David, echoed repeatedly by the Arab League, individual fedayeen organizations, and PLO constituent bodies,[23] reflected widespread fears concerning the impact of the Egyptian-Israeli-American "alliance" on Palestinian national/territorial aspirations. Such concerns, exacerbated by the 1981 US-Israeli *Memorandum of Understanding*, 1982 Israeli "Operation Peace for Galilee," and 1985 Israeli attack on the PLO's Tunis headquarters,[24] prompted Palestinian leaders to reemphasize the necessity of armed struggle, particularly within Israel and the Occupied Territories.[25] However, neither increasingly vitriolic rhetoric nor such high profile incidents as the TWA and Achille Lauro hijackings prompted Israeli officials to revise assessments concerning Palestinian terrorism's international strategic implications. While Defense Minister Sharon noted the PLO's impact on Israel's international diplomatic and political interests,[26] Prime Minister Begin insisted that PLO-sponsored terrorism was "not a threat to the existence of the state" and that "Operation Peace for Galilee's" destruction of the PLO's Lebanese assets had created the opportunity for "many years of establishing peace treaties and peaceful relations with the various Arab countries."[27]

Prior to the first Palestinian intifada's eruption in December 1987, neither Israeli policymakers nor the general public had transitioned fully from Phase III to Phase V in their relationship with Palestinian terror. While nearly twenty years of victimization had established terrorism's domestic political salience, terror remained at worst only an episodic irritant to the pursuit of such critical Israeli strategic objectives as normalizing relations with its Arab neighbors and strengthening political, military, and economic ties with the United States. Israeli leaders, while characterizing terrorism as "a question of life or death" that threatened "the lives of civilians . . . day after day, week after week, month after month," addressed the issue primarily as a domestic security concern; the Cabinet professed confidence in the Israeli Defense Force's ability to manage what was described as an "internal security" matter. While the PLO's disruptive presence in Lebanon prompted Israel's 1982 invasion, Begin downplayed the organization's longterm strategic significance, declaring that the terrorist "problem will be solved" by "Operation Peace for Galilee."[28]

The first Palestinian intifada catalyzed significant change both in the nature of the Palestinian terrorist threat and in Israel's perspective on it. Although Arafat and the PLO's executive leadership lauded "the heroic uprising of our steadfast people," promised that the Intifada was "the beginning of a new stage of confronting the Zionist-imperialist settlement onslaught," and seized upon the uprising to proclaim "the establishment of the State of Palestine," they failed to prevent the emergence of Hamas, an Islamist organization which argued that "the Palestinian problem is a religious problem, and should be dealt with on this basis." Emphasizing that "[t]here is no solution for the Palestinian question except through Jihad," it focused on cultivating an "Islamic consciousness among the masses" necessary to confront the Israeli occupation.[29]

Arafat's efforts to forestall "a haemorrhage in popular support to the Islamists" that would undermine the PLO's "position and power as leader of the Palestinian national movement" centered on securing the international diplomatic support necessary to establish the newly proclaimed State of Palestine as a tangible reality for those living under occupation.[30] Such a strategy was predicated upon transforming the PLO's terrorist image, an effort pursued most dramatically in a 1988 speech before the UN General Assembly. Denouncing the use of "violence, force, or terrorism" against the "political independence and the territorial integrity of any other state," Arafat "categorically reject[ed] all forms of terrorism, including individual, group, and state terrorism."[31] He subsequently called upon Palestinians to exercise "more and more revolutionary discipline," and implored "all our organizations—Hamas, Fatah, the Popular Front (for the Liberation of Palestine), the [Popular] Democratic Front (for the Liberation of Palestine), the [Islamic] Jihad, the communists, the (Palestinian Popular) Struggle Front, [and] the Palestinian Front"— to "fight against anarchy" and unite behind a cohesive "front."[32] The Reagan administration responded positively to such pronouncements, entering into an unprecedented "substantive dialogue with PLO representatives."[33]

As the Intifada claimed growing numbers of civilian casualties, spawned ideological, radical, and fundamentalist movements, and led to direct US-PLO negotiations, Israel's relationship with Palestinian terror increasingly manifested Phase V-type characteristics. The government's "iron fist" policy, adopted shortly after the Intifada's outbreak and characterized by the punishing use of force against those suspected of planning or participating in violent actions, testified to the domestic political imperative to crush an increasingly deadly mass terrorist campaign.[34] While exacerbating domestic security concerns, Intifada-related terrorism also empowered those Islamic organizations most threatening to Israel's international strategic interests. Unlike Arafat's secular, nationalist Fatah, an organization that grudgingly had come to accept Israel's existence in hopes of securing a Palestinian "mini-state," fundamentalist parties promised nothing less than the total "liberation of Palestine."[35] Buchanan, noting Israeli fears that a "leadership vacuum . . . in the territories" was being "rapidly filled by Islamists such as Hamas," stressed that the Rabin government's pursuit of negotiations with its Arab neighbors reflected concerns that the "radicalization of the *intifada*," dominated by "implacable foe[s]" who "eschewed accommodation and assumed the mantle of existential confrontation," risked transforming "a popular outpouring of Palestinian frustration and anger within the confines of civil disobedience to a more extreme form of struggle involving armed confrontation, and indiscriminate suicidal terror." Rabin particularly feared that Iran's "megalomaniacal ambitions in empire-building" might prompt closer ties between itself and Palestinian Islamist terrorists, contributing to what Buchanan characterized as Iran's "long-term strategic existential" threat to the Jewish state.[36]

That an increasingly dangerous Palestinian terrorist threat was coupled with the initiation of US-PLO discussions was deeply troubling to Israeli leaders. Prime Minister Shamir observed, "we were forced to disagree strenuously with the recent US decision regarding a dialogue with the PLO which, as far as we see and know, has not changed its character or ways, its malicious covenant and the terrorism that it perpetrates."[37] Soviet communism's collapse and the corresponding "reconfiguration of the international structure from a bipolar to a unipolar one" increased Israel's uncertainty about its "future relationship with the US" and "the US's Middle Eastern strategic policies and economic commitments."[38] Such anxieties were heightened by Washington's efforts both to minimize Israeli involvement in the 1991 Gulf War and to court Palestinian participation in post-War diplomacy. The Bush administration's October 1991 *Letter of Assurances* to the Palestinians was especially worrisome, indicating that the "United States has long believed that Palestinian participation [in the peace process] is critical to the success of our efforts" to secure "a comprehensive, just and lasting peace in the region," committing the US to "launch a political negotiation process that directly involves Palestinians and offers a pathway for achieving the legitimate political rights of the Palestinian people and for participation in the determination of their future," and promising "Palestinian involvement in any bilateral or multilateral negotiations on refugees and in all multilateral negotiations."[39]

Rabin's 1992 election and ascendance of his Labor Party reflected in part "a growing acceptance by a significant proportion of the Israeli electorate and political establishment that the *status quo ante* was unsustainable," and that "negotiating a deal with the Palestinians, including the PLO, would not only materially affect their daily lives in removing an element of uncertainty and fear of random violence, it would also preclude more politically divisive settlements such as with Syria," while undermining Islamists' growing appeal.[40] Rabin's pledge to "pursue peace as if there were no terrorism, and fight terrorism as if there were no peace process," reflected efforts simultaneously to respond to domestic concerns while seeking the political accommodation with the PLO necessary "to resolve the core conflict [Israeli-Palestinian] and make peace with its neighbours before the Iranian threat became real."[41] While he may not have believed Palestinian terror to be "an existential threat to Israel," Rabin recognized both the Israeli public's "knee-jerk response to Palestinian violence" and the relationship between terror and the Islamic fundamentalist threat. He observed, "Our struggle against murderous Islamic terror is also meant to awaken the world which is lying (in) slumber. We call on all nations and all people to devote their attention to the great danger inherent in Islamic fundamentalism. That is the real and serious danger which threatens the peace of the world in the forthcoming years. The danger of death is at our doorstep. And just as the state of Israel was the first to perceive the Iraqi nuclear threat, so today we stand in the line of fire against the danger of fundamentalist Islam."[42]

The *Oslo Accords*, reflecting Rabin's conviction that "'real peace here will come only when the Arabs move' from their grudging acceptance of 'the fact of our existence' to an appreciation of Israel's 'right to exist,'"[43] established the broad parameters of Israel's Palestinian policy from September 1993 until the eruption of the al-Aqsa Intifada in September 2000. While stressing that "any PLO agreement or accord with Hamas on the possibility of continuing Hamas terror with the approval of the PLO" was unacceptable, Rabin looked to the newly created, Arafat-led PA to provide critical support in combating "opposition to peace" led by "radical" Islamist "rejectionist organizations."[44] Noting Arafat's recognition of Israel's right "to exist in peace and security," acceptance of UN Security Council Resolutions 242 and 338, and renunciation of "the use of terrorism and other acts of violence," Rabin anticipated the PA contributing to a "political solution" while fighting "an all-out war against all those continuing the violence and terror."[45] Recognizing that there "is no end to the goals of Hamas and other terrorism—every citizen, every Israeli in the territories and within the Green Line, every bus and every home is a target for its murderous intentions," and that "[t]housands of hidden and exposed paths lead from the territories into Israel. We cannot hermetically seal the territory," he highlighted a PA police force's value in ensuring "public order" and helping prevent terrorism from "stop[ping] the peace convoy."[46]

Rabin's assassination in November 1995 and the subsequent election of Netanyahu prompted a significant reevaluation of Israel's approach to Palestinian terror. Rabin's distinction between the "new" Palestinian Islamic terrorism and the "old" Palestinian national, secular terrorism had little relevance for a Likud government skeptical that either Arafat or the PA had abandoned their terrorist roots. Critical of *Oslo*'s very premise of "land for peace" negotiations, Netanyahu refused to address "final status" issues with an Arafat dominated PA, prompting Palestinians increasingly to question the PA's ability to deliver a Palestinian state through a negotiating process.[47]

While Netanyahu's successor, Ehud Barak, expressed concern that terrorism threatened "the personal security of all residents of Israel," he, in language similar to Rabin's, stressed his government's "historic obligation to take advantage of the 'window of opportunity' which has opened before us in order to bring long-term security and peace to Israel."[48] While emphasizing his determination to "conduct an all-out war against terrorist organizations and the initiators and perpetrators of terrorism," he pledged to pursue a "permanent settlement" by "work[ing] with the elected Palestinian leadership, under Chairman Yasser Arafat, in partnership and respect."[49] However, Arafat proved less than an ideal interlocutor. Confronted by growing popular disaffection with the fruits of the Oslo process, he could ill afford to clamp down on increasingly popular Islamist organizations, nor to accept suboptimal Israeli concessions on Jerusalem and the West Bank proffered at the July 2000 Camp David negotiations. Barak came to recognize all too clearly the impact of ascendant "extremist elements" on Arafat and the PA's policy options.[50]

Arafat's embrace of the al-Aqsa Intifada confirmed for Israeli policymakers and citizens alike their suspicions about his ostensible renunciation of terror and acceptance of the Jewish state. Yoel Marcus, writing in *Ha'aretz*, voiced widespread concerns,

> The Oslo agreement, which returned Arafat to his homeland from his life of exile and ceaseless wandering, was designed to bring about conciliation between the Palestinians and the Israelis. However, to this day, Arafat has not managed, has not wanted or has not been able to break the habit of constantly

using the slogan about Palestine being redeemed only through blood and fire. Instead of leading his people down the road to conciliation with Israel, he is leading them down the road to terrorism, murder and anti-Semitic incitement.[51]

Arafat's fiery rhetoric only heightened anxieties. Praising the al-Aqsa "martyrs," he observed, "Our people of revolutionary struggle, the people of the glorious *intifada*, whose waves will only stop with victory, pledge to every Arab, Muslim, Christian, and friend to continue their struggle using all legitimate means to reach victory." Abandoning his previous emphasis on the Israeli-Palestinian conflict's secular character, he decried Sharon's "desecrat[ion]" of the al-Aqsa mosque as a "premeditated step" that "added" a "new, religious, dimension . . . to the Arab-Israeli struggle," a dimension whose "repercussions" were particularly "difficult . . . to contain."[52]

Marwan Barghuti, Fatah's Secretary-General of the West Bank, similarly applauded the Intifada, observing,

> What would be the point of a return to calm? We were calm for seven years in order to give a chance to the negotiations, of which I have been a keen supporter. But the Israelis used that time in order to negotiate interim agreements which were never implemented and to continue their policy of a fait accompli on the ground: The new settlements, the expropriations, the confiscation of land, the keeping of prisoners in the jails. Why should calm now be restored? So that they can resume the same policy? . . . After seven years, we have experience of the Israelis; we have had hundreds of meetings with them: They never let go of anything without being obliged to do so by force.[53]

His characterization of the Fatah-Islamist relationship was particularly worrisome to Israelis, "The Islamists—Hamas and Jihad—are in the [Intifada's] local committees' coordinating body called the 'Committee of National and Islamic Political Forces.' Sometimes they have their own activities, as we do, but, on the whole, we cooperate well; we are very united. *Fatah* is leading the movement not because it is afraid of being outflanked by the Islamists but because it is its duty."[54]

While Sharon recognized the domestic political implications of escalating civilian casualties and suicide attacks, 9/11 eased concerns that Washington might be tempted to distance itself from Israel and aggressively pursue a two state solution in an effort to support the PA and undercut Islamist terrorists. Bush's Manichean "war on terror," privileging those friends and allies willing to embrace hard line anti-terror policies, provided great latitude for pursuing unyielding, confrontational, and increasingly militaristic approaches toward both Hamas-style extremists and the PA alike. Sharon's post-9/11 preoccupation with Palestinian terrorism's domestic political and security implications and relative lack of concern with its international strategic import—characteristics more typical of Phase III than of Phase V—were critical in defining the context within which the *Road Map* was evaluated.

Palestinians

Although *terrorism* entered the vernacular of Israeli-Palestinian relations only in the late 1960s, Palestinians experienced Israeli policies as terroristic as early as 1948. Arafat's November 1974 UN General Assembly speech recounted Palestinians' victimization at the hands of the new Jewish state, observing, "Just as colonialism used religion, colour, race and language to justify the people's exploitation and its cruel subjugation by terror and discrimination, so too were these methods employed as Palestine was usurped and its people hounded from their national homeland." He noted that although the UN's 1947 "partition resolution granted the colonialist settlers 54 percent of the land of Palestine, their dissatisfaction with the decision prompted them to wage a war of terror against the civilian Arab population. They occupied 81 percent of the total area of Palestine, uprooting a million Arabs. Thus, they occupied 524 Arab towns and villages, of which they destroyed 385, completely obliterating them in the process. Having done so, they built their own settlements and colonies on the ruins of our farms and our groves." Characterizing Zionism as an "imperialistic, colonialist, racist" ideology, Arafat condemned Israeli efforts "to hide the terrorism and tyranny of their acts" and reminded the UN that the "Zionist terrorism which was waged against the Palestinian people to evict them from their country and usurp their land is on record in your documents." He recalled that "[t]housands of our people have been assassinated in their villages and towns; tens of thousands of others have been forced by rifle and artillery fire to leave their homes and the crops they have sown in the lands of their fathers," argued that the "small number of Palestinian Arabs whom the Zionists did not succeed in uprooting in 1948 . . . have been subject to all forms of racial discrimination and terror," lamented that "terrorism even reached our sacred places in our beloved city of peace, Jerusalem," insisted that the "record of Zionist terrorism in south Lebanon" would "shock even the most hardened," and observed that terrorism "was even directed against the olive tree in my country, which they saw as a symbol of our spirit, a flag, and which reminded them of the indigenous inhabitants of the land, a living reminder that the land is Palestinian. Hence they uprooted or killed it by neglect, or used it for firewood." He criticized "the acts of terror perpetrated on those of our people who remained under occupation in Sinai and the Golan Heights," noting that the "criminal bombardment of the Bahr al-Baqar School and the Abu Za'bal factory in Egypt are but two such unforgettable acts of terrorism," and observing that the "total destruction of the city of Quneitra is yet another tangible instance of systematic terrorism." In the face of such "acts of barbarism" and "terrorism in their grimmest forms," Arafat implored the GA to resist Israeli efforts to label as *terrorism* Palestinians' legitimate struggle against Zionist aggression, and to support the PLO's "resolve to build a new world . . . a world free of colonialism, imperialism, neo-colonialism and racism in all its forms, including Zionism."[55]

Premised upon equating *Zionism, racism, colonialism, aggression*, and *US imperialism* with Israeli *terrorism*, Arafat's remarks reflected Palestinians' post-1948 relationship with Israeli terror. Traumatized by Israel's dislocation of non-

Jews during the 1948 and 1967 wars, Palestinians perceived terror to be an ongoing threat both to "Palestinianism" and to their national/territorial objectives. As a sub-state actor, Palestinians perceived little distinction between terrorism's "international" strategic and "domestic" political and security implications. While the PLO's domestic political and security objectives centered on ameliorating the social, economic, and physical hardships inflicted by Israeli terror, its pursuit of statehood sought to counter Israeli terrorism's demoralization, isolation, and marginalization of those living under "colonial" rule. The "convergence of strategic necessity and political imperative" that distinguishes an actor's Phase V relationship to terror thus characterized Palestinians' experience with Israeli terrorism from the founding of the Jewish state.

Such Phase V tendencies were reinforced by what Arafat described as the post-Camp David "attack" by the "tripartite alliance" of Carter, Begin, and Sadat "on our people in the occupied land by means of fascist, mean and oppressive measures in addition to the confiscation of land, building of settlements and terrorism such as deportation of the population, arrest and mass punishment against towns and villages as well as confiscation of springs."[56] Echoing Arafat's criticism of Israel's "mounting war of attrition" and "terrorist and hellish plan" against the "Lebanese and Palestinian peoples," the PNC issued a statement "strongly condemn[ing] terrorism and international terrorism, especially the Zionist official and organized terrorism against the Palestinian people, the PLO and the people of Lebanon, as well as American imperialist terrorism against the world liberation movements."[57] Appealing for support from the Soviet Union, nonaligned countries, and Western Europe, it emphasized Palestinians' vulnerability to "the organized and official terrorism of Israel and the US."[58] Arafat's 1985 *Declaration on Terrorism*, contrasting Zionist aggression with Palestinians' struggle "to cling to peace," stressed the PLO's commitment to "an international conference on peace in the Middle East," "the right of all states in the region to exist within safe and internationally recognized borders," and the PNC's unequivocal condemnation of "all acts of terrorism." Observing that "terminating the occupation and putting limits on its [Israel's] policies is the one way to achieve peace and security in the region," it "implore[d] all peaceloving powers in all parts of the world to stand beside it [the PLO] as it takes this step to participate in ridding the world of the phenomenon of terrorism," and called upon "the international community to force Israel to stop all of its acts of terrorism both inside and outside (Palestine)."[59]

Israel's self-proclaimed "iron fist" response to the first Palestinian intifada elicited particularly vitriolic condemnation. The PLO's Executive Committee noted that despite "[h]erds of settlers [being] sent to practice bloody terrorism against our people," the Intifada demonstrated "that all fascist Zionist crimes, terrorism, and repression cannot save the criminal occupation from its inevitable crisis and fate; that is, their defeat and removal from the sacred Palestinian land, the land of fathers and grandfathers." Vowing that "crimes and terrorism cannot defeat our people's determination and steadfastness. Such crimes and terrorism will increase the Zionists' impasse and isolation and expose the collusion of their protectors in the U.S. Administration," it "call[ed] upon international and friendly bodies to provide more support and backing for our struggling masses and our just cause, particularly in confronting the organized and official war of terrorism and the crimes perpetrated against our people by the fascist and racist Zionist occupation authorities."[60] The Unified National Command of the Intifada, echoing the Executive Committee's outrage at "the fascist racist terrorism inflicted upon the masses" and at the Zionist's "savage terrorism against our people, children, and women," decried the "Nazi methods being perpetrated by the occupation authorities against our masses, our prisoners, and our deportees." It declared that the "stone revolution" "cannot be ended or liquidated by the breaking of bones, fascist killing and terrorism, mass arrests, or economic harassment."[61]

The PNC added its voice to the anti-Israel chorus. Condemning Jerusalem's "organized, fascist official terrorism,"[62] it observed,

> Our people have stood fast against all the attempts of our enemy's authorities to end our revolution, and those authorities have tried everything at their disposal; they have used terrorism, they have imprisoned us, they have sent us into exile, they have desecrated our holy places and restricted our religious freedoms, they have demolished our homes, they have killed us indiscriminately, and premeditatedly, they have sent bands of armed settlers into our villages and camps, they have burned our crops, they have cut off our water and power supplies, they have beaten our women and children, they have used toxic gases that have caused many deaths and abortions, they have waged an ignorance war (sic) against us by closing our schools and universities.[63]

In proclaiming "the establishment of the State of Palestine," it recalled that "the occupation of Palestine and parts of other Arab territories by Israeli forces, the willed dispossession and expulsion from their ancestral homes of the majority of Palestine's civilian inhabitants, was achieved by organized terror." It stressed the Intifada's potential to "set siege to the mind of official Israel, which has for too long relied exclusively upon myth and terror to deny Palestinian existence altogether," and demanded that Israel renounce forever "the threat or use of force, violence and terrorism against [Palestinian] territorial integrity or political independence."[64]

Arafat's indictment of Israel's Intifada-related policies was particularly scathing. Denouncing the "illegitimate terrorism of the occupier," he implored the European Parliament to recognize that "[o]ur people, including their leaders, cadres, and citizens, have invariably been the target of organized Israeli state terrorism as practiced directly or indirectly by armed settlers acting alongside troops in full view of all." He emphasized that despite Palestinians' condemnation of "terrorism in all its forms and from whatever source,"

> an unchecked Israel continued to practice all forms of terrorism, including state terrorism, against the Palestinian people and their leaders within the occupied territories and in every corner of the globe. This terrorism reached its climax with the bombardment of my headquarters at Hammam al-Shatt in Tunis and the assassination of Brother Abu Jihad, my deputy and one of the most prominent symbols of Palestinian leadership, who was gunned down in front of his

family in Tunis. Israel also perpetrated acts of piracy against civilian shipping in the high seas and in international waters and assassinated our leaders and cadres in Cyprus, Athens, and elsewhere.

Arafat catalogued the terroristic nature of

> the iron fist policy, including the use of plastic and rubber bullets, live ammunition, internationally-banned suffocating gases, the burning and burial of people alive, miscarriages, the breaking of bones, the murder of prisoners, the torture of some detainees to death, the murder of children, the demolition of homes, collective punishments, inhuman mass detention centers, mass administrative arrests without trial or charge, deportation, desecration of Muslim and Christian sanctuaries, and a series of other practices which go against the principles set in Nuremberg.[65]

His December 1988 UN General Assembly address reminded the international community of the PNC's "rejection of terrorism of all kinds . . . including state terrorism," declared that "[a]ll forces of repression and terrorism cannot dissuade the people from their firm belief in their right to their homeland and in the values of justice, peace, love, and tolerant coexistence," and observed, "That the world is rallying around our just cause to achieve just peace brilliantly indicates that the world realizes in no vague terms who is the executioner and who is the victim, who is the aggressor and who is aggressed upon, and who is the struggler for freedom and peace and who is the terrorist."[66]

However, Palestinian participation in the Madrid Peace Conference and commitment to the *Oslo Accords* created unprecedented fissures within the PLO over the appropriate response to Israeli terror. Its Executive Committee, dominated by Arafat's Fatah, emphasized *Oslo*'s potential to enlist US support in pressuring Israel to accept binding limitations on its use of anti-Palestinian terror. Arafat, having recognized Israel's right "to exist in peace and security," called upon the "international community in its entirety to help the parties overcome the tremendous difficulties which are still standing in the way of reaching a final and comprehensive settlement."[67] He applauded the 1994 *Cairo Agreement*'s demand that Israel "take all measures necessary to prevent . . . hostile acts emanating from the Settlements and directed against Palestinians," while accepting both parties' commitment "to prevent acts of terrorism, crime and hostilities directed against each other, against individuals falling under the other's authority and against their property, and . . . [to] take legal measures against offenders."[68] He likewise endorsed the 1995 *Interim Agreement on the West Bank and Gaza Strip*'s insistence on a "mutual commitment to act . . . immediately, efficiently and effectively against acts or threats of terrorism, violence or incitement, whether committed by Palestinians or Israelis."[69]

Such commitments, undertaken in the context of ongoing settlement activities, provoked sharp criticism of the PLO's executive leadership. Mahmoud Darwish, resigning in protest from the PLO's Executive Committee, observed, "We have taken two generations to their death in the project of liberation and independence, and it now appears as if we are abandoning them completely, leaving them to the winds of the new wilderness." Pronouncing the PLO "finished," he decried *Oslo*'s fracturing of the "Palestinian cause and the Palestinian people."[70] Hani al-Hasan voiced similar concerns, criticizing the *Accords* for "stripping the organization of all that it represents" and the PLO for relying "on the Jewish state's good will" in "agreeing to stop the *intifada*." He especially indicted PLO leaders for buttressing the Israeli occupation, observing, "proponents of the Gaza-Jericho deal have been entrusted with the task of punishing anyone who resorts to violence. It is strange that a Palestinian leader should undertake to stop the resistance in, say, Nablus or Hebron (or the West Bank) which will remain under Israeli occupation for at least five years. Hence Gaza-Jericho advocates will be the allies of the Israeli security forces over the next five years."[71]

Rabin's assassination and the ascendance of Netanyahu's hard-line Likud government broadened and deepened Palestinian skepticism that *Oslo* indeed would rein in Israeli terror; viscerally opposed to negotiating with an Arafat-led Palestinian Authority, Netanyahu shared none of his predecessor's willingness to accommodate Palestinian demands. While echoing widespread frustration at *Oslo*'s inability to deliver "territory," "honor," and improvements in "economic and social well-being," Hamas and Islamic Jihad were especially incensed at the PA's complicity in suppressing resistance to Israeli occupation.[72] The 1998 *Wye River Memorandum* provoked particular outrage. While reaffirming "[b]oth sides . . . vital interest" in combating terrorism through "comprehensive" measures targeting "terrorists, the terror support structure, and the environment conducive to the support of terror," it remained silent about Israeli terror, focusing instead on "the Palestinian side's implementation of its responsibilities for security [and] security cooperation." In addition to insisting that the PA "outlaw and combat terrorist organizations," "prohibit illegal weapons," and "prevent incitement," it called for establishing a US-Palestinian committee "to review the steps being taken to eliminate terrorist [cells] and the support structure that plans, finances, supplies and abets terror" and to "evaluate information pertinent to the decisions on prosecution, punishment or other legal measures which affect the status of individuals suspected of abetting or perpetrating acts of violence and terror." A US-Palestinian-Israeli committee was to "monitor cases of possible incitement to violence or terror," "make recommendations and reports on how to prevent such incitement," assess "current threats, deal with any impediments to effective security cooperation and coordination and address the steps being taken to combat terror and terrorist organizations."[73] Such collusion with the Israeli occupier and its American patron *against* the Palestinian resistance was anathema to growing numbers of Palestinians within the Occupied Territories, as well as to those organizations hostile to the PA-orchestrated Oslo process.

While *Oslo* had intensified intra-Palestinian discord about the trajectory of Israeli-Palestinian relations, the al-Aqsa Intifada proved a remarkable catalyst for transcending such differences. The *Accord*'s principal architects, notably Arafat and Fatah's leadership, retreated immediately to pre-*Oslo* rhetoric. Noting the impact of "an iron-clad and stifling siege by the Israeli war machine against more than 3 million Palestinians," Arafat demanded that Israel be "forced to submit to international legitimacy, implement the signed agreements, stop aggression, open the international border posts, lift the siege on our cities and people, and withdraw from all the occupied Palestinian Arab territories." He acknowledged Islamists' longstanding concerns, including Israel's "licentiously attacking the worshippers in its mosques and those defending its honor and sanctity," "attempting to Judaize holy Jerusalem and its Christian and Islamic holy places," and "imposing a siege on Bethlehem."[74] Highlighting Israel's ongoing settlement activities, expropriations, and land seizures, Barghuti vowed that there "will never again be either a 1948 or a 1967; they will not be able to expel us *en masse*."[75]

United States

Perceptions of transnational terrorism's domestic political and international strategic irrelevance defined US thinking prior to 1970. Kidnappings of US officials and businessmen in Latin America in the late 1960s were addressed "primarily as a 'local' problem involving efforts by leftist guerrillas to secure the freedom of imprisoned colleagues" or to extort ransom, while airline hijacking was perceived as "a means of obtaining political asylum by hijackers who wanted merely to change the plane's destination." Domestic attention centered not on transnational terror but on escalating politically motivated violence within the US, including assassinations, riots, and kidnappings.[76]

Such a Phase I orientation evolved dramatically during the early 1970s. The PFLP's September 1970 multiple hijacking operation was one of several watershed events, sensitizing the Nixon White House to terrorism's impact on vital national interests, including managing the Arab-Israeli conflict, improving US-Arab relations, and insuring Jordan's stability.[77] Kissinger told Nixon, "The September crisis in Jordan brought to the fore the issue of how the Palestinians can be dealt with in a peace settlement." While noting that the "U.S. is not rushing to support the Palestinians," he acknowledged that "we like everyone else recognize the need to find some way to bring them into the settlement process." He stressed to the US ambassador to Jordan "our belief that it (is) likely to be desirable that Palestinians at some appropriate stage become participants in the negotiating process as well as partners in any peace settlement if that peace settlement is to stick." Indicating that "the US has very much in mind the interests of the Palestinians in any negotiation and in any settlement," he emphasized that "increasing attention to the Palestinian factor will be required since if we were to disregard it, this would tend to dash hopes of those whom we believe hold moderate views."[78]

While King Hussein's crushing defeat of the PLO temporarily relieved such Phase IV anxieties, the Munich Olympic hostage crisis and Khartoum Saudi embassy seizure reengaged the Administration's strategic attention, threatening US efforts to promote Egyptian-Israeli negotiations, forestall a Soviet-Egyptian rapprochement, and cultivate improved ties with moderate Arab states.[79] Secretary of State Rogers, noting "the serious implications for international order of Black September Organization," stressed that "continuation of BSO activities will make USG's (US government's) task in seeking a peaceful settlement for Arab-Israeli conflict much more complex, difficult and lengthy." Kissinger indicated that "a peace settlement ultimately depends on the Palestinians," while Joseph Sisco concluded that a "durable peace . . . in the area" was predicated on addressing Palestinians' "legitimate interests" and "aspirations." The Cabinet Committee to Combat Terrorism (CCCT), expressing concern that "the Arabs feel they have discovered a new technique (terrorism) with which they feel they can keep us off balance," asserted, "In the long run, a modus vivendi in the Middle East would be the best antidote."[80] The American Embassy in Tel Aviv highlighted terrorism's growing strategic import, observing, the "major success that Black September has gained (is) sidetracking of American efforts towards peace by setting brush fires which must be put out first but which are not fundamental to problem." In Khartoum's aftermath it observed, "In long run, answer to Palestinian terrorism continues to lie only in a settlement between Israel and Arab nations that is sufficiently acceptable to allow them to turn to peaceful development and to disown, in actuality and not merely in statements made privately to American ears, violence of radical fedayeen groups."[81]

While Munich prompted the Administration to rethink terrorism's international strategic significance, it also engendered a newfound appreciation of its growing, if episodic, domestic political salience. Acknowledging Phase II imperatives at least to appear to "do something," Rogers advised Nixon "to dramatize the seriousness of your concern about the problem of terrorism," while the CCCT's Working Group stressed "the desirability of Executive Branch moves to forestall Congressional action which might not have desirable contents."[82] Nixon's "frenetic anti-terror efforts after Munich" reflected such advice, demonstrating a clear recognition of "the political value of an *ostensibly* strong anti-terror policy." One observer noted, "Prior to the 1972 election . . . Nixon's desire to cultivate Jewish support, coupled with Congressional calls following Munich for stricter measures against state supporters of terrorism, created particularly strong incentives to *appear* responsive to the terrorist threat."[83]

Highlighting "the growing menace of international terrorism" and his commitment "to taking every step necessary to end the vicious threat of terror both here and abroad," Nixon pursued a variety of high profile initiatives in Munich's aftermath. The CCCT was established "to coordinate the government's response to terrorism," while its Working Group and Emergency Watch Group were to facilitate intelligence dissemination among government agencies, develop "precautionary measures," and "devise procedures for reacting swiftly and effectively to acts of terrorism and . . . measures to prevent such acts." Efforts also focused on "enhancing security for airports and airlines, tightening screening of visa applications and initiating transit visa requirements, expanding protection of foreign diplomats, their families, and their premises, seeking stronger anti-hijacking legislation, and developing more effective procedures for safeguarding nuclear materials."[84] Such high visibility measures likewise characterized the Administration's international anti-terror policies, including:

> seeking UN General Assembly adoption of a resolution on terrorism, an anti-terrorism convention, and a convention to protect diplomats; engaging in con-

sultations with the Organization of American States; strengthening the antiterrorist capabilities of countries belonging to CENTO and SEATO; pursuing discussions within NATO to enhance the security of international civil aviation, the safety of diplomats and foreign officials, and the 'protection of innocent people from the spread of international terrorism to countries not involved in a dispute giving rise to acts of terrorism'; bolstering nuclear materials safeguards in Europe; supporting more effective anti-terror actions by the Council of Europe; negotiating an anti-hijacking agreement with Cuba; convening a world conference by the International Civil Aviation Organization (ICAO); . . . attempting to secure a commitment by Interpol's General Assembly 'to focus on terrorism as an international police problem'; . . . [and emphasizing] to the Arab governments that (they) . . . cannot evade responsibility for acts of fedayeen terrorism so long as they do not take steps to deny support and facilities to them.[85]

That Nixon's post-Munich anti-terror efforts were rooted primarily in domestic political rather than international strategic calculations was reflected in "the CCCT's failure to convene after its initial meeting," "the lack of authority given to the chair of the Working Group (WG) over participating agencies and departments," "Nixon's appointment of Rogers to chair the CCCT, his decision to give the State Department the leadership role in its operations, and Kissinger's nonparticipation in either CCCT or WG activities." Nixon's awarding of the terrorist portfolio to Rogers and the State Department rather than to Kissinger, who by late 1972 "had assumed operational control over all areas of US foreign policy considered important by Nixon—relations with the Soviet Union and the PRC [People's Republic of China], negotiations to end the Vietnam War, and policy toward the Middle East"—was particularly telling. Similarly, Kissinger's ready acceptance of Rogers' ostensible bureaucratic victory testified to terrorism's relative insignificance within the Administration's strategic universe.[86]

However, the Yom Kippur War's aftermath prompted a significant reassessment about the extent to which transnational terrorism, particularly that of the fedayeen, posed serious threats to US strategic interests. Although Kissinger was loathe to include Palestinians in his "step-by-step" diplomacy—he minimized "the so-called Palestinian problem," argued that at "this stage, involving the PLO was incompatible with the interests of any of the parties to the Middle East conflict," and observed that "[e]ven should some PLO leader accept Resolution 242 and the legal right of Israel to exist . . . the dynamics of the movement made it unlikely that such moderation could be maintained indefinitely"—he and Nixon recognized that efforts to initiate negotiations involving Israel, Egypt, Syria, and Jordan, as well as secure an early end to the Arab oil embargo, were predicated "both upon the willingness and ability of frontline Arab states to moderate their demands and upon Israel recognizing the benefits of negotiation."[87] While Palestinian extremism constrained Arab latitude to pursue land-for-peace discussions with Israel, the "ability of any Israeli government to accept the kind of territorial concessions necessary for peace depended on Palestinians refraining from terrorist operations"; as the US Embassy in Tel Aviv observed in February 1974, "Israeli public opinion will not be able to take another Kiryat Shmona (a terrorist attack) for long time to come. When one stops to consider enormity of what USG (US government) is hoping to accomplish through Israelis over next half year, seriousness of any fedayeen resurgence for our Mid East strategy becomes apalling (sic)."[88]

Reflecting such strategic concerns, Kissinger authorized two meetings between Lieutenant General Vernon Walters, Deputy Director of the CIA, and a "close associate" of Arafat's, the first in November 1973 preceding the Geneva Conference, the second in March 1974 prior to Israeli-Syrian negotiations. Kissinger noted that the initial meeting sought "to gain time and to prevent radical assaults on the early peace process" by "encourag[ing] PLO quiescence in the delicate postwar phase when we were assembling the Geneva Conference and preparing for Egyptian-Israeli disengagement," while the subsequent meeting "played for time . . . by telling the PLO leader that we were not ready for further contacts until after a Syrian disengagement," helped "ease the decision of various OPEC fence-sitters with respect to the oil embargo," and "calm[ed] the atmosphere for the planned Syrian shuttle." Nixon also emphasized to Arab leaders that pursuing "the legitimate interests of the Palestinian people" depended on controlling terrorism and marginalizing radical elements. A July 1974 memo from Alfred Atherton, Jr. to Kissinger clarified Administration thinking about the fedayeen terrorist threat, observing, "the U.S. should now engage itself more actively in the Palestinian issue, working with the moderate Arab Governments and perhaps having direct contacts with some elements of the PLO in order to minimize the disruptive influence of the Palestinians upon Arab negotiating positions and to seek to curb terrorist activity against Israel." It noted, "Although the Palestinians have yet to unite decisively on a position, . . . the time has come to devise a strategy for drawing some elements of the PLO into the political process and trying to isolate the radicals."[89]

Although Palestinian terrorism had yet to become either "a commonplace occurrence directly impacting domestic perceptions of security and wellbeing" or "an issue of vital and ongoing domestic concern"[90]—critical Phase III characteristics—by 1975–1976 it commanded far more attention from the media, mass public, and Congress than it had during Nixon's tenure. The PLO, Arafat, fedayeen organizations, and prominent individuals such as Ilich Ramirez Sanchez ("Carlos the Jackal") received extensive network coverage emphasizing Palestinians' contribution to the "dread plague" of transnational terrorism, reinforcing the "Palestinian as terrorist" perspective, and highlighting Palestinian involvement in such terrorist spectaculars as the 1975 kidnapping of OPEC oil ministers and 1976 Entebbe hijacking. The *Christian Science Monitor* reported on CIA concerns that, while "foreign terrorist groups are planning to step up their attacks on American targets abroad in the near future," "the odds are that the impact of . . . terror will be more sharply felt in the United States in the years just ahead."[91] That such coverage increasingly resonated with the electorate was apparent in the thunderous applause given to Jimmy Carter's comments during the 1976 Democratic national convention that "[p]eace is not the mere absence of war. Peace is action to stamp out international terrorism"; Tom Wicker, a prominent journalist, observed that the public was "outraged by terrorist tactics and their consequences."[92] Congress likewise demonstrated growing concern with Palestinian leadership of an increasingly dangerous transnational terrorist threat. Hearings before subcommittees of the Senate Judiciary Committee and the House Committee on International Relations addressed "international terrorism," "terroristic activity," and "international terrorism in the Middle East," examined the PLO's relationships with other transnational terrorist organizations, and assessed Palestinian terrorism's impact on US diplomatic objectives, while legislation sought to enhance the safety of internationally protected persons, promote multilateral sanctions against states shielding terrorists from prosecution, and eliminate military assistance to state sponsors of terror.[93]

Internal memos reflected the Administration's sensitivity to terrorism's heightened political salience, advising Ford to "strengthen Executive Branch efforts to combat terrorism . . . now before a major incident turns this latent problem into a major public issue," recognize the CCCT's value in providing "a tangible expression of the President's concern with the still very acute problem of worldwide terrorism," and address Congressional concerns in an "active and meticulous fashion." The White House "worked diligently to secure Congressional support for domestic and international legal measures to combat terrorism," while developing "procedures for 'responding to acts of terrorism against Americans abroad' that recognized that a 'cardinal rule of (terrorism) task force management is to do the maximum to see that the family, employer and Congressional acquaintances have no legitimate complaints about (any) rescue operation.'" Ford was particularly solicitous toward the American Jewish community following Israel's Entebbe rescue operation, stressing his commitment "to international action to combat terrorism," vowing "never [to] capitulate to terrorism," and promising US leadership in "stamp[ing] out terrorism wherever (it) may occur."[94]

Although Ford and Kissinger lamented Palestinian terror's potential to "sabotage" diplomatic progress, radicalize Palestinians, complicate relations with Israel and Arab moderates, and enhance Soviet regional influence, they "perceived no imperative to satisfy Palestinian political ambitions, address 'Palestinian interests' prior to Arab-Israeli negotiations, or permit Arafat and the PLO an autonomous role within the step-by-step process."[95] Robert Fearey, chair of the CCCT's Working Group, articulated the White House position that "(t)erroristic activity, while sometimes reaching serious proportions, is not sufficient in and of itself to disrupt [US-sponsored] negotiations unless a key Arab leader should be assassinated."[96] The 1975 US-Israeli *Memorandum of Agreement* reflected the Administration's strategic design, declaring, "The United States will continue to adhere to its present policy with respect to the Palestine Liberation Organization, whereby it will not recognize or negotiate with the Palestine Liberation Organization so long as the Palestine Liberation Organization does not recognize Israel's right to exist and does not accept Security Council Resolutions 242 and 338."[97] In addition to precluding PLO participation in step-by-step diplomacy, the *Memorandum* signaled Ford's conviction that the US, as Israel's "de facto ally," must "consult fully and seek to concert its position and strategy at the Geneva Peace Conference" with Jerusalem and, "if necessary, vote against any initiative in the Security Council to alter adversely the terms of reference of the Geneva Peace Conference or to change Resolutions 242 and 338 in ways which are incompatible with their original purpose."[98]

Several aspects of the Administration's approach to Palestinian terrorism proved particularly enduring. First, its characterization of Arafat, the PLO, and individual fedayeen organizations as *Arab terrorists*, *Arab guerrillas*, and *Arab extremists* committed to "the liquidation of Israel and all pro-western Arab regimes" resonated among the American media, Congress, and general public. Ford stressed Palestinians' "cruelty and bloodletting against fellow Arabs," "brutal resort to terrorism," and "collaboration with the Communist bloc of nations," while Kissinger highlighted the PLO's "capacity for assassination and producing civil turmoil," "terror against individuals or groups identified with peace negotiations," embrace of "radical and pro-Soviet" policies, and commitment to "the destruction of Israel."[99] In contrast, the White House characterized such Israeli actions as assassinations, home demolitions, and settlement construction not as *violence* but rather as *retaliation, justifiable responses*, and *security measures*.[100] Buchanan, acknowledging such rhetorical disparities, noted Israel's success in shaping "political discourse largely in its favour." He observed, "Such a manipulation of geopolitical realities has meant that Israel can, as the representative of the Israeli people, utilize more extensive violent tactics and strategies, and be no more mindful of civilian innocence, international law, and the authority of the United Nations than the Palestinians, and their representatives, the PLO." He concluded,

> What the international structure and the geopolitical framework enables Israel to achieve is the opportunity to claim plausible deniability for any of its immoral and violent actions, thus allowing it to continue virtually without let or hindrance, in much the same way that Palestinian violence is surrounded by self-righteous vituperation. This control of the terms and nature of the discourse has allowed Israel to achieve a 'kind of polemical plausibility' to her 'refusal to deal with the most legitimate Palestinian representatives and political organisation, contending that it will not negotiate with 'terrorists''.[101]

Second, Palestinian terrorism's threat to US strategic interests was addressed through a policy of diplomatically marginalizing the PLO "to create the *possibility* for both Israel and the Arab states to pursue bilateral talks." Kissinger, fearing the PLO's disruptive influence, refused to permit its involvement in step-by-step negotiations absent prior peace agreements between Israel and its Arab neighbors. While Ford's briefing materials acknowledged that "any final peace settlement must include the interests of the Palestinians and a solution to the Palestinian problem," they emphasized that "Israel cannot be expected to deal with terrorist groups which will not even acknowledge Israel's right to exist."[102] Ford concurred, noting, "any extreme radicalism/terrorism by elements of the Palestinian community made it more difficult to arrange any face-to-face negotiations between the Israelis and the Palestinians. Terrorism by any group makes it more difficult for reasonable people to try to resolve questions that are in dispute."[103]

Finally, national security and foreign policy bureaucracies devoted unprecedented attention to counterterrorism efforts, focusing particularly on combating the Palestinian threat. Noting that "a new outbreak of international terrorism" could threaten both "the fabric of society" and "world peace and order," Ford supported a series of anti-terror studies and operational initiatives. The Central Intelligence Agency's Office of Political Research produced an exhaustive report warning that "transnational and international terror" would impact the US itself in the immediate future, "impinge more directly on US interests and options with respect to a broad range of critical (international) issue areas," and remain a "potentially gravely unsettling problem for the world community." Emphasizing that "the trend toward greater international contact and cooperation among terrorist groups that has already markedly enhanced the operational capabilities of some of the organizations involved seems likely to gain further momentum," it cautioned that "the wave of the future seems to be toward the development of a complex support base for transnational terrorist activity that is largely independent of—and quite resistant to control by—the state-centered international system." The CCCT's Working Group, expressing particular concern about Palestinian success in promoting "increasingly effective cooperation among leading terrorist groups worldwide," utilized the newly created Anti-Terrorism Research and Development Committee to "identify ongoing anti-terrorism related research and development activities" and "explore possible new avenues of R&D that might help with this problem." The Terrorism Special Action Group, created within the NSC system, served "as a management vehicle for the President in terrorism crisis situations requiring his attention," facilitated "coordination within the Executive Office of the President," provided "advice and assistance to the President," and acted "as a White House coordinating agency for interface with the Cabinet Committee to Combat Terrorism." While the Defense Department emphasized understanding "the political dynamics of Palestinian terrorist movements," the Army initiated "a research program aimed at developing an anti-ballistic missile (ABM) system capable of protecting American cities from nuclear attack by small 'third world' nations or terrorist organizations."[104]

The State Department, expressing growing concern about "possible acts of terrorism in the United States with international ramifications," the increasing "scale and sophistication of terrorist activities," and Moscow's provision of "military and ideological training and weapons to Palestinian terrorists," was particularly active in counterterror efforts. Its newly established Office for Combating Terrorism was charged with providing "an effective link between the policy and the operational aspects of the Department's efforts in combatting international terrorism," while an enhanced Command Center was to be developed to provide "an automated, comprehensive data bank which would comprise intelligence data on domestic and international terrorism from all sources." Special attention was directed toward identifying "new legal instruments to combat international terrorism," developing "detailed data on host country laws and policies concerning international terrorism," exploring possible revisions of "existing bilateral and multilateral agreements and other international legal controls so as to increase their effectiveness in combatting terrorism," and working collaboratively with NATO, the European Community, United Nations, International Civil Aviation Organization, and Interpol to develop innovative anti-terror programs.[105]

A series of high profile terrorist operations—including the 1983 bombing of US Marine headquarters in Beirut, 1985 hijacking of TWA flight 847, seizure of the Achille Lauro cruise ship, and attacks on El Al ticket counters in the Rome and Vienna airports, 1986 bombing of a West Berlin discotheque and attack on TWA flight 840, and series of kidnappings of Americans in Lebanon—prompted key Reagan administration officials to emphasize terrorism's growing domestic political and international strategic significance. Secretary of State George Shultz, noting that the public was "more concerned about terrorism than any other issue" and that escalating terrorist operations had created a "momentum [that] was disturbing," stressed the need for a coherent "strategy" to prevail over the "weapon of unconventional war" targeting "the democracies of the West." He advocated developing "a better understanding of terrorism and how to counter it," cultivating more "reliable intelligence," improving "security measures at U.S. embassies," strengthening "international efforts to improve airline safety," pressuring "states that sponsored terrorism to stop," "streamlin[ing] international legal procedures," and "promot[ing] closer cooperation among law enforcement agencies."[106] Emphasizing the need "to think long, hard, and seriously about more active means of defense—about defense through appropriate preventive or preemptive actions against terrorists before they strike,"[107] he argued,

> We cannot allow ourselves to become the Hamlet of nations, worrying endlessly over whether and how to respond. A great nation with global responsibilities cannot afford to be hamstrung by confusion and indecisiveness. Fighting terrorism will not be a clean or pleasant contest, but we have no choice. . . . We must reach a consensus in this country that our responses should go beyond passive defense to consider means of active prevention, preemption, and retaliation. Our goal must be to prevent and deter future terrorist acts. . . . The public must understand *before the fact* that occasions will come when their government must act before each and every fact is known—and the decisions cannot be tied to the opinion polls.[108]

Speaking before the National Defense University in January 1986, he observed, "There should be no confusion about the status of nations that sponsor terrorism against Americans and American property. There is substantial legal authority for the view that a state which supports terrorist or subversive attacks against another state, or which supports or encourages terrorist planning and other activities within its own territory, is responsible for such attacks. Such conduct can amount to an ongoing armed aggression against the other state under international law."[109]

Although Shultz observed that by 1986 terrorism figured "very prominently on the international agenda," he encountered significant obstacles in translating his concerns "into action at home." Noting that "our thinking about terrorism was confused," he struggled to dispel both the "odious" and "dangerous" myth that "[i]f you want to get at terrorism, you have to get at its 'root causes'" and the mistaken belief, captured in the mantra, "[o]ne man's terrorist is another man's freedom fighter," that "terrorist acts could be justified and legitimized—and that somehow *we* were to blame."[110] Emphasizing that "force—or the threat of force," was critical in countering terrorism, he lamented that "[c]aution and worry and inhibition were paralyzing an effective response to terrorism: on Capitol Hill and in the Pentagon, among Democrats and Republicans, on the left and on the right, all too many people of influence and authority seemed to have an endless litany of reasons to refrain from the use of power as an instrument of American foreign policy." Secretary of Defense Caspar Weinberger was subjected to particularly scathing criticism, accused of carrying the "Vietnam syndrome" "to an absurd level" by counseling "inaction bordering on paralysis" and by buttressing the Defense Department's "deep philosophical opposition to using our military for counterterrorist operations." Shultz asserted that the "executive branch was itself so fragmented that it was impossible to orchestrate all counterterrorist efforts effectively or even to get agreement that there should be a specific counterterrorist effort."[111]

Shultz nonetheless noted that by mid-1986 "our war against terrorism and the policy that informed it were taking shape in an effective way: those who argued that terrorism was justified because of economic or political grievances now knew they would be taken on whenever they put this argument out. Our legal position had been carefully developed and articulated. Most importantly, we had shown that we possessed the will to take military action against a state found to be directly supporting terrorism. We had achieved an unprecedented sense of unity among the major democracies on cooperative approaches to stopping terrorism." Reagan echoed Shultz, noting during the 1985 TWA 847 crisis, "America will never make concessions to terrorists—to do so would only invite more terrorism—, nor will we ask nor pressure any other government to do so"; following the US raid on Libya in 1986 he stressed, "Today we have done what we had to do. If necessary, we shall do it again. . . . We Americans are slow to anger. We always seek peaceful avenues before resorting to the use of force—and we did. . . . Despite our repeated warnings, Qadhafi continued his reckless policy of intimidation, his relentless pursuit of terror. He counted on America to be passive. He counted wrong. I warned that there should be no place on Earth where terrorists can rest and train and practice their deadly skills. I meant it. I said that we would act with others, if possible, and alone if necessary to ensure that terrorists have no sanctuary anywhere. Tonight, we have."[112]

The Administration embraced the Nixon era practice of labeling Palestinian violence *terrorism* and Israeli violence *retaliation*. The PLO, characterized as among "the most violent and radical elements around," was described as "a serious threat to our national security and to the lives of American citizens," while Arafat was accused of being an "accessory" to PLO terror.[113] Shultz, observing that "[w]henever even a glimmer of peace emerged in the Middle East, radical Palestinians and rejectionist states would step up their assaults on innocent people," insisted that "Palestinians must renounce terrorism and violence" should they ever hope to "present themselves as a viable negotiating partner."[114] In contrast, IDF and Mossad operations, including large scale military incursions, airstrikes, and targeted assassinations, invariably were described as "retaliatory" measures, while such settlement activities as land confiscations, forced evictions, and house demolitions—measures experienced as terroristic by Palestinians on a daily basis—were characterized only as "obstacle[s] to peace."[115]

The PLO's official renunciation of terror on 14 December 1988 prompted the US to pursue an unprecedented "substantive dialogue with PLO representatives."[116] While careful to reassure Israel that "the fundamental basis of our approach to a Middle East settlement has not changed" and that "American bipartisan support for Israel is a great and an enduring achievement . . . for America's national interest," the incoming George H.W. Bush administration stressed that "Palestinian participation is vital to any successful [peace] process."[117] Should Palestinians "speak with one voice for peace," "[a]mend the covenant" calling for Israel's destruction, and "[t]ranslate the dialogue of violence in the *intifadah* into a dialogue of politics and diplomacy," Bush expressed support for Palestinian involvement in "all multilateral negotiations," including the Madrid Peace Conference.[118]

The 1993 *Oslo Accords*, punctuated by Rabin and Arafat's historic handshake on the White House lawn, temporarily transformed US perceptions about Arafat, the PLO, and Palestinian terror. Arafat and the PA's recognition of Israel's right to exist and commitment to meaningful anti-terror efforts minimized both Phase III concerns about Palestinian terrorism's impact on domestic security and wellbeing and Phase IV anxieties about its international strategic significance. However, Clinton, while applauding Arafat for "fully, finally and forever [rejecting] the passages in the Palestinian Charter calling for the destruction of Israel" and "for being willing to change course and for being strong enough to stay with what is right," reminded the PA's President that terrorism "must become a fact of the past. It must never be a part of your future. Let me say this as clearly as I can: no matter how sharp a grievance or how deep a hurt, there is no justification for killing innocents." He stressed that "a secure, just and lasting peace" was predicated upon "the courage of Palestinians to take action against all those who resort to and support violence and terrorism" and "the courage of Palestinians to confiscate illegal weapons of war and terror."[119]

The September 2000 eruption of the extraordinarily lethal al-Aqsa Intifada, an uprising marked by extensive use of suicide bombers against civilian targets, engaged the American media, Congress, pro-Israeli interest groups, and public in a fashion reminiscent of the high profile Palestinian terrorism of the early 1970s. Juxtaposed against the hopes of the *Oslo* era, such violence was particularly disconcerting. Expressing Americans' profound distress, Clinton lamented the "tragic cycle of violence" and called for an end to Palestinians' "culture of violence and the culture of incitement." Emphasizing that "[s]uch conduct is inconsistent with the Palestinian leadership's commitment to Oslo's nonviolent path to peace and its persistence sends the wrong message to the Israeli people," he stressed that terrorism, whether sanctioned by the PA or conducted by "independent" actors "who don't want this peace to work," "shattered the confidence in the peace process," made "it much more difficult for [the Israeli people] to support their leaders in making the compromises necessary to get a lasting agreement," and encouraged "the enemies of peace [who] know they can drive the Israelis to close the borders if they can blow up enough bombs." In contrast to such indictments of PA policies, Clinton refrained from criticizing the Barak government, instead reiterating Washington's commitment to "preserving Israel's qualitative edge in military superiority"; he emphasized that "there will be no lasting peace or regional stability without a strong and secure Israel, secure enough to make peace, strong enough to deter the adversaries which will still be there, even if a peace is made in complete good faith."[120] Perhaps equally important, he avoided characterizing as *terrorism* Israeli house demolitions, land seizures, targeted assassinations, and military incursions into refugee camps, reserving such an appellation only for Palestinian violence.

The terrorist attacks of September 11, 2001 catapulted the US into a Phase V relationship with transnational terrorism, profoundly impacting its approach to Palestinian and Israeli violence alike. As terrorism assumed "direct, significant, and longterm international strategic, as well as domestic political and security, implications," George W. Bush confronted "overwhelming, and often conflicting, pressures to provide both visible and effective management of the terrorist threat."[121] Efforts to remove the Taliban from power in Afghanistan, capture or kill Osama bin-Laden, and encourage both NATO and the UN to pursue more effective anti-terror measures were couched in the rhetoric of an "either with us or against us" "War on Terror." Addressing the Intifada as a particularly serious threat to a valued democratic ally, Bush provided a "green light" for Sharon's sweeping anti-terror measures, including attacks on refugee camps, reoccupation of Palestinian cities in the Occupied Territories, collective punishments, and assassinations of Palestinian leaders suspected of terrorist activities. Such an approach marked the final delegitimization of the PA, which became, as had the PLO before it, perceived as a terrorist-tainted organization unfit for conventional diplomacy.

ANALYSIS

The readiness of Israeli, Palestinian, and US policymakers "to exploit opportunities, confront hard choices, and make fair and mutual concessions" to secure peace has been, and will continue to be, predicated significantly upon their perceptions of the pendular dynamic of terror.[122] Recognizing that "similar acts of terror will elicit different responses as strategic and political conditions evolve and their relative influence varies" highlights the extent to which prospects for negotiated peace depend upon "the relationship among terrorist actions, the international strategic perspective and goals of elite decisionmakers, and key features of the domestic political environment." As transitions occur both between and within different phases of an actor's relationship with transnational terror, the policy options available to decisionmakers may fluctuate dramatically.[123] Seizing opportunities created by such flux while avoiding ill-conceived, poorly timed initiatives demands a rigorous and nuanced understanding of the phases within which Israeli, Palestinian, and US policymakers are functioning at any given time.

Pre-Intifada I

Palestinians' high profile *acts de presence* against Israeli targets, beginning in 1968 and continuing through the mid-1980s, were marked by exceptional brutality and callous disregard for innocents, including women, children, and the elderly. Israeli perceptions of Palestinians as impoverished refugees were replaced by images of bomb throwing, gun wielding terrorists. Public fear and anger, coupled with a refusal to acknowledge Palestinians' distinct "national identity,"[124] generated intense pressure on government leaders to pursue aggressive counterterror, anti-fedayeen policies, including assassinating top Palestinian leaders.[125] While Rabin, Meir's successor, sought to resolve key disagreements with the Palestinians, the extent to which terrorism had poisoned Israeli sentiment permitted only the most tentative and highly secret overtures.[126] Such Phase III constraints were reflected in Likud's 1977 party platform. Echoing Rabin's earlier refusal to "negotiate with terrorist organizations," it decried the "murderous (Palestinian) organizations," vowing to "eliminate" them and "to prevent them from carrying out their bloody deeds."[127] Reflecting both the "transformation of transnational terror into an issue of vital and ongoing domestic concern" and personal revulsion at Palestinian actions,[128] Begin and his Likud successor, Yitzhak Shamir, relentlessly sought to isolate Palestinians and prevent them from engaging in conventional diplomatic intercourse.

Israeli leaders' pre-Intifada tendency to discount Palestinian terrorism's international strategic significance provided no incentive to ignore domestic political sentiment and pursue a negotiated settlement. Prior to the Yom Kippur War, fedayeen terror was dismissed as an unpleasant irritant that could be managed "without real difficulty."[129] Israel's increasingly close economic, military, and political relationship with the US mitigated concerns about its growing international isolation, while the 1967 War's decisive outcome generated unprecedented confidence about Israel's regional supremacy. Although the 1974 Rabat Summit threatened to enhance the PLO's ability "to disrupt any progress towards peace," the 1979 Egyptian-Israeli peace treaty effectively neutralized a key Palestinian sponsor, specifically enjoining Cairo from supporting "violence" against the Jewish state and requiring that it bring "perpetrators . . . to justice."[130] Israel's expulsion of Arafat and the PLO from Lebanon in 1982 reinforced perceptions about Palestinians' relative insignificance, enabling Begin and his successor to focus on solidifying peace with Egypt, exploring negotiations with Jordan, and cementing ties with the US.

If Israel's Phase III relationship with Palestinian terror presented neither opportunity nor incentive to negotiate with the PLO, Palestinians' Phase V experience with Israeli terror precluded conventional diplomatic intercourse with the "Zionist enemy." Outraged at Israel's attempt to obliterate Palestinians' national identity through its 1967 "war of terror" and subsequent settlement efforts in the Occupied Territories, the 12th Palestine National Council rejected "any plan for the establishment of a Palestine entity the price of which is recognition (of Israel), conciliation (with it), secure borders, (or) renunciation of the national right"; the PFLP similarly opposed "all proposed forms of settlement," refusing to recognize even "the existence of Israel."[131] Arafat, responding to intense domestic pressures, delivered a scathing indictment of "Zionist terrorism" before the UN General Assembly in 1974, condemned Israeli "terrorist" policies in the Occupied Territories following the Camp David *Frameworks*, and indicted Israel's "terrorist and hellish" Lebanese policy in the late 1970s.[132] Substantive overtures toward Israel, neither strategically attractive nor politically tenable, were forsaken in favor of armed confrontation and resistance.

Although evolving significantly from 1968 to the outbreak of the first Intifada in 1987, the US relationship with Palestinian terror provided the White House neither incentive nor opportunity to facilitate Israeli-Palestinian negotiations. While Palestinian terror's lack of domestic political salience and international strategic relevance prior to 1970 afforded Nixon typical Phase I latitude in addressing the Palestinian issue, both he and Kissinger perceived few benefits in promoting Palestinian national/territorial objectives through US-sanctioned Israeli-Palestinian dialogue, preferring instead to marginalize the PLO, strengthen ties with Israel, and cultivate relationships with moderate Arab regimes. Such an approach remained largely unchanged subsequent to the emergence of Phase IV-type concerns following the PFLP's 1970 multiple hijacking operation and BSO's 1972 Munich Olympic hostage seizure. The Administration, while acknowledging the need "at some appropriate stage" to "bring them [Palestinians] into the settlement process," exercised its Phase IV discretion by continuing to exclude the PLO from "step-by-step" regional diplomacy. Nascent domestic pressures were addressed by creating the symbolically expedient CCCT and by pursuing practical measures to secure international civil aviation, protect foreign diplomats, safeguard nuclear materials, and tighten visa requirements.[133] The Reagan administration, perceiving PLO-sanctioned terrorism within the context of Soviet, Libyan, Syrian, and Iranian terrorist activities, expressed growing concerns about transnational terrorism's international strategic implications, including its potential to sabotage regional diplomatic initiatives. Stressing its commitment to a global "war against terrorism" and to a policy of "active prevention, preemption, and retaliation," the White House insisted upon the PLO's exclusion from conventional diplomatic fora absent its unequivocal renunciation of terror.[134] Events such as the TWA and Achille Lauro hijackings episodically engaged public attention, bolstering support for the Administration's aggressive, Phase IV-inspired, counterterror approach.

Intifada I- *Oslo Accords*

The period 1987–1991 witnessed the unprecedented development of a Phase V Israeli relationship to Palestinian terror. While the Intifada heightened domestic pressures to control escalating violence, Hamas and its Islamist counterparts' success in exploiting popular discontent with Arafat and the PLO posed new and increasingly complex strategic challenges. Hamas's call for the total "liberation of Palestine," emphasis on the religious dimension of the "Palestinian problem," and call for Jihad against the Israeli occupiers threatened to unleash a campaign of indiscriminate terror likely to exacerbate Israeli difficulties in controlling the Occupied Territories and to bolster Iranian efforts to cultivate fundamentalist movements threatening to Jerusalem.[135] Arafat's renunciation of terror before the UN General Assembly in December 1988 further complicated strategic assessments. In addition to prompting unprecedented, direct, and substantive US-PLO discussions—a development which threatened to attenuate the political, economic, and military support upon which Israeli security had come to depend—Arafat's position emboldened Islamic extremists opposed to any accommodation with Israel or its US patron.

Although confronting both domestic political and international strategic imperatives to address the terrorist threat, Prime Minister Rabin leveraged his impeccable military reputation to work effectively within Phase V constraints. While vowing to "fight terrorism as if there were no peace process"—a pledge necessitated by public anger and bitterness about ongoing terrorist attacks—he quietly engaged the PLO in direct talks.[136] Seeking to capitalize both on Arafat's fears about growing Islamist popularity and on the PLO's quest to be included in conventional diplomatic negotiations, he successfully orchestrated the 1993 *Oslo Accords*. Arafat and the PLO were given powerful incentives to reign in Islamic terror, including most significantly the opportunity to direct the new Palestinian Authority, and thus become a critical instrument in addressing Rabin's terror-related domestic political and international security concerns.

While Palestinians' Phase V relationship with Israeli terror remained unchanged in the late 1980s–early 1990s, Arafat confronted increasingly complex pressures concerning effective management of Israeli violence. Recognizing the need to address outrage over Israel's "fascist official terrorism" and "iron fist" suppression of Intifada I, he condemned US-sanctioned Israeli terrorism and openly supported Saddam Hussein during the 1991 Gulf War.[137] However, the importance of achieving tangible progress toward statehood given the PLO's competition with increasingly popular Islamic militants prompted Arafat's categorical rejection of "all forms of terrorism," support of the US-sponsored, Israeli endorsed, Madrid Peace Conference, and willingness to negotiate the *Oslo Accords*, an agreement proffering the possibility of achieving Palestinian statehood *and* eliminating Israeli terror.[138] The secrecy surrounding *Oslo*'s negotiation testified to the Phase V constraints operating on both Arafat, the architect of modern day Palestinianism, and Rabin, one of Israel's most revered war heroes.

Although the Intifada and emergence of Islamist terrorist organizations highlighted Palestinian terror's ongoing threat to US regional strategic interests, Arafat's official renunciation of terror prompted Washington's development of a more nuanced Phase IV perspective. Despite skepticism about the PLO's *bona fides* as a negotiating partner and commitment to respect internationally negotiated accords, Reagan acknowledged a potentially meaningful split within the Palestinian community. Arafat's PLO, the erstwhile symbol of Palestinian terror, was to be given an opportunity to earn its place at the negotiating table by transforming public pronouncements into substantive anti-terror actions, while Hamas-type terrorist organizations were to be marginalized and combated by all available means. Such a policy reversal—demonstrated most dramatically by the initiation of US-PLO discussions—by an administration noted for characterizing Palestinians, the PLO, and Arafat as *terrorists* sent a powerful signal to the American public that terror no longer was the *modus operandi* of mainstream Palestinian institutions, but rather only an instrument of "extremist" elements.

While the incoming George H.W. Bush administration expressed frustration at the PLO's inability or unwillingness to "discipline" "constituent" organizations that perpetrated terrorist actions, it continued to embrace the moderate PLO/radical Islamic terrorist distinction. Bush noted that US-PLO exchanges "about the political and security situation in the region" had "contributed to progress in the peace process," applauded the PLO's public condemnation of "attacks against civilians in principle," and stressed that Palestinian participation in the Madrid Peace Conference was necessary "to launch" direct negotiations with Israel.[139] While abandoning the blanket use of *terrorist* to characterize Palestinians in favor of its more limited application to radical groups implied no necessary diminution of the Phase IV terrorist threat for US policymakers, it created unprecedented *Oslo*-type opportunities to employ cooptation and "divide and rule" anti-terror tactics.

Oslo-Intifada II

While remaining firmly rooted in Phase V throughout the post-*Oslo*, pre-Intifada II period, Israel's relationship to Palestinian terror experienced a series of dramatic intra-phase transitions impacting the potential for sustained, productive negotiations with the PA. Although Rabin, Netanyahu, and Barak agreed that radical Islamic terror's Hizbollah-like tactics threatened "every" Israeli citizen, fueled "rejectionist" opposition to *Oslo*, and undermined the PA's legitimacy within the Occupied Territories,[140] their divergent assessments of Arafat and the PA contributed to marked differences in managing the terrorist threat. Rabin and Barak, convinced that containing Palestinian terror necessitated identifying a sufficiently motivated and capable Palestinian partner, reluctantly embraced the newly established PA. Arguing that Arafat had broken decisively from the PLO's terrorist past and had a significant stake in preventing Islamic extremists from derailing efforts to establish a Palestinian state, they actively pursued a series of negotiations with their newfound Palestinian interlocutor.[141] In contrast, Netanyahu acknowledged no meaningful distinction between the PA and radical Islamic groups' perspective on terror. His antipathy to the PA dramatically slowed diplomatic progress, undermining the Authority's domestic legitimacy as Palestinians increasingly questioned the efficacy of negotiations. Rabin, Netanyahu, and Barak's sequential pursuit of divergent anti-terror policies contributed to disconcertingly abrupt intra-Phase V pendular flux, and thus to periodic, albeit brief, moments of diplomatic opportunity.

Such intra-Phase V pendular flux likewise defined Palestinians' approach to Israeli terror in the post-*Oslo*, pre-Intifada II period. Arafat's initial commitment to *Oslo*'s diplomatic path reflected the PA's pressing need to counter Hamas's growing popular appeal by securing immediate and tangible territorial, political, economic, and security benefits for Palestinians in the Occupied Territories. Such a strategy, predicated upon Israel abandoning land confiscations, house demolitions, assassinations, and settlement construction, appeared vindicated by Jerusalem's commitment in the *Cairo Agreement* and *Interim Agreement on the West Bank and Gaza Strip* to "take all measures necessary in order to prevent acts of terrorism."[142] While Rabin never accepted Palestinians' conception of Israeli "terrorism," his commitment to expanding PA purview over Gaza and the West Bank and to addressing in a timely manner "final status" issues afforded hope that Arafat's approach would yield near term dividends.

However, such expectations proved both short-lived and illusory, undermining the PA's anti-Islamist strategy. Rabin's assassination, followed by the ascendance of a Netanyahu government opposed to *Oslo* and insistent upon Israel's historical and religious claims to Judea and Samaria, emboldened Arafat's anti-*Oslo* critics. Islamic Jihad and Hamas highlighted PA-Israeli collaboration against Palestinian resistance organizations, Israel's ongoing terrorist activities, and Netanyahu's failure to adhere to *Oslo*-era commitments. Reluctant to abandon a negotiating process in which he had invested such political capital and personal prestige, Arafat responded to such criticism by coupling rhetorical support for negotiations with a refusal to take decisive action against the increasingly popular Islamic resistance parties. While participating in the July 2000 Camp David talks reflected a final effort to salvage *Oslo* under the far more conciliatory Barak-led Israeli government, Arafat's refusal to accept unprecedented concessions on Jerusalem, the Occupied Territories, and the nature of a two state solution testified to the extent to which intra-Phase V pendular flux during the Netanyahu administration had foreclosed the diplomatic option; by 2000, a "negotiated solution" demanded virtual Israeli capitulation.

Arafat and Rabin's historic handshake in September 1993 precipitated a rapid transition from a Phase IV to a Phase II US relationship to Palestinian terror, a development that provided significant policy latitude to the new Clinton administration. Rabin's pledge to include the PLO, the erstwhile symbol of Palestinian terror, "within the Middle East peace process" transformed perceptions about Palestinian terror's domestic political salience *and* international strategic significance.[143] While Islamist groups rejected *Oslo* and insisted on continuing terrorist operations, their relative lack of resources and visibility commanded only episodic public attention. Clinton, accepting the sincerity of Arafat and the PLO's anti-terrorism commitments, reevaluated Palestinian terror's threat to US strategic interests. He emphasized that it was "profoundly wrong to equate Palestinians in particular and Islam in general with terrorism, or to see a fundamental conflict between Islam and the West. For the vast majority of the more than one billion Muslims in the world, tolerance is an article of faith and terrorism a travesty of faith"; he cautioned, "the act of a few can falsify the image of the many."[144] Such a redrawing of "definitional boundaries" reflected both Clinton's domestic latitude in applying the terrorist label and his assessment of Palestinian terror's diminished strategic significance. Such a Phase II perspective, one that informed US policy until the al-Aqsa Intifada's outbreak in September 2000, permitted concerted intervention on behalf of Israeli-Palestinian negotiations.

Intifada II- *Road Map*

The al-Aqsa Intifada's devastating violence, including extensive suicide bombings against civilian targets, prompted shell-shocked Israelis to replace Barak with Ariel Sharon, Likud's hardline leader. Claiming an electoral mandate for radical change in the government's approach to Palestinian terror, Sharon unabashedly abandoned *Oslo*, dismissing Arafat as an unrepentant terrorist with whom Israel no longer would negotiate;[145] in addition, he ordered the IDF to conduct massive anti-terror operations in select refugee camps, crippled PA security capabilities, and authorized high profile assassinations. Although reflecting public anger and frustration, Sharon's aggressive policies also were premised on his oft-stated belief that Arafat, the PLO, and the PA posed "a political threat to the very existence of the State of Israel";[146] he stressed both the strategic threat inherent in a Palestinian state in Gaza and the West Bank and the tactical necessity of crushing Palestinian terror. Such convergence of domestic political pressure and international strategic perspective generated especially pronounced intra-Phase V pendular flux as Barak's expectant optimism preceding the Camp David talks yielded to Sharon's unflinching embrace of the military instrument.

Arafat's domestic political vulnerabilities, heightened by Camp David's high profile failure, created overwhelming pressures to support the al-Aqsa uprising and abandon diplomacy as the PA's principal anti-terror strategy. Arafat publicly questioned the peace process that he had championed through *Oslo*, noting that it "has suffered from the absence of the balance needed to offer real chances for the progress of this process and the reaching of effective results in it." Condemning Israel's "mass extermination campaign against our people," which included "massacr[ing]" innocent civilians, destroying agricultural produce, demolishing houses, and razing colleges, he pledged support for the Intifada's "revolutionary struggle" to secure an independent Palestinian state with Jerusalem as its capital.[147] Such a break from *Oslo* completed the intra-Phase V pendular flux begun during Netanyahu's tenure toward a violence rather than diplomacy centered anti-terror strategy.

The al-Aqsa Intifada, coupled with Arafat's "pledge" that Palestinians' "revolutionary struggle . . . will only stop with victory,"[148] shattered Clinton's hope that *Oslo* had altered irrevocably Palestinian terror's strategic significance. Embraced yet again by mainstream Palestinian leaders, terrorism threatened US interests in regional stability, Israeli security and wellbeing, and improved relations with the Arab world. Although Clinton argued that the Intifada "demonstrate[d] the futility of force or terrorism as an ultimate solution," he acknowledged that the violence "has shattered the confidence in the peace process" and "has raised questions in some people's minds about whether Palestinians and Israelis could ever really live and work together, support each other's peace and prosperity and security." He observed that it was a "heartbreaking" time, both for himself and for all those "who have believed for eight years in the Oslo process."[149]

The United States' al-Aqsa-induced Phase IV perspective on Palestinian terror was transformed instantly by al-Qaeda's devastating attacks of September 11, 2001. Highlighting Western democracies' vulnerability to well financed, operationally sophisticated transnational terrorist organizations, 9/11 established terrorism's "direct, significant, and longterm international strategic, as well as domestic political and security, implications."[150] Confronting an unprecedented threat to global political, economic, and military interests, as well as to domestic security and wellbeing, Bush announced an open-ended "war on terror" dependent upon securing unwavering political, diplomatic, and intelligence related support from friends and allies, all of whom were to enjoy significant latitude in addressing their own particular terrorist threats. That the transition to Phase V obviated any near term possibility that Israel would be pressured by its American ally to negotiate with the PA was apparent in Bush's acquiescence to Sharon's sweeping anti-terror initiatives, including perhaps most importantly his relentless efforts to isolate and punish Arafat, the elected Palestinian president.

THE *ROAD MAP FOR PEACE*

Reflecting an emerging consensus among the US, EU, Russia, and the UN that the Israeli-Palestinian impasse demanded immediate attention, efforts began in mid-2002 to develop what would be presented in April 2003 to Israel and the Palestinian Authority as the *Road Map for Peace*. While prompted by shared concerns about the confluence of the al-Aqsa Intifada's intensifying violence and al-Qaeda's emergence as a transnational terrorist organization with unprecedented global reach, the *Road Map* nonetheless failed to overcome Quartet members' significant and longstanding differences. Indeed, both procedural and substantive disagreements became increasingly pronounced as the *Road Map* unfolded, revealed in differing perspectives on empowered multilateral versus mediated bilateral negotiations, incremental versus comprehensive peacemaking strategies, and formulations for resolving such final status issues as Jerusalem, borders, settlements, and refugees. The failure of Israel, the PA, and the US to exploit opportunities afforded by terrorism's pendular flux further compromised prospects for success.

ROAD MAP'S ORIGINS—2001–2002

Context

Echoing EU, Russian, and UN concerns about escalating Israeli-Palestinian violence,[1] George W. Bush noted that the "tragic cycle of incitement, provocation and violence has gone on far too long," observed that "the violence must cease in order for there to be any meaningful dialogue in the Middle East," and argued that "in order for the region to be peaceful and hopeful, there must be a resolution to the Palestinian-Israeli conflict."[2] Focusing on those "people in the Middle East who would use terror as a weapon to derail any peace process," he warned that "this terrible destruction of human life is not the correct path to follow" and vowed "to rout out terror" in pursuit of "peace."[3]

Bush's conviction that fighting terror was "the calling of our time" prompted a fundamental reassessment of "America's traditional acceptance of Arab autocracies as useful security partners" and a willingness "to engage more seriously than any previous administration with the issue of whether and how the United States can promote democracy in the Middle East."[4] "[A]cceptance of friendly autocrats" over the "promotion of democratic change," an approach premised on "security considerations, dependence on Arab oil, and the fact that the United States had little leverage to force reforms on regimes whose cooperation it needed to maintain peace in the region and to secure access to abundant and cheap oil," yielded to a new emphasis on "political and economic reform and democratization as policy goals in the Middle East."[5] EU policy likewise reflected post-9/11 considerations. Accepting European Commissioner Christopher Patten's argument that "fostering human rights should become an integral part of the fight against terrorism," the EU promised increased assistance to Euro-Mediterranean Partnership countries that implemented national human rights action plans, while stressing in its new *security* strategy that "the best protection of our security is a world of well-governed democratic states." German Foreign Minister Joschka Fischer, discussing his government's new Task Force for Dialogue with the Islamic World, similarly observed, "security is a broader concept in this fight against terrorism: social and cultural modernization, as well as democracy . . . are of almost greater importance (than traditional security issues)." Britain's "new Arab reform strategy" emphasized establishing "a number of programs, including a reform-oriented fund for engaging with the Islamic world," and creating "a new cross-Whitehall conflict prevention fund, with governance, security sector reform, and 'engagement with political movements' outlined as priority areas," while France "increased its democracy and governance spending to 10 percent of its overall aid in the Middle East and North Africa" and pursued "an enhanced *zone de solidarite prioritaire* program that included Algeria, Lebanon, Morocco, the Palestinian Territories, Tunisia, and Yemen."[6]

While the al-Aqsa Intifada prompted growing concerns about regional stability and the plight of innocent civilians,[7] and 9/11 heightened attention to links between good governance and minimizing the terrorist violence so destructive to Israeli-Palestinian relations, Bush's "regime change" rhetoric toward Iraq exposed deep fissures between the US and UN, key European allies, and the broader Arab world. Rejecting White House arguments in favor of preemptive intervention,[8] the UN, France, Germany, and neighboring Arab states cautioned that an unprovoked US attack risked fragmenting Iraq, destabilizing the region, and compromising multilateral efforts to resolve the Israeli-Palestinian conflict. The international community's concerns were expressed most pointedly by Arab commentators, including the Jordanian press: "The first objective (of US policy toward Iraq) is to serve Israel and implement its Sharonist wish of striking off the map a pivotal Arab country, thus giving Israel full dominance over the Arab region for an indefinite period of time. . . . Hence the first thing that the alternative Iraqi government will do, either voluntarily or under coercion, is to recognize Israel and unconditionally exchange diplomatic representation with it. The rest of the Arab countries would fall like domino chips"; "It is natural for the United States and Britain to view Baghdad's acceptance of the return of inspectors as a tactical maneuver because their real goal goes beyond the return of inspectors"; and, "what does Bush have to say about the so-called Israeli democracy, which has produced the worst kind of far-right, extremist government, led by General Ariel Sharon, who is committed to continued occupation, the demolition of more Palestinian houses, the expropriation of Palestinian land, the assassination of Palestinian activists, ethnic cleansing and all-out state terrorism?" Egyptian journalists made similar arguments: "The claims of the American media, endlessly reiterated—concerning Iraq's alleged possession of weapons of mass destruction that pose threats to US interests, the need to replace the present dictatorship with a truly democratic order—are no more than colorful confetti, thrown with the intention of diverting attention away from Washington's real objective, which is no more, and no less, than to secure access to Iraqi oil, and to ensure that Saudi Arabia and other Gulf countries no longer produce organizations like Bin-Laden's Al-Qaeda"; "The US is not the country that people of this region can rely upon to generate a foreign climate conducive to fostering and supporting a true process of democratization. The U.S. has a long record of supporting dictatorships and of plotting to overthrow democratically elected governments. Whenever the defense of democratic values has come into conflict with the defense of US interests, the latter always win out"; and, "Now we are being told that Saddam is not a democrat, is not nice at all really, is actually a tyrant who gasses his own people. How nice to hear this two decades after the event in Khalabje, from the very governments who supported him in his first Gulf War against Iran. It did not seem to bother them then, or at any time in the past two decades."[9]

Differences over Iraq were exacerbated both by EU, Russian, and UN resistance to Bush's unilateralist tendencies and by disagreements concerning global warming, ballistic missile defense, international trade, Iran, and North Korea. The EU, confronted by a US administration dismissive of "old" Europe's continuing vitality and relevance, especially feared a damaging attenuation of both trans-Atlantic and intra-EU relationships, while Putin questioned the impact of rapidly escalating US military expenditures, Washington's fascination with China, and White House contempt for UN multilateralism on his efforts to reestablish Russia's international stature; the UN struggled to maintain its relevance in increasingly uncertain diplomatic times.

Process

As Quartet members focused increasingly on the Israeli-Palestinian conflict in late 2001–early 2002, significant differences emerged over procedural issues, one of the most intractable of which concerned the very nature of the Quartet's role in pursuing peace. Insisting that neither the Quartet nor its individual members attempt "to force" a peace settlement or "the adoption of a mechanism on which both parties did not agree," Bush stressed that a "lasting peace in the region will come only when the parties agree directly on its terms";[10] he argued that the US "cannot impose a timetable, nor settlement on the parties if they're unwilling to accept it," but rather must seek "to facilitate the party's work in finding their own solution to peace."[11] US Special Envoy David Satterfield highlighted the principals' responsibility "themselves to take necessary steps to bring an end to this very dangerous situation."[12]

In contrast, the EU, Russia, and UN advocated a more engaged, interventionist approach. European Commission President Romano Prodi committed the EU to "step[ping] up its already active role" in efforts to achieve "peace in the Middle East," German Chancellor Gerhard Schroder noted that "there cannot be peace in the Middle East without the United States of America . . . being active in this field," and Putin stressed that "[p]eace will not come to the Middle East on its own."[13] Christopher Patten highlighted the EU's "on the ground" efforts in countering both Palestinians' "totally unacceptable, horrendous acts of terrorism" and Israel's refusal to "respect the international standards of behaviour that we have all agreed to uphold," including refraining from "trampling over the Geneva Convention, and any notion of international law," "blockading an entire population, withholding tax revenues, extra-judicial killings, destruction of infrastructure and arable land," "denying medical services to those in need," "indiscriminate shelling of refugee camps, the humiliating treatment of prisoners, and wanton destruction of public and private property."[14] He also supported helping the PA to remain "alive as the legitimate governing body that provides essential services to the Palestinian people and only partner for peace with Israel" and to undertake much needed institution building and reform initiatives.[15]

Differences over the nature and extent of Quartet intervention were compounded by unresolved debates concerning incremental versus comprehensive approaches to Middle East peacemaking. Adhering to Kissinger's step-by-step formula, Bush rejected immediate consideration of "final status issues" in favor of "encourag[ing] a series of reciprocal and parallel steps by both sides that will halt the escalation of violence, provide safety and security for civilians on both sides, and restore normalcy to the lives of everyone in the region."[16] Establishing such a "foundation for peace" demanded efforts to "develop the institutions necessary so that a Palestinian state can emerge that will be at peace with Israel," including the critical "first step" of creating "a security force that actually keeps the security."[17] Bush and Assistant for National Security Affairs Condoleezza Rice urged "both parties" to implement the May 2001 *Mitchell Report*'s call for "an immediate and unconditional halt to violence followed by a period of calm for confidence-building measures to be implemented, including a total freeze on Jewish settlement, *before* a resumption of final status talks";[18] Rice noted that the "Mitchell process" established a "step by step" "road map for meaningful negotiations toward a final status," while Bush observed that the *Mitchell Report* "provides a path to return to peace negotiations based on United Nations Security Council Resolutions 242, 338, and the Madrid Conference."[19]

While the EU, Russia, and Secretary-General similarly endorsed "a return to the Mitchell Recommendations. No ifs and no buts," called upon the PA and Arafat to do "everything in their power to put an end to terrorist attacks against innocent people," and agreed "that there can be no military solution to the crisis.

Negotiation is the only way forward," they feared that Washington's insistence upon satisfying extensive preconditions prior to commencing final status negotiations was a recipe for continued stalemate. Prodi reflected such concerns, arguing, "It is clear that previous mediation efforts have failed and we need new mediation. . . . We can't get out of this situation with any other, partial solutions. . . . A solution can be found only if everyone is around one table—EU, US, Russia, Arab Ligue, Israel, Palestine—to analyse together a global plan for peace in the Middle East."[20]

Substance

Although the Bush administration's acknowledgment that "two states living in peace, side by side," was "the only solution to this conflict" resonated with EU, Russian, and UN officials who long had argued that "by the end of the day, certainly there is going to be an independent Palestinian state,"[21] such a "common vision" did little to overcome substantive differences concerning both "final status" issues and approaches to resolving the ongoing Israeli-Palestinian crisis.[22] While reiterating longstanding positions on settlements, refugees, Jerusalem, and borders, Bush focused on addressing immediate obstacles to resuming high level Israeli-Palestinian contacts. Questioning Arafat's commitment to establishing a state "based on the principles that are critical to freedom and prosperity: democracy and open markets, the rule of law, transparent and accountable administration and respect for individual liberties and civil society," he insisted that Palestinians "develop the institutions necessary so that a Palestinian state can emerge that will be at peace with Israel."[23] Attacking Arafat's failure to "condemn and thwart terrorist activities," and arguing that eliminating those "who would use terror as a weapon to derail any peace process" was the "key" to regional peace, Bush demanded that Arafat and the PA "act on [their] condemnation of terror," "speak out against violence in a language that the Palestinians can understand," "arrest and bring to justice" terrorists and their supporters, and undertake "sustained action to prevent future terrorist attacks."[24] He also insisted that Arafat "perform" and "do his job," noting that he "hasn't earned my respect yet. He must earn my respect by leading. And there are a lot of people, a lot of Palestinians who are suffering, and now is the time for him to step up."[25] Emphasizing that the PA's President had "let the Palestinian people down. He hasn't delivered. He had a chance to secure the peace as a result of the hard work of President Clinton and he didn't. He had a chance to fight terror and he hasn't," Bush contrasted Arafat's "disappointing" leadership and past failures "to grab the peace" with Sharon's commitment to "the notion of two states living side by side"; indeed, he praised Sharon as "a man of peace" committed to a negotiated settlement.[26]

While recognizing Arafat's shortcomings, particularly his failure to "apprehend extremists" and "fight those terrorist groups that are opposed to peace," the EU, Russia, and Secretary-General held Israel primarily responsible for the Israeli-Palestinian deadlock. Christopher Patten voiced widespread concerns that an Israeli "policy based on repression and force" created the appearance of seeking not only "the elimination of terror but the elimination of the Palestinian Authority and any achievements of the Oslo Accords," while failing to bring "lasting security to Israel's population." Focusing on Israel's "rapid expansion of settlements," "non-implementation of agreed withdrawals from areas in the West Bank," and ongoing violations of international humanitarian law, he observed, "until Israeli politicians sign up once again to the principles behind the Oslo peace process, until they sign up to a real Palestinian state, until they recognise Palestinians' legitimate political ambitions, unfortunately the violence will continue."[27] Pledging "to keep open the channels for dialogue with Israel," Patten implored Sharon to abandon a posture of not "listening to any outside advice" nor "taking any account of what the world has been saying from the Security Council to the Pope."[28] He reminded Israel that while this "isn't a hostile world against Israel, it's a world that wants to see Israel able to exist behind secure frontiers," "the lack of proportion, to put it mildly, which Israel is displaying" toward Palestinians was unlikely "to secure political stability and a secure world for Israeli citizens," while violating "much" of what Israeli democracy "stands for."[29]

Such criticism contrasted sharply with perspectives on the PA and "its elected President."[30] Arguing that creating a "viable Palestinian State" demanded working "closely with the Palestinian Authority on reforming its institutions and creating an efficient and transparent administration and government," Patten urged Europe to "be in the vanguard of a concerted international development plan for the Palestinians," provide the budgetary support necessary to prevent the PA's "financial collapse," and adopt a pragmatic approach toward dealings with Arafat. Acknowledging the "Arafat dilemma," he observed, "We can't choose the leader of the Palestinian territories, the leader of the Palestinian Authority. . . . If we don't negotiate with him [Arafat], who are we negotiating with? When Chairman Arafat wasn't allowed to go to the Beirut Arab League Summit, who spoke for the Palestinians then? Not somebody who was more moderate than him but somebody who was more extreme than him." Prodi concluded, the "Palestinian Authority under its elected leader, Mr. Arafat, is the only valid interlocutor for Israel."[31]

ROAD MAP'S FORMULATION—2002–2003

Context

US efforts "to push the Israeli-Palestinian crisis into the background to focus on its 'war on terror' and a possible strike on Iraq" prompted renewed efforts in mid-2002 to revive the moribund Middle East peace process.[32] Stung by increasingly strident criticism of both his Iraq and Intifada-related policies, Bush pledged immediate efforts to deescalate the Israeli-Palestinian crisis while utilizing "regime change" in Iraq to facilitate a permanent, comprehensive Israeli-Palestinian-Arab settlement. His 24 June 2002 address established the foundation for such efforts. Declaring support for a Quartet-inspired Israeli-Palestinian settlement "within three years,"[33] Bush sought to enhance US visibility and influence over the Israeli-Palestinian crisis, defuse concerns about US unilateralist tendencies, and, perhaps most importantly, refocus the international community's attention away from the Israeli-Palestinian conflict—now under the active purview of an unprecedentedly broad and powerful international coalition—to the urgent problem of Saddam Hussein and weapons of mass destruction. Pressure also was applied privately to Sharon to limit military "incursions" in the West Bank, ease "restrictions on Palestinians' day to day functioning," and release VAT receipts to the PA, while Security Council measures were tolerated demanding Israel's immediate cessation of "measures in and around Ramallah including the destruction of Palestinian civilian and security infrastructure" and "the expeditious withdrawal of the Israeli occupying forces from Palestinian cities towards the return to the positions held prior to September 2000."[34] While highlighting Bush's commitment "to work intensively . . . to realize the vision of a Palestinian state" and secure "a final peace between Israel and Lebanon, and Israel and Syria that supports peace and fights terror," top Administration officials stressed the link between regime change in Iraq and prospects for comprehensive Middle East peace. Vice-President Dick Cheney promised, "Regime change in Iraq would bring about a number of benefits to the region . . . Extremists in the region would have to rethink their strategy of jihad. Moderates throughout the region would take heart. And our ability to advance the Israeli-Palestinian process would be enhanced, just as it was following the liberation of Kuwait in 1991."[35]

Focused on preventing the increasingly lethal cycle of violence from precipitating both general regional conflict and a humanitarian disaster—particular attention was directed toward Palestinian suicide bombings and terrorist operations and Israel's policy of targeted assassinations, house demolitions, and military incursions into Palestinian population centers in the West Bank and Gaza—the EU, Russia, and the UN intensified peacemaking initiatives by mid-2002. Noting their "grave concern about the current serious situation in the Middle East," including the "deepening" "humanitarian crisis facing the Palestinian people,"[36] Russia and the EU stressed an empowered Quartet's role in facilitating negotiations through providing technical assistance, budgetary support, development aid, and diplomatic offices. Kofi Annan, expressing concern over escalating casualties on both sides, characterized the Israeli-Palestinian conflict as one of the most significant "current threats to world peace, where true leadership and effective action are badly needed," lamented the "atmosphere of gloom and defeatism [that] has descended" on the Middle East, implored the Quartet to assume a more engaged role in peacemaking efforts, and called upon the international community to relieve Palestinian suffering.[37]

Process

While generating renewed hope about prospects for peace, Bush's landmark 24 June 2002 speech highlighted critical rifts between the US and its Quartet partners over procedural issues, including the Quartet's very role in the peace process. Although reaffirming that "real peace" could be achieved only "through a settlement negotiated between the parties," Bush declared that US engagement in the peace process and "support for the creation of a provisional state of Palestine" depended upon Palestinians "embrac[ing] democracy, confront[ing] corruption," developing "new leaders, new institutions and new security arrangements," and creating a parliament with the "full authority of a legislative body." Indicting "Palestinian authorities" for "encouraging, not opposing terror," and for concentrating power "in the hands of an unaccountable few," Bush observed, "*I* laid out a way forward for Palestinians, the Israelis, the Arab world and all the rest of us . . . [a]nd it said basically . . . there needs to be a new constitution, there needs to be elections, there needs to be balance of power, there needs to be new security forces, there needs to be transparency amongst financial institutions. I also made it plenty clear that if there [sic] leadership [is] compromised by terror, we won't be on the path to peace."[38]

Bush focused on developing a "detailed plan" for securing his two state vision which included establishing effective Palestinian security forces and creating a Palestinian constitution that would ensure "that the institutions of a new state are bigger than any one person."[39] Such a "plan" soon emerged as the State Department's *Road Map*, a document Bush characterized "as a part of the vision that I described. It is a way forward. It sets conditions. It's a results-oriented document."[40] That Bush remained committed to the traditional US preference for mediated bilateral, rather than empowered multilateral third party, negotiations was reflected most clearly in the draft *Road Map*'s support for international conferences only *after* satisfaction of its stringent Phase I requirements;[41] he observed, "*Eventually* there will be a peace conference, but there needs to be steps leading up to the peace conference, where all of us do our jobs about putting those institutions in place that will lead to peace, so we all have confidence."[42]

The extent to which Bush envisioned a peace process similar to that which followed the Yom Kippur War—one in which the Quartet's role would be primarily symbolic—was revealed by the Administration's effective "impos[ition]" of "its own draft road map on the Quartet" and by its absolute control over the timing of the document's release.[43] Thwarting his Quartet partners' calls for the *Road Map*'s presentation "to the parties in the near future,"[44] Bush delayed acting until after both Mahmoud Abbas's installation as the PA's first empowered Prime Minister *and* his appointment of a new government. While arguing that such measures were necessary to afford Israel and the Quartet "a credible and responsible partner" in the peace process, White House insistence on preconditions for the *Road Map*'s release raised concerns about the *Road Map* being manipulated first to regain "diplomatic momentum as a new U.N. resolution to authorize a war on Iraq seemed doomed," and subsequently "to help allay Arab anger over the US-led war in Iraq by focusing on Israeli-Palestinian peacemaking."[45]

While acknowledging the importance of Bush's 24 June 2002 statement and encouraging US engagement in the peace process, the EU, Russia, and the UN resisted subservience to their American partner, instead supporting the Quartet's pledge to make "all possible efforts to realize the goals of reform, security and peace," insistence that "progress in the political, security, economic, humanitarian, and institution-building fields must proceed together, hand-in-hand," and endorsement of initiatives such as the International Task Force on Palestinian Reform (ITFR) in helping to establish the foundation of a "democratic Palestinian state characterized by the rule of law, separation of powers, and a vibrant free market economy" through the strengthening of "civil society, financial accountability, local government, the market economy, elections, and judicial and administrative reform."[46] The EU, insisting that the Quartet move beyond "talk" to addressing the "continuing violence which is threatening to widen the gap further between Israelis and Palestinians," took the lead in urging prompt adoption and release of the *Road Map* while promising tangible assistance to the peace process.[47] In addition to providing the PA direct budgetary support of approximately 10 million euros/month, the EU utilized development assistance both to the PA and to Palestinian nongovernmental organizations to promote health, infrastructure, the environment, human rights, food security, the judiciary, NGO co-financing, and private sector business opportunities.[48] Christopher Patten, stressing that "a well-governed Palestinian State that follows democratic principles and operates in a predictable and transparent way on the basis of market economy rules is the best guarantee for its neighbors, and in particular for Israel," emphasized the EU's role in

> creating a constitutional government by shaping the institutions foreseen in the [Palestinian] Basic Law and making them efficient and accountable . . . establishing a truly independent judiciary and a harmonised national legal and regulatory framework more suitable to a free society and market, as well as abolishing state security courts . . . establishing democratic participatory politics and a pluralist society by creating a more effective Legislative Council that would exercise enforceable oversight and decision-making authority, and which would be responsible for receiving and implementing the external audit findings of a statutorily established General Control Institute . . . and encouraging financial openness and accountability.[49]

In addition to exposing differences between the US and its Quartet partners over third parties' responsibilities in facilitating peace, Bush's 24 June 2002 address highlighted fundamental disagreements concerning the efficacy of incremental versus comprehensive diplomatic approaches. Acknowledging the "deep anger and despair of the Palestinian people," Bush observed, "For decades you've been treated as pawns in the Middle East conflict. Your interests have been held hostage to a comprehensive peace agreement that never seems to come." While endorsing a final settlement, the parameters of which included establishing a Palestinian state "living side by side in peace and security" with Israel, he argued that premature consideration of "final status issues" was doomed to fail. His "deeply" held belief that Israel needed "a reformed, responsible Palestinian partner" to achieve the security upon which an acceptable agreement depended commended the *Road Map*'s incremental, phased approach:[50] Phase I demanded that the PA "form a new cabinet that would appoint a PM [Prime Minister], declare the cessation of the armed intifada, halt all violence, and hold parliamentary elections—in that order," that Israel withdraw "to 9/00 positions" and "halt all settlement activity (including natural growth) 'consistent with the Mitchell report,'" and that Egypt and Jordan return their ambassadors to Israel; Phase II required the Quartet to establish "a monitoring body to oversee Palestinian security cooperation, hold an international conference to discuss Palestinian economic recovery, and mediate negotiations on the establishment of a state with provisional borders"; Phase III called for convening a second international conference "to endorse the provisional state, relaunch final status negotiations . . . and take steps to restart Israeli peace talks with Lebanon and Syria." While indicating the possibility of achieving a final settlement "within three years," Bush refused to sanction final status negotiations absent Palestinian political, economic, and institutional reform, as well as PA success in combating terror and violence.[51]

More pessimistic than the US about prospects for Kissinger-style "step-by-step" diplomacy, the EU, Russia, and Secretary-General feared that such an approach privileged US mediated bilateral diplomacy, provided Israel opportunity for additional settlement expansion, and risked further marginalizing Palestinian moderates as prospects for Palestinian statehood receded into the ever more distant future. Observing that the "sequential approach of the past, in my judgment, has not worked," and arguing that peace could be realized "only if we move rapidly and in parallel on all fronts,"[52] Kofi Annan applauded the *Road Map*'s goal of a comprehensive regional peace, including Israel, Lebanon, Syria, and the Palestinians, endorsed its insistence on "parallel" steps for "both parties" and commitment to "a monitoring mechanism to ensure that both parties are performing," and supported its ambitious three year timetable for completion.[53] Russia echoed the Secretary-General, stressing the urgency of achieving "a comprehensive peace on all tracks, including the Syrian-Israeli and Lebanese-Israeli tracks."[54]

Substance

The commitment by *all* Quartet members to a two state solution provided the foundation upon which the *Road Map* ultimately was constructed. Observing in June 2002 that it "is untenable for Israeli citizens to live in terror. It is untenable for Palestinians to live in squalor and occupation. And the current situation offers no prospect that life will improve," Bush declared, "My vision is two states, living side by side in peace and security."[55] He stressed that while an independent Palestinian state would afford Palestinians an opportunity for "[p]rosperity and freedom and dignity," Israel also "has a large stake in the success of a democratic Palestine. Permanent occupation threatens Israel's identity and democracy. A stable, peaceful Palestinian state is necessary to achieve the security that Israel longs for." As the *Road Map*'s official release approached, Bush observed, "We have reached a hopeful moment of progress toward the vision of Middle East peace that I outlined last June. I spoke of a day when two states, Israel and Palestine, will live side by side in peace and security. . . . There can be no peace for either side in the Middle East unless there is freedom for both."[56]

Kofi Annan likewise spoke repeatedly about realizing "the vision of two states, Israel and Palestinian, living side by side," emphasizing that the "Road Map's goal of two states, a secure and prosperous Israel and an independent, viable, sovereign and democratic Palestine, living side-by-side in peace and security, must be the focus of our energies and efforts."[57] Danish Foreign Minister Per Stig Moeller, reaffirming the EU's two states "vision," observed, "It's very important for European Union that the people in the area know they will get two states which have to live quietly, peacefully, side by side." He noted, "What we are trying to do is pave the way to the two states. And that's why we have endorsed this road map and worked with this road map, because it's good thing with a vision, but you must know how to go there. . . . And I think it's very important that Israel know it will live there forever in security. But they can only have that security if they give a political solution to the Palestinians, that the Palestinians know that their day will come where they get the state." Russia and the EU, in a joint statement on the Middle East, endorsed Quartet efforts to realize "the vision of two States, Israel and independent, viable and democratic Palestine, living side by side in peace and security."[58]

While sharing a general commitment to a two state solution, Quartet members' prescriptions for achieving that goal differed markedly. Relentlessly focused on terror as the principal obstacle to a negotiated peace, Bush vowed that a "Palestinian state will never be created by terror."[59] He stressed that leaders "actually committed to peace will end incitement to violence in official media, and publicly denounce homicide bombings. . . . Leaders who want to be included in the peace process must show by their deeds an undivided support for peace."[60] Condemning Arafat and the PA for having "encourage[ed]" and "trafficked with terrorists," he observed, "there are some who will say . . . there's only one person [Arafat] that could conceivably make this [establishment of a Palestinian state] happen from the Palestinian side. I just simply don't believe that. I believe there's all kinds of brilliant and smart and capable Palestinians that, given a chance, given a chance to emerge—and by the way, people committed to peace—and given the chance to articulate that vision of peace will do so."[61] He called upon the PA to develop a security force "designed to fight off terror, not designed to serve the whims and interests . . . of one person," while emphasizing that an independent Palestinian state must be reformed, peaceful, and founded on a constitution guaranteeing that the new state's institutions were "bigger than any one person."[62]

While insisting on substantial progress from the PA prior to commencing "final status" negotiations, Bush refrained from placing similar demands on Israel. He indicated that Jerusalem was expected to "work toward a final status agreement," "take concrete steps to support the emergence of a viable and credible Palestinian state," and "withdraw fully to positions . . . held prior to September 28, 2000" only *after* "new Palestinian institutions and new leaders emerge, demonstrating real performance on security and reform." The sequential nature of US demands was reflected most clearly in Bush's indication that the *Road*

Map's Phase I prohibition on "all settlement activity" would become operative only after "progress is made toward peace."[63]

Unwilling to outline terms of a final settlement, Bush instead articulated fundamental principles upon which "core issues" must be addressed "if there is to be real peace." Emphasizing his commitment "to implementing our road map toward peace," he observed, "Our efforts are guided by clear principles: We believe that all people in the Middle East—Arab and Israeli alike—deserve to live in dignity, under free and honest governments. We believe that people who live in freedom are more likely to reject bitterness, blind hatred and terror; and are far more likely to turn their energy toward reconciliation, reform and development."[64] While acknowledging the need to "resolve questions concerning Jerusalem," "the plight and future of Palestinian refugees," "final borders," and "other aspects" of a sovereign Palestinian state "through a settlement negotiated between the parties, based on U.N. Resolutions 242 and 338," the White House indicated only that its "rock solid" relationship with Israel would continue to inform its position on such issues.[65] That Israel was reassured by such support was reflected in Sharon's observation that "we never had such relations with any President of the United States as we have with you, and we never had such cooperation in everything as we have with the current administration."[66]

Although the EU, Russia, and Secretary-General repeatedly condemned Palestinian terror and called upon the PA to pursue "necessary reforms, including within its security services," they, unlike the US, refused either to isolate Arafat diplomatically or to place the onus for stalemate on the Palestinians.[67] The EU Commission stressed Israeli culpability in "severely disrupt[ing]" the PA's "basic administrative capacity," and thus its ability to pursue those reforms necessary for it to become the "credible and responsible partner" demanded by Israel. It called upon Sharon to "make it easier for humanitarian workers to do their job in the Palestinian territories," "allow full, safe, and unfettered access to those in desperate need who depend on international assistance," and remove "obstacles to the reform and peace process—notably by ending curfews, closures and the withholding of tax revenues."[68] The EU and Russia issued a joint statement emphasizing that both "the reform effort and the political process must include measures by Israel, consistent with its legitimate security concerns, to improve the lives of Palestinians. These should include allowing resumption of normal economic activity, facilitating the movement of goods, people, and essential services, and the lifting of curfews and closures." The International Task Force on Palestinian Reform, functioning under the Quartet's aegis, noted that "the continued violence and terror, continued restrictions on the movement of persons and goods, and deterioration of the humanitarian situation constitute a significant hindrance to reforms"; it stressed that maintaining "momentum in the reform process" depended upon Israel's "immediate resumption of monthly transfers of Palestinian tax revenues and transfer of arrearages."[69]

In addition to supporting Palestinian humanitarian operations, development projects, institutional reform, health sector initiatives, private sector development, electoral preparations, and budgetary obligations,[70] the EU, Russia, and Secretary-General consistently endorsed the PA's stance on final status issues.

The EU and Russia's *Final Statement on the Middle East* declared that an "independent" and "viable" Palestinian state depended upon Israel's immediate cessation of "settlement activities in the Occupied Territories," while calling upon "all parties to live up to their responsibilities to seek a just and comprehensive settlement to the conflict, based on UN Security Council resolutions 242, 338, and 1397, the Madrid terms of reference, the principle of land for peace, and implementation of all existing agreements and understandings between the parties."[71] Such terms of reference, privileging direct negotiations "between the parties concerned under appropriate auspices,"[72] afforded no justification for such unilateral Israeli measures as annexation, land confiscation, expulsion of resident populations, or settlement expansion. Kofi Annan, sympathetic to Palestinian positions on settlements, borders, refugees, and Jerusalem, endorsed PA demands that "all" Security Council and General Assembly resolutions "be implemented . . . across the board," while Per Stig Moeller, representing the EU presidency, cautioned that Israeli settlements threatened to leave Palestinians with a state looking "like Swiss cheese."[73]

ROAD MAP'S IMPLEMENTATION—2003–2005

Context

Quartet efforts to achieve the *Road Map*'s goal of "a comprehensive settlement of the Israeli-Palestinian conflict by 2005" reflected both shared concerns stemming from the US-led war in Iraq and fears that continued deterioration in Israeli-Palestinian relations threatened critical strategic, economic, and political interests. Russian Foreign Minister Igor Ivanov expressed the widespread conviction that "progress on the Palestinian-Israeli front . . . will have a positive impact on an Iraq settlement, and vice versa." Arguing that the "problems of a settlement in Iraq and the Middle East are closely interwoven and interlinked," he urged that both "an Iraq settlement and the implementation of the road map should be taken forward as rapidly as possible."[74] Confronted by an increasingly deadly and costly Iraqi insurgency, growing hostility within the broader Middle East, strained relations with NATO allies, and increasing isolation from the global community, the US anticipated significant dividends from shepherding the internationally endorsed *Road Map* to a successful conclusion. Similarly, the EU and Russia recognized the *Road Map*'s potential both to ameliorate Iraq-related intra-European discord and to ease relations with Washington, while Kofi Annan and the UN, stung by accusations of impotence (the Iraq War), corruption (Oil-for-Food program), and unresponsiveness (Darfur crisis), seized upon the *Road Map* at least partly as an opportunity to demonstrate anew their relevance, integrity, and effectiveness by facilitating the emergence of "a secure and prosperous Israel and an independent, viable, sovereign and democratic Palestine."[75]

In addition to addressing Iraq-related issues, the *Road Map* afforded a significant opportunity to reverse the seemingly inexorable escalation of Israeli-Palestinian hostilities. Fearing the polarizing impact of Palestinian suicide attacks and Intifada-related violence, Israeli military and counterterror operations, and such unilateral measures as Jerusalem's construction of the "separation barrier," the Quartet lauded the *Road Map*'s two-state vision for buttressing embattled moderates on both sides. Arguing that the *Road Map* offered a "historic window of opportunity" "after a terrible period of death and destruction on both sides of the conflict," Annan cautioned Israelis and Palestinians alike not to "allow extremists to dictate the future," while Russia's special peace envoy Andre Vidovin stressed the need to address "the deterioration [in Israeli-Palestinian relations] we have seen for the past two years."[76] EU Commission President Prodi expressed hope that the *Road Map* could "re-launch the Peace Process," provide "an important stabilising factor for the entire region," and realize "the vision of a two-state solution"; Christopher Patten observed, "Too much blood has been shed: it is imperative to re-energise the quest for peace without further delay. . . . It is in the interest of both parties to start making rapid progress to implement the provisions of the Road Map with the support of the international community."[77] While highlighting the extent to which both "Israelis and Palestinians have suffered from the terror and violence, and from the loss of hope in a better future of peace and security," Bush emphasized that in "an age of global terror and weapons of mass destruction what happens in the Middle East greatly matters to America. The bitterness of that region can bring violence and suffering to our own cities. The advance of freedom and peace in the Middle East would drain this bitterness and increase our own security."[78] Describing the *Road Map* as "a starting point toward achieving the vision of two states, a secure State of Israel and a viable, peaceful, and democratic Palestine, that I set out on June 24, 2002," *and* as "a framework for progress towards lasting peace and security in the Middle East," he urged "Israelis and Palestinians to work with us and with other members of the international community, and above all directly with each other to immediately end the violence and return to a path of peace."[79]

Process

While Mahmoud Abbas's confirmation as the PA's first Prime Minister paved the way for the *Road Map*'s formal presentation to Israel and the Palestinians on 30 April 2003, fundamental disagreements concerning the nature and extent of Quartet influence over negotiations, parallel versus sequential obligations, unilateral measures, and the timetable for completion continued to divide Israelis from Palestinians and the US from its Quartet partners.

Palestinians

The PA, in stark contrast to Israel, recognized opportunities afforded both by US-mediated bilateral negotiations *and* by a multilateral, Quartet-centered peace process. Applauding Bush's "vision of two states" and commitment to ending the Israeli occupation,[80] it called "on the US Administration to force the Israeli government to implement the road map," "bring all the parties back to the negotiating table on the basis of the road map," and apply "enough pressure on the Israeli government to end its aggression against the Palestinians, comply with the international legality resolutions, and honour the agreements signed with the Palestinians."[81] Senior Palestinian negotiator Sa'ib Urayqat emphasized the value of Palestinian-US dialogue in developing "action plans, implementation mechanisms and timetables for the implementation of the road map," while the PA insisted that Washington "propose a mechanism of implementation and a time-table and dispatch monitoring teams if it really wants the road map to be implemented accurately and honestly."[82] Both Abbas and Information Minister Nabil Amr stressed the US role in preventing Israel from "drown[ing] the road map with their own interpretations and attempts to impose amendments" and in guaranteeing that it "be implemented as it is."[83]

While endorsing Washington's "basic role" in the *Road Map* "process," the PA also supported the Quartet's multilateral efforts. Urayqat stressed the Quartet's "responsibility" to establish "a time-table, monitoring teams and mechanisms of implementation," as well as determine "whether to move from one stage [of the *Road Map*] to another";[84] he called upon Europe to "breathe new life into the Quartet, put the road map back on the table and work closely with the United States. The Europeans must tell the USA: We are partners, allies; you must take our geopolitical situation into account, our interests in the Middle East. We must solve this problem peacefully. This situation cannot continue."[85] Abbas, speaking as Arafat's newly elected successor, urged the Quartet "to play a direct role in sponsoring the implementation of the road map and preventing our entry once again into the labyrinths of preconditions that seek to disrupt its implementation."[86]

Whether implemented primarily by the US or the Quartet, Palestinian officials unequivocally endorsed the *Road Map*. Arafat declared, "The Palestinian leadership and the Palestinian National Authority announced their welcome and acceptance of the road map because it fulfils many of our basic goals, represented by ensuring the withdrawal of the Israel troops from our Palestinian land to the 1967 borders and the establishment of an independent Palestinian state. This international map represents all the international resolutions and legitimacy and requires us to meet certain political and security obligations, to which we have announced our commitment without any hesitation." He acknowledged the "duty of our leadership, authority and the PLC (Palestinian Legislative Council) to take legal, security and political measures" to ensure "full adherence to the peace option and the road map."[87] Abbas likewise stressed Palestinians' commitment "to each and every item in the road map," pledging to abide by its "letter and spirit" with "no reservations."[88]

Such support, however, was predicated upon Israeli adherence to the *Road Map*'s "methodology" of "parallel" obligations. Minister of Cabinet Affairs Yasir Abd-Rabbuh, rejecting Israeli demands "that the Palestinian side should first do what it has to do from the security side, and after that Israel would do what it has to do," stressed that the "road map says there should be steps in parallel and one side should not impose conditions on the other side." He called upon Israel "to issue a statement, as stipulated by the road map, to stop all forms of violence against the Palestinian people, accept an independent Palestinian state and stop incitement," and upon the PA to "issue a reciprocal statement," after which "steps would begin in parallel." Abbas similarly observed, "It is inconceivable to ask only us to implement our obligations, while the settlement building is continuing and the wall [Israel's separation barrier] is extending into Palestinian territory . . . and also while the closures, blockades, arrests and all forms of violations are continuing against our people."[89] Emphasizing that Palestinian "security measures in isolation from a serious political framework will not be enough to entrench security and open the horizons of peace," he insisted upon a "reciprocal commitment according to the original text of the plan as drafted by the Quartet."[90]

The PA also demanded a *negotiated* resolution of all outstanding issues, arguing that "security, peace, and stability will not be realized without reaching an agreement with the PLO leadership"; it observed, the "Israeli prime minister has been elected by the Israeli people and we must deal with him. We have no other option. We must have meetings every day, every hour and every minute. Unless we talk, we shall be the losers but so will the Jews."[91] Urayqat, noting that Israel's preference for unilateral measures "means cancelling the negotiations, turning negotiations into dictates and imposing facts on the ground," chastised Sharon's government for wanting "to restrict my expectations, dictate their conditions; they do not want to negotiate with me. They know better than I do what is good for me. They want to negotiate with their Labor Party, with their religious parties, with the United States, with the EU, with Belgium, with everybody, and then come to me and say, 'Listen boy, this is what is good for you. We are going to continue occupying parts of your country, we are going to keep the settlements, we are going to leave the wall standing, and if you do not accept that, we will call you a terrorist, as we did Arafat.'"[92] PA officials, discussing unilateral Gaza withdrawal, stressed their "full readiness to *coordinate* with the Israeli side provided that withdrawal . . . is considered a basic part of the road map," was not "used as an excuse to expand settlements in the West Bank and Jerusalem or entrench occupation in other West Bank and Gaza areas," and was "an integral part of the road map, an integral part of the peace process."[93] They were equally insistent that Israel abandon construction of the "racist segregation wall," targeted assassinations, and settlement expansion.[94]

Deeply skeptical of Israel's commitment to Palestinian statehood and fearing a replay of the aborted *Oslo* process, Palestinians insisted upon transitioning quickly from the *Road Map*'s Phase I focus on security, normalizing Palestinian life, and institution building to establishing an independent Palestinian state and resolving final status issues. Abbas, stressing that "at any minute the whole situation could implode," advocated "start[ing] now to discuss all issues mentioned in the road map" "rather than wait[ing] for the third phase." He emphasized "our full readiness to resume the final status talks," "our political readiness to reach a comprehensive agreement on the different issues," and the need immediately to work "together to reach a final and permanent solution—one that would resolve all outstanding issues."[95] Urayqat likewise noted the PA's sense of urgency, observing in early 2005, "We, the moderate Palestinians, are sinking. If the situation remains with no prospects, within five years, there will be no one left here . . . to talk to."[96] Arguing that only rapid implementation of the *Road Map* "as an inseparable whole" would create "prospects for real peace," he warned that a "policy of small steps" risked "the whole region" being "condemned and handed over to the extremists."[97]

Israel

While Palestinians perceived opportunity to achieve longstanding national/territorial objectives through a US-dominated *Road Map* process, Israel looked to Washington to safeguard its "vital political and security interests" from "dangerous" "political initiatives" arising in the *Road Map*'s context.[98] Its very acceptance of the *Road Map* was predicated on the US publicly committing to address "fully and seriously" Israel's "real concerns" during the *Road Map*'s implementation, agreeing that any "future settlement will be reached through agreement and direct negotiations between the two parties, in accordance with the vision outlined by President Bush in his 24 June (2002) address," and acknowledging the Israeli Cabinet's fourteen "reservations" to the plan.[99] Fearing that the "world will not permit the stalemate to continue" and that a "stalemate will sooner or later lead to political initiatives that are dangerous for Israel," Sharon looked to the US "to repel such initiatives," particularly given the "broad international support" for pressuring Israel to "remove its demand that the Palestinians fight terrorism" prior to initiating "political negotiations."[100] Reflecting the Cabinet's rejection of Quartet "involvement with issues pertaining to the final settlement," including "settlement in Judea, Samaria and Gaza," "the status of the Palestinian Authority and its institutions in Jerusalem, and all other matters whose substance relates to the final settlement," Sharon sought US assistance in blocking Russia from securing UN Security Council endorsement of the *Road Map*. He declared, "From our point of view . . . the decision by the Security Council would be a decision hostile towards Israel. . . . Efforts to transfer the road map for consideration by the UN Security Council pose an extremely serious problem for Israel. Israel is categorically opposed to such an attempt. We believe that such an act would endanger the road map plan itself."[101]

Although most comfortable working "in full coordination" with the US,[102] Israel insisted on its right to pursue unilateral measures, reinterpreting or deviating from the US-authored *Road Map* as necessary to protect vital national interests. The Cabinet's September 2003 decision to "remove" Arafat, taken against the backdrop of calls by the *Jerusalem Post* to "kill" the PA President as a demonstration "that the tool of terror is unacceptable,"[103] was particularly troubling to Bush, who characterized the Cabinet's action as "unhelpful" to the *Road Map*'s prospects.[104] Similarly, despite US insistence that Sharon's unilateral Gaza disengagement plan "doesn't replace the road map," Sharon told *Yediot Ahronot*, "we are . . . not following the road-map. I am not ready for this . . . The disengagement plan relieves Israel of pressures to adopt one plan or another that would be dangerous for it." He noted, "Right now, there is no roadmap because there is no Palestinian partner. Since a vacuum would have been dangerous, there was a need for another initiative that will park us in a position where we'll be able—if and when there is a partner that is ready to fight terror, institute reforms and change the leadership—to return to the road-map."[105] Sharon's senior aide, Dov Weissglas, acknowledged, "We launched the disengagement plan (DP) in order to freeze the political process indefinitely. . . . In fact, this entire package involving the Palestinian state has been taken off our agenda indefinitely. The plan provides the amount of formaldehyde that is necessary . . . so there will not be a political process with the Palestinians."[106]

Sharon shared none of the PA's enthusiasm either for the *Road Map*'s parallel obligations language or for its ambitious timetable, insisting that the "underlying concept of the road map is that only security will bring about peace—and in that order. Without achieving full security, which includes the dismantling of the terrorist organizations, real lasting peace cannot be achieved. This is the essence of the road map. The reverse concept, according to which the actual signing of a peace agreement will somehow bring about peace, has already been tried and was a failure."[107] Insisting that "[o]nly after the Palestinians fulfil their obligations—primarily a real fight against terrorism, the dismantling of its infrastructure—can we proceed towards negotiations based on the road map,"[108] Sharon continued to demand over two years *after* the *Road Map*'s official launch that Abbas "take additional steps to disarm terror organisations, stop incitement, or we can't move forward from the *pre*-road map stage."[109] Sharon's advisors, emphasizing the need for sequential negotiations, argued, "the road map has two parts, two stages. The first stage consists of a total Palestinian commitment to eradicate terrorism and set up a reformed authority, and the second stage is the political process. It is only with a reformed authority that the State of Israel will sit down at a negotiating table to discuss a permanent status agreement on all the well-known issues."[110]

Neither Sharon nor the Cabinet envisioned a rapid transition beyond the *Road Map*'s security oriented Phase I. While insisting that "the Roadmap will not state that Israel must cease violence and incitement against the Palestinians," the Cabinet's 25 May 2003 *Statement on Road Map and 14 Reservations* declared, "Both at the commencement of and during the process, and as a condition to its continuance, calm will be maintained. The Palestinians will dismantle the existing security organizations and implement security reforms during the course of which new organizations will be formed and act to combat terror, violence and incitement (incitement must cease immediately and the Palestinian Authority must educate for peace). These organizations will engage in genuine prevention of terror and violence through arrests, interrogations, prevention and the enforcement of the legal groundwork for investigations, prosecutions and punishment." It continued, "In the first phase of the plan and as a condition for progress to the second phase, the Palestinians will complete the dismantling of terrorist organizations . . . and their infrastructure, collection of all illegal weapons and their transfer to a third party[,] . . . cessation of weapons smuggling and weapons production inside the Palestinian Authority, activation of the full prevention apparatus and cessation of incitement. There will be no progress to the second phase without the fulfillment of *all* above-mentioned conditions relating to the war against terror." It stressed that the "first condition for progress will be the *complete* cessation of terror, violence and incitement," indicated that "formation of a new [Palestinian] leadership constitutes a condition for progress to the second phase," and declared that "[f]ull performance will be a condition for progress between phases and for progress within phases."[111]

Although Sharon promised that "the government of Israel led by Likud will be willing to do its part to enable the establishment of an independent Palestinian state," he insisted first on the creation of "a new, democratic Palestinian (National) Authority" (PNA) that "turns away from terrorism," halts "incitement," roots out "terrorist infrastructures," and collects weapons.[112] Endorsing the *Road Map* as "a balanced plan for progressing *gradually* towards peace," he and his advisors justified unilateral measures such as Gaza disengagement as necessary to guarantee Israeli "security" during an "*interim period*" prior to the emergence of "an appropriate, reformed" PNA "which has eradicated terrorism and is ready to go on to enforce law and order and prevent future terrorism." Weissglas similarly stressed the *Road Map*'s sequential, incremental approach, declaring that only "if and when [Palestinians] uphold their commitments under the road map's Chapter I" would Israel "be required to address its fundamental existential issues, such as borders, Jerusalem, refugees, settlements and so forth"; indeed, he argued that "Chapter 3 of the road map says that its emergence depends on the *complete, perfect* execution of Chapter 1."[113]

United States

While acknowledging both the Quartet's role in promoting "peaceful coexistence in the Middle East" and the "special responsibilities" of "all states in the region" to "support the building of the institutions of a Palestinian state," "fight terrorism, and cut off all forms of assistance to individuals and groups engaged in terrorism," and "begin now to move toward more normal relations with the State of Israel," Bush insisted that "all final status issues must be negotiated between the parties," promised that the US would "not prejudice the outcome of those negotiations," and refused to permit "any attempt by anyone to impose any other plan."[114] He stressed that achieving Israeli-Palestinian peace was "a matter of the highest priority" and a "primary objective" of his administration, and committed the US to doing "that which is necessary to help move the [peace] process forward."[115] While emphasizing that "the role of the United States will be to continue to urge both parties to make the sacrifices necessary—sacrifice meaning that Israel must withdraw from the settlements, there must be contiguous territory for a Palestinian state—into which a Palestinian state can grow. The Palestinians, in their part, must continue to work hard to fight any terrorist activities within the territories," Bush vowed to help Palestinians "develop democratic political institutions, build security institutions dedicated to maintaining law and order, . . . and promote a free and prosperous economy," pledged $350 million "to support Palestinian political, economic, and security reforms," and advocated establishing a joint US-PA "Palestine Economic Development Group."[116]

Frustrated by the *Road Map*'s failure "to get everything moving" and supportive of Israel's "right to defend itself against terrorism, including to take actions against terrorist organizations,"[117] Bush displayed great tolerance for Israel's most controversial unilateral initiatives. While publicly reminding Sharon to avoid actions that "pre-judge" negotiations or "prejudice any final status issues," the White House praised his Gaza disengagement plan as "a bold and historic initiative that can make an important contribution to peace," an opportunity for "all sides . . . to reinvigorate progress on the *Road Map*," and a chance "to begin the process of the development of a Palestinian state."[118] Condoleezza Rice, responding to criticism that the plan represented a dangerous deviation from the *Road Map*, observed, "The President remains completely committed to the road map as the viable way to get to a two-state solution. But when you have the Israeli Prime Minister come to you and say, we'll withdraw unilaterally from the Gaza and from four West Bank settlements, we believe that that is worth doing . . . All of the negotiations that we've had over many, many years, we've never been able to see the Palestinians actually recover land. If the Sharon plan or some version of it goes forward, then the Palestinians will begin to recover land. . . . We believe that the Palestinians need an opportunity to build the institutions of their state."[119]

Although threatening the *Road Map*'s objective of establishing a *viable* Palestinian state within the context of a two state solution, Israel's decision to construct a "separation barrier" through parts of the West Bank elicited a similarly muted US response. While acknowledging that "the fence is a sensitive issue," "should be a security rather than a political barrier," and "should be temporary rather than permanent,"[120] Bush refrained from calling either for an immediate halt to its construction or for its removal. Praising Sharon's "visionary leadership" for "taking difficult steps to improve the lives of people across the Middle East," he pledged only to help "make sure that the fence sends the right signal that not only is security important, but the ability for the Palestinians to live a normal life is important, as well."[121]

The White House was sympathetic to Israeli concerns about the *Road Map*'s emphasis on parallel obligations, "clear phases, timelines, [and] target dates," and commitment to achieving a "comprehensive settlement" by December 2005.[122] Arguing that creating "a peaceful Palestinian state and the long-term security of the Israeli people both depend on defeating the threat of terrorist groups and ending incitement and hatred," Bush stressed that "the *starting point* for a prosperous and peaceful Middle East must be the rejection of terror," emphasized that "'the' most important condition for peace to prevail is for all parties to fight off terror . . . [and] dismantle organizations whose intent is to destroy the vision of peace," and called upon "all sides [to] do all in their power to defeat the determined enemies of peace, such as Hamas and other terrorist groups."[123] While acknowledging that "[a]ll sides of this conflict have duties," and stressing that "the more progress there's made on terror, the more progress there will be made on difficult issues," he indicated that the "*first* reform must be the dismantling of terrorist organizations."[124] He dismissed the *Road Map*'s demand that Israel "immediately" freeze "all settlement activity" and dismantle "settlement outposts erected since March 2001," arguing instead that Israel need act only "*as progress is made*" by the PA in fulfilling its Phase I commitments, including undertaking "an *immediate* cessation of armed activity and all acts of violence against Israelis anywhere," acting "decisively against terror, including sustained, targeted and effective operations to stop terrorism and dismantle terrorist capabilities and infrastructure," pursuing "comprehensive and fundamental political reform that includes a strong parliamentary democracy and an empowered prime minister," and insuring that "all official Palestinian institutions . . . end incitement against Israel."[125] Bush reminded the PA that the "alternative (to the peace plan) is more death and destruction and letting the terrorists win and let those that have no interest in a Palestinian state win."[126] While calling on Israel to "take tangible steps now to ease the suffering of Palestinians and to show respect for their dignity,"[127] he refrained from insisting upon Israeli compliance with Phase I obligations prior to the PA fulfilling its terror related commitments.

While indicating that achieving the *Road Map*'s two-state goal by December 2005 was "realistic," Bush stressed that the "pace of progress will depend strictly on the performance of the parties."[128] Empathizing with Sharon's incremental tendencies, he noted, "I think what is necessary to achieve the vision of two states living side by side in peace is for there to be progress. . . . until he sees more progress, he doesn't have confidence. . . . I'm convinced the place to earn—to gain that confidence is to succeed in the Gaza. . . . And when that happens, then all of a sudden, I think we'll have a different frame of mind."[129] Secretary of State Colin Powell, sharing Bush's belief that *the* precondition for progress was a "peaceful" PA committed to "providing hope for its people," discounted a rapid transition to Phase II's multilateral conference approach, observing, "At the moment, we do not have a Palestinian Government that is seen as a partner who could participate in such a conference. So it is a possibility; it is an idea that is out there, but I do not see any immediate prospects of holding such a conference."[130]

EU, Russia, and UN

The EU, Russia, and the UN seized upon the *Road Map*'s formal presentation as a long awaited opportunity to assert their respective political, diplomatic, and economic influence over what was envisioned to be a genuinely multilateral peace initiative. While even such strident critics of US foreign policy as German Chancellor Gerhard Schroder acknowledged that "a solution [to the Israeli-Palestinian conflict] can only ever be mentioned and conceived if there is a strong involvement of the United States of America," EU officials stressed both the Quartet's role in forging "a common position" on the peace process and EU readiness to "make a useful contribution" to Quartet efforts.[131] Christopher Patten highlighted the EU's role in keeping "a Palestinian administration alive" and in supporting the "institution-building and reform" that would "make a viable Palestinian state a reality one day and in the short term make the Palestinian territories a better, safer neighbour for Israel."[132] His successor, Dr. Benita Ferrero-Waldner, identified three "priorities" for EU-sponsored reform: promoting a "well functioning judiciary and court system," developing "a better electoral legal framework" for future Palestinian elections, and creating an "anti-corruption task force" that would "further improve public financial management."[133] The EU also stressed its ability to "contribute to the Roadmap's monitoring process," arguing that "it is clear that every member of the Quartet is capable of contributing more in the area of monitoring rather than in other areas."[134] It also noted its willingness to utilize a variety of instruments, including the Euro-Mediterranean Partnership, International Task Force on Palestinian Reform, "Neighbourhood Policy," and Member State's bilateral programs, to provide "badly needed humanitarian assistance" and support for development initiatives;[135] Ferrero-Waldner, noting the Palestinians' "need to see the fruits of peace," committed the EU to "make funds available to help deliver tangible improvement in living conditions, to build up the Palestinians' government capacity, and support the reconstruction of infrastructure and basic services."[136]

Insisting that a Quartet directed multilateral peace process was "the only realistic programme for a Palestinian-Israeli settlement," Russia anticipated the Quartet functioning as "a finely tuned mechanism that enables Russia, the USA, the EU and the UN, as the international community's most eminent representatives, to have a positive influence on the sides to the conflict."[137] It stressed that the "vicious spiral of violence" demanded Quartet action beyond facilitating the "sharing [of] opinions" and "monitoring the implementation of obligations,"[138] including "tak[ing] the lead" in "end[ing] the stalemate in the process of Palestinian-Israeli negotiations" and advocating for an international conference to expedite the *Road Map*'s implementation.[139] Arguing that "it will not be possible to break the circle of violence without a decisive interference of the international community," Foreign Minister Igor Ivanov called upon "the international community, acting through the 'Quartet' or the UN Security Council, [to] present the parties to the conflict with tough conditions for the implementation of all aspects of the 'road map.'"[140] Deputy Foreign Minister Yuriy Fedotov likewise observed, "a good deal will depend on the world community's readiness to exert greater pressure on the sides to fulfil their obligations in terms of the 'road map,'" while his successor, Aleksandr Saltanov, called on the Quartet to offer "suggested compromise solutions" for resolving the "cardinal problems of the final status, such as Jerusalem, refugees and borders."[141]

While recognizing the Quartet's role in promoting the "unity" of international efforts, Moscow vowed "to take a more active part, as far as it is possible on our side, in the process of resolving the Middle East issue."[142] Reflecting a commitment "to work with all sides concerned," but "primarily with the Israelis and Palestinians,"[143] Ivanov and Fedotov undertook Russia's "first fully-fledged mission" to the Middle East in three years in July-August 2003, visiting Jordan, Syria, Lebanon, Egypt, Israel, and the PA.[144] Conversations with Palestinian leaders addressed bilateral relations, Israel's withdrawal from Gaza, humanitarian assistance to residents of the Occupied Territories, and "coordinated efforts by the Palestinian National Authority to consistently promote negotiations with Israel," while unprecedented, high level discussions with Israeli officials focused on cooperating "fruitfully in fighting with terrorism, the settlement of regional crises, and the solution of acute social and economic problems."[145] Despite ongoing differences with the PA over anti-terror and reform strategies and with Israel over violations of "the norms of international law" and Security Council endorsement of the *Road Map*, Moscow emphasized that its "active contacts with Israel, as well as relations with the Palestinians and Arab countries," were helping "to normalize the situation in the Middle East as soon as possible and put the Arab-Israeli conflict into the framework of political settlement."[146]

The Secretary-General, emphasizing that the "two parties seem unable to find their way out of the current quagmire without outside help," called upon the Quartet, functioning as a true "partnership," to help "the parties to shoulder their responsibilities to their peoples." Arguing that "at any one stage, the influence of one or the other of the [Quartet] members with one or the other of the parties may be greater than that of another," he stressed that "each member brings something to the table" and that "[a]ll of us . . . have a role to play."[147] While citing the EU's "considerable influence on the Palestinian side," US sway over Israel, and Quartet success in promoting Palestinian reform,[148] Annan pledged that the "United Nations and its agencies [would] continue to help the [Palestinian] Authority build up its [governance] capacity," promised UN support for "new" coordinating mechanisms to enhance security and for "the security forces of the Palestinian Authority," and indicated that the UN would "do our part" to promote peace by alleviating Palestinian "suffering and providing economic opportunity" through insuring that international aid mechanisms were "as effective as possible."[149]

Neither the EU, Russia, nor the UN was prepared to abandon the *Road Map*'s language of parallel obligations, tolerate unilateral actions that prejudged final status issues, or accept non-comprehensive approaches to peace. The EU declared, "It is crucial that parallel progress is made in the political, economic and security fields," stressed the "need to address political, economic/humanitarian and security issues simultaneously," and indicated that reform of Palestinian institutions should not "be regarded as condition for moving on politically." It urged both sides to honor, immediately and without preconditions, their Phase I commitments. Israel was "to withdraw its military forces, to stop extra-judicial killings, to lift closures and all restrictions imposed on the Palestinian people, and to freeze settlement activities and dismantle settlements," while the PA was "to show determination in the fight against extremist violence and to confront individuals and groups conducting and planning terrorist attacks."[150] Russia, emphasizing that "all the sides' actions must be taken in line with the sequence set out in the road map," observed, the "only real way out of the current extremely explosive situation . . . is going back to the fulfillment of the road map plan obligations by all sides."[151] It urged the PA to "put an end to terror" and to "complete the creation of a stable Palestinian government which is able to fulfill Palestinian obligations according to 'the road map' as well as to conduct reforms,"[152] while encouraging Israel to "reject the nonproportional use of force [and] nonjudicial reprisals," "take effective steps to ease economic hardship of the Palestinian people," and freeze settlement activity.[153] Kofi Annan, speaking on behalf of the Quartet, stated, "Each party must do more to address, immediately and *simultaneously*, the core concerns of the other as described in the road map";[154] the UN's Special Coordinator for the Middle East Peace Process, Alvaro de Soto, likewise called upon both parties to fulfill their respective parallel obligations, including an Israeli freeze on settlement construction and PA clampdown on terrorist organizations.[155]

EU officials adamantly rejected any party taking "unilateral measures that might prejudice the outcome of negotiations on the final settlement," declaring, "Any final agreement must be reached through negotiations between the two parties."[156] Particular concern was expressed that Israel's "ongoing illegal settlement activities and land confiscations for the construction of the so-called security fence" were "obstacle[s] to peace . . . threatening to render the two-State solution physically impossible."[157] The EU's General Affairs and External Relations Council, although recognizing Israel's legitimate right "to self-defense in the face of terrorist attacks against its citizens," implored Jerusalem "to reverse the settlement policy and activity, to dismantle settlements built after March 2001 and to freeze the construction of the separation fence."[158] The EU insisted that Gaza disengagement take "place in the context of the Roadmap, is a step towards a two State solution, [involves] no transfer of settlement activity to the West Bank, [includes] a negotiated handover of responsibility to the Palestinian Authority, and [requires] facilitation of rehabilitation and reconstruction [in Gaza] by Israel."[159]

Russia was equally insistent that "both sides refrain from unilateral steps pre-empting solutions to the final status issues."[160] Arguing that "unilateral steps must not predetermine the final settlement, which can be reached only through direct negotiations and mutually acceptable agreements between the parties," it characterized settlement activity and the barrier as "counter to the spirit and the letter of the 'road map,'" and as likely to create "additional obstacles on the path to peace between Israelis and Palestinians."[161] It insisted that disengagement "be carried out in the context of the 'road map' implementation," correspond "completely" to the *Road Map*, "be linked to further moves within the framework of the 'road map,'" and not "be followed by active expansion of settlements in the West Bank."[162]

The Secretary-General likewise observed, "Attempts by either side to resolve this drawn-out conflict unilaterally could actually foment more anger and violence. There is no substitute for the two parties sitting down and working out with each other the details of an agreement that both peoples can live with."[163] He reminded Israelis and Palestinians that "they are partners in this endeavour and can only succeed or fail together," urged "everyone . . . to refrain from any actions that would be detrimental to the resumption of negotiations and implementation of the Road Map, or that could prejudge the resolution of final status issues," and called for "an end" to "unilateral measures of one kind or another," including "[t]errorist attacks against civilians, arbitrary assassinations, arrests and detentions, house demolitions, stifling closures and blockages, [and] settlement activities."[164] He criticized the separation barrier's construction as "a deeply counterproductive act" that "could damage the longer term prospects for peace by making the creation of an independent, viable and contiguous Palestinian state more difficult," argued that "continued settlement expansion . . . could prejudge the resolution of final status issues," and insisted that Gaza disengagement "be seen as part of a broader process . . . consistent with the Road Map" and be conducted "directly and fully" with the PA.[165] Prior to the disengagement plan's implementation, Alvaro de Soto observed, "The unease, suspicion and cynicism that bedevil Israeli-Palestinian relations can be attributed in large part to the fact that the disengagement is not taking place within an unequivocally agreed framework for the next steps toward the overall solution to which both sides claim adherence, i.e., two states living alongside each other in peace."[166]

The EU, Russia, and the UN rejected US-style incrementalism, advocating instead decisive action on behalf of a comprehensive settlement. Declaring that "[t]ime is of the essence: concrete action and results are needed now," the EU argued that "the only way to end the conflict" was for the international community to "move boldly with the Israeli government to establish its commitment to the two-State solution; and with the Palestinians to establish their commitment to security and reform."[167] In addition to addressing the Israeli-Palestinian conflict, the Quartet was urged to "play an active role in pursuing the goal of a comprehensive regional peace," including facilitating "a solution to the [*Road Map*'s] Israeli-Syrian and Israeli-Lebanese tracks."[168] Sergei Lavrov stressed Moscow's commitment "to making progress as rapidly as possible towards implementing the relevant UN resolutions and the road map," while Foreign Ministry spokesman Alexander Yakovenko called for "an acceleration of the transition to the second stage of the Road Map, during which an independent Palestinian state should be proclaimed."[169] The Kremlin, stressing that "observance of the 'road map' should lead to a comprehensive settlement in the interests not only of the Israelis and Palestinians, but also of all the people of the Middle East," argued that negotiations must include "not only the Palestinian dossier, but also the Syrian and Lebanese tracks of the peace process."[170] As Putin observed, "We are in favour of overcoming the lengthy stagnation in the Syrian and Lebanese areas of the peace process. No general settlement in the Middle East can be attained without the Golan Heights being returned to Syria and without the disputed issues between Israel and Lebanon being resolved"; Yuriy Fedotov concurred, noting, "Russia's idea of creating the 'road maps' on the Syrian and Lebanese tracks of the Middle East settlement will remain in force. We cannot move forwards without them."[171] The Secretary-General, expressing concern over the stagnating peace process, argued, "It seems to me that bold steps, in keeping with the Road Map, are now necessary to salvage peace. Small steps have not worked. They are unlikely to work in the future." Indicating that to "further delay the implementation of the Road Map is unacceptable, since time is not on our side," Annan emphasized the *Road Map*'s mandate both to resolve the Israeli-Palestinian conflict and to ensure that "the whole region" achieve "peace and security" and "move on to have a normal, neighbourly relationship."[172]

Substance

The *Road Map*'s rhetoric of "comprehensive settlement" and "final, permanent status resolution" prompted Palestinians, Israelis, and Quartet members alike to focus anew on such critical issues as settlements, borders, Jerusalem, and refugees. Unfortunately, having achieved unprecedented consensus on both a framework for negotiations and a two-state solution, Palestinians, the EU, Russia, and the UN remained in seemingly intractable conflict with Israel and the US over the basic character and attributes of a future Palestinian state.

Palestinians, anxious to address final status issues with "the seriousness and interest they deserve," expressed growing concern that Sharon was pursuing a policy of "dismemberment and imposing a fait accompli by imposing facts on the ground, leading to . . . geographical enclaves in the West Bank," "turning Gaza into a prison," and "dropping the files of Jerusalem, borders, settlements and refugees."[173] Observing that Palestinians' vision of "a sovereign, independent Palestinian state, with East Jerusalem as its capital, and a just, agreed solution of the refugee question on the basis of the U.N. Resolution 194 . . . cannot be realized if Israel continues to grab Palestinian land," Abbas argued, "If the settlement activities in Palestinian land and construction of the so-called separation wall on confiscated Palestinian land continue, we might soon find ourselves at a situation where the foundation of peace, a free Palestine state, living side-by-side in peace and security [with] Israel is a factual impossibility."[174] Sa'ib Urayqat questioned, "If the issue of Jerusalem, the issue of borders, the issue of water and the issue of settlements are determined by the Israeli wall and settlements, what is left for negotiation? How do you translate President Bush's two-state solution to a realistic political track, while the land that's supposed to constitute a Palestinian state is eaten up by settlements and walls?"[175] Declaring that "peace and settling are on parallel lines and will not meet," and insisting that the "Israeli government must choose between peace and the settlements,"[176] Palestinian leaders criticized Israeli plans to construct thousands of new homes in the West Bank, annex large settlement blocs as part of any final status agreement, and use Gaza withdrawal "as an excuse to expand settlements in the West Bank and Jerusalem."[177]

Distress over settlements was linked closely to concerns about final borders and Jerusalem. While accepting a state of Israel that "accounts for 78 percent of what was Palestine," the PA insisted upon "recognition of our state in the remaining 22 percent: the West Bank, Gaza and East Jerusalem."[178] Arafat stressed that any settlement be premised on "the 4 June 1967 borders" and "ensure that Jerusalem remain the capital of both Israel and Palestine," while cautioning that Israel would "never find a Palestinian partner who will accept its proposals for setting up Palestinian bantustans and cantons on half of the West Bank's area while maintaining Israeli control over the borders and the water resources."[179] Prime Minister Ahmad Quray criticized Israeli annexation of West Bank settlements as compromising "geographical contiguity," threatening to turn any Palestinian state into "a mere laughing stock."[180] The separation barrier drew particular fire for "isolating Jerusalem, displacing the residents and seizing their properties," and "eras[ing] its historical, religious Arab and Islamic identity" in order to "judaize the city prior to annexing it."[181] The PA also insisted upon refugees' "right of return," arguing that Resolution 194 established the legal framework for resolving refugees' status. Abbas rejected "resettlement outside the homeland," endorsing Foreign Affairs Minister Nabil Sha'th's observation, "The right of return is no longer imaginary or mythical. It is an integral part of the Arab peace plan, which has now become the term of reference of the road map plan. . . . Let me be clear: Return to the homeland includes return to both the independent Palestinian state and the Palestinian cities in Israel."[182]

The EU, long critical of the Israeli occupation,[183] argued that "the rapidly expanding settlement activities—and the so-called security wall which is expanding into the West Bank"—threatened "to make a solution based on the coexistence of two States physically impossible."[184] Javier Solana, affirming the EU's refusal to recognize "any change to the pre-1967 borders other than those arrived at by agreement between the parties," declared, "We recognise Israel's right to defend itself, but, on legal and humanitarian grounds, the Fence [separation barrier] should not be built on territory that is not in Israel." The EU also stressed the need for "a fair solution to the complex issue of Jerusalem" and for an "agreed, just, fair and realistic solution" to the refugee problem.[185] Russia likewise expressed concern that "[s]ettlement activity, like the construction of the so-called 'protective wall,' . . . runs counter to the spirit and the letter of the 'road map,'" "raise[d] a question mark over the creation of a Palestinian state," "violate[d] the principle of its territorial continuity," and posed "serious obstacles on the path to a settlement."[186] A joint Russian-Palestinian statement highlighted both parties' longstanding adherence to "the principle of the inadmissibility of acquiring territories by force," declaring, "The settlement should be of a comprehensive nature and include the liberation of *all* the Arab territories occupied in 1967, including East Jerusalem."[187] Kofi Annan echoed the EU and Russia's pro-Palestinian positions. Observing that "settlements are a clear breach of the Fourth Geneva Convention and also contradict Israel's commitments under the Quartet's Road Map," he insisted that Israel's "right and duty to protect its people against terrorist attacks" not " be carried out in a way that is in contradiction of international law, that could damage the longer term prospects for peace by making the creation of an independent, viable and contiguous Palestinian state more difficult, or that increases suffering among the Palestinian people."[188] Criticizing "both the security wall and settlements in the West Bank built on Palestinian land as serious obstacles to the achievement of a two-State solution," he urged Israel "to dismantle outposts established since March 2001, immediately freeze all settlement activity, including natural growth of settlements, and stop the construction of the barrier in the occupied Palestinian territory." He concluded, "In the midst of the Road Map process, when each party should be making good faith confidence-building gestures, the barrier's construction in the West Bank cannot . . . be seen as anything but a deeply counterproductive act. The placing of most of the structure on occupied Palestinian land could impair future negotiations."[189]

While Sharon's unprecedented acknowledgment that "keeping 3.5 million Palestinians under occupation is bad for Israel, bad for the Palestinians and bad for the Israeli economy" was reflected in his commitment to give up "some" of the Jewish settlements "under the terms of a permanent agreement," he insisted that "the major population centers in Judea and Samaria will be part of the state of Israel."[190] Violating his commitment to Bush to insure "no construction beyond the existing construction lines, no expropriation of land for construction, no special economic incentives, no construction of new settlements," Sharon pursued vigorous efforts to "strengthen and develop" the five West Bank settlement blocs that Israel intended to keep "forever": Maaleh Adumim, Givat Zeev, and the Etzion bloc near Jerusalem, and Ariel and Kiryat Arba in the West Bank's interior.[191] He expressed particular interest in insuring "contiguity" between Maale Adumim and East Jerusalem, promoting a plan to build 3500 homes linking the two areas;[192] a Foreign Ministry spokesman observed, "Building in a place where there is an international consensus that it's going to stay in Israel in no way undermines the ability of the Palestinians to create a viable, contiguous Palestinian state."[193]

Sharon's declaration that Palestinians should "govern themselves in their own state, a democratic state with territorial contiguity in Judea and Samaria,"[194] was belied by his steadfast refusal to return to the pre-1967 borders.[195] Committed only to a Palestinian mini-state constituting Gaza and 40 percent of the West Bank, he acknowledged the importance of Gaza disengagement and the security barrier in insuring Israeli "control in those parts of Eretz Yisrael that will constitute an inseparable part of the State of Israel under any future arrangement."[196] The Israeli Cabinet's conditional acceptance of the *Road Map* on 25 May 2003 was similarly uncompromising, including an absolute rejection of Palestinian refugees' "right of return." Declaring that "both during and subsequent to the political process, the resolution of the issue of the refugees will not include their entry into or settlement within the State of Israel," it stressed that the "waiver of any right of return for Palestinian refugees to the State of Israel" was necessary to guarantee "Israel's right to exist as a Jewish state."[197] It likewise indicated no flexibility on the issue of Jerusalem, a stance that defined Sharon's approach throughout the 2003–2005 period.[198]

Long sympathetic to Israeli arguments concerning final status issues, Bush provided critical support to Sharon on settlements, borders, and refugees. While calling on Israel to "freeze settlement activity," "remove unauthorized outposts," "meet its road map obligations regarding settlements in the West Bank," and refrain from "any activity that contravenes road map obligations or prejudice[s] final status negotiations," he supported Sharon's refusal *ever* to abandon certain settlements, declaring, "In light of new realities on the ground, including already existing major Israeli population centers, it is unrealistic to expect that the outcome of final status negotiations will be a full and complete return to the armistice lines of 1949."[199] Recognizing that "the realities on the ground and in the region have changed greatly over the last several decades," Bush stressed that while a Palestinian state of "scattered territories will not work," Israel's "population centers" in the Occupied Territories "must be taken into account in any final status negotiations."²⁰⁰ He likewise refrained from insisting Israel abandon the separation fence, instead reminding Sharon only that it "should be a security rather than political barrier, should be temporary rather than permanent, and . . . [should] not prejudice any final status issues including final borders."²⁰¹ Bush was equally solicitous concerning Israel's rejection of Resolution 194's insistence on Palestinian refugees' "right of return." Declaring that such a "right" risked demographic suicide for the Jewish state, he observed, "It seems clear that an agreed, just, fair and realistic framework for a solution to the Palestinian refugee issue as part of any final status agreement will need to be found through the establishment of a Palestinian state, and the settling of Palestinian refugees there, rather than in Israel."²⁰²

Terror

While reflecting the Quartet's growing preoccupation with terrorism, the *Road Map*'s demand for the mutual cessation of violence contributed as well to Israeli and Palestinian reassessments of terrorism's domestic political and international strategic significance. Functioning within a Phase V context characterized by mutual hostility, distrust, and expectations of conflict, Israeli and PA decisionmakers confronted the reality that neither a policy of confrontation nor accommodation appeared certain to satisfy constituent demands while protecting vital international interests. While such ambiguity prompted both parties to consider transitioning from armed conflict to renewed negotiations, neither Sharon nor the PA proved adept at exploiting such potential pendular flux. Unable to recognize one another's sensitivity to changing international strategic and domestic political conditions, they failed to identify and leverage periods of *shared* interest in non-confrontational relations, and in so doing created nearly insuperable obstacles to the *Road Map*'s implementation.

Confronted by the US-authored *Road Map*'s two state objective and "parallel obligations" language, as well as by Washington's concern that its Iraq agenda not be hamstrung by a failure to address the Israeli-Palestinian conflict, Sharon recognized the escalating international strategic implications of addressing Palestinian terror, and particularly the need for immediate action on behalf of the ostensibly anti-terror *Road Map*. However, while Israel's rapid transition from a Phase III to a Phase V relationship with Palestinian terrorism focused renewed attention on US-Israeli relations, neither Sharon nor his cabinet, reflecting both domestic political constraints and personal convictions, were willing to negotiate "under fire," insisting instead on conditions of "absolute quiet" and the "complete cessation of terror."²⁰³ Forced to navigate Phase V's complex and oftentimes competing demands, Sharon opted to endorse the *Road Map*'s two state objective—he indicated that the "time has come to divide this piece of land between us and the Palestinians"—*and* unilaterally to define a pre-*Road Map* phase during which Palestinians would be required to maintain "calm" prior to Israel commencing the *Road Map* process itself.²⁰⁴ Creating the appearance of diplomatic engagement while minimizing the need for immediate action was accompanied by domestic efforts to portray the *Road Map* as an anti-terror initiative, the success of which was necessary to forestall costly unilateral military, economic, and security measures.

Insisting that the PA achieve rapid, demonstrable progress in combating terror while simultaneously endorsing the *Road Map* enabled Sharon to forestall confrontation with Washington, placate the sixty percent of Israelis supportive of the *Road Map* and of resuming negotiations with the Palestinians,[205] and maintain Likud's confrontational, unilateralist anti-terror strategy.[206] However, Arafat's sabotage of the newly installed Abbas government and support for renewed violence prompted Sharon to dismiss any Arafat-tainted PA as "an obstacle to peace" with whom it was impossible to conduct *Road Map* envisioned negotiations.[207] Characterizing the present "stalemate" as "extremely dangerous for Israel," Sharon proposed a unilateral disengagement plan from Gaza in which Israel would withdraw "from areas which we know will not remain under Israeli control under any permanent arrangement to be signed in future and which cause severe friction between Israelis and Palestinians." He and his advisors argued that such a measure would establish "a physical barrier for assisting in the defence of Israeli citizens," while helping "preserve and stabilize the State of Israel's condition until that time when, we all hope and pray, the preconditions are met by the Palestinians." Dov Weissglas acknowledged the impact of public pressure for more effective management of the terrorist threat, observing, "when the road map unfortunately reached an impasse that was imposed on us by the Palestinians, there was no political process whatsoever, terrorism intensified and the national mood was reflected, among other things, in fads such as the Geneva plan and the refuseniks. All these were undoubtedly phenomena that drew our attention to the need to carry out a move to stabilize security and strengthen the hope and faith among Israelis." He reasoned, "A prime minister has to be attentive to the voice of every group, to every sign, be it big or small. It's his job. The fact that we took into consideration what we believed to be signs of waning national fortitude is precisely the reason people get paid to read the signs and draw conclusions."[208] The disengagement plan served its objectives well, greeted by the US as an effort to reenergize the *Road Map* and by Israelis as an attempt to reduce terrorism.[209]

However, Arafat's November 2004 death unexpectedly complicated Jerusalem's counterterror approach. Having long argued that an Arafat-led PA foreclosed *Road Map*-style peace efforts,[210] Sharon suddenly confronted both a Bush administration insistent upon pursuing direct negotiations with Arafat's successor, the moderate Mahmoud Abbas, and an Israeli public optimistic about prospects for a political settlement and willing to explore unprecedented methods to achieve it; indeed, nearly half of Israelis expressed a readiness to negotiate with Hamas if necessary to reach a "compromise settlement," a dramatic increase from the twenty percent that had supported such efforts shortly before Arafat's death.[211] Responding to such pressures, Sharon vowed "to make progress in the contacts on the implementation of the road map" and to explore the potential for Israeli-PA coordination on "various actions pertaining to the disengagement plan."[212] However, he indicated that, while Abbas represented "a departure from Yasser Arafat's strategy of terror"—he noted that "encouraging signs" could be detected from the new Palestinian leadership—the PA "must take additional steps to disarm terror organisations, stop incitement, or we can't move forward from the pre-road map stage."[213] Defense Minister Shaul Mufaz observed, "we are dealing with a different leadership, whose intentions, in my opinion, are—generally speaking—positive, but have not yet been fully translated into action against terrorism," while Ehud Olmert argued that a "PNA crackdown on terror is a prerequisite for restarting negotiations."[214]

While Palestinians had maintained a Phase V relationship with Israeli terror since the traumatic events of 1948, the *Road Map* catalyzed transition away from the al-Aqsa Intifada's confrontational approach to more accommodative efforts. Arafat, Abbas, Quray, and other top PA officials recognized both the *Road Map*'s potential for helping Palestinians realize their most cherished national objectives and the perils of rejecting such a widely supported international initiative. Arafat highlighted the *Road Map*'s promise to fulfill "many of our basic goals," including "ensuring the withdrawal of the Israel troops from our Palestinian land to the 1967 borders and the establishment of an independent Palestinian state," while Abbas stressed Palestinians' commitment to the *Road Map* as a "strategic" choice to pursue a "just peace . . . through negotiation in order to restore Palestinian national rights," including "establishing the Palestinian state on the 1967 borders with holy Jerusalem as its capital and reaching a just solution that will be approved (by the two sides) to the refugees issue."[215] Sensitive to the Intifada's failure to forestall continued settlement expansion and construction of the separation barrier, Abbas argued that "[t]ime is becoming our greatest enemy" and urged the *Road Map*'s rapid implementation.[216] While reiterating their condemnation of terrorism and the targeting of "civilians on both sides," Arafat and Abbas insisted that Israel not "avoid resuming the peace negotiations" either by "casting aspersions on the Palestinian leadership and accusing it of not being a peace partner" or by attempting "to portray as terrorism any normal struggle against injustice or military occupation."[217] Sa'ib Urayqat argued, "you can react in two ways [to such violence.] Either you use the attacks as a pretext for doing nothing more for peace, or you use them to activate the peace process." Stressing that "the only thing that can stop this violence, this vicious circle, is a meaningful peace process that will revive hope in the minds of Palestinians and Israelis," he cautioned against Israeli tendencies to dismiss the very possibility of negotiations with *any* Palestinian interlocutor, observing, "Look, if Mother Teresa were elected Palestinian president, if Thomas Jefferson were president of our parliament, if Mahatma Gandhi got my job as leader of the negotiating team, I am sure that the Israeli government would still find a way to accuse us of terrorism."[218] Palestinian officials insisted that the Quartet establish "definite and clear implementation mechanisms," convene an international conference as quickly as possible, pressure Israel to fulfill its obligations under the *Road Map*, including halting "violence against Palestinians in all places," ending settlement activities, and abandoning construction of the separation barrier, and demand that such unilateral measures as Gaza disengagement be implemented as "part of the road map and not an operation that destroys the road map or prepares for an alternative project."[219]

Although the PA's embrace of the *Road Map* reflected an evolving international strategic context, it was prompted as well by Arafat and Abbas's sensitivity to changing domestic political conditions. While the public's increasingly vocal criticism of PA corruption and attraction to Hamas and the Islamist parties heightened concerns about Fatah's political vulnerability,[220] both Arafat and Abbas were particularly attuned to growing frustrations with the failure of Intifada-style confrontation to end the Israeli occupation and establish an independent Palestinian state.[221] Such popular disaffection was reflected in Palestinians' willingness to abandon rigid adherence to a "violence only" approach in favor of a "try and see" attitude toward *both* conciliation and confrontation; the public thus supported armed attacks against soldiers and settlers *and* an immediate ceasefire and return to negotiations,[222] argued both that "armed confrontations have helped achieve Palestinian national rights in ways that negotiations could not" *and* that Fatah was better able than Hamas to secure an acceptable settlement with Israel,[223] and endorsed the *Road Map* while expressing skepticism that it would lead to a political settlement with Sharon's Israel.[224] As one analyst observed, such apparent contradictions seemed "to reflect street thinking that the Palestinians have more than one option in the search for their vital needs: ceasefire and negotiations is one while armed confrontation is another."[225] Arafat, seeking to avoid the perils of overcommitment and overidentification either with conciliatory or confrontational strategies—lessons learned from *Oslo* and the al-Aqsa Intifada—endorsed the *Road Map*, condemned terror, and indicated Palestinians' readiness to fulfill their obligations to Israel, while criticizing Jerusalem's conditional acceptance of the *Road Map*, failure to adhere to prior commitments, and continued use of terroristic violence against Palestinians.[226]

Abbas's January 2005 election as Arafat's successor accelerated the PA's transition toward a more accommodative approach toward Israeli terror. Seeking to capitalize on the majority of Palestinians hopeful that Arafat's death would increase "the chances for reaching a political settlement" and supportive of comprehensive negotiations,[227] Abbas reaffirmed the PA's commitment to the *Road Map* and pledged concerted efforts to promote a ceasefire among Palestinian militants, unify the PA's security agencies, and establish "the rule of law."[228] However, he also recognized Palestinians' skepticism about reaching a settlement with Sharon *and* deep-rooted faith in the efficacy of violence; seventy-five percent of Palestinians believed Sharon's Gaza disengagement plan was "a victory for the Palestinian armed struggle against Israel," a victory credited to Hamas rather than to Fatah or the PA.[229] He thus tempered support for *Road Map* sanctioned security measures, direct negotiations, and PA reform with reminders to Israel and the Quartet that such efforts were "in danger of retreat and perhaps collapse if they are not protected by a serious political process between us and the Israelis." He cautioned, "Welcoming and supporting Palestinian democracy is an important thing, but this support will remain incomplete if it is not backed by the endeavour to end the occupation with all its manifestations and measures so that it will be possible for this democracy to continue and prosper."[230] Urayqat noted the threat to moderate Palestinians in the absence of a "meaningful peace process" and an end to occupation, observing that Abbas "wants to conduct a policy of peace and negotiation with determination. He has had the courage to condemn radical groups. But what he can do depends on what Israel and the United States give him to convince his people with." Recalling that Abbas "was prime minister for three months and came out against violence, but Israel did not give him a chance," he expressed "hope that things will be different this time," warning that the *Road Map*'s failure risked fueling extremist tendencies throughout the region."[231]

Washington's Phase V relationship to terrorism throughout the *Road Map* period, a product of the devastating attacks of September 11, 2001, was defined by the Bush administration's unwavering commitment to a global "war on terror" and by the American public's demand for decisive action to protect its security and wellbeing. Bush highlighted the unique and far-reaching nature of the terrorist threat, observing, "Terrorist movements seek to intimidate free peoples and reverse the course of history by committing dramatic acts of murder." Refusing "to live in a world dominated by fear," he vowed, "We will not be intimidated . . . terrorists will not stop the march of freedom. . . . Spreading liberty for the sake of peace is the cause of all mankind. This approach not only reduces a danger to free peoples; it honors the dignity of all peoples, by placing human rights and human freedom at the center of our agenda." He argued that "a narrow definition of security is not enough. While confronting a present threat, we have accepted the long-term challenge of spreading hope and liberty and prosperity as the great alternatives to terror. As we defeat the agents of terror, we will also remove the sources of terror." Bush particularly focused on Middle East terrorism's impact on American security, noting, "In the long run, we cannot live in peace and safety if the Middle East continues to produce ideologies of murder, and terrorists who seek the deadliest weapons. Regimes that terrorize their own people will not hesitate to support terror abroad."[232] Emphasizing that in "an age of global terror and weapons of mass destruction what happens in the Middle East greatly matters to America. The bitterness of that region can bring violence and suffering to our own cities," he argued that the "advance of freedom and peace in the Middle East would drain this bitterness and increase our own security," and that "a transformed Middle East would benefit the entire world."[233]

Equating Palestinian violence with terrorism, the White House relentlessly criticized Arafat's failure to fight terror, indicated that establishing a Palestinian state depended upon "fighting terror" and "deal[ing] harshly with Hamas and the killers," and stressed that "'the' most important condition for peace to prevail is for all parties to fight off terror."[234] While highlighting Palestinians' responsibility for preventing "suiciders and killers" from "blow[ing] up" the *Road Map* process, Bush expressed optimism that Abbas, characterized as a "good man" "committed to peace" and to "rout[ing] out terror," would become an interlocutor with whom the US and Israel could work productively.[235] In contrast to the unyielding demands placed on the PA, Israel was given wide latitude in determining how best "to defend itself against terrorism," including those measures to be taken "against terrorist organizations."[236] Bush repeatedly praised Sharon's commitment to peace,[237] while resisting EU, Russian, and UN efforts to characterize as terroristic Israel's policy of targeted assassinations, house demolitions, and military reoccupation of portions of the West Bank and Gaza.

Bush's confrontational approach to combating terrorism was buttressed by a post-9/11 domestic political environment extraordinarily attuned to the terrorist threat, supportive of aggressive, proactive counterterror measures, unflinchingly hostile toward Arafat and the PA, and sympathetic toward Israel and its security challenges.[238] While Americans had demonstrated little sustained concern about terrorism prior to 9/11,[239] al-Qaeda's attacks instantly transformed counterterror policy into a domestic and international priority. The public overwhelmingly endorsed "using American military force against groups in other countries that have committed international terrorist acts," regardless of whether or not they were implicated in 9/11. It likewise supported Israeli efforts to "do whatever is necessary to find and destroy terrorists who threaten serious harm to its citizens or nation," including using "pre-emptive force against terrorists and their safe havens."[240] The public's willingness to give Israel free rein in combating Palestinian terror reflected in part its sharply contrasting perceptions of Israel and the PA; while Sharon's Likud government was considered a valuable and loyal ally in the "war on terror," Arafat's PA was condemned for seeking to "destroy Israel" and for promoting "the current violence."[241]

CONCLUSION

NATURE OF CONFLICT

The *Road Map*'s attempt to facilitate "a final and comprehensive settlement of the Israeli-Palestinian conflict by 2005" confronted the inherent difficulties associated with reconceptualizing an "inter-ethnic," "existential," and "high intensity" conflict characterized by decades-long efforts by both parties to destroy "the other side's claim to legitimacy and to exist as a sovereign entity in the land of Israel/Palestine." Transitioning from perceptions of "conflict" to those of "dispute"—critical to achieving a negotiated outcome—was complicated by competing "psychologies of victimhood" rooted in historic threats to both parties' "ontological human needs." The al-Aqsa Intifada's mutual violence served only to exacerbate the chasm separating the current "military/political phase—the unmanageable stage," in Israeli-Palestinian relations from both the "conflict management phase—the reduction stage," and the "conflict resolution stage—the peace stage," proffered by the *Road Map*.[1]

Polling data from the post-2000 Camp David, pre-2003 *Road Map* period highlighted the enormity of the Quartet's challenge in developing a peace initiative perceived by Palestinians and Israelis alike as relevant to advancing their national interests. While Palestinians overwhelmingly supported both the *Road Map*'s two state objective and "reconciliation between the two peoples after peace and statehood," they remained fervently attached "to the same land, to the same water, to the same air" as Israelis;[2] fewer than 10% of those surveyed supported a curriculum "which educates school children to give up irredentist aspirations," 51% rejected as "too much of a compromise" a settlement in which Palestinians would receive "96% of the West Bank and the Gaza Strip, and a territorial exchange involving the remaining 4%, where most settlers live, with unspecified Israeli territory," and over 40% of refugees in the West Bank, Gaza, Lebanon, and Jordan preferred to "remain a refugee" if they could not return to their "original residence" but instead were "allowed to live elsewhere in Israel."[3] Israelis expressed similar support both for the *Road Map* and for "reconciliation between peoples under conditions of peace and the existence of a Palestinian state."[4] However, they likewise resisted relinquishing longstanding territorial claims. Barak suffered withering criticism for offering "too much of a compromise" on the Occupied Territories, this despite proposing to annex five major settlement blocs and up to ten percent of the West Bank, as well as insisting upon Israel's unilateral right to determine those refugees permitted the "right of return." Israelis also were ambivalent about revising school curricula to recognize a future Palestinian state, and adamantly opposed any retreat from East Jerusalem.[5]

Committed to historically rooted, non-negotiable positions, neither Palestinians nor Israelis demonstrated great confidence in peaceful accommodation. Over 40% of Palestinians thought "reconciliation" was "not possible ever,"[6] while nearly 70% discounted prospects for a "lasting peace" as "impossible" or "definitely impossible."[7] Israelis similarly anticipated continuing "armed confrontation" and "conflictual and violent" relations for the next five to ten years; indeed, only 15% of the public thought a "lasting peace" with Palestinians to be "definitely possible," while nearly 50% thought that even in the context of a peace agreement "full reconciliation between the two peoples" was "not possible ever" or would occur only "in many generations to come."[8]

ROAD MAP'S ACCEPTANCE

Reflecting divergent strategic objectives and tactical preferences, Palestinian and Israeli perceptions of the *Road Map* differed significantly. While procedurally focused, the *Road Map*'s over-arching commitment to a two-state solution, emphasis on "reciprocal" obligations, insistence on the "unconditional cessation of violence," and enthusiastic endorsement by the US encouraged Palestinians to believe that their quest for an independent, sovereign, and viable state was within reach. The conviction that "armed confrontations have so far helped achieve Palestinian national rights in ways that negotiations could not" increasingly was coupled with a willingness to explore alternatives to the failed Intifada.[9] The PA was particularly hopeful that its immediate and unconditional acceptance of the *Road Map* would buttress US willingness to pressure Israel to accept a two-state solution.[10]

The *Road Map*'s potential to deliver within the year "an independent Palestinian state with provisional borders and attributes of sovereignty," improve Palestinians' socioeconomic and security situation, and provide a framework for resolving all final status issues also afforded Arafat, Fatah, and the PA a powerful weapon in their battle for Palestinians' political allegiance. Confronting a significant and longterm deterioration in his personal popularity,[11] a growing Islamist challenge to Fatah,[12] a conflict weary public,[13] and increasingly strident calls for "fundamental political reform in the PA,"[14] Arafat recognized the political imperative of securing Palestinians' most pressing national/territorial objectives. Both he and newly elected Prime Minister Mahmoud Abbas thus sought to distinguish clearly between the tangible results promised by Fatah/PA moderation and the unproductive rhetoric of violence espoused by Islamic extremists. Abbas, highlighting the importance of establishing "a Palestinian state with Jerusalem as its capital," insuring the state's "geographic unity," and ending settlement activity, endorsed both the *Road Map*'s two-state objective and its call for immediate and mutual cessation of violence.[15] Indicting Hamas and Islamic Jihad's rejection of the *Road Map* and reliance on terroristic violence,[16] he observed, "We denounce terrorism by any party and in all its forms, both because of our religious and moral traditions and because we are convinced that such methods do not lend support to a just cause like ours, but rather destroy it."[17] While highlighting the *Road Map*'s potential for "incorporating Hamas, Islamic Jihad and other organizations into political life and making them part of it—namely, turning them into political parties,"[18] he pledged, "Ending the armed chaos, which carries a direct threat to the security of the citizen, will be one of our fundamental missions. There is no place for weapons except in the hands of the government."[19]

The *Road Map*'s Phase I demand that Palestinians "reiterat[e] Israel's right to exist in peace and security" and accept "an immediate and unconditional ceasefire to end armed activity and all acts of violence against Israelis everywhere" was the type of limited "normalization" measure particularly appealing to Sharon. While skeptical of the *Road Map*'s innovative and redistributive implications,[20] he recognized its potential to address the public's pervasive insecurity,[21] desire to mitigate the Intifada's economic impact,[22] and readiness to open "a political process" with the Palestinians.[23] In addition, the *Road Map* offered a mechanism for postponing painful decisions concerning permanent disposition of the Occupied Territories. Buchanan captured Israel's dilemma, observing, "maintaining control over the Arabs of the West Bank and Gaza would inevitably involve Israel in acts of repression and in depriving the Palestinians of civil rights, which would erode the democratic nature of Israel's regime and society. If Israel annexed the territories and conferred citizenship on the Palestinians, the high birthrate of the latter would quickly bring about the loss of the Jewish majority in Israel, and though the state might be democratic, Israel would cease to be a Jewish and Zionist state."[24] While the *Road Map* proffered the possibility that the Territories' status would be addressed as early as January 2004, Sharon's insistence that Palestinians fulfill *all* of their Phase I obligations, including most importantly the *complete* cessation of violence, prior to Israel taking *any* steps involving the occupation, effectively insured that Phase I's security concerns would eclipse for the foreseeable future Phases II and III's territorial agenda.

Sharon's endorsement of the *Road Map* also reflected his government's commitment to the US-Israeli special relationship. While opposed to the *Road Map*'s rhetoric of "reciprocal" obligations, "timelines," and "target dates," he recognized the risks of simply dismissing the US-authored plan. Electing "to accept the steps set out in the road map" rather than the *Road Map* itself, attach fourteen reservations and clarifications to its "acceptance," and reject compromise on such a critical issue as refugees' "right of return", Sharon's cabinet sought both to reassure Washington that Israel would "not be an impediment to implementing the road map" and to reinterpret its provisions to reflect Israeli concerns.[25]

ROAD MAP'S EVALUATION

The *Road Map*'s April 2003-December 2005 timeframe, while marked by such watershed events as Arafat's death, Israel's unilateral withdrawal from Gaza and parts of the northern West Bank, and Sharon's defection from Likud, witnessed precious little progress toward achieving "a final and comprehensive settlement of the Israeli-Palestinian conflict." Neither Israel nor the PA proved willing and able to complete even their Phase I obligations, while the Quartet largely abdicated its assistance, facilitation, and monitoring functions. Israel thus remained as deeply entrenched in the West Bank as ever—the separation barrier testified to its *status quo ante* approach—while the Abbas-led PA, struggling to establish it *bona fides* vis-à-vis Israel and the Quartet in the face of relentless pressure from Hamas and Fatah dissidents, proved incapable of decisive action.

Drafting

The *Road Map*'s failure can be attributed to several key factors, one of the most significant of which was Washington's dominant role in its drafting. Buchanan, noting that "[b]oth the forums and the processes of conflict resolution are usually 'biased to some degree toward the interests of those who create them,'" emphasized that successful conflict resolution demands that "the needs of all the interested parties [be met] in designing the process by which they will try to settle their differences." He argued, "Through inclusion and participation many objectives are accomplished: 'ownership' of the process is encouraged, greater participation by parties in the process of resolving the problem influences the kind of behaviour that parties will use later in the problem-solving process, positive working relationships are built that help to create 'elegant options and implement the chosen solution effectively, and permit facilitators to build sufficient credibility to serve in an impartial role.'"[26] US insistence on the principals' exclusion from the *Road Map*'s development thus militated against Israelis and Palestinians alike perceiving an ownership stake in the initiative, buttressed Islamic extremists' "*Road Map* as US conspiracy" argument, and heightened Jerusalem's fear of a Quartet-imposed settlement. Similarly, Washington's refusal to countenance a multilaterally oriented drafting process attenuated Russian, EU, and UN readiness to undertake concerted action within the Quartet framework. Divergent motivations—the US sought to mitigate opposition to regime change in Iraq, bolster the "war on terror," and enhance Israeli security, while its Quartet partners focused on alleviating Palestinian suffering, promoting regional security through a two state solution, and strengthening their political position vis-à-vis the US—only heightened Quartet members' willingness to forsake coordinated, consensus driven action in favor of a "go it alone" approach.

Process

Fundamental differences over procedural issues likewise plagued the *Road Map*'s implementation. Its timetable elicited particularly intense disagreements. Palestinians, anxious to achieve statehood as rapidly as possible and fearful of *Oslo*-type deadline slippages, embraced the *Road Map*'s rhetoric of "clear phases, timelines, [and] target dates." The EU, Russia, and Secretary-General, focused on the *Road Map*'s innovative and redistributive objectives, likewise endorsed an ambitious implementation timetable. In contrast, Israel and the US, fearing artificial deadlines and the risks of premature transition among the *Road Map*'s phases, stressed the need to normalize Israeli-Palestinian relations prior to transitioning toward a two state solution, and thus highlighted the *Road Map*'s references to "benchmarks" and "performance." The *Road Map*'s constructive ambiguity proved unable to transcend such competing perspectives.

The *Road Map*'s rhetoric of "parallel" obligations similarly failed to resolve fundamental disagreements concerning the principals' respective responsibilities. Israel, fixated on terrorist threats to personal security, insisted that the PA fulfill *all* of its Phase I commitments, including declaring "an unequivocal end to violence and terrorism" and developing the institutional capabilities necessary for "sustained, targeted and effective operations aimed at confronting all those engaged in terror," prior to its assumption of *any* responsibilities. Such a sequential understanding of obligation—one shared by a US sympathetic to Israel's terror-related insecurities—was rejected by the PA and its Quartet supporters as a precondition driven approach guaranteed to produce stalemate, particularly given Sharon's insistence upon the "complete" cessation of violence prior to undertaking *any* action; they argued that only the *Road Map*'s "parallel" and "reciprocal" obligations approach could nurture and sustain a *mutual* commitment to peace and reconciliation.

The debate over parallel versus sequential performance mirrored longstanding differences over the wisdom of incremental versus comprehensive peacemaking strategies. Accepting Kissinger's argument that comprehensive multilateral negotiations would produce deadlock and ever increasing frustration,[27] both the US and Israeli governments had endorsed since the early 1970s an incremental, "step-by-step" peace process. The Egyptian-Israeli rapprochement, Israeli-Palestinian *Oslo Accords*, and Israeli-Jordanian *Peace Treaty* seemingly vindicated such an approach, marginalizing extremists, promising participants the enhanced security and economic benefits of normalized relations, and establishing a momentum for peace predicated on mutual fulfillment of obligations. Such incrementalism was embodied most clearly in Phase I's emphasis on establishing a foundation for peace by "ending terror and violence, normalizing Palestinian life, and building Palestinian institutions." While supporting such efforts, Palestinians, the EU, Russia, and Secretary-General stressed the importance of linking attempts to deescalate the Israeli-Palestinian crisis with achieving *immediate* progress both in establishing a Palestinian state and in facilitating broader regional peace initiatives; Palestinians' decades-long exclusion from negotiations between Israel and its Arab neighbors heightened concerns that Israel might abandon the *Road Map* after its Phase I security objectives had been achieved. The PA and non-US Quartet members thus emphasized the need for a rapid transition from Phase I to Phases II and III, while highlighting the *Road Map*'s commitment both to securing a "final and comprehensive permanent status agreement that ends the Israel-Palestinian conflict in 2005" and to serving as "a vital element of international efforts to promote a comprehensive peace on all tracks, including the Syrian-Israeli and Lebanese-Israeli tracks," "to be achieved as soon as possible."[28]

Reconciling divergent conceptions about the Quartet's role in implementing the *Road Map* likewise proved problematic. Cognizant of Israel's relative economic, military, and political advantages, the PA eagerly anticipated an activist Quartet shepherding a Palestinian state into being. The *Road Map* gave reason for optimism, calling on the Quartet to "assist and facilitate implementation of the plan," "meet regularly at senior levels to evaluate the parties' performance on implementation of the plan," engage in "informal monitoring and consult with the parties on establishment of a formal monitoring mechanism and its implementation," and convene two international conferences, the first "to support Palestinian economic recovery and launch a process, leading to establishment of an independent Palestinian state with provisional borders," the second "to endorse agreement reached on an independent Palestinian state with provisional borders and formally to launch a process with the active, sustained, and operational support of the Quartet, leading to a final, permanent status resolution in 2005." The EU, Russia, and the UN, historically interested but largely impotent observers of the Israeli-Palestinian conflict, relished the opportunities afforded by the *Road Map*'s ostensible commitment to empowered multilateralism. However, Sharon, fearing both an interventionist Quartet and the international conference model of conflict resolution, highlighted the *Road Map*'s commitment to "direct discussions between the parties," "a settlement negotiated between the parties," and the Quartet acting only "in consultation with the parties." The US, loathe to relinquish it historically pivotal position to its pro-Palestinian Quartet partners and sensitive to Israel's concern that "negotiations within the framework of an international conference" invariably would place Jerusalem "in an inferior position strategically, tactically and numerically,"[29] supported its ally's preference for mediated bilateral negotiations.

Terms of Reference

Compounding uncertainties about the Quartet's responsibilities were disagreements about the terms of reference upon which *Road Map*-sanctioned negotiations should be conducted. The PA, supported by the EU, Russia, and Secretary-General, emphasized that "international legitimacy" demanded adherence to *all* relevant internationally endorsed documents, including UN Security Council and General Assembly Resolutions, and support for constructive regionally endorsed peace initiatives. It argued against selective or distorted application of generally accepted principles concerning "land for peace," refugee rights, and administration of the Occupied Territories, while urging sensitivity to well intentioned efforts by Saudi Arabia, Jordan, Egypt, and the Arab League. While encouraged by the *Road Map*'s reference to "the principle of land for peace" and to Saudi Crown Prince Abdullah's peace proposal, its failure to mention General Assembly Resolution 194 detailing refugees' "right of return," the 1949 *Geneva Convention* governing administration of occupied territories, and the extent of Israeli withdrawal obligations under UNSCR 242 caused significant concern. In contrast, Israel and the US took comfort in the *Road Map*'s reference to UNSCR 338 and its call for direct negotiations between the parties, insistence upon abiding by "agreements previously reached by the parties," and silence concerning Israeli and US adherence to Security Council and General Assembly resolutions, international legal instruments, and multilateral initiatives perceived as impacting negatively either the negotiating process or Israel's future security.

Substance

The *Road Map* suffered as well from the limits of its process driven approach. While expressing unprecedented commitment to a two state solution, it focused on articulating processes, procedures, and mechanisms for pursuing a diplomatic settlement rather than on resolving historically intractable final status issues and bridging the chasm separating Israeli and Palestinian conceptions of peace within a two state framework. The resulting disjunction between the *Road Map*'s rhetoric of an expedited, performance driven, multilaterally administered peace process and the reality of Washington's refusal to pressure its Israeli ally to modify longstanding, internationally problematic positions left unresolved the conflict between the Middle East and Mediterranean paradigms for advancing regional "peace, development, democratisation, and integration." Reflecting post-WWII US efforts to secure "reliable and cheap oil supplies" and establish Israel as "*primus inter pares* in regional terms," the Middle East paradigm was "at heart a geopolitical arrangement for the benefit of, primarily, the USA, but also the USA's principal allies (namely Israel) and those deemed friendly by the USA such as Saudi Arabia, the Gulf States and Egypt." US attempts to promote Israeli-Palestinian conflict resolution thus could be interpreted as "the articulation of a *pax americana*, which is the culmination of a US-Israeli geopolitical strategy to engage Arab and non-Arab states of the region in a mutual management arrangement which combines bilateral and multilateral economic and security cooperation." In contrast, the Mediterranean paradigm stressed "the development of a partnership between the Europeans, the people of the Middle East and the North Africans, based on mutual concerns and benefits, with no one region dominating the other in a partner-client relationship." Peace efforts emphasized "dialogue and interaction among governmental and non-governmental actors in search for problem-solving and maximizing cooperation between Europe and the Middle East," as well as "the absence of the USA as a principal part of the equation, with the concomitant lessening of the dominating impact of Israel, and Israel's presence, on inter-regional relations."[30]

While the *Road Map* failed to resolve latent tensions between the US and its Quartet partners over the shape of a potential settlement and provided no indication that Washington was prepared to accept an agreement contrary to Israel's oft-stated positions, just as importantly it failed to narrow Israeli-Palestinian differences over the nature of any future "peace".[31] Palestinians, having struggled to establish an independent, sovereign, and viable state for nearly sixty years, overwhelmingly supported establishing "open borders" and "joint Palestinian-Israeli economic institutions and ventures" between Jerusalem and a future Palestinian state, while rejecting a peace defined by "joint political institutions leading to an Israeli-Palestinian confederation," social interaction with Israeli colleagues, tolerance inspired school reform, and legal measures against incitement.[32] In contrast, Israelis, while more concerned about the security threats inherent in "open borders," were willing to pursue "friendship," "forgiveness," and "tolerance" as the most effective guarantees of long term peace and security. They expressed notable support—"given a state of peace"—for "cultural changes in education and public discourse and social interaction," including endorsing curricular reform countering "irredentist aspirations," adopting anti-incitement legislation, and inviting "a Palestinian colleague to their home."[33]

The *Road Map*'s emphasis on "two state" rhetoric rather than on substantive proposals for surmounting critical differences over refugees, Jerusalem, settlements, and borders was exploited by extremists on both sides. Hamas was particularly adept at playing upon the 35-40% of Palestinians opposed to the *Road Map*, the 60-70% who believed that "armed confrontations have helped achieve Palestinians' national rights in ways that negotiations could not," and the overwhelming majority committed to establishing "an independent and secure Palestinian state" as *the* most important national interest.[34] Abbas, recognizing public support for Hamas's participation in PA-Israeli negotiations and opposition to clamping down "against militants who continue to carry out attacks inside Israel" after ceasefire agreements,[35] attempted unsuccessfully to convince Hamas that its participation in "political life" would be "the best thing both for us and for them."[36]

Although domestically far stronger than his Palestinian counterpart, Sharon likewise struggled to marginalize extremist elements in the context of the *Road Map*'s silence concerning details of a final settlement. Confronting a public skeptical about the underspecified *Road Map*,[37] he turned to unilateral disengagement to secure vital national interests while enhancing perceptions of personal security. However, lacking the US-led Quartet's imprimatur, he encountered particularly intense resistance. While 70% of Israelis supported vigorous measures against "extreme Israeli elements in the West Bank and Gaza Strip" and two-thirds "the dismantling of most settlements in the West Bank and Gaza Strip as part of a peace agreement,"[38] approximately 30% opposed the Gaza Disengagement Plan,[39] 14% of whom believed that "disengagement should be resisted by all means."[40] While greater substantive specificity and elaboration would have had little impact on such intra-societal rifts, a US-endorsed *Road Map* that meaningfully tackled final status issues would have provided Sharon

Pendular Dynamic of Terror

While the *Road Map*'s failure can readily be attributed to the disjunction between Quartet rhetoric sympathetic to Palestinian, EU, Russian, and UN concerns and the reality of staunch US support for Israel, the limits of its process oriented approach in the context of competing procedural perspectives, and its refusal to confront substantively the existentially defined conflict, the parties' inability to identify, manage, and exploit the pendular dynamic of terror may be equally significant. Despite oft-repeated assertions by Sharon, Arafat, Abbas, and Bush that terrorism precluded the very possibility of negotiations, the dynamic relationship among terrorist actions, the international strategic perspective of policymakers, and the domestic political environment may result in terror *either* foreclosing negotiations *or* creating unanticipated possibilities. Recognizing and exploiting oftentimes fleeting moments of opportunity while avoiding ill-advised diplomatic initiatives is especially critical to resolving Israeli-Palestinian-type conflicts.

The pendular dynamic of terror has two distinct manifestations, both of which reflect evolving relationships among a state's international strategic interests, domestic political circumstances, and terrorist actions. First, it produces changes in perceptions of constraint, opportunity, and imperative as a state's relationship to terrorism fluctuates among five distinct phases. Phases I, II, and IV, in which terrorism has yet to engage domestic constituencies on an ongoing basis, typically afford policymakers greater latitude, including the discretion to pursue accommodative diplomacy. In contrast, Phases III and V, characterized by an "assertive, vocal, and knowledgeable public," "attentive and activist" legislature and media, and "engaged and insistent interest group community," place significant demands on decisionmakers to utilize "punitive, confrontational, and non-concessionary policies" to address a terrorist threat perceived to be direct, pressing, and consequential.[42] Second, the pendular dynamic may prompt reevaluations of the effectiveness or appropriateness of counterterror efforts as a result of intra-phase transitions. Such fluctuations may occur incrementally, reflecting evolving perspectives on the relative efficacy of force and diplomacy, or suddenly, typically in response to such paradigm altering events as the collapse of high profile negotiations, dramatic escalation of violence, or unanticipated diplomatic success. While the rapidity of flux impacts both the frequency with which diplomatic "windows of opportunity" arise and their duration, the amplitude of transition affects the intensity with which a particular approach, whether confrontational or accommodative, will be pursued. High amplitude fluctuations heighten the imperative for action and concomitant commitment of government resources, while low amplitude transitions demand neither significant policy adjustments nor additional capabilities.

Policymakers must be particularly adept at exploiting those fleeting moments of diplomatic opportunity generated by intra-phase flux in Phases III and

V. Given both phases default preference for accommodating domestic political pressures through punitive, aggressive, and confrontational tactics, seizing upon that all-too-rare confluence of circumstances by which *all* parties possess both the will and capability to abandon seemingly ineffectual policies is critical to achieving a negotiated settlement. Failure to recognize the opportunity afforded by episodic disillusionment with confrontational policies risks alienating potential interlocutors, empowering extremists, and precipitating renewed intra-phase flux in favor of non-accommodative policies. Identifying a state's current relationship to terrorism, as well as its recent inter and intra-phase transitions, thus is critical to distinguishing moments of diplomatic possibility from periods of unpromising constraint.

Israelis, Palestinians, and Americans experienced significant, albeit unproductive, intra-phase flux during the April 2003–December 2005 *Road Map* period. While such transitions challenged prevailing conceptions about the utility of violence and potential for peaceful conflict resolution, policymakers' failure to apply the "I-M-E" formula—identify pendular flux, manage confrontation, and exploit opportunity—proved disastrous. As opportunities were squandered to resolve procedural and substantive differences, surmount historical animosities, and minimize extremists' disruptive potential, risks mounted for a potentially catastrophic reversal of pendular flux toward renewed emphasis on violence and conflict.

Ariel Sharon, an archetype of the strong, decisive, charismatic leader best suited to implementing "I-M-E," neither appreciated the import of Palestinians' growing interest in negotiations nor Israelis' readiness to accept innovative and distasteful measures, including negotiating with Hamas, on behalf of peace. Confident of US support for aggressive counterterror policies, attracted to such unilateral initiatives as the West Bank separation barrier, Gaza withdrawal, and settlement consolidation, and skeptical of the PA's commitment to peace, Sharon clung to deeply held beliefs that the Israeli-Palestinian conflict was managed most effectively not through negotiations but rather through "iron fist" policies. Although acknowledging the potential significance of Abbas's January 2005 election, Sharon displayed little sense of urgency in reaching out to his Palestinian counterpart. Content to insist that Abbas prove both the sincerity of his peaceful intentions and ability to reign in extremist groups *prior* to initiating negotiations, and blind to the impact of unilateral, militaristic measures on the pendular dynamic and prospects for future negotiations, he made few concessions, clinging to the fiction that Israel could choose the moment at which to engage Palestinians diplomatically. While Sharon's "wait and see" complacency toward negotiations had begun to shift by late 2005—evidenced most clearly by his creation of the centrist Kadima party—Fatah's splintering and Hamas's ascendance threatened once again to reorient the PA toward a "confrontation only" approach, leaving Israel with no viable negotiating partner. Sharon's massive stroke and departure from office in early 2006 revealed only too clearly the risks of delay in exploiting pendular moments of opportunity.

PA leadership—Arafat prior to November 2004, Abbas afterwards—proved similarly inept at pursuing "I-M-E". Arafat, having committed to "I-M-E" in the early *Oslo* period with devastating national and personal political consequences, focused during the *Road Map* period not on "I-M-E" but rather on managing conflict with Israel with an eye toward outflanking Fatah's Islamist rivals. Failing to identify pendular flux supportive of more accommodative policies toward Israel, he called upon Palestinians to resist by *all* means the Israeli occupation, avoided clamping down on terrorist organizations, and, most importantly, ignored Palestinians' growing weariness, sense of despair, and readiness to explore alternative approaches to achieving national/territorial objectives. While Arafat's domestic political perceptions encouraged adherence to Intifada-type policies, Abbas recognized clearly both the moment of diplomatic opportunity and the imperative for immediate action. Arguing that "[t]ime is becoming our greatest enemy,"[43] he emphasized the need to seize upon unprecedented circumstances—US and Israeli support for a two state solution, active and coordinated engagement of the US, EU, Russia, and the UN on behalf of comprehensive regional peace, and Palestinian willingness to explore non-violent tactics—to push for rapid diplomatic progress. While unequivocally renouncing terror and advocating reform of PA security forces, Abbas sought to manage intra-Palestinian discord not by crushing Islamist organizations but rather by co-opting them into the political process. Unfortunately, his own political weakness—he clearly lacked Arafat's "father of the revolution" stature—coupled with Sharon's complacency about the PA President's need to deliver immediate and tangible benefits to his conflict weary constituents, emboldened both Islamic extremists and Fatah dissidents. Abbas's failure to project the aura of political authority necessary both to control violence and negotiate peace undermined his ability to resolve the Israeli-Palestinian conflict prior to the inevitable closing of the diplomatic "window of opportunity."

Uniquely positioned to advance the negotiated peace envisioned in its own *Road Map* initiative, the Bush White House nonetheless failed to apply "I-M-E" to necessary effect. While cognizant that intra-Phase V pendular flux had created for *both* Israelis and Palestinians a moment of great diplomatic opportunity, Bush's inability to transcend either Washington's post-1967 historical approach to the region—one characterized by unwavering support for Israel and insistence upon a US-dominated, bilateral, incremental peace process—or his own post-9/11 reliance on military force in combating terrorism, undermined US efforts to secure the *Road Map*'s objectives. White House tolerance for Israeli deviations from the *Road Map*—including rejecting parallel obligations, comprehensive negotiations, and meaningful Quartet involvement, expanding settlements, constructing the separation barrier, and preferencing unilateral measures such as Gaza disengagement over bilaterally negotiated agreements—was particularly damaging to attempts to manage confrontation. Israel's policy of targeted assassinations, house demolitions, and collective punishments similarly compromised both the PA's effectiveness in countering Islamist criticism of the *Road Map* and Quartet attempts to encourage negotiations. Confronted by ongoing Palestinian violence, Bush endorsed Sharon's uncompromising, militarily oriented, policy and refusal to negotiate except under conditions of "absolute quiet." While resonating with Americans, as well as with many Israelis, such an approach demanded that PA leaders assume the onerous and politically untenable burden of crushing popular extremist groups in hopes of securing uncertain future national/territorial benefits. White House insistence upon such measures—a reflection of its misunderstanding of the fleeting nature of pendular opportunity—threatened the *Road Map*'s objective of securing a "two state solution to the Israeli-Palestinian conflict" through "*reciprocal* steps by the two parties in the political, security, economic, humanitarian, and institution-building fields."[44]

Introduction

1. See "A Performance-Based Road Map to a Permanent Two-State Solution to the Israeli-Palestinian Conflict," 30 April 2003, in http://www.state.gov/, accessed 23 August 2004.
2. See *Road Map*.
3. See *Road Map*.
4. See *Road Map*.
5. See *Road Map*.
6. See *Road Map*.
7. See *Road Map*. Emphasis added.
8. Andrew S. Buchanan, *Peace with Justice: A History of the Israeli-Palestinian Declaration of Principles on Interim Self-Government Arrangements* (New York: St. Martin's Press, 2000), 11. Emphasis in original.
9. Buchanan, *Peace with Justice*, 12, 53.
10. Buchanan, *Peace with Justice*, 14–15, 28.
11. According to Craig and George, in contrast to normalization agreements that "terminate an abnormal situation in relations between two or more parties," redistributive agreements "benefit one side at the expense of the other," while innovative agreements "set up new arrangements or undertakings that benefit both parties (though not necessarily equally)." Gordon A. Craig and Alexander L. George, *Force and Statecraft: Diplomatic Problems of Our Time: third edition* (New York: Oxford University Press, 1995), 165.
12. See *Road Map*.
13. Buchanan, *Peace with Justice*, 3, 14.
14. Buchanan, *Peace with Justice*, 83, 34, 4.
15. Buchanan, *Peace with Justice*, 28. They recognized that Israeli-Palestinian type conflicts that involve "painful losses, in lives, in territory, in justice and in legitimacy are the most resistant to traditional methods of diplomatic or political mediation and negotiation." Buchanan, *Peace with Justice*, 14.
16. "Marwan Barghuti: 'The Israelis Must Leave the Territories' (October 26, 2000)," in *The Israel-Arab Reader: A Documentary History of the Middle East Conflict, sixth revised edition*, Walter Laqueur and Barry Rubin, eds., (New York: Penguin Books, 2001), 561.
17. See Buchanan, *Peace with Justice*, 45.
18. "*UN Security Council*: Resolution 242 (November 22, 1967)," in *Israel-Arab Reader*, Laqueur and Rubin, eds., 116; "*UN General Assembly:* Resolution 194 (December 11, 1948)," in *Israel-Arab Reader*, Laqueur and Rubin, eds., 85. Resolution 242 acknowledged such a settlement as critical to securing "a just and lasting peace in the Middle East."
19. See, for example, "The Venice European Declaration, 13 June 1980," in *The Israeli-Palestinian Conflict: a documentary record, 1967–1990*, Yehuda Lukacs, ed. (Cambridge, Great Britain: Cambridge University Press, 1992), 19; "The Madrid European Declaration, 27 June 1989," in *Israeli-Palestinian Conflict*, Lukacs, ed., 51–53. See also "UN Security Council Resolution 605, 22 December 1987," in *Israeli-Palestinian Conflict*, Lukacs, ed., 30–31; "UN Security Council Resolution 607, 5 January 1988," in *Israeli-Palestinian Conflict*, Lukacs, ed., 31–32.
20. Derick L. Hulme, Jr., *Palestinian Terrorism and U.S. Foreign Policy, 1969–1977: Dynamics of Response* (Lewiston, New York: Edwin Mellen Press, 2004), 24.

21. See, for example, "President Ronald Reagan Peace Plan, 1 September 1982," in *Israeli-Palestinian Conflict*, Lukacs, ed., 72–78.

22. Hulme, *Palestinian Terrorism*, 17.

23. "'This is the Plan,' Secretary of State George Shultz's Peace Proposal, 18 March 1988," in *Israeli-Palestinian Conflict*, Lukacs, ed., 105, 104. Emphasis added.

24. See *Road Map*.

25. "Venice Declaration," in *Israeli-Palestinian Conflict*, 18.

26. The US historically had viewed the UN with a mixture of contempt and indifference, (See Hulme, *Palestinian Terrorism*, 115) repeatedly rejecting UN efforts to convene an international conference on the Middle East and criticizing its pro-Palestinian, anti-Israeli bias. (See, for example, "This is the Plan," in *Israeli-Palestinian Conflict*, 105.)

27. See, for example, "UN General Assembly Resolution 41/43 D, 2 December 1986," in *Israeli-Palestinian Conflict*, Lukacs, ed., 26, which was supported overwhelmingly by European states.

28. Hulme, *Palestinian Terrorism*, 144.

29. "Statement on the Problem in the Middle East, Soviet Foreign Minister Gromyko, 25 September 1979," in *Israeli-Palestinian Conflict*, Lukacs, ed., 17.

30. "Soviet Communist Party Chairman Leonid Brezhnev's Position on Arab-Israeli Peace, 23 February 1981," in *Israeli-Palestinian Conflict*, Lukacs, ed., 19.

31. "The Soviet Union's Proposals on a Middle East Settlement, 29 July 1984," in *Israeli-Palestinian Conflict*, Lukacs, ed., 22; "Speech of President Mikhail Gorbachev on Relations with Israel, 24 April 1987," in *Israeli-Palestinian Conflict*, Lukacs, ed., 29. Emphasis added.

32. "Near East: Chance for a Historic Compromise, Soviet Foreign Minister Eduard Shevardnadze, Cairo, 23 February 1989," in *Israeli-Palestinian Conflict*, Lukacs, ed., 39, 42, 45, 46, 47.

33. See, for example, "Statement by The European Community Foreign Ministers, Brussels, 6 November 1973," in *Israeli-Palestinian Conflict*, Lukacs, ed., 14.

34. "Venice Declaration," in *Israeli-Palestinian Conflict*, 18. It particularly focused on securing Palestinians' "legitimate rights," including that of self-determination.

35. "The Brussels European Declaration, 23 February 1987," in *Israeli-Palestinian Conflict*, Lukacs, ed., 27.

36. See, for example, "Madrid Declaration," in *Israeli-Palestinian Conflict*, 52.

37. Hulme, *Palestinian Terrorism*, 135.

38. See, for example, "UN General Assembly Resolution A/43/L.53, Geneva, 14 December 1988," in *Israeli-Palestinian Conflict*, Lukacs, ed., 35.

39. See, for example, "UNGA Res. 41/43 D," in *Israeli-Palestinian Conflict*, 26.

40. See *Road Map*.

41. Laura Zittrain Eisenberg and Neil Caplan, "The Israeli-Palestinian Peace Process in Historical Perspective," in *The Middle East Peace Process: Interdisciplinary Perspectives,* Ilan Peleg, ed. (Albany, New York: State University of New York Press, 1998), 4–5. Such "other" purposes included negotiating "for appearances, trying to impress upon a powerful third party their willingness to resolve matters, as opposed to the extremist, uncompromising posture of the other side." Eisenberg and Caplan, "The Israeli-Palestinian Peace Process," in *The Middle East Peace Process*, 5.

42. Hulme, *Palestinian Terrorism*, 125.

43. For Kissinger's concerns, see Hulme, *Palestinian Terrorism*, 123, 125, 149.

44. See *Road Map*.

45. See *Road Map*.

46. Hulme, *Palestinian Terrorism*, 30.

47. "Soviet Foreign Minister Andrei Gromyko: On the Camp David Agreement (September 25, 1979)," in *Israel-Arab Reader*, Laqueur and Rubin, eds., 229–230.

48. "Brezhnev's Position," in *Israeli-Palestinian Conflict*, Lukacs, 19. Soviet dismay reflected particular bitterness at Washington's embrace of Sadat's bilateral initiative to Israel *subsequent* to the 1 October 1977 US-USSR *Joint Statement* that had endorsed a "comprehensive [settlement] incorporating all parties concerned and all questions," and that had declared, "The United States and the Soviet Union believe that the only right and effective way for achieving a fundamental solution to all aspects of the Middle East problem in its entirety is by negotiations within the framework of the Geneva Peace Conference . . . with participation in its work of the representatives of all the parties involved in the conflict including those of the Palestinian people." "Joint Statement by the Governments of the US and the USSR, 1 October 1977," in *Israeli-Palestinian Conflict*, Lukacs, ed., 16.

49. "Soviet Union's Proposals, 29 July 1984," in *Israeli-Palestinian Conflict*, 23.

50. "Gorbachev on Relations with Israel," in *Israeli-Palestinian Conflict*, Lukacs, ed., 29; "Statement on the Middle East by President Mikhail Gorbachev Following the Moscow Summit, 1 June 1988," in *Israeli-Palestinian Conflict*, Lukacs, ed., 33.

51. See *Road Map*.

52. See, for example, "Madrid Declaration," in *Israeli-Palestinian Conflict*, 52.

53. See, for example, "Venice Declaration," in *Israeli-Palestinian Conflict*, 18.

54. See "UN Security Council Resolution 242, 22 November 1967," in *Israeli-Palestinian Conflict*, Lukacs, ed., 1–2.

55. See, for example, "UNGA Res. 41/43 D," in *Israeli-Palestinian Conflict*, 26.

56. "UNGA Res. 41/43 D," in *Israeli-Palestinian Conflict*, Lukacs, 26; "UN General Assembly Resolution 3236, 22 November 1974," in *Israeli-Palestinian Conflict*, Lukacs, ed., 15.

57. Hulme, *Palestinian Terrorism*, 144; "UN General Assembly Resolution 3236, 22 November 1974," in *Israeli-Palestinian Conflict*, 15.

58. Hulme, *Palestinian Terrorism*, 135–136.

59. Concerns about US unilateralism were particularly evident in the Security Council's steadfast opposition to supporting military action against Iraq. Opposition included such "permanent five" members as France and China, erstwhile US allies Germany and Canada, and states from the developing world.

60. See Buchanan, *Peace with Justice*, 14–16.

61. Buchanan, *Peace with Justice*, 30, 14.

62. Buchanan, *Peace with Justice*, 15.

63. Hulme, *Palestinian Terrorism*, 201, 205, 213.

64. Hulme, *Palestinian Terrorism*, 11.

65. Hulme, *Palestinian Terrorism*, 11.

66. Hulme, *Palestinian Terrorism*, 214, 11, 215–216.

67. Hulme, *Palestinian Terrorism*, 12, 218.

Context—Process

1. See Buchanan, *Peace with Justice*, 56.

2. Hulme, *Palestinian Terrorism*, 16.

3. Hulme, *Palestinian Terrorism*, 22. He observed, "if they want a settlement, they have to come to us. No one else can deliver." Hulme, *Palestinian Terrorism*, 29.

4. Hulme, *Palestinian Terrorism*, 16.

5. Ibid., 29–30. Kissinger's aides acknowledged that Geneva's multilateral forum "would buy time and provide a public cover, while we seek to manipulate the parties into secret talks on the difficult issues." Hulme, *Palestinian Terrorism*, 30.

6. Hulme, *Palestinian Terrorism*, 128–129.

7. "Reagan Plan," in *Israeli-Palestinian Conflict*, 75.

8. Ibid., 73. He indicated his commitment to "follow[ing] the broad guidelines" of previous administrations. "Reagan Plan," in *Israeli-Palestinian Conflict*, 73.

9. "This is the Plan," in *Israeli-Palestinian Conflict*, 104, 105.

10. "US Policy on an International Middle East Peace Conference, 13 January 1984," in *Israeli-Palestinian Conflict*, Lukacs, ed., 81.

11. Buchanan, *Peace with Justice*, 65–66, 89–91. The EU and UN participated only as conference observers.

12. Eisenberg and Caplan, "The Israeli-Palestinian Peace Process," in *The Middle East Peace Process*, Peleg, ed., 11. See "*Israel and Jordan:* Peace Treaty (October 26, 1994)," in *Israel-Arab Reader*, Laqueur and Rubin, eds., 477–486; "*Israel and Palestinian Authority:* Hebron Accords (January 15, 1997)," in *Israel-Arab Reader*, Laqueur and Rubin, eds., 522–523; "*Israel and Palestinian Authority:* The Wye River Agreement Signing Ceremony (October 23, 1998)," in *Israel-Arab Reader*, Laqueur and Rubin, eds., 529–534; "*U.S. President Bill Clinton:* Statement after the Camp David Peace Talks (July 25, 2000)," in *Israel-Arab Reader*, Laqueur and Rubin, eds., 551–556.

13. Hulme, *Palestinian Terrorism*, 115, 17, 61, 15.

14. See "European Community Foreign Ministers, 6 November 1973," in *Israeli-Palestinian Conflict*, Lukacs, ed., 14. The Foreign Ministers stressed "the ties of all kinds which have long linked them to the littoral States of the South and East of the Mediterranean." "European Community Foreign Ministers, 6 November 1973," in *Israeli-Palestinian Conflict*, 14.

15. Hulme, *Palestinian Terrorism*, 143.

16. See Henry Kissinger, *Years of Upheaval* (Boston: Little, Brown and Company, 1982), Chapters V, XVI.

17. "Venice European Declaration," in *Israeli-Palestinian Conflict*, 18–19.

18. "The Brussels European Declaration, 23 February 1987," in *Israeli-Palestinian Conflict*, 27; "Madrid European Declaration, 27 June 1989," in *Israeli-Palestinian Conflict*, 52.

19. See Buchanan, *Peace with Justice*, 69–70.

20. Hulme, *Palestinian Terrorism*, 88. Fulbright also criticized the US for surrendering "much of . . . (its) freedom of action to the bellicose whims" of Israel. Hulme, *Palestinian Terrorism*, 88.

21. Hulme, *Palestinian Terrorism*, 14, 22.

22. Hulme, *Palestinian Terrorism*, 132, 22, 125.

23. "Memorandum of Agreement between the Governments of Israel and the United States, September 1975," in *Israeli-Palestinian Conflict*, Lukacs, ed., 60.

24. "Reagan Plan," in *Israeli-Palestinian Conflict*, 72–78, esp. 75, 77.

25. "U.S. Letter of Assurances to the Palestinians (October 18, 1991)," in *Israel-Arab Reader*, Laqueur and Rubin, eds., 387.

26. "*U.S. President Bill Clinton, Israeli Prime Minister Ehud Barak, Syrian Foreign Minister Faruk al-Shara:* Speeches at the Renewal of Syrian-Israeli Negotiations (December 15, 1999)," in *Israel-Arab Reader*, Laqueur and Rubin, eds., 545–546.

27. "*U.S. President Bill Clinton:* The Clinton Plan (December 23, 2000)," in *Israel-Arab Reader*, Laqueur and Rubin, eds., 562–564.

28. "*U.S. President Bill Clinton:* Summarizing His Experience with the Peace Process (January 7, 2001)," in *Israel-Arab Reader*, Laqueur and Rubin, eds., 574.
29. "Clinton, December 26, 2000," in *Israel-Arab Reader*, 562–564.
30. Hulme, *Palestinian Terrorism*, 31.
31. Hulme, *Palestinian Terrorism*, 16–17, 123, 149.
32. "Deputy Assistant Secretary of State Harold H. Saunders, Statement on the Palestinians, 12 November 1975," in *Israeli-Palestinian Conflict*, Lukacs, ed., 65.
33. "Joint Statement," in *Israeli-Palestinian Conflict*, 16.
34. "Statement to the Israeli Knesset by President Sadat, 20 November 1977," in *Israeli-Palestinian Conflict*, Lukacs, ed., 140, 137.
35. See "*Camp David Summit Meeting:* Frameworks for Peace (September 17, 1978)," in *Israel-Arab Reader*, Laqueur and Rubin, eds., 222–228.
36. "Arab League Summit Conference Declaration, Tripoli, 5 December 1977," in *Israeli-Palestinian Conflict*, Lukacs, ed., 467.
37. "Arab League Summit Conference, Final Statement, Baghdad, 5 November 1978," in *Israeli-Palestinian Conflict*, Lukacs, ed., 471; "Arab League Summit Conference Resolutions, Baghdad, 31 March 1979," in *Israeli-Palestinian Conflict*, Lukacs, ed., 473–477.
38. "Six-Point Programme," in *Israeli-Palestinian Conflict*, Lukacs, ed., 335–336.
39. "Palestine National Council, 23 January 1979," in *Israeli-Palestinian Conflict*, Lukacs, ed., 339, 342; "PLO Executive Committee, 5 October 1979," in *Israeli-Palestinian Conflict*, Lukacs, ed., 344; "*PLO Chairman Yasir Arafat:* Interview on Camp David (November 19, 1979)," in *Israel-Arab Reader*, Laqueur and Rubin, eds., 230–231.
40. "Summit of Anti-Sadat 'Steadfastness and Confrontation Front', Damascus, 23 September 1978," in *Israeli-Palestinian Conflict*, Lukacs, ed., 470; "*Syrian President Hafiz al-Asad:* Speech (March 8, 1980)," in *Israel-Arab Reader*, Laqueur and Rubin, eds., 231–232.
41. "*Israeli Prime Minister Yitzhak Shamir and Palestinian Delegation Leader Haydar Abd al-Shafi:* Speeches at the Madrid Peace Conference (October 21, 1991)," in *Israel-Arab Reader*, Laqueur and Rubin, eds., 391.
42. Buchanan, *Peace with Justice*, 90.
43. See Buchanan, *Peace with Justice*, 71–89, especially 77. Israeli Prime Minister Yitzhak Rabin recognized the value of such talks, observing, "by not dealing with the PLO in the immediate future, the rise of absolutist, Islamic fundamentalism would result." Buchanan, *Peace with Justice*, 159.
44. "*Syrian President Hafiz al-Asad and U.S. President Bill Clinton:* Statement on Their Meeting (January 16, 1994)," in *Israel-Arab Reader*, Laqueur and Rubin, eds., 441.
45. "*Israel and Jordan*: The Washington Agreement (July 26, 1994)," in *Israel-Arab Reader*, 467; "*Israel and Jordan* (October 26, 1994)," in *Israel-Arab Reader*, 477–486.
46. "*Asad and Clinton,* January 16, 1994," in *Israel-Arab Reader*, 440.
47. "*Clinton, Barak, and al-Shara,* December 15, 1999," in *Israel-Arab Reader*, 545–548. This was the "highest level meeting ever" between the two states.
48. Hulme, *Palestinian Terrorism*, 150. He had observed, for example, "Deep down, Egypt had no Palestinian vocation; it had to overcome nationalist impulses to dedicate itself to that cause." Quoted in Hulme, *Palestinian Terrorism*, 62.
49. See Hulme, *Palestinian Terrorism*, 37.
50. Hulme, *Palestinian Terrorism*, 37, 39, 40.
51. Hulme, *Palestinian Terrorism*, 42, 43.
52. Hulme, *Palestinian Terrorism*, 135–136.
53. Hulme, *Palestinian Terrorism*, 44.

54. Hulme, *Palestinian Terrorism*, 46, 139.

55. "Palestine National Council, 23 January 1979," in *Israeli-Palestinian Conflict*, 340; "The Fourth General Conference of the Palestine Liberation Movement, Fatah, Political Program, 31 May 1980," in *Israeli-Palestinian Conflict*, Lukacs, ed., 345; "PLO Executive Committee, 7 March 1986," in *Israeli-Palestinian Conflict*, Lukacs, ed., 383; "Statement by the PLO Central Committee, 9 January 1988," in *Israeli-Palestinian Conflict*, Lukacs, ed., 392.

56. "The Covenant of Hamas (The Islamic Resistance Movement in the West Bank), 18 August 1988," in *Israeli-Palestinian Conflict*, Lukacs, ed., 401, 402.

57. "Arafat, 13 December 1988," in *Israeli-Palestinian Conflict*, Lukacs, ed., 420–433, esp. 431; "Palestine National Council, 15 November 1988," in *Israeli-Palestinian Conflict*, Lukacs, ed., 415–420. Arafat had issued a similar "condemnation of all acts of terrorism" in 1985. See "Arafat, 7 November 1985," in *Israeli-Palestinian Conflict*, Lukacs, ed., 370.

58. "Arafat, 13 December 1988," in *Israeli-Palestinian Conflict*, 426.

59. "Arafat, 15 December 1988," in *Israeli-Palestinian Conflict*, Lukacs, ed., 434; "Arafat, 13 December 1988," in *Israeli-Palestinian Conflict*, 431. The PNC argued that the Intifada had "turned the aim of Palestinian independence into a feasible program." "*Palestine National Council*: Political Communiqué (September 28, 1991), in *Israel-Arab Reader*, Laqueur and Rubin, eds., 381.

60. "*Israel and PLO:* Agreed Minutes to the Declaration of Principles on Interim Self-Government Arrangements (September 13, 1993)," in *Israel-Arab Reader*, Laqueur and Rubin, eds., 424.

61. "*Israel and PLO:* Cairo Agreement (March 4, 1994)," in *Israel-Arab Reader*, Laqueur and Rubin, eds., 449, 452. Israel accepted the same responsibilities concerning preventing terrorism, crime, and hostilities toward Palestinians.

62. See "*Israel and Palestinian Authority:* Interim Agreement on the West Bank and Gaza Strip (September 28, 1995)," in *Israel-Arab Reader*, Laqueur and Rubin, eds., 502–521; "*Israel and Palestinian Authority,* January 15, 1997," in *Israel-Arab Reader*, 522–523; "*Israel and Palestinian Authority,* October 23, 1998," in *Israel-Arab Reader*, 529–534.

63. "*PLO Chairman Yasir Arafat:* Speech at the Arab Summit (October 21, 2000)," in *Israel-Arab Reader*, Laqueur and Rubin, eds., 557.

64. See Buchanan, *Peace with Justice*, 3.

65. Menachem Begin, as quoted in "*Israeli Prime Minister Menachem Begin:* The Wars of No Alternative and Operation Peace for the Galilee (August 8, 1982)," in *Israel-Arab Reader*, Laqueur and Rubin, eds., 255.

66. Hulme, *Palestinian Terrorism*, 44; Simon Reeve, *One Day in September: the full story of the 1972 Munich Olympics Massacre and the Israeli revenge operation "Wrath of God"* (New York: Arcade Publishing, 2000). Nixon was supportive of such efforts "to crush the fedayeen," as was Kissinger, who expressed particular concern about terrorism's impact on Israeli society: "In early February 1969 Israeli sources reported that 1,288 incidents of sabotage and terrorism had taken place in the year and a half from the Six Day War to the end of 1968: 920 incidents on the Jordanian front, 166 on the Egyptian border, 37 on the cease-fire line with Syria, 35 on the Lebanese border, and 130 in Gaza. Israeli losses for the same period were reported as 234 dead and 765 wounded among military personnel and 47 dead and 330 wounded among civilians—a staggering total for a country with a population of 2.5 million, equivalent to over 20,000 dead and 100,000 wounded for a nation the size of America." Hulme, *Palestinian Terrorism*, 53, 51–52.

67. "*Israeli Prime Minister Menachem Begin*: The Wars of No Alternative and Operation Peace for the Galilee (August 8, 1982)," in *Israel-Arab Reader*, Laqueur and Rubin, eds., 255.
68. "*Israeli Defense Minister Ariel Sharon*: Israel's Security (December 15, 1981)," in *Israel-Arab Reader*, Laqueur and Rubin, eds., 240–243.
69. "*Begin,* August 8, 1982," in *Israel-Arab Reader*, 254–257.
70. Buchanan, *Peace with Justice*, 84.
71. "*Unified National Leadership of the Intifada:* Calls No. 12, 16, and 18 (April–May 1988)," in *Israel-Arab Reader*, Laqueur and Rubin, eds., 337.
72. "*Israeli Prime Minster Yitzhak Rabin:* Speech to Knesset (September 21, 1993)," in *Israel-Arab Reader*, Laqueur and Rubin, eds., 429.
73. He observed that by early 1994, 219 Israelis and 2156 Palestinians had been killed, while 7872 Israelis and 25,000 Palestinians had been wounded. "*Israeli Prime Minister Yitzhak Rabin:* Speech to Knesset (April 18, 1994)," in *Israel-Arab Reader*, Laqueur and Rubin, eds., 462.
74. "*Yitzhak Rabin:* Speech to Knesset (April 18, 1994)," in *Israel-Arab Reader*, 464.
75. See, for example, "*PLO Chairman Yasir Arafat (Abu Ammar):* An Interview (August 1969)," in *Israel-Arab Reader*, Laqueur and Rubin, eds., 137.
76. "Palestine National Assembly, 17 July 1968," in *Israeli-Palestinian Conflict*, Lukacs, ed., 297. See also Hulme, *Palestinian Terrorism*, 39–41.
77. Hulme, *Palestinian Terrorism*, 105. This "status" was symbolized most powerfully by the UN General Assembly's invitation in 1974 to the PLO to participate as an "observer" in its deliberations.
78. "Statement by Prime Minister Yitzhak Rabin, Following the Rabat Conference, 5 November 1974," in *Israeli-Palestinian Conflict*, Lukacs, ed., 189; "Israel's Cabinet, 21 July 1974," in *Israeli-Palestinian Conflict*, Lukacs, ed., 187; "*The Likud Party:* Platform (March 1977)," in *Israel-Arab Reader*, Laqueur and Rubin, eds., 207.
79. "*Israeli Foreign Minister Yitzhak Shamir:* Israel's Role in a Changing Middle East (Spring 1982)," in *Israel-Arab Reader*, Laqueur and Rubin, eds., 246.
80. "Statement by Prime Minister Yitzhak Shamir on Yasser Arafat's Speech to the UN, 13 December 1988," in *Israeli-Palestinian Conflict*, Lukacs, ed., 215–216.
81. "Policy Guidelines, 23 December 1988," in *Israeli-Palestinian Conflict*, Lukacs, ed., 219; "Israeli Foreign Ministry, 15 November 1988," in *Israeli-Palestinian Conflict*, Lukacs, ed., 218. See as well "Shamir, 23 December 1988," in *Israeli-Palestinian Conflict*, Lukacs, ed., 223.
82. See Buchanan, *Peace with Justice*, 91–94; "*Israel and PLO,* September 13, 1993," in *Israel-Arab Reader*, Laqueur and Rubin, eds., 425.
83. "*Rabin,* September 21, 1993," in *Israel-Arab Reader*, 431.
84. Buchanan, *Peace with Justice*, 156. Rabin, observing that "there never were, and there is no settlement without a partner," decried making "proposals with no partner." "*Rabin,* April 18, 1994," in *Israel-Arab Reader*, 462.
85. Buchanan, *Peace with Justice*, 159, 156–158.
86. "*Israeli Prime Minister Ehud Barak:* Presentation of the Government to the Knesset (July 6, 1999)," in *Israel-Arab Reader*, Laqueur and Rubin, eds., 542.
87. "*Israeli Prime Minister Ehud Barak:* Statement after the Camp David Talks (July 25, 2000)," in *Israel-Arab Reader*, Laqueur and Rubin, eds., 555–556. He indicated, "We cannot impose it [peace] upon them. We are ready, and if a partner will be there, there will be peace." "*Barak,* July 25, 2000," in *Israel-Arab Reader*, 555–556.

88. *"Barak,* July 25, 2000," in *Israel-Arab Reader,* 555–556. Sharon focused particular attention on Arafat's continuing support of terrorist violence, including his praise for "the glorious *intifada,* whose waves will only stop with victory." *"Arafat,* October 21, 2000," in *Israel-Arab Reader,* 559.

89. Hulme, *Palestinian Terrorism,* 111.

90. Hulme, *Palestinian Terrorism,* 191, 63, 116.

91. Hulme, *Palestinian Terrorism,* 184.

92. Hulme, *Palestinian Terrorism,* 198.

93. Buchanan, *Peace with Justice,* 34.

94. Hulme, *Palestinian Terrorism,* 199. Although the Arab League Summit at Rabat had declared in October 1974 that the PLO was "the sole legitimate representative of the Palestinian people," ("Arab League Summit Conference Communiqué, Rabat, 29 October 1974," in *Israeli-Palestinian Conflict,* Lukacs, ed., 464.) US officials remained adamant that "[w]e cannot envision or urge a negotiation between two parties as long as one professed to hold the objective of eliminating the other—rather than the objective of negotiating peace with it," while clinging to the "belief that Jordan would be a logical negotiator for the Palestinian related issues." ("Saunders, 12 November 1975," in *Israeli-Palestinian Conflict,* 64.)

95. "Memorandum of Agreement, September 1975," in *Israeli-Palestinian Conflict,* 60. It also indicated that the US would "consult fully and seek to concert its position and strategy at the Geneva Peace Conference on this issue with the Government of Israel."

96. "Carter, 4 January 1978," in *Israeli-Palestinian Conflict,* Lukacs, ed., 71.

97. *"Camp David,* September 17, 1978," in *Israel-Arab Reader,* Laqueur and Rubin, eds., 223–224. Egypt, Israel, and Jordan were given such responsibilities.

98. "Statement by State Department Spokesman Bernard Kalb on the Legitimate Rights of the Palestinian People, 15 February 1985," in *Israeli-Palestinian Conflict,* Lukacs, ed., 82; "Statement by Secretary of State George Shultz on Jordan and the Peace Process, 19 June 1985," in *Israeli-Palestinian Conflict,* Lukacs, ed., 84. See also "Shultz, 16 September 1988," in *Israeli-Palestinian Conflict,* Lukacs, ed., 111; *"U.S. Secretary of State George Shultz:* Congressional Testimony (July 12, 1982)," in *Israel-Arab Reader,* Laqueur and Rubin, eds., 253. Both the 1982 *Reagan Plan* and 1998 *Shultz Plan* highlighted the need for Palestinian involvement in peace efforts. See "Reagan Plan," in *Israeli-Palestinian Conflict,* 76; *"U.S. Secretary of State George Shultz:* Plan (March 6, 1988)," in *Israel-Arab Reader,* Laqueur and Rubin, eds., 322.

99. "Speech by Secretary of State George Shultz before American-Israel Public Affairs Committee, Washington, DC, 17 May 1987," in *Israeli-Palestinian Conflict,* Lukacs, ed., 87–88.

100. "Arafat, 13 December 1988," in *Israeli-Palestinian Conflict,* 431; "Arafat, 15 December 1988," in *Israeli-Palestinian Conflict,* Lukacs, 434.

101. "Shultz, 14 December 1988," in *Israeli-Palestinian Conflict,* Lukacs, ed., 119–120; "Statement by President George Bush on Suspension of the Dialogue Between the US and the PLO, 20 June 1990," in *Israeli-Palestinian Conflict,* Lukacs, ed., 134–35.

102. "Shamir, 5 July 1989," in *Israeli-Palestinian Conflict,* Lukacs, ed., 249. Prime Minister Shamir also indicated that US willingness to talk to the PLO "encroaches on US credibility in our eyes." "Shamir, 5 July 1989," in *Israeli-Palestinian Conflict,* 249.

103. Buchanan, *Peace with Justice,* 70–71.

104. *"Clinton,* January 7, 2001," in *Israel-Arab Reader,* 576.

105. Hulme, *Palestinian Terrorism,* 41–43.

106. Hulme, *Palestinian Terrorism*, 44–46. The "Rejection Front" included the PFLP, PFLP-GC, Palestine Popular Struggle Front, Iraqi Ba'ath, and Arab Liberation Front.

107. *"George Habash:* Interview (August 3, 1974)," in *Israel-Arab Reader*, Laqueur and Rubin, eds., 170, 168; Hulme, *Palestinian Terrorism*, 139.

108. Hulme, *Palestinian Terrorism*, 139–140. These operations included an unsuccessful missile attack on an El Al plane in Nairobi, Kenya, in January 1976 and the hijacking of an Air France plane to Entebbe, Uganda, in June 1976.

109. "Arafat, 13 November 1974," in *Israeli-Palestinian Conflict*, Lukacs, ed., 326–329.

110. "Arafat, 7 November 1985," in *Israeli-Palestinian Conflict*, 370–371. Emphasis added.

111. "Arafat, 13 September 1988," in *Israeli-Palestinian Conflict*, Lukacs, ed., 410.

112. "Arafat, 13 December 1988," in *Israeli-Palestinian Conflict*, 431. He "salute[d]" those "who have been accused by their executioners and colonialists of being terrorists during the battles for the liberation of their land from the yoke of colonialism."

113. "PLO's Central Council, 16 October 1989," in *Israeli-Palestinian Conflict*, Lukacs, ed., 444. Emphasis added.

114. *"Israel and PLO,* September 13, 1993," in *Israel-Arab Reader*, 424. See as well *"Israel and PLO,* March 4, 1994," in *Israel-Arab Reader*, 452; *"Israel and Palestinian Authority,* September 28, 1995," in *Israel-Arab Reader*, 503–504, 512–513; *"Israel and Palestinian Authority,* January 15, 1997," in *Israel-Arab Reader*, 523; *"Israel and Palestinian Authority,* October 23, 1998," in *Israel-Arab Reader*, 530, 532.

115. *"Arafat,* October 21, 2000," in *Israel-Arab Reader*, 557, 559.

116. See Hulme, *Palestinian Terrorism*, 42–43, 46, 140.

117. "Arafat, 13 November 1974," in *Israeli-Palestinian Conflict*, 333.

118. *"PLO Chairman Yasir Arafat:* Speech to Palestine National Council (February 14, 1983)," in *Israel-Arab Reader*, Laqueur and Rubin, eds., 275.

119. *"PLO Chairman Yasir Arafat:* Speech on the Intifada (September 1989)," in *Israel-Arab Reader*, Laqueur and Rubin, eds., 363, 367; *"Arafat,* October 21, 2000," in *Israel-Arab Reader*, 556, 559.

120. "Six-Point Programme, 4 December 1977," in *Israeli-Palestinian Conflict*, 335–336; "The Fourth General Conference of the Palestine Liberation Movement, Fatah, Political Program, 31 May 1980," in *Israeli-Palestinian Conflict*, 346–348.

121. *"Arafat,* September 1989," in *Israel-Arab Reader*, 365. See as well *"PLO Executive Committee:* Statement on the Intifada (April 1988)," in *Israel-Arab Reader*, Laqueur and Rubin, eds., 323–326.

122. See, for example, *"Arafat,* October 21, 2000," in *Israel-Arab Reader*, 556–560.

123. The PLO had been recognized by Arab leaders as the "sole legitimate representative of the Palestinian people," established diplomatic relationships with countries from Africa, Asia, Western Europe, Latin America, and the Soviet bloc, and been invited by the UN General Assembly, International Labour Organization, World Health Organization, and numerous other international bodies to participate in their work as an "official observer." Hulme, *Palestinian Terrorism*, 135.

124. Hulme, *Palestinian Terrorism*, 139, 135–136.

125. "Arafat, 13 December 1988," in *Israeli-Palestinian Conflict*, 420–433; *"Israel and PLO,* September 13, 1993," in *Israel-Arab Reader*, 424–425.

126. "Address by the Labor Party's Leader Shimon Peres Proposing a Non-Confidence Motion to the Knesset, 15 March 1990," in *Israeli-Palestinian Conflict*, Lukacs, ed., 254.

127. *"Israeli Prime Minister Yitzhak Rabin:* Inaugural Speech (July 13, 1992)," in *Israel-Arab Reader*, Laqueur and Rubin, eds., 403–407.

128. *"Israel and PLO:* Declaration of Principles on Interim Self-Government Arrangements ['The Oslo Agreement'] (September 13, 1993)," in *Israel-Arab Reader*, Laqueur and Rubin, eds., 413–422; *"Israel and PLO:* Agreed Minutes, September 13, 1993," in *Israel-Arab Reader*, 422–425. See as well *"Israel and PLO:* March 4, 1994," in *Israel-Arab Reader*, Laqueur and Rubin, eds., 442–455.

129. *"Barak,* July 6, 1999," in *Israel-Arab Reader*, 542; *"Israeli Government:* Basic Guidelines (July 1999)," in *Israel-Arab Reader*, Laqueur and Rubin, eds., 544.

130. *"Israeli Prime Minister Ehud Barak:* Leaving for the Camp David Talks (July 10, 2000)," in *Israel-Arab Reader*, Laqueur and Rubin, eds., 550. Rabin had made a similar commitment concerning Israeli-Syrian negotiations. See *"Rabin,* April 18, 1994," in *Israel-Arab Reader*, 461.

131. While Fatah's principle of "harmonization" sought to encourage cooperation among the fedayeen, it precluded imposing a common political/military strategy on non-Fatah actors. Kissinger, recognizing the "severe internal divisions" among the PLO's "many divergent elements," observed, "Even should some PLO leader accept Resolution 242 and the legal right of Israel to exist . . . the dynamics of the movement made it unlikely that such moderation could be maintained indefinitely." Hulme, *Palestinian Terrorism*, 41, 63, 247, n.308.

132. Arafat rejected the 1968 *Palestinian National Covenant*'s position that armed struggle was "the only way to liberate Palestine," arguing that "armed struggle complements political struggle" and insisting that "the PLO will struggle by every means, the foremost (i.e. *not the only one*) of which is armed struggle to liberate Palestinian land." "Palestine National Covenant, 1968," in *Israeli-Palestinian Conflict*, Lukacs, ed., 292; *"Arafat:* [February 14, 1983]," in *Israel-Arab Reader*, 275; Hulme, *Palestinian Terrorism*, 45. Emphasis added.

133. Arafat, in opposition to Rejection Front members, persuaded the PNC to accept a "mini-state" formula. Hulme, *Palestinian Terrorism*, 45.

134. Hulme, *Palestinian Terrorism*, 41–46.

135. See, for example, "Statement by the PFLP Announcing its Withdrawal from the Executive Committee of the PLO, 26 September 1974," in *Israeli-Palestinian Conflict*, Lukacs, ed., 312–313; *"Habash:* (August 3, 1974)," in *Israel-Arab Reader*, 166–171.

136. Hulme, *Palestinian Terrorism*, 138, 139.

137. "Covenant of Hamas," in *Israeli-Palestinian Conflict*, 400, 401, 403.

138. "Arafat, 13 September 1988," in *Israeli-Palestinian Conflict*, 403–411; "Arafat, 13 December 1988," in *Israeli-Palestinian Conflict*, 420–433.

139. See "Covenant of Hamas, 18 August 1988," in *Israeli-Palestinian Conflict*, 402.

140. *"Mahmoud Darwish:* Resigning from the PLO Executive Committee (August 1993)," in *Israel-Arab Reader*, Laqueur and Rubin, eds., 411–413.

141. *"Hani al-Hasan:* Opposition to the Israel-PLO Accord (October 9, 1993)," in *Israel-Arab Reader*, Laqueur and Rubin, eds., 435–436.

142. *"Arafat,* October 21, 2000," in *Israel-Arab Reader*, 559, 556.

143. See "UNSCR 242, 22 November 1967," in *Israeli-Palestinian Conflict*, 1–2.

144. *"Camp David,* September 17, 1978," in *Israel-Arab Reader*, 222–227.

145. Limited progress had occurred through the *Interim Agreement on the West Bank and Gaza Strip* (28 September 1995), *Hebron Accords* (15 January 1997), *Wye River Memorandum* (23 October 1998), and Camp David Talks (July 2000), although significant differences remained concerning such "final status" issues as Jerusalem, refu-

gees, settlements, and borders. See *"Israel and Palestinian Authority,* September 28, 1995," in *Israel-Arab Reader,* 502–521; *"Israel and Palestinian Authority,* January 15, 1997," in *Israel-Arab Reader,* 522–523; *"Israel and Palestinian Authority,* October 23, 1998," in *Israel-Arab Reader,* 529–534.

Context—Substance

1. See *Road Map*.
2. See Craig and George, *Force and Statecraft,* 170, for discussion of the "optimizing" negotiation strategy.
3. Hulme, *Palestinian Terrorism,* 36.
4. "Statement Issued by Israel's Cabinet Insisting that Jordan Represents the Palestinians in Negotiations, 21 July 1974," in *Israeli-Palestinian Conflict,* 187. See as well Hulme, *Palestinian Terrorism,* 234, n.154.
5. "Fundamental Policy Guidelines of the Government of Israel as Approved by the Knesset, 5 August 1981," in *Israeli-Palestinian Conflict,* Lukacs, ed., 199.
6. *"Shamir:* Spring 1982," in *Israel-Arab Reader,* 244. Emphasis in original. See as well, "Text of Israel's Communiqué on the Reagan Plan, 2 September 1982," in *Israeli-Palestinian Conflict,* Lukacs, ed., 202; "Basic Policy Guidelines of the Government of Israel, 13 September 1984," in *Israeli-Palestinian Conflict,* Lukacs, ed., 204.
7. *"Palestine National Council:* Declaration of Independence (November 15, 1988)," in *Israel-Arab Reader,* Laqueur and Rubin, eds., 354–358; "Statement by Secretary of State George Shultz on Dialogue with the PLO, 14 December 1988," in *Israeli-Palestinian Conflict,* 119; "Statement by President Ronald Reagan on Relations with the PLO, 14 December 1988," in *Israeli-Palestinian Conflict,* Lukacs, ed., 120.
8. "Basic Policy Guidelines of the Government of Israel, 23 December 1988," in *Israeli-Palestinian Conflict,* 219; "Statement by the Israeli Foreign Ministry on the Decisions of the 19th Palestine National Council, 15 November 1988," in *Israeli-Palestinian Conflict,* 218.
9. "Address by Prime Minister Yitzhak Shamir to the Knesset, 23 December 1988," in *Israeli-Palestinian Conflict,* Lukacs, ed., 221. See as well, "A Peace Initiative by the Government of Israel, 14 May 1989," in *Israeli-Palestinian Conflict,* Lukacs, ed., 236. Expressing support for Camp David's autonomy approach, Shamir vowed, "yes; but never an Arab-Palestinian state!" "Address by Prime Minister Yitzhak Shamir to the Likud Party's Central Committee, 5 July 1989," in *Israeli-Palestinian Conflict,* Lukacs, ed., 249.
10. Buchanan, *Peace with Justice,* 71.
11. *"Rabin,* July 13, 1992," in *Israel-Arab Reader,* 404.
12. *"Barak,* July 10, 2000," in *Israel-Arab Reader,* 550–551.
13. "The Palestine National Covenant, 1968," in *Israeli-Palestinian Conflict,* 294, 292. Zionism was characterized as "a political movement organically related to world Imperialism," while the "Palestinian personality" was described as "an innate, persistent characteristic that does not disappear." "The Palestine National Covenant, 1968," in *Israeli-Palestinian Conflict,* 294, 292.
14. "Statement Issued by the Palestine Liberation Organization Rejecting UN Resolution 242, 23 November 1967," in *Israeli-Palestinian Conflict,* Lukacs, ed., 290; *"Fatah:* The Seven Points (January 1969)," in *Israel-Arab Reader,* Laqueur and Rubin, eds., 130–131.

15. "Palestine National Assembly Political Resolutions, 17 July 1968," in *Israeli-Palestinian Conflict*, 299, 298, 301. See as well "Palestine National Council, Political Program, 12 January 1973," in *Israeli-Palestinian Conflict*, Lukacs, ed., 303–304.

16. Hulme, *Palestinian Terrorism*, 45.

17. See, for example, "Statements by General Secretary of the PDFLP Naif Hawatmah Defending the Establishment of a Palestinian National Authority in Territories Liberated from Israeli Occupation, 24 February 1974," in *Israeli-Palestinian Conflict*, Lukacs, ed., 307–308.

18. "Palestine National Council, Political Program, 8 June 1974," in *Israeli-Palestinian Conflict*, Lukacs, ed., 309.

19. *"George Habash:* Interview (August 3, 1974)," in *Israel-Arab Reader*, Laqueur and Rubin, eds., 168; "Six-Point Programme Agreed to by the Various Palestinian Organizations Calling for the Formation of a 'Steadfastness and Confrontation Front' in Opposition to Sadat's Negotiations with Israel, 4 December 1977," in *Israeli-Palestinian Conflict*, 335–336.

20. "Letter from PLO Executive Committee to Delegate Walter Fauntroy, 5 October 1979," in *Israeli-Palestinian Conflict*, 345. Emphasis added. See also Hulme, *Palestinian Terrorism*, 45.

21. "Statement by the PLO's Executive Committee on the Amman Accord, 19 February 1985," in *Israeli-Palestinian Conflict*, Lukacs, ed., 369.

22. "Declaration by Yasser Arafat on Terrorism, Cairo, 7 November 1985," in *Israeli-Palestinian Conflict*, 370.

23. "PLO view: Prospects of a Palestinian-Israeli Settlement, by PLO Spokesman Bassam Abu-Sharif, 18 June 1988," in *Israeli-Palestinian Conflict*, Lukacs, ed., 397–399.

24. "Yasser Arafat's Geneva Press Statement, 15 December 1988," in *Israeli-Palestinian Conflict*, 434. See as well "Address by Yasser Arafat to the UN General Assembly, Geneva, 13 December 1988," in *Israeli-Palestinian Conflict*, 421–433; "Letter Sent by Yasser Arafat to the Emergency World Jewish Leadership Peace Conference, Jerusalem, 17 February 1990," in *Israeli-Palestinian Conflict*, Lukacs, ed., 450.

25. "Address of Yasser Arafat to the European Parliament, 13 September 1988," in *Israeli-Palestinian Conflict*, 408; "Arafat to UN, Geneva, 1988," in *Israeli-Palestinian Conflict*, 424; "Arafat, Geneva Press, 1988," in *Israeli-Palestinian Conflict*, 434.

26. "Palestine National Council, Political Communiqué, Algiers, 15 November 1988," in *Israeli-Palestinian Conflict*, 419; "*Israel and PLO*, September 13, 1993," in *Israel-Arab Reader*, 424.

27. Hulme, *Palestinian Terrorism*, 145, 61, 52–53.

28. "President Jimmy Carter, Statement on Recognition of Palestinians, 4 January 1978," in *Israeli-Palestinian Conflict*, 71; "Joint Statement," in *Israeli-Palestinian Conflict*, 16; "President Jimmy Carter, on Middle East Peace, 16 March 1977," in *Israeli-Palestinian Conflict*, Lukacs, ed., 70.

29. "*Camp David,* September 17, 1978," in *Israel-Arab Reader*, 224. Such "autonomy" was not to include control over borders or security.

30. "Reagan Peace Plan," in *Israeli-Palestinian Conflict*, 73, 75. It advocated a five year transition period "to prove to the Palestinians that they can run their own affairs, and that such Palestinian autonomy poses no threat to Israel's security." "Reagan Peace Plan," in *Israeli-Palestinian Conflict*, 76.

31. "Text of 'Talking Points' Sent to Prime Minister Menachem Begin by President Ronald Reagan, 8 September 1982," in *Israeli-Palestinian Conflict*, 79; "Reagan Peace Plan," in *Israeli-Palestinian Conflict*, 76.

32. "Arrival Statements by Secretary of State George Shultz During his Visit to the Middle East, Cairo, 3 June 1988; Amman, 4 June 1988; Tel Aviv, 5 June 1988," in *Israeli-Palestinian Conflict*, Lukacs, ed., 109; "Address by Secretary of State George Shultz Before the Washington Institute for Near East Policy, 16 September 1988," in *Israeli-Palestinian Conflict*, 112–114.

33. "Statement by President George Bush Following his Meeting with Prime Minister Yitzhak Shamir, Washington, DC, 6 April 1989," in *Israeli-Palestinian Conflict*, Lukacs, ed., 122–123.

34. "Address by Secretary of State James Baker Before the American-Israel Public Affairs Committee, 22 May 1989," in *Israeli-Palestinian Conflict*, Lukacs, ed., 126.

35. "U.S. Letter, October 18, 1991," in *Israel-Arab Reader*, 387.

36. "*Clinton,* December 23, 2000," in *Israel-Arab Reader*, 564; "*Clinton,* January 7, 2001," in *Israel-Arab Reader*, 577.

37. "The Nine-Point Peace Plan, Israel's Foreign Minister Abba Eban, 8 October 1968," in *Israeli-Palestinian Conflict*, Lukacs, ed., 173, 178, 174. Eban echoed Prime Minister Eshkol's argument following the 1967 War that the ceasefire lines had created a "constant threat to Israel's security." "Principles Guiding Israel's Policy in the Aftermath of the June 1967 War, Prime Minister Levi Eshkol, 9 August 1967," in *Israeli-Palestinian Conflict*, Lukacs, ed., 171.

38. "Israel's Foreign Minister Abba Eban, Knesset Statement on Occupied Territories, 13 May 1969," in *Israeli-Palestinian Conflict*, Lukacs, ed., 181.

39. "*Israeli Prime Minister Golda Meir:* Statement in the Knesset (October 23, 1973)," in *Israel-Arab Reader*, Laqueur and Rubin, eds., 156.

40. "The Allon Plan, Article by Israeli Foreign Minister Yigal Allon Reiterating his Plan for Peace, October 1976," in *Israeli-Palestinian Conflict*, Lukacs, ed., 190–91, 195.

41. "*Shamir,* Spring 1982," in *Israel-Arab Reader*, 245.

42. "*Shamir and al-Shafi,* October 21, 1991," in *Israel-Arab Reader*, 392–393. Emphasis added.

43. "*Rabin,* April 18, 1994," in *Israel-Arab Reader*, 461; "*Barak,* July 6, 1999," in *Israel-Arab Reader*, 542; "*Israeli Government,* July 1999," in *Israel-Arab Reader*, 544; "*Barak,* July 10, 2000," in *Israel-Arab Reader*, 550.

44. "President Johnson, Statement on Principles for Peace, 19 June 1967," in *Israeli-Palestinian Conflict*, Lukacs, ed., 54. While he argued that "the political independence and territorial integrity of all the states in the area must be assured," he observed, "We are not the ones to say where other nations should draw lines between them that will assure each the greatest security." "Johnson, 19 June 1967," in *Israeli-Palestinian Conflict*, 54.

45. "The Rogers Plan, 9 December 1969," in *Israeli-Palestinian Conflict*, Lukacs, ed., 58–59.

46. Hulme, *Palestinian Terrorism*, 129. He observed, while "(m)ost Americans are willing to take great risks to preserve the state of Israel . . . they are not willing to take great risks to preserve Israeli conquests." Hulme, *Palestinian Terrorism*, 131.

47. Hulme, *Palestinian Terrorism*, 17. He noted, "Had we wished to pursue the 1967 boundaries, we could have done it much more easily without any need for ambiguity. We could have joined the EEC in October 1973 and done it directly. Instead we decided upon the step-by-step approach to avoid just this and ease the pressure on Israel." Hulme, *Palestinian Terrorism*, 132–133.

48. Hulme, *Palestinian Terrorism,* 122. Kissinger observed that Israeli inflexibility during the 1975 Egyptian-Israeli negotiations prompted Ford to consider "making America's ultimate threat" of proposing a "comprehensive peace plan, including borders, and present it publicly." However, sensitive to the "intolerable situation that existed immedi-

ately before the outbreak of the Six-Day War," Ford also expressed the belief that "Israel should not withdraw from a single inch of occupied territory unless there is a real peace treaty and credible evidence that the Arabs will normalize relations." Hulme, *Palestinian Terrorism*, 128, 122.

49. "'Toward Peace in the Middle East,' Brookings Institution Report, December 1975," in *Israeli-Palestinian Conflict*, Lukacs, ed., 66; "Carter, 16 March 1977," in *Israeli-Palestinian Conflict*, 70.

50. "Reagan Peace Plan, 1 September 1982," in *Israeli-Palestinian Conflict*, 75–77.

51. "Shultz, 16 September 1988," in *Israeli-Palestinian Conflict*, 112.

52. "US Senators' Letter to Secretary of State George Shultz, 3 March 1988," in *Israeli-Palestinian Conflict*, Lukacs, ed., 102.

53. "U.S. Letter, October 18, 1991," in *Israel-Arab Reader*, 385, 387; "James Baker, 22 May 1989," in *Israeli-Palestinian Conflict*, 125.

54. "*Clinton,* December 23, 2000," in *Israel-Arab Reader*, 562; "*Clinton,* January 7, 2001," in *Israel-Arab Reader*, 577.

55. "Allon Plan," in *Israeli-Palestinian Conflict*, 196; "The 'Galili Plan'—Statement by Government Ministers of the Israeli Labor Party on Proposed Policy in the Occupied Territories, August 1973," in *Israeli-Palestinian Conflict*, Lukacs, ed., 186.

56. "Likud, March 1977," in *Israel-Arab Reader*, 206, 207.

57. "*Begin,* December 28, 1977," in *Israel-Arab Reader*, Laqueur and Rubin, eds., 219–220. See as well Buchanan, *Peace with Justice*, 78.

58. "Policy Guidelines, 5 August 1981," in *Israeli-Palestinian Conflict*, 199. See as well "Policy Guidelines, 13 September 1984," in *Israeli-Palestinian Conflict*, 204, and "Policy Guidelines, 23 December 1988," in *Israeli-Palestinian Conflict*, 219, that discussed efforts to establish additional settlements.

59. "*Sharon,* December 15, 1981," in *Israel-Arab Reader*, 242.

60. "*Shamir,* Spring 1982," in *Israel-Arab Reader*, 245.

61. "Shamir, 23 December 1988," in *Israeli-Palestinian Conflict*, 221–222. See as well "Statement by Prime Minister Yitzhak Shamir on the Israeli Peace Initiative," 17 May 1989, in *Israeli-Palestinian Conflict*, Lukacs, ed., 243, where Shamir, noting the 80,000 settlers living in Judea and Samaria in 1989, observed, "may they multiply." In addition, see "Shamir, 5 July 1989," in *Israeli-Palestinian Conflict*, 249, where Shamir promised that "any Jew who so wishes will be able to settle anywhere throughout Eretz-Israel . . . [and] will enjoy support from and protection by the Government of Israel."

62. See "Address by The Labor Party's Leader Shimon Peres Proposing a Non-Confidence Motion to the Knesset, 15 March 1990," in *Israeli-Palestinian Conflict*, Lukacs, ed., 257; "*Rabin,* July 13, 1992," in *Israel-Arab Reader*, 406.

63. "*Rabin,* September 21, 1993," in *Israel-Arab Reader*, 432.

64. "*Israeli Government,* July 1999," in *Israel-Arab Reader*, 545.

65. "*Barak,* July 10, 2000," in *Israel-Arab Reader*, 550. His position mirrored that of Shimon Peres, who had observed previously, "We [the Labor Party] never suggested that existing settlements in the territories be evacuated." "Peres, 15 March 1990," in *Israeli-Palestinian Conflict*, 257.

66. "Palestine National Council, 12 January 1973," in *Israeli-Palestinian Conflict*, 303, 305.

67. "*West Bank-Gaza Palestinian Leaders:* Fourteen Points (January 14, 1988)," in *Israel-Arab Reader*, Laqueur and Rubin, eds., 319; "Arafat, 13 December 1988," in *Israeli-Palestinian Conflict*, 429; "Palestine National Council, 15 November 1988," in *Israeli-Palestinian Conflict*, 419.

68. *"Israeli Prime Minister Yitzhak Rabin, PLO Chairman Yasir Arafat, and Israeli Foreign Minister Shimon Peres:* Speeches Accepting the Nobel Peace Prize (December 10, 1994)," in *Israel-Arab Reader*, Laqueur and Rubin, eds., 494; *"Israel and Palestinian Authority,* September 28, 1995," in *Israel-Arab Reader*, 520.

69. *"Palestine National Council:* Political Communiqué (September 28, 1991)," in *Israel-Arab Reader*, Laqueur and Rubin, eds., 382.

70. See *"Barak,* July 10, 2000," in *Israel-Arab Reader*, 550; *"The Palestinian Negotiating Team:* Remarks and Questions Regarding the Clinton Plan (January 2, 2001)," in *Israel-Arab Reader*, Laqueur and Rubin, eds., 568–569.

71. "Ambassador William W. Scranton, Statements on Occupied Territories, 23 March 1976," in *Israeli-Palestinian Conflict*, Lukacs, ed., 68, 69. Article 49 of the *Fourth Geneva Convention* states, "The Occupying Power shall not deport or transfer parts of its own civilian population into the territory it occupies." Should there have been any uncertainty concerning US policy, Scranton declared that an occupying power was to "maintain the occupied area as intact and unaltered as possible, without interfering with the customary life of the area." ("Scranton, 23 March 1976," in *Israeli-Palestinian Conflict*, 69.) Kissinger similarly had observed, "US policy has been not to accept any changes in the Occupied Territories because their future is an issue to be resolved through negotiations and not unilaterally by one side or the other." Hulme, *Palestinian Terrorism*, 273, n.699.

72. Hulme, *Palestinian Terrorism*, 121, 130–131.

73. "Reagan Peace Plan," in *Israeli-Palestinian Conflict*, 76.

74. "Statement by President Ronald Reagan on the Establishment of New Israeli Settlements, 27 August 1983," in *Israeli-Palestinian Conflict*, Lukacs, ed., 80; "Shultz, 16 September 1988," in *Israeli-Palestinian Conflict*, 113; "Talking Points," in *Israeli-Palestinian Conflict*, 78.

75. "Statement by President George Bush on Jewish Settlements in the West Bank and East Jerusalem, 3 March 1990," in *Israeli-Palestinian Conflict*, Lukacs, ed., 133.

76. "U.S. Letter, October 18, 1991," in *Israel-Arab Reader*, 387–388; "Baker, 22 May 1989," in *Israeli-Palestinian Conflict*, 128.

77. *"Clinton,* January 7, 2001," in *Israel-Arab Reader*, 576; *"Clinton,* December 23, 2000," in *Israel-Arab Reader*, 562.

78. *"UNGA:* Resolution 194, December 11, 1948," in *Israel-Arab Reader*, 85.

79. "Palestine National Council, 8 June 1974," in *Israeli-Palestinian Conflict*, 308; "Six-Point Programme," in *Israeli-Palestinian Conflict*, 335.

80. "Statement, PLO, 23 November 1967," in *Israeli-Palestinian Conflict*, 290–291; "Palestine National Council, Political and Organizational Program, 23 January 1979," in *Israeli-Palestinian Conflict*, 339, 340; "PLO, 5 October 1979," in *Israeli-Palestinian Conflict*, 344.

81. "Palestinian National Council, Political Statement, 21 April 1981," in *Israeli-Palestinian Conflict*, Lukacs, ed., 354; "Palestinian National Council Political Resolutions, 22 February 1983," in *Israeli-Palestinian Conflict*, Lukacs, ed., 361; "Palestine National Council, Political Statement, Amman, 29 November 1984," in *Israeli-Palestinian Conflict*, Lukacs, ed., 366; "Palestine National Council, Resolutions of the Political Committee, Algiers, 26 April 1987," in *Israeli-Palestinian Conflict*, Lukacs, ed., 385; "Palestine National Council, 15 November 1988," in *Israeli-Palestinian Conflict*, 418, 420.

82. *"PLO Executive Committee:* April 1988," in *Israel-Arab Reader*, 325; "PLO's Executive Committee, 19 February 1985," in *Israeli-Palestinian Conflict*, 369; *"Unified*

National Leadership: April–May 1988," in *Israel-Arab Reader*, Laqueur and Rubin, eds., 332–333.

83. "Arafat, 13 December 1988," in *Israeli-Palestinian Conflict*, 425.

84. "Fateh Fifth General Congress, Political Program, 8 August 1989," in *Israeli-Palestinian Conflict*, Lukacs, ed., 441.

85. "Statement by the PLO's Central Council, Baghdad, 16 October 1989," in *Israeli-Palestinian Conflict*, 446. See as well the PNC's declaration in September 1991 that the refugee issue must be resolved "in accordance with UN resolutions, especially Resolution 194." *"Palestine National Council,* September 28, 1991," in *Israel-Arab Reader*, 382.

86. "Arafat, 17 February 1990," in *Israeli-Palestinian Conflict*, 451.

87. *"Palestinian Negotiating Team,* January 2, 2001," in *Israel-Arab Reader*, 570–571.

88. "Principles, Eshkol, 1967," in *Israeli-Palestinian Conflict*, 171; "The Nine-Point Peace Plan, Israel's Foreign Minister Abba Eban, 8 October 1968," in *Israeli-Palestinian Conflict*, Lukacs, ed., 179.

89. See, for example, *"Israeli Government:* Fundamental Policy Guidelines (August 5, 1981)," in *Israel-Arab Reader*, Laqueur and Rubin, eds., 233–234; "Policy Guidelines, 13 September 1984," in *Israeli-Palestinian Conflict*, 203–204; "Policy Guidelines, 23 December 1988," in *Israeli-Palestinian Conflict*, 218–219. Neither Camp David's "framework" for addressing "the Palestinian problem in all its aspects" (*"Camp David,* September 17, 1978," in *Israel-Arab Reader*, 222–225) nor such 1980s peace initiatives as the *Reagan Plan* prompted Israeli leaders to revisit refugee policy.

90. *"Rabin,* July 13, 1992," in *Israel-Arab Reader*, 404.

91. See *"Barak,* July 10, 2000," in *Israel-Arab Reader*, 550 (Emphasis added.); *"Barak,* July 25, 2000," in *Israel-Arab Reader*, 555.

92. "Rogers Plan," in *Israeli-Palestinian Conflict*, 59. He stressed the need for a "just settlement" of the refugee problem, without which there could be "no real peace," and advocated United Nations Relief and Works Agency (UNRWA) assistance to alleviate "bitterness and frustration" and "channel the Palestinian movement toward the constructive goals of peace and development." Hulme, *Palestinian Terrorism*, 51, 57.

93. Hulme, *Palestinian Terrorism*, 51.

94. "Carter, 16 March 1977," in *Israeli-Palestinian Conflict*, 70; "Carter, 4 January 1978," in *Israeli-Palestinian Conflict*, 71; *"Camp David,* September 17, 1978," in *Israel-Arab Reader*, 222–227.

95. "Reagan Plan," in *Israeli-Palestinian Conflict*, 74–75. Vernon Walters, U.S. Ambassador to the UN, emphasized that "Palestinian demands will have to accommodate the reality of Israel's existence and security needs." "Address by Ambassador Vernon A. Walters to the 43rd Session of the UN General Assembly, Geneva, 14 December 1988," in *Israeli-Palestinian Conflict*, Lukacs, ed., 118–119.

96. Indeed, "refugees" was not included as a "final status issue" in talking points sent by Reagan to Menachem Begin and key Arab leaders immediately following the *Reagan Plan*'s launch. "Talking Points, 8 September 1982," in *Israeli-Palestinian Conflict*, 78–80.

97. "Bush, 6 April 1989," in *Israeli-Palestinian Conflict*, 123; *"U.S. Letter,* October 18, 1991," in *Israel-Arab Reader*, 385. See as well comments by Secretary of State James Baker in "Baker, 22 May 1989," in *Israeli-Palestinian Conflict*, 123–129.

98. *"U.S. President Bill Clinton:* Speech to the Palestinian Leadership (December 14, 1998)," in *Israel-Arab Reader*, Laqueur and Rubin, eds., 537, 540.

99. *"Clinton,* December 23, 2000," in *Israel-Arab Reader*, 564.

100. "*Clinton,* January 7, 2001," in *Israel-Arab Reader,* 578, 577; "*Clinton,* December 23, 2000," in *Israel-Arab Reader,* 563.

101. "Nine-Point Plan," in *Israeli-Palestinian Conflict,* 179; "Israel's Foreign Minister Abba Eban, Knesset Statement on Occupied Territories, 13 May 1969," in *Israeli-Palestinian Conflict,* 181.

102. "Allon Plan," in *Israeli-Palestinian Conflict,* 194. Emphasis in original. See also the comments of Menachem Begin, who noted the need to insure "free admission for all believers to the places sacred to them." "*Israeli Prime Minister Menachem Begin:* Autonomy Plan for the West Bank and Gaza Strip (December 28, 1977)," in *Israel-Arab Reader,* 219.

103. "Law Enacted by Israel's Knesset Proclaiming Jerusalem the Capital of Israel, 29 July 1980," in *Israeli-Palestinian Conflict,* Lukacs, ed., 198.

104. "Shamir, 5 July 1989," in *Israeli-Palestinian Conflict,* 250–251; "Shamir, 23 December 1988," in *Israeli-Palestinian Conflict,* 222.

105. "Peres, 15 March 1990," in *Israeli-Palestinian Conflict,* 259.

106. Only such minor parties as Hadash and the Arab Democratic Party advocated repartitioning Jerusalem. See "The Arab Democratic Party Platform, 1988," in *Israeli-Palestinian Conflict,* Lukacs, ed., 271; "The Hadash Party Platform, 1988," in *Israeli-Palestinian Conflict,* Lukacs, ed., 272–273.

107. See "Policy Guidelines, 5 August 1981," in *Israeli-Palestinian Conflict,* 200; "Policy Guidelines, 13 September 1984," in *Israeli-Palestinian Conflict,* 203; "Policy Guidelines, 23 December 1988," in *Israeli-Palestinian Conflict,* 218–219.

108. "Address by Prime Minister Yitzhak Shamir at the Knesset in Response to the Non-Confidence Motion, 15 March 1990," in *Israeli-Palestinian Conflict,* Lukacs, ed., 266. See as well "Shamir, 5 July 1989," in *Israeli-Palestinian Conflict,* 250, 251; "Policy Guidelines, 5 August 1981," in *Israeli-Palestinian Conflict,* 200; "Israel's Communiqué," in *Israeli-Palestinian Conflict,* Lukacs, ed., 200–201; "Basic Policy Guidelines of the Government of Israel, 10 June 1990," in *Israeli-Palestinian Conflict,* Lukacs, ed., 270.

109. "*Shamir and al-Shafi,* October 21, 1991," in *Israel-Arab Reader,* 389.

110. "*Rabin,* July 13, 1992," in *Israel-Arab Reader,* 406. Rabin noted his particular commitment to Jerusalem, as one of its native sons. "*Rabin,* July 13, 1992," in *Israel-Arab Reader,* 406.

111. "*U.S. President Bill Clinton, Israeli Prime Minister Yitzhak Rabin, and PLO Chairman Yasir Arafat:* Speeches at the Signing of the Israeli-PLO Declaration of Principles (September 13, 1993)," in *Israel-Arab Reader,* Laqueur and Rubin, eds., 426; "*Rabin,* September 21, 1993," in *Israel-Arab Reader,* 431–432. He highlighted the "eternalness of Jerusalem as Israel's capital." "*Rabin,* September 21, 1993," in *Israel-Arab Reader,* 431.

112. See *Oslo* (1993), *Cairo* (1994), the *Interim Agreement on the West Bank and Gaza* (1995), *Hebron* (1997) and *Wye River* (1998).

113. "*Barak,* July 10, 2000," in *Israel-Arab Reader,* 550; "*Israeli Government,* July 1999," in *Israel-Arab Reader,* 545.

114. "*Barak,* July 25, 2000," in *Israel-Arab Reader,* Laqueur and Rubin, eds., 554–55.

115. "*PLO Executive Committee,* April 1988," in *Israel-Arab Reader,* 325.

116. "Palestine National Covenant," in *Israeli-Palestinian Conflict,* 294, 292.

117. "Palestine National Assembly, 17 July 1968," in *Israeli-Palestinian Conflict,* 298, 296.

118. "Speech by Yasser Arafat to the UN General Assembly, 13 November 1974," in *Israeli-Palestinian Conflict,* 327, 331.

119. "Statement Issued by the Government of Israel Responding to the US-USSR Joint Declaration on the Middle East, 1 October 1977," in *Israeli-Palestinian Conflict*, Lukacs, ed., 198; "Statement by the West Bank National Conference, Beit Hanina, 1 October 1978," in *Israeli-Palestinian Conflict*, Lukacs, ed., 339.

120. "Palestinian National Council, 21 April 1981," in *Israeli-Palestinian Conflict*, Lukacs, ed., 351–352.

121. *"Arafat,* February 14, 1983," in *Israel-Arab Reader*, 274.

122. "PLO's Executive Committee, 19 February 1985," in *Israeli-Palestinian Conflict*, 369; "PLO Executive Committee Statement, 7 March 1986," in *Israeli-Palestinian Conflict*, 383.

123. See, for example, *"West Bank-Gaza Palestinian Leaders,* January 14, 1988," in *Israel-Arab Reader*, 317–319; "The Covenant of Hamas, 18 August 1988," in *Israeli-Palestinian Conflict*, 400–403.

124. "The Palestinian Declaration of Independence, 15 November 1988," in *Israeli-Palestinian Conflict*, Lukacs, ed., 413; "Palestine National Council, 15 November 1988," in *Israeli-Palestinian Conflict*, 419–420.

125. *"Arafat,* September 1989," in *Israel-Arab Reader*, 367. See as well statements by Fatah ("Fateh, 8 August 1989," in *Israeli-Palestinian Conflict*, 441–444) and the PLO's Central Council ("PLO's Central Council, 16 October 1989," in *Israeli-Palestinian Conflict*, 444–447).

126. *"Palestine National Council,* September 28, 1991," in *Israel-Arab Reader*, 382, 384.

127. *"Shamir and al-Shafi,* October 21, 1991," in *Israel-Arab Reader*, 400, 395.

128. *"Israel and PLO:* Declaration, September 13, 1993," in *Israel-Arab Reader*, 418. See also *"Israel and Palestinian Authority,* September 28, 1995," in *Israel-Arab Reader*, 505.

129. *"Barak,* July 25, 2000," in *Israel-Arab Reader*, 555.

130. *"PLO Chairman Yasir Arafat:* Speech for Fatah's Anniversary (December 31, 1992)," in *Israel-Arab Reader*, Laqueur and Rubin, eds., 408; *"Palestinian Negotiating Team,* January 2, 2001," in *Israel-Arab Reader*, 567, 570.

131. "Johnson, 19 June 1967," in *Israeli-Palestinian Conflict*, 55.

132. "Scranton, 23 March 1976," in *Israeli-Palestinian Conflict*, 68.

133. "Rogers Plan," in *Israeli-Palestinian Conflict*, 59–60. See also Hulme, *Palestinian Terrorism*, 220–221, n.23.

134. "Scranton, 23 March 1976," in *Israeli-Palestinian Conflict*, 68–69.

135. "U.S. Letter, October 18, 1991," in *Israel-Arab Reader*, 386–387; "Reagan Plan," in *Israeli-Palestinian Conflict*, 77; "Bush, 3 March 1990," in *Israeli-Palestinian Conflict*, 133. They likewise agreed that "Palestinians of east Jerusalem should be able to participate by voting in the elections for an interim self-governing authority." "U.S. Letter, October 18, 1991," in *Israel-Arab Reader*, 387.

136. *"Clinton,* January 7, 2001," in *Israel-Arab Reader*, 578; *"Clinton,* December 14, 1998," in *Israel-Arab Reader*, 540; "Address by Prime Minister Yitzhak Shamir at the Knesset in Response to the Non-Confidence Motion, 15 March 1990," in *Israeli-Palestinian Conflict*, Lukacs, ed., 266.

137. *"Clinton,* December 23, 2000," in *Israel-Arab Reader*, 563; *"Clinton,* January 7, 2001," in *Israel-Arab Reader*, 578–579.

Context—Terrorism

1. Buchanan, *Peace with Justice*, 53.

2. "'This is the Plan,' Shultz's Peace Proposal, 18 March 1988," in *Israeli-Palestinian Conflict*, 104.
3. Buchanan, *Peace with Justice*, 25, 11, 14.
4. Hulme, *Palestinian Terrorism*, 11, ii.
5. Hulme, *Palestinian Terrorism*, 213–214, 11.
6. Hulme, *Palestinian Terrorism*, 215.
7. Hulme, *Palestinian Terrorism*, 215–216.
8. Hulme, *Palestinian Terrorism*, 216, 12, 217.
9. Hulme, *Palestinian Terrorism*, 217, 12, 218.
10. "*Y. Harkabi:* Fatah's Doctrine (December 1968)," in *Israel-Arab Reader*, Laqueur and Rubin, eds., 122, 123, 126–127, 129, 124, 121.
11. Hulme, *Palestinian Terrorism*, 51.
12. See Hulme, *Palestinian Terrorism*, 45–46, 138–140.
13. Hulme, *Palestinian Terrorism*, 241, n.243.
14. Hulme, *Palestinian Terrorism*, 135.
15. "Rabin, 5 November 1974," in *Israeli-Palestinian Conflict*, 188–189.
16. Hulme, *Palestinian Terrorism*, 135.
17. "Rabin, 5 November 1974," in *Israeli-Palestinian Conflict*, 188–189.
18. See, for example, "Rabin, 5 November 1974," in *Israeli-Palestinian Conflict*, 189. However, despite their public opposition to negotiating with terrorist organizations, Israeli leaders participated in tentative, highly secret, discussions with Palestinian representatives. Preliminary conversations involving General Mattityahu Peled and Palestinians Issam Sartawi and Abbu Jiryis occurred between July 1976 and May 1977. Addressing such fundamental issues as Israel's right to exist, territorial boundaries, and Jewish immigration to Israel, the talks explored potential openings for more conventional diplomatic exchange. Hulme, *Palestinian Terrorism*, 137.
19. Hulme, *Palestinian Terrorism*, 44; "Galili Plan, August 1973," in *Israeli-Palestinian Conflict*, 186; *"The Likud Party:* Platform (March 1977)," in *Israel-Arab Reader*, 207.
20. "Galili Plan, August 1973," in *Israeli-Palestinian Conflict*, 185.
21. "Rabin, 5 November 1974," in *Israeli-Palestinian Conflict*, 189. Begin's Likud party promised to "strive to eliminate these murderous organizations in order to prevent them from carrying out their bloody deeds." "*Likud,* March 1977," in *Israel-Arab Reader*, 207.
22. "*Likud,* March 1977," in *Israel-Arab Reader*, 207; "*Camp David,* September 17, 1978," in *Israel-Arab Reader*, 225; "*Egypt and Israel:* Peace Treaty (March 26, 1979)," in *Israel-Arab Reader*, Laqueur and Rubin, eds., 228.
23. "*PLO Chairman Yasir Arafat:* Interview on Camp David (November 19, 1979)," in *Israel-Arab Reader*, 230–231; "Arab League, 5 November 1978," in *Israeli-Palestinian Conflict*, 470–473; "Arab League, 31 March 1979," in *Israeli-Palestinian Conflict*, 473–477; "Steadfastness and Confrontation Front, 23 September 1978," in *Israeli-Palestinian Conflict*, 469–470; "PLO, 5 October 1979," in *Israeli-Palestinian Conflict*, 344–345.
24. See "*U.S. and Israel:* Memorandum of Understanding (November 30, 1981)," in *Israel-Arab Reader*, Laqueur and Rubin, eds., 238–239; "*Begin,* August 8, 1982," in *Israel-Arab Reader*, 254–257; "Arafat, 7 November 1985," in *Israeli-Palestinian Conflict*, 370.
25. See "*Arafat,* February 14, 1983," in *Israel-Arab Reader*, 274–276; "Fourth General Conference, 31 May 1980," in *Israeli-Palestinian Conflict*, 345–349; "Arafat, 7 November 1985," in *Israeli-Palestinian Conflict*, 370–371.

26. "*Sharon,* December 15, 1981," in *Israel-Arab Reader,* Laqueur and Rubin, eds., 240–241. He also noted its impact on "domestic stability" and "security." "*Sharon,* December 15, 1981," in *Israel-Arab Reader,* 240–241.

27. "Begin, August 8, 1982," in *Israel-Arab Reader,* 256–257.

28. "Israel's Communiqué, 2 September 1982," in *Israeli-Palestinian Conflict,* 201; "*Begin:* August 8, 1982," in *Israel-Arab Reader,* 256.

29. "PLO Central Committee, 9 January 1988," in *Israeli-Palestinian Conflict,* 391, 392; "Palestinian Declaration of Independence, 15 November 1988," in *Israeli-Palestinian Conflict,* 413; "Covenant of Hamas, 18 August 1988," in *Israeli-Palestinian Conflict,* 403, 401–402.

30. Buchanan, *Peace with Justice,* 143.

31. "Arafat, 13 December 1988," in *Israeli-Palestinian Conflict,* 429; "Arafat, 15 December 1988," in *Israeli-Palestinian Conflict,* 434.

32. "*Arafat,* September 1989," in *Israel-Arab Reader,* 365–367.

33. "Reagan, 14 December 1988," in *Israeli-Palestinian Conflict,* 120.

34. "*Rabin,* April 18, 1994," in *Israel-Arab Reader,* 462.

35. "Covenant of Hamas, 18 August 1988," in *Israeli-Palestinian Conflict,* 402, 400.

36. Buchanan, *Peace with Justice,* 156, 158.

37. "Address by Prime Minister Yitzhak Shamir to the Knesset, 23 December 1988," in *Israeli-Palestinian Conflict,* 222–223.

38. Buchanan, *Peace with Justice,* 142.

39. "U.S. Letter, October 18, 1991," in *Israel-Arab Reader,* 385–386.

40. Buchanan, *Peace with Justice,* 142, 147.

41. Ibid., 150, 158. Future Prime Minister Ehud Barak voiced similar concerns, observing, "We have no control over whether Iran will have non conventional nuclear capabilities in another ten years . . . [However,] [g]iven this long-term uncertainty, it is not an exaggerated risk to attempt to relax the conflict in our immediate circle, including with Lebanon and Syria . . . as long as we do not waive our vital security interests." He noted, "On one hand, the Palestinians are weak. On the other hand, they are perceived by (Israeli) citizens to be the source of terror and day-to-day frictions, and they legitimise pan-Arab hostility toward Israel. As long as we reduce (Palestinian) terror without damaging any of Israel's vital interests by smoothing relations with them, it will be more difficult to motivate hostile acts against us from Benghazi to Teheran." Buchanan, *Peace with Justice,* 154.

42. Buchanan, *Peace with Justice,* 150, 159.

43. Ibid., 141–142. He also observed, "Our power can guarantee us as a fact probably forever, but who wants to live like that?" Buchanan, *Peace with Justice,* 142.

44. "*Rabin,* April 18, 1994," in *Israel-Arab Reader,* 460, 463. Rabin acknowledged both "a willingness for peace on the other side" and a need to avoid the "well-understood . . . danger contained in freezing the situation." "*Rabin,* April 18, 1994," in *Israel-Arab Reader,* 460, 462.

45. "*Israel and PLO:* Agreed Minutes, September 13, 1993," in *Israel-Arab Reader,* 424; "*Rabin,* April 18, 1994," in *Israel-Arab Reader,* 462–464.

46. "*Rabin,* April 18, 1994," in *Israel-Arab Reader,* 463–464; "*Israel and PLO:* Declaration, September 13, 1993," in *Israel-Arab Reader,* 414.

47. Such concerns had been expressed by a significant element of the Palestinian population within days of *Oslo*'s conclusion. See "*Hasan,* October 9, 1993," in *Israel-Arab Reader,* 435–436; "*West Bank-Gaza Palestinian Leaders:* Memorandum to Chairman Yasir Arafat (November 1993)," in *Israel-Arab Reader,* Laqueur and Rubin, eds., 436–439. Such skepticism increased Palestinian support for Hamas.

48. "*Israeli Government*, July 1999," in *Israel-Arab Reader*, 544; "*Barak*, July 6, 1999," in *Israel-Arab Reader*, 542.

49. "*Israeli* Government, July 1999," in *Israel-Arab Reader*, 544; "*Barak*, July 6, 1999," in *Israel-Arab Reader*, 542.

50. "*Barak*, July 25, 2000," in *Israel-Arab Reader*, 554–556.

51. "*Yoel Marcus:* 'If They Want It, They'll Take It' (December 26, 2000)," in *Israel-Arab Reader*, Laqueur and Rubin, eds., 565.

52. "*Arafat*, October 21, 2000," in *Israel-Arab Reader*, 557, 559, 556. Speaking before the UN General Assembly in 1974 he had noted, "The roots of the Palestine question . . . do not stem from any conflict between two religions or two nationalisms. . . . It is the cause of people deprived of its homeland, dispersed and uprooted, the majority of whom live in exile and in refugee camps." He observed, "We distinguish between Judaism and Zionism. While we maintain our opposition to the colonialist Zionist movement, we respect the Jewish faith. . . . since its inception, our revolution has not been motivated by racial or religious factors. Its target has never been the Jew, as a person, but racist Zionism and aggression." "Arafat, 13 November 1974," in *Israeli-Palestinian Conflict*, 324, 326.

53. "*Barghuti*, October 26, 2000," in *Israel-Arab Reader*, 560–561.

54. "*Barghuti*, October 26, 2000," in *Israel-Arab Reader*, 561.

55. "Arafat, 13 November 1974," in *Israeli-Palestinian Conflict*, 322–24, 326–30, 318.

56. "*PLO Chairman Yasir Arafat:* Interview on Camp David (November 19, 1979)," in *Israel-Arab Reader*, 230.

57. "*Arafat,* November 19, 1979," in *Israel-Arab Reader*, 230; "Palestinian National Council, 21 April 1981," in *Israeli-Palestinian Conflict*, 356.

58. "Palestinian National Council, 22 February 1983," in *Israeli-Palestinian Conflict*, 362.

59. "Arafat, 7 November 1985," in *Israeli-Palestinian Conflict*, 370–371.

60. "*PLO Executive Committee:* On the Intifada (December 1987)," in *Israel-Arab Reader*, Laqueur and Rubin, eds., 315; "*PLO Executive Committee,* April 1988," in *Israel-Arab Reader*, 325.

61. "*PLO Executive Committee,* April 1988," in *Israel-Arab Reader*, 324–325; "*Unified National Leadership,* April-May 1988," in *Israel-Arab Reader*, 337, 326.

62. "Palestine National Council, 15 November 1988," in *Israeli-Palestinian Conflict*, 419.

63. Ibid., 416.

64. "Palestinian Declaration of Independence, 15 November 1988," in *Israeli-Palestinian Conflict*, 412–414.

65. "Arafat, 13 September 1988," in *Israeli-Palestinian Conflict*, 410, 406.

66. "Arafat, 13 December 1988," in *Israeli-Palestinian Conflict*, 431, 426.

67. "*Israel and PLO:* Agreed Minutes, September 13, 1993," in *Israel-Arab Reader*, 424; "*Clinton, Rabin, and Arafat,* September 13, 1993," in *Israel-Arab Reader*, 427.

68. "*Israel and PLO,* March 4, 1994," in *Israel-Arab Reader*, 452.

69. "*Israel and Palestinian Authority,* September 28, 1995," in *Israel-Arab Reader*, 503-504.

70. "*Darwish,* August 1993," in *Israel-Arab Reader*, 412, 411.

71. "*Hasan,* October 9, 1993," in *Israel-Arab Reader*, 435–436.

72. See, for example, "*Sufyan Abu-Zayidah:* Interview (January 27, 1995)," in *Israel-Arab Reader*, Laqueur and Rubin, eds., 499–500.

73. "*Israel and Palestinian Authority,* October 23, 1998," in *Israel-Arab Reader*, 530–532.
74. "*Arafat,* October 21, 2000," in *Israel-Arab Reader*, 557–558.
75. "*Barghuti,* October 26, 2000," in *Israel-Arab Reader*, 562.
76. Hulme, *Palestinian Terrorism*, 107, 71.
77. Hulme, *Palestinian Terrorism*, 109, 50, 53.
78. Hulme, *Palestinian Terrorism*, 55.
79. Hulme, *Palestinian Terrorism*, 110, 56–59.
80. Hulme, *Palestinian Terrorism*, 111, 61.
81. Ibid., 111–112. Recognizing terrorism's potential to assume unwarranted strategic significance, it argued, "We must continue to work for a peace settlement, and we must continue to fight terrorism, but the latter must be seen in perspective, as a part and not the major part of the whole, and must not be allowed to become the dominant factor in US policy formation." Hulme, *Palestinian Terrorism*, 112.
82. Hulme, *Palestinian Terrorism*, 72.
83. Hulme, *Palestinian Terrorism*, 112. Emphasis in original.
84. Hulme, *Palestinian Terrorism*, 113.
85. Hulme, *Palestinian Terrorism*, 114.
86. Ibid., 114–5. Kissinger loathed Rogers, and was particularly contemptuous of his lack of strategic vision and poor tactical judgment.
87. Hulme, *Palestinian Terrorism*, 61–63.
88. Hulme, *Palestinian Terrorism*, 116.
89. Hulme, *Palestinian Terrorism*, 64, 116, 65. Emphasis in original.
90. Hulme, *Palestinian Terrorism*, 215, 12.
91. Hulme, *Palestinian Terrorism*, 176–179.
92. Hulme, *Palestinian Terrorism*, 196–197.
93. Hulme, *Palestinian Terrorism*, 172–173.
94. Hulme, *Palestinian Terrorism*, 197–198.
95. Hulme, *Palestinian Terrorism*, 146–147, 143, 196.
96. Hulme, *Palestinian Terrorism*, 173.
97. "Memorandum of Agreement, September 1975," in *Israeli-Palestinian Conflict*, 60. This was despite Arab leaders unanimously recognizing the PLO as the "sole legitimate representative of the Palestinian people" in October 1974 and the UN General Assembly inviting its participation "in the sessions and the work of the General Assembly in the capacity of observer" in November 1974. Hulme, *Palestinian Terrorism*, 135.
98. Hulme, *Palestinian Terrorism*, 121; "Memorandum of Agreement, September 1975," in *Israeli-Palestinian Conflict*, 60.
99. Hulme, *Palestinian Terrorism*, 145–146.
100. See, for example, the comments of Harold Saunders, Deputy Assistant Secretary of State for Near Eastern and South Asian Affairs, who highlighted Palestinians use of terror against Americans, Israelis, and "others," while ignoring those Israeli practices considered by Palestinians to be terroristic. "Saunders, 12 November 1975," in *Israeli-Palestinian Conflict*, 64.
101. Buchanan, *Peace with Justice*, 34.
102. Hulme, *Palestinian Terrorism*, 149, 148, 199. Emphasis in original. They also recognized that "the Palestinian dimension of the Arab-Israeli conflict is the heart of that conflict," accepted that "the legitimate interests of the Palestinian Arabs must be taken into account in the negotiation of an Arab-Israeli peace," and stressed that "the problem of the Palestinians will have to be addressed before there can be real peace." Hulme, *Palestinian Terrorism*, 196, 198–199.

103. Hulme, *Palestinian Terrorism*, 198.
104. Hulme, *Palestinian Terrorism*, 191, 186–190.
105. Hulme, *Palestinian Terrorism*, 189–190, 187, 194–195.
106. George P. Shultz, *Turmoil and Triumph: My Years as Secretary of State* (New York: Charles Scribner's Sons, 1993), 687, 652–653, 643.
107. Shultz, *Turmoil and Triumph*, 647.
108. Shultz, *Turmoil and Triumph*, 648. Emphasis in original.
109. Shultz, *Turmoil and Triumph*, 678.
110. Shultz, *Turmoil and Triumph*, 687, 647, 645, 676. Emphasis in original.
111. Shultz, *Turmoil and Triumph*, 650–651, 647. In addition to opposition from Weinberger and the Joint Chiefs of Staff, Shultz also encountered resistance to his hard-line policies from Vice-President George Bush. Shultz, *Turmoil and Triumph*, 648, 664.
112. Shultz, *Turmoil and Triumph*, 688, 658, 686.
113. "Shultz, 17 May 1987," in *Israeli-Palestinian Conflict*, 88; "Statement by the State Department on the Rejection of PLO Chairman Yasser Arafat's Visa Application to the US, 26 November 1988," in *Israeli-Palestinian Conflict*, Lukacs, ed., 116.
114. Shultz, *Turmoil and Triumph*, 646; "Shultz, 16 September 1988," in *Israeli-Palestinian Conflict*, Lukacs, ed., 114. He insisted that "people who engage in terror do not want peace or justice, and people who want peace and justice do not engage in terror." Shultz, *Turmoil and Triumph*, 646.
115. "Statement by President Ronald Reagan on the Establishment of New Israeli Settlements, 27 August 1983," in *Israeli-Palestinian Conflict*, Lukacs, ed., 80. Israelis were urged only to "find a way to respond to expressions of Palestinian grievances" without "suppressing political expression and arresting or deporting those who speak out." "Shultz, 16 September 1988," in *Israeli-Palestinian Conflict*, 114.
116. "Reagan, 14 December 1988," in *Israeli-Palestinian Conflict*, 120. See "Shultz, 14 December 1988," in *Israeli-Palestinian Conflict*, 119, where the US accepted such a "renunciation".
117. "Bush, 6 April 1989," in *Israeli-Palestinian Conflict*, 122; "Baker, 22 May 1989," in *Israeli-Palestinian Conflict*, 123; "Bush, 20 June 1990," in *Israeli-Palestinian Conflict*, 135.
118. "Address by Secretary of State James Baker Before the American-Israel Public Affairs Committee, Washington, DC, 22 May 1989," in *Israeli-Palestinian Conflict*, Lukacs, ed., 128; "U.S. Letter, October 18, 1991," in *Israel-Arab Reader*, 385, 386.
119. "*Clinton*, December 14, 1998," in *Israel-Arab Reader*, 538, 536, 539, 540.
120. "*Clinton*, January 7, 2001," in *Israel-Arab Reader*, 574–576.
121. Hulme, *Palestinian Terrorism*, 217, 12.
122. "This is the Plan, 18 March 1988," in *Israeli-Palestinian Conflict*, 104.
123. Hulme, *Palestinian Terrorism*, 11, ii.
124. Prime Minister Golda Meir likewise observed, "It was not as if there was a Palestinian people in Palestine and we came and threw them out and took their country away from them. They did not exist." Quoted in Hulme, *Palestinian Terrorism*, 36.
125. Hulme, *Palestinian Terrorism*, 44. The Mossad was created at least partly to perform this function.
126. See Hulme, *Palestinian Terrorism*, 137.
127. "Rabin, 5 November 1974," in *Israeli-Palestinian Conflict*, 189; "*Likud*, March 1977," in *Israel-Arab Reader*, 207.
128. Hulme, *Palestinian Terrorism*, 12.
129. Hulme, *Palestinian Terrorism*, 241, n.243.

130. "Rabin, 5 November 1974," in *Israeli-Palestinian Conflict*, Lukacs, 188; "*Egypt and Israel,* March 26, 1979," in *Israel-Arab Reader*, 228.

131. Hulme, *Palestinian Terrorism*, 137–138.

132. "Speech by Yasser Arafat to the UN General Assembly, 13 November 1974," in *Israeli-Palestinian Conflict*, Lukacs, ed., 327; "*Arafat,* November 19, 1979," in *Israel-Arab Reader*, 230.

133. Hulme, *Palestinian Terrorism*, 55, 113. Ford deviated little from Nixon's approach, excluding the PLO from US-sponsored Arab-Israeli negotiations, while domestically emphasizing his "tangible" commitment to combating terror. See Hulme, *Palestinian Terrorism*, 186–195.

134. Shultz, *Turmoil and Triumph*, 688, 686, 648. Secretary of State Shultz characterized terrorism as a "war against the democracies of the West." Shultz, *Turmoil and Triumph*, 643. The Administration particularly emphasized Arafat's complicity in terrorism against Americans.

135. "Covenant of Hamas, 18 August 1988," in *Israeli-Palestinian Conflict*, 401–403. See also Buchanan, *Peace with Justice*, 158.

136. Buchanan, *Peace with Justice*, 150.

137. "Palestine National Council, 15 November 1988," in *Israeli-Palestinian Conflict*, 419; "Arafat, 13 December 1988," in *Israeli-Palestinian Conflict*, 420–434.

138. "Arafat, 13 December 1988," in *Israeli-Palestinian Conflict*, 434. Mutual commitments were undertaken "to live in peaceful coexistence" and to resolve differences "by negotiations." "*Israel and PLO:* Declaration, September 13, 1993," in *Israel-Arab Reader*, 413, 417.

139. "Bush, 20 June 1990," in *Israeli-Palestinian Conflict*, 134; "U.S. Letter, October 18, 1991," in *Israel-Arab Reader*, 386.

140. See, for example, "*Rabin,* April 18, 1994," in *Israel-Arab Reader*, 463; "*Israeli Government,* July 1999," in *Israel-Arab Reader*, 544.

141. They nonetheless reassured the public of their commitment to "an all-out war against terrorist organizations and the initiators and perpetrators of terrorism." "*Israeli Government,* July 1999," in *Israel-Arab Reader*, 544; Buchanan, *Peace with Justice*, 150.

142. "*Israel and PLO,* March 4, 1994," in *Israel-Arab Reader*, 452.

143. "*Israel and PLO:* Agreed Minutes, September 13, 1993," in *Israel-Arab Reader*, 425.

144. "*Clinton,* December 14, 1998," in *Israel-Arab Reader*, 539.

145. Indeed, he confined Arafat to his Ramallah compound and threatened him with exile or assassination.

146. See, for example, "*Sharon,* December 15, 1981," in *Israel-Arab Reader*, 240.

147. "*Arafat,* October 21, 2000," in *Israel-Arab Reader*, 557–559.

148. "*Arafat,* October 21, 2000," in *Israel-Arab Reader*, 559.

149. "*Clinton,* January 7, 2001," in *Israel-Arab Reader*, 575, 574.

150. Hulme, *Palestinian Terrorism*, 217.

The *Road Map For Peace*

1. See, for example, "President Prodi and Commissioner Patten Receive Emissary of Israeli PM Elect Sharon", Europa, 16 February 2001, in http://www.europa.eu.int/, accessed 16 August 2005. European Commission President Romano Prodi warned in March 2002, "War must be avoided as a matter of urgency now before we reach a point of no return." "Statements of the President of the Commission concerning the speech of Presi-

dent Bush 05/04/2002," Europa, 3 April 2002 and 29 March 2002, in http://www.europa.eu.int/, accessed 16 August 2005.

2. "Press Conference by the President", Office of the Press Secretary, 29 March 2001, in http://www.whitehouse.gov/, accessed 14 June 2005; "President Bush Meets with German Chancellor Schroder", Office of the Press Secretary, 23 May 2002, in http://www.whitehouse.gov/, accessed 17 August 2005.

3. "Statement by the President on the Middle East", Office of the Press Secretary, 28 April 2002, in http://www.whitehouse.gov/, accessed 17 August 2005; "President Meets with Muslim Leaders", Office of the Press Secretary, 26 September 2001, in http://www.whitehouse.gov/, accessed 14 June 2005. See also "President to Meet With Israeli Prime Minister Sunday: Remarks by the President Upon Return from Camp David", Office of the Press Secretary, 2 December 2001, in http://www.whitehouse.gov/, accessed 14 June 2005.

4. "President Bush, Secretary Powell Discuss Middle East", Office of the Press Secretary, 18 April 2002, in http://www.whitehouse.gov/, accessed 17 August 2005; Thomas Carothers, "Choosing a Strategy," in *Uncharted Journey: Promoting Democracy in the Middle East*, Thomas Carothers and Marina Ottaway, eds., (Washington: Carnegie Endowment for International Peace, 2005), 193.

5. Marina Ottaway, "The Problem of Credibility," in *Uncharted Journey,* Carothers and Ottaway, eds., 176–177; Michele Dunne, "Integrating Democracy into the U.S. Policy Agenda," in *Uncharted Journey,* Carothers and Ottaway, eds., 209.

6. Richard Youngs, "Europe's Uncertain Pursuit of Middle East Reform," in *Uncharted Journey,* Carothers and Ottaway, eds., 234.

7. See, for example, "Press Conference by the President", 29 March 2001, where Bush noted that "the escalating violence . . . [was] claiming the lives of innocent civilians on both sides."

8. For comments by Bush justifying preemptive action see, "President Bush Meets with German Chancellor Schroder," 23 May 2002, where he characterized Hussein as "a dangerous man," "a dictator who gassed his own people," and as someone with "a history of incredible human rights violations."

9. Ottaway, "Problem of Credibility," in *Uncharted Journey,* Carothers and Ottaway, eds., 179–180.

10. "Press Conference by the President", 29 March 2001. See also "President Discusses Economy, Middle East Following Cabinet Meeting", Office of the Press Secretary, 31 July 2002, in http://www.whitehouse.gov/, accessed 17 August 2005.

11. "Press Conference by the President", 29 March 2001.

12. "U.S. Envoy Says Only Mitchell Plan Can Stop Violence", Deutsche Presse-Agentur, 9 August 2001, in http://web.lexis-nexis.com/, accessed 23 August 2005.

13. "Romano Prodi Congratulates Ariel Sharon", Europa, 29 January 2003, in http://www.europa.eu.int/, accessed 16 August 2005; "President Bush Meets with German Chancellor Schroder," 23 May 2002; "President Bush, President Putin Release Joint Statement on Middle East", Office of the Press Secretary, 24 May 2002, in http://www.whitehouse.gov/, accessed 17 August 2005.

14. "Situation in the Middle East: Speech by the Rt. Hon. Christopher Patten, External Relations Commissioner," Europa, 9 April 2002, in http://www.europa.eu.int/, accessed 16 August 2005; "Comments on the situation in the Middle East: Interview with Rt. Hon. Christopher Patten, External Relations Commissioner," Europa, 10 April 2002, in http://www.europa.eu.int/, accessed 16 August 2005. He condemned such actions as suicide bombings as "wrong at every time, in every place. Wrong always. Wrong everywhere." "Situation in the Middle East, Christopher Patten," 9 April 2002.

15. "European commission welcomes Arafat announcement of elections and reforms and signature of Law on Independence of the Judiciary," Europa, 16 May 2002, in http://www.europa.eu.int/, accessed 16 August 2005. See also "Statement to the Foreign Affairs Committee on EU budgetary assistance to the Palestinian Authority: Statement by the Rt. Hon. Christopher Patten, External Relations Commissioner," Europa, 19 June 2002, in http://www.europa.eu.int/, accessed 16 August 2005. Noting that Israeli security operations had destroyed "the basic fabric of administration in the Palestinian territories" and "knocked [the PA] to smithereens," he was particularly fearful that Palestinians might descend into anarchy. "Statement to the Foreign Affairs Committee, Christopher Patten," 19 June 2002; "Comments on the situation in the Middle East: Christopher Patten," 10 April 2002.

16. "Press Conference by the President", 29 March 2001. Bush similarly rejected rigid deadlines and timetables as likely to distort peacemaking efforts.

17. "Press Conference by the President", 29 March 2001; "President Discusses Missile Tests in Pakistan and Middle East", Office of the Press Secretary, 26 May 2002, in http://www.whitehouse.gov/, accessed 17 August 2005. See also "President to Meet With Israeli Prime Minister Sunday," 2 December 2001.

18. "US Pushing for Israel-Palestinian Talks: Rice", AFX News Limited, AFX-Asia, 16 October 2001, in http://web.lexis-nexis.com/, accessed 23 August 2005. Emphasis added.

19. "US Pushing for Israel-Palestinian Talks," 16 October 2001; "Statement by the President: Terrorist Bombing in Jerusalem", Office of the Press Secretary, 9 August 2001, in http://www.whitehouse.gov/, accessed 14 June 2005.

20. "Chris Patten Commissioner for External Relations welcomes Statement from President Bush on the Middle East", Europa, 5 April 2002, in http://www.europa.eu.int/, accessed 16 August 2005; "Statements of the President of the Commission concerning the speech of President Bush 05/04/2002," 3 April 2002 and 29 March 2002.

21. "President Bush, Secretary Powell Discuss Middle East", Office of the Press Secretary, 18 April 2002, in http://www.whitehouse.gov/, accessed 17 August 2005. See as well "US Pushing for Israel-Palestinian Talks," 16 October 2001, where Condoleezza Rice highlighted Bush's "clearly and publicly announced" belief that "a Palestinian state in the Middle East is necessary."

22. See, for example, "President Bush Meets with European Leaders", Office of the Press Secretary, 2 May 2002, in http://www.whitehouse.gov/, accessed 17 August 2005; "President Bush Meets with Egyptian President Mubarak", Office of the Press Secretary, 8 June 2002, in http://www.whitehouse.gov/, accessed 17 August 2005.

23. "President Bush Meets with European Leaders," 2 May 2002; "President Discusses Missile Tests in Pakistan and Middle East," 26 May 2002.

24. "Statement by the President on the Middle East," 28 April 2002; "President Discusses Missile Tests in Pakistan and Middle East," 26 May 2002; "President Bush, Secretary Powell Discuss Middle East," 18 April 2002; "Press Conference by the President", 29 March 2001; "Statement by the President," 9 August 2001. See as well "President Bush Meets with Egyptian President Mubarak," 8 June 2002; "US Pushing for Israel-Palestinian Talks," 16 October 2001. Colin Powell likewise demanded that "Palestinian leaders not only denounce violence, but take action to act against those who continue to encourage violence and perform acts of terrorism and violence. The terrorism, violence has to stop." "President Bush, Secretary Powell Discuss Middle East," 18 April 2002.

25. "Statement by the President on the Middle East," 28 April 2002. See as well "President Bush Meets with European Leaders," 2 May 2002.

26. "President Discusses Missile Tests in Pakistan and Middle East," 26 May 2002; "President Bush Meets with European Leaders," 2 May 2002; "President Bush, Secretary Powell Discuss Middle East," 18 April 2002; "Press Conference by the President", 29 March 2001.

27. "Statement to the Foreign Affairs Committee, Christopher Patten," 19 June 2002; "Situation in the Middle East, Christopher Patten," 9 April 2002; "Comments on the situation in the Middle East: Christopher Patten," 10 April 2002.

28. "Situation in the Middle East, Christopher Patten," 9 April 2002; "Comments on the situation in the Middle East: Christopher Patten," 10 April 2002.

29. "Comments on the situation in the Middle East: Christopher Patten," 10 April 2002; "Situation in the Middle East, Christopher Patten," 9 April 2002.

30. See, for example, "Situation in the Middle East, Christopher Patten," 9 April 2002.

31. "European commission welcomes Arafat announcement," 16 May 2002; "Statement to the Foreign Affairs Committee, Christopher Patten," 19 June 2002; "Comments on the situation in the Middle East: Interview with Rt. Hon. Christopher Patten, External Relations Commissioner," Europa, 10 April 2002, in http://www.europa.eu.int/, accessed 16 August 2005; "Statements of the President of the Commission concerning the speech of President Bush 05/04/2002," 3 April 2002 and 29 March 2002. "Clear, concrete and tangible conditions" were attached to such assistance in an effort to promote necessary institutional reform. Patten also stressed the "need for organised structures to run the Palestinian territories and represent the Palestinian people in peace talks and internationally." "Statement to the Foreign Affairs Committee, Christopher Patten," 19 June 2002; "Situation in the Middle East, Christopher Patten," 9 April 2002.

32. Michele K. Esposito, "Quarterly Update on Conflict and Diplomacy", *Journal of Palestine Studies* XXXII, no. 2 (Winter 2003): 120.

33. "President Bush Calls for New Palestinian Leadership", Office of the Press Secretary, 24 June 2002, in http://www.whitehouse.gov/, accessed 17 August 2005.

34. Esposito, "Quarterly Update on Conflict and Diplomacy," 122–123; UNSCR 1435, 9/24/2002, in http://daccessdds.un.org/. Natan Sharansky, a Knesset member, observed in September 2002 that Israel "didn't correctly assess . . . how much the U.S. has already started counting down to the strike against Iraq. . . . This [pressure on Israel] is the result." Esposito, "Quarterly Update on Conflict and Diplomacy," 122.

35. "President Bush Calls for New Palestinian Leadership," 24 June 2002; Esposito, "Quarterly Update on Conflict and Diplomacy," 137.

36. "Joint Statement on the Middle East: 10th EU-Russia Summit," Europa, 11 November 2002, in http://www.europa.eu.int/, accessed 16 August 2005; "Commission approves EUR 29 million in support of Palestinian reform efforts and in response to the deteriorating situation on the ground," Europa, 28 October 2002, in http://www.europa.eu.int/, accessed 16 August 2005. Christopher Patten characterized "conditions" in the Occupied Territories as "extremely like war." "Statement to the Foreign Affairs Committee, Christopher Patten," 19 June 2002.

37. Esposito, "Quarterly Update on Conflict and Diplomacy," 139. By November 2002, over 2000 Palestinians and approximately 650 Israelis had been killed since the al-Aqsa Intifada's beginning in September 2000. Esposito, "Quarterly Update on Conflict and Diplomacy," 126.

38. "President Bush Calls for New Palestinian Leadership," 24 June 2002; "President Reiterates Path for Peace in Middle East: Remarks by the President and Prime Minister Blair", Office of the Press Secretary, 26 June 2002, in http://www.whitehouse.gov/,

accessed 17 August 2005. Emphasis added. Responding to a question about Arafat's possible reelection in January 2003 elections, Bush remarked, "I meant what I said, that there needs to be change. If people are interested in peace, something else has got to happen." "President Reiterates Path for Peace in Middle East", 26 June 2002.

39. "President Discusses Economy, Middle East Following Cabinet Meeting," 31 July 2002; "President Bush, King Abdullah Discuss Middle East Peace: Remarks by the President and His Majesty King Abdullah of the Hashemite Kingdom of Jordan", Office of the Press Secretary, 1 August 2002, in http://www.whitehouse.gov/, accessed 17 August 2005.

40. "President Welcomes Quartet Principals to White House: Remarks by President Bush, Secretary General Kofi Annan, Danish Foreign Minister Per Stig Moeller, and Russian Foreign Minister Igor Ivanov in Photo Opportunity with the Quartet Principals", Office of the Press Secretary, 20 December 2002, in http://www.whitehouse.gov/, accessed 17 August 2005.

41. Esposito, "Quarterly Update on Conflict and Diplomacy," 124.

42. "President Discusses Economy, Middle East Following Cabinet Meeting," 31 July 2002. Emphasis added. Bush did support certain multilateral mechanisms, including the US-dominated International Task Force on Palestinian Reform, which included Quartet representatives and such key donors as Japan, Norway, the International Monetary Fund, and the World Bank. Esposito, "Quarterly Update on Conflict and Diplomacy," 129; "Statement of the Middle East Quartet", Europa, 16 July 2002, in http://www.europa.eu.int/, accessed 16 August 2005.

43. Esposito, "Quarterly Update on Conflict and Diplomacy," 139.

44. "Joint Statement by the Quartet", UN News Centre, 20 December 2002, in http://www0.un.org/, accessed 9 August 2005; "President Welcomes Quartet Principals to White House," 20 December 2002.

45. "President Discusses Roadmap for Peace in the Middle East", Office of the Press Secretary, 14 March 2003, in http://www.whitehouse.gov/, accessed 17 August 2005; "1st Lead: Bush Announces Mideast Peace Road Map to be Delivered", Deutsche Presse-Agentur, 14 March 2003, in http://web.lexis-nexis.com/, accessed 23 August 2005; "Israel Out to Change 'Road Map'", Nationwide News Pty Limited, The Sunday Times (Perth, Australia), 13 April 2003, in http://web.lexis-nexis.com/, accessed 23 August 2005.

46. "Statement of the Middle East Quartet", 16 July 2002. See also "Joint Statement by the Quartet", 20 December 2002.

47. "E.U. says pressing ahead with quartet Mideast peace plan," Deutsche Presse-Agentur, 19 November 2002, in http://web.lexis-nexis.com/, accessed 23 August 2005; Esposito, "Quarterly Update on Conflict and Diplomacy," 139. See as well "Joint Statement on the Middle East: 10th EU-Russia Summit," 11 November 2002. Russia likewise urged immediate action on the *Road Map*, while Kofi Annan implored Bush "to press ahead with the Roadmap" as rapidly as possible. See "Joint Statement on the Middle East: 10th EU-Russia Summit," 11 November 2002; "Russia Calls for Urgent Meeting of Mideast Mediators", Deutsche Presse-Agentur, 28 January 2003, in http://web.lexis-nexis.com/, accessed 23 August 2005; "Quartet to Approve Israeli-Palestinian Peace Plan in February: Russia", Xinhua News Agency, Xinhua General News Service, 23 December 2002, in http://web.lexis-nexis.com/, accessed 23 August 2005; "Secretary-General's Remarks to a Delegation of Visiting Palestinian Journalists (unofficial transcript)", Secretary-General Office of the Spokesman, 31 March 2003, in http://www0.un.org/, accessed 9 August 2005.

48. "Commission approves EUR 29 million," 28 October 2002.

49. "Statement to the Foreign Affairs Committee, Christopher Patten," 19 June 2002.
50. "President Bush Calls for New Palestinian Leadership," 24 June 2002.
51. Esposito, "Quarterly Update on Conflict and Diplomacy," 124; Bush, "President Bush Calls for New Palestinian Leadership." See also "Text of U.S.-E.U. Declaration Supporting Peace, Progress, and Reform in the Broader Middle East and in the Mediterranean", Office of the Press Secretary, 26 June 2004, in http://www.whitehouse.gov/, accessed 17 August 2005; "President Bush, King Abdullah Discuss Middle East Peace," 1 August 2002; "President Discusses Roadmap for Peace in the Middle East," 14 March 2003.
52. "Secretary-General's Remarks to a Delegation of Visiting Palestinian Journalists (unofficial transcript)", 31 March 2003; Esposito, "Quarterly Update on Conflict and Diplomacy," 139.
53. "Secretary-General's Remarks to a Delegation of Visiting Palestinian Journalists (unofficial transcript)", 31 March 2003.
54. "Joint Statement on the Middle East: 10th EU-Russia Summit," 11 November 2002.
55. "President Bush Calls for New Palestinian Leadership," 24 June 2002. Bush reiterated his commitment "to a vision of two states respecting each other, two states living side by side in peace," in meetings with such diverse leaders as Ariel Sharon, ("President Bush Welcomes Prime Minister Sharon to White House", Office of the Press Secretary, 16 October 2002, in http://www.whitehouse.gov/, accessed 17 August 2005) Jordan's King Abdullah, ("President Bush, King Abdullah Discuss Middle East Peace," 1 August 2002) and the foreign ministers of Egypt and Saudi Arabia. "President Meets with Foreign Ministers of Egypt, Jordan, and Saudi Arabia", Office of the Press Secretary, 18 July 2002, in http://www.whitehouse.gov/, accessed 17 August 2005).
56. "President Bush Calls for New Palestinian Leadership," 24 June 2002; "President Discusses Roadmap for Peace in the Middle East," 14 March 2003.
57. "President Welcomes Quartet Principals to White House," 20 December 2002; "Pledging UN Support for Road Map, Annan Appeals for All to 'Stay the Course'", UN News Centre, 30 April 2003, in http://www0.un.org/, accessed 9 August 2005.
58. "President Welcomes Quartet Principals to White House," 20 December 2002; "Joint Statement on the Middle East: 10th EU-Russia Summit," 11 November 2002.
59. "President Bush Calls for New Palestinian Leadership," 24 June 2002. Bush stressed terrorists' efforts to "deny the dreams of the many" by destroying "efforts toward peace in the Middle East." "President Welcomes Quartet Principals to White House," 20 December 2002; "President Condemns Terrorist Attack in Israel", Office of the Press Secretary, 5 January 2003, in http://www.whitehouse.gov/, accessed 17 August 2005.
60. "President Bush Calls for New Palestinian Leadership," 24 June 2002. He noted, "All who genuinely seek peace in the region must join in the effort to stop terror." "President Condemns Terrorist Attack in Israel," 5 January 2003.
61. "President Bush Calls for New Palestinian Leadership," 24 June 2002; "President Bush, King Abdullah Discuss Middle East Peace," 1 August 2002. Bush refused even to consider a ceremonial role for Arafat in an independent Palestinian state. "President Meets with Foreign Ministers of Egypt, Jordan, and Saudi Arabia", 18 July 2002.
62. "President Bush, King Abdullah Discuss Middle East Peace," 1 August 2002. He indicated that genuine "reform" required "action against terrorism." "President Bush Calls for New Palestinian Leadership," 24 June 2002. He also stressed that a Palestinian state was to "abandon forever the use of terror." "President Discusses Roadmap for Peace in the Middle East," 14 March 2003.

63. "President Bush Calls for New Palestinian Leadership," 24 June 2002; "President Discusses Roadmap for Peace in the Middle East," 14 March 2003.

64. "President Bush Calls for New Palestinian Leadership," 24 June 2002; "President Discusses Roadmap for Peace in the Middle East," 14 March 2003.

65. "President Bush Calls for New Palestinian Leadership," 24 June 2002; "Statement by the Press Secretary: Election of Ariel Sharon as Prime Minister of Israel", Office of the Press Secretary, 6 February 2001, in http://www.whitehouse.gov/, accessed 14 June 2005.

66. "President Bush Welcomes Prime Minister Sharon to White House," 16 October 2002.

67. See, for example, "Joint Statement on the Middle East: 10th EU-Russia Summit," 11 November 2002. The EU's foreign policy chief, Javier Solana, ignored Sharon's request not to meet with Arafat. Esposito, "Quarterly Update on Conflict and Diplomacy," 139.

68. "Commission decides on emergency rehabilitation of administrative infrastructure of Palestinian Authority," Europa, 27 June 2002, in http://www.europa.eu.int/, accessed 16 August 2005; "President Discusses Roadmap for Peace in the Middle East," 14 March 2003; "Commission approves EUR 29 million," 28 October 2002; "European Commission approves EUR 5.45 million to support Palestinian reform, plus EUR 2.5 million for election observation mission," Europa, 17 December 2002, in http://www.europa.eu.int/, accessed 16 August 2005. See as well "Statement of Chris Patten, Commissioner for External Relations, on partial release of tax revenues by Israel to the Palestinian Authority," Europa, 25 July 2002, in http://www.europa.eu.int/, accessed 16 August 2005.

69. "Joint Statement on the Middle East: 10th EU-Russia Summit," 11 November 2002; "Statement of the Task Force on Palestinian Reform," Europa, 14–15 November 2002, in http://www.europa.eu.int/, accessed 16 August 2005.

70. "Commission approves EUR 29 million," 28 October 2002; "European Commission approves EUR 5.45 million," 17 December 2002.

71. "Joint Statement on the Middle East: 10th EU-Russia Summit," 11 November 2002.

72. See, for example, UNSCR 338 in "UN Security Council Resolution 338, Concerning the October War, 22 October 1973," in *Israeli-Palestinian Conflict*, Lukacs, ed., 13.

73. "Secretary-General's Remarks (unofficial transcript)", 31 March 2003; "Powell Acknowledges No Movement Likely Until Israeli Elections", Deutsche Presse-Agentur, 18 December 2002, in http://web.lexis-nexis.com/, accessed 23 August 2005.

74. "Russian Foreign Minister Denies Mideast-For-Iraq Deal With Washington", Financial Times Information, Global News Wire- Asia Africa Intelligence Wire, BBC Monitoring/BBC, BBC Monitoring International Reports, 21 May 2003, in http://web.lexis-nexis.com/, accessed 23 August 2005.

75. "Israeli-Palestinian Road Map Plan is 'Historic Window of Opportunity'- Annan", UN News Centre, 8 May 2003, in http://www.un.org/, accessed 9 August 2005.

76. "Israeli-Palestinian Road Map Plan is 'Historic Window of Opportunity'- Annan", 8 May 2003; "Russia Tells Palestinians Get a Government or Suffer More", Deutsche Presse-Agentur, 22 April 2003, in http://web.lexis-nexis.com/, accessed 23 August 2005.

77. "European Commission welcomes Quartet's presentation of the Middle East Road Map," Europa, 30 April 2003, in http://www.europa.eu.int/, accessed 16 August 2005.

78. "Statement on the Middle East: Statement by the President on the Middle East", Office of the Press Secretary, 30 April 2003, in http://www.whitehouse.gov/, accessed 17 August 2005; "President Bush Presses for Peace in the Middle East", Office of the Press Secretary, 9 May 2003, in http://www.whitehouse.gov/, accessed 17 August 2005.

79. "Statement on the Middle East," 30 April 2003.

80. "Palestinian Minister Says US, Quartet Need to Fulfil Road Map Responsibilities", Financial Times Information, Global News Wire- Asia Africa Intelligence Wire, BBC Monitoring/BBC, BBC Monitoring International Reports, 20 February 2004, in http://web.lexis-nexis.com/, accessed 23 August 2005.

81. "Palestinians Ask for US Clarification of Policy on Israeli Settlements", Financial Times Information, Global News Wire- Asia Africa Intelligence Wire, BBC Monitoring/BBC, BBC Monitoring International Reports, 23 August 2004, in http://web.lexis-nexis.com/, accessed 23 August 2005; "Palestinian Negotiator on Elections, Prospects of Road Map", Financial Times Information, Global News Wire- Asia Africa Intelligence Wire, BBC Monitoring/BBC, BBC Monitoring International Reports, 10 January 2005, in http://web.lexis-nexis.com/, accessed 23 August 2005; "PLO Official Says US Not Pressuring Israel Enough, Urges Greater EU Role", Financial Times Information, Global News Wire- Asia Africa Intelligence Wire, BBC Monitoring/BBC, BBC Monitoring International Reports, 1 September 2003, in http://web.lexis-nexis.com/, accessed 23 August 2005. See as well "Palestinian Premier Warns of 'Explosion of the Situation' in Territories", Financial Times Information, Global News Wire- Asia Africa Intelligence Wire, BBC Monitoring/BBC, BBC Monitoring International Reports, 5 June 2005, in http://web.lexis-nexis.com/, accessed 23 August 2005.

82. "Palestinian Minister Urayqat Hopes Israeli Withdrawal to Be Part of Road Map", Financial Times Information, Global News Wire- Asia Africa Intelligence Wire, BBC Monitoring/BBC, BBC Monitoring International Reports, 16 May 2004, in http://web.lexis-nexis.com/, accessed 23 August 2005; "Palestinian Minister Says US, Quartet Need to Fulfil Road Map Responsibilities," 20 February 2004.

83. "Palestinian Minister Insists Road Map Must be Implemented 'As it is'", Financial Times Information, Global News Wire- Asia Africa Intelligence Wire, BBC Monitoring/BBC, BBC Monitoring International Reports, 28 May 2003, in http://web.lexis-nexis.com/, accessed 23 August 2005. See "Powell Says US Ready for Mideast Peace", Xinhua News Agency, Xinhua General News Service, 3 April 2003, in http://web.lexis-nexis.com/, accessed 23 August 2005.

84. "New Palestinian President Underlines Commitment to Road Map", Financial Times Information, Global News Wire- Asia Africa Intelligence Wire, BBC Monitoring/BBC, BBC Monitoring International Reports, 15 January 2005, in http://web.lexis-nexis.com/, accessed 23 August 2005; "Palestinian Minister Says US, Quartet Need to Fulfil Road Map Responsibilities," 20 February 2004. See also "Palestinian Authority Welcomes UN Resolution on Road Map", Financial Times Information, Global News Wire- Asia Africa Intelligence Wire, BBC Monitoring/BBC, BBC Monitoring International Reports, 20 November 2003, in http://web.lexis-nexis.com/, accessed 23 August 2005; "Palestinians Say Road Map Progress Depends on Active Quartet Role", Financial Times Information, Global News Wire- Asia Africa Intelligence Wire, BBC Monitoring/BBC, BBC Monitoring International Reports, 7 January 2004, in http://web.lexis-nexis.com/, accessed 23 August 2005; "Palestinian Official Discusses Developments with UN, US, Russian Envoys", Financial Times Information, Global News Wire- Asia Africa Intelligence Wire, BBC Monitoring/BBC, BBC Monitoring International Reports, 10 November 2003, in http://web.lexis-nexis.com/, accessed 23 August 2005; "Palestinian Officials React to Quartet Recommendations", Financial Times Information, Global

News Wire- Asia Africa Intelligence Wire, BBC Monitoring/BBC, BBC Monitoring International Reports, 26 September 2003, in http://web.lexis-nexis.com/, accessed 23 August 2005; "Palestinian Minister Urges Quartet to Stop Israeli Settlement Activity", Financial Times Information, Global News Wire- Asia Africa Intelligence Wire, BBC Monitoring/BBC, BBC Monitoring International Reports, 27 January 2005, in http://web.lexis-nexis.com/, accessed 23 August 2005.

85. "Palestinian Negotiator on Elections, Prospects of Road Map," 10 January 2005. Prime Minister Ahmad Quray noted Britain's particular importance in enhancing EU influence in the Quartet Committee given its "good relations with the United States." "Palestinian Premier Stresses Need for International Forces in Gaza", Financial Times Information, Global News Wire- Asia Africa Intelligence Wire, BBC Monitoring/BBC, BBC Monitoring International Reports, 8 March 2004, in http://web.lexis-nexis.com/, accessed 23 August 2005. See as well "Palestinian Minister Notes Need for UK Pressure on US Over Sharon Plan", Financial Times Information, Global News Wire- Asia Africa Intelligence Wire, BBC Monitoring/BBC, BBC Monitoring International Reports, 4 May 2004, in http://web.lexis-nexis.com/, accessed 23 August 2005. Arafat also highlighted Russian efforts on the Quartet's behalf, thanking Putin for his "comprehensive support" of the peace process and "solidarity with our Palestinian people." "Arafat Asks Russia to Help Oversee Road Map Implementation", Financial Times Information, Global News Wire- Asia Africa Intelligence Wire, BBC Monitoring/BBC, BBC Monitoring International Reports, 14 July 2003, in http://web.lexis-nexis.com/, accessed 23 August 2005; "Arafat Thanks Russian President for Effort in Securing UN Road Map Resolution", Financial Times Information, Global News Wire- Asia Africa Intelligence Wire, BBC Monitoring/BBC, BBC Monitoring International Reports, 21 November 2003, in http://web.lexis-nexis.com/, accessed 23 August 2005.

86. "New Palestinian President Underlines Commitment to Road Map," 15 January 2005.

87. "Arafat Calls for Palestinian Commitment to Road Map", Financial Times Information, Global News Wire- Asia Africa Intelligence Wire, BBC Monitoring/BBC, BBC Monitoring International Reports, 12 November 2003, in http://web.lexis-nexis.com/, accessed 23 August 2005.

88. "Palestinian Leader Abbas, Italian Foreign Minister Discuss Gaza Pull-Out", Financial Times Information, Global News Wire- Asia Africa Intelligence Wire, BBC Monitoring/BBC, BBC Monitoring International Reports, 23 December 2004, in http://web.lexis-nexis.com/, accessed 23 August 2005.

89. "Palestinian Minister: Israel Replacing Road Map Steps With 'Formalities'", Financial Times Information, Global News Wire- Asia Africa Intelligence Wire, BBC Monitoring/BBC, BBC Monitoring International Reports, 30 May 2003, in http://web.lexis-nexis.com/, accessed 23 August 2005; "New Palestinian President Underlines Commitment to Road Map," 15 January 2005.

90. "Palestinian Leader Addresses London Meeting, Demands Adherence to Road Map", Financial Times Information, Global News Wire- Asia Africa Intelligence Wire, BBC Monitoring/BBC, BBC Monitoring International Reports, 1 March 2005, in http://web.lexis-nexis.com/, accessed 23 August 2005. This echoed the PA's insistence that "all the parties" fulfill their *Road Map* obligations. "New Palestinian President Underlines Commitment to Road Map," 15 January 2005.

91. "Arafat's Adviser Says No Peace, Stability Without Agreement with PLO", Financial Times Information, Global News Wire, 2 October 2003, in http://web.lexis-nexis.com/, accessed 23 August 2005; "Palestinian PM Tells Russian TV We Must Deal with Sharon", Financial Times Information, Global News Wire- Asia Africa Intelligence

Wire, BBC Monitoring/BBC, BBC Monitoring International Reports, 8 July 2003, in http://web.lexis-nexis.com/, accessed 23 August 2005.

92. "Palestinian Minister Says US, Quartet Need to Fulfil Road Map Responsibilities," 20 February 2004; "Palestinian Negotiator on Elections, Prospects of Road Map," 10 January 2005.

93. "Palestinian Premier Says No Peace Without Final-Status Talks", Financial Times Information, Global News Wire- Asia Africa Intelligence Wire, BBC Monitoring/BBC, BBC Monitoring International Reports, 22 May 2005, in http://web.lexis-nexis.com/, accessed 23 August 2005 (Emphasis added.); "Palestinian Minister says No Israeli Plan to Withdraw from Gaza", Financial Times Information, Global News Wire- Asia Africa Intelligence Wire, BBC Monitoring/BBC, BBC Monitoring International Reports, 13 March 2004, in http://web.lexis-nexis.com/, accessed 23 August 2005. See also "Palestinians, Egyptians Envoy Discuss Mideast Peace Ahead of Abbas-Sharon Meeting", Financial Times Information, Global News Wire- Asia Africa Intelligence Wire, BBC Monitoring/BBC, BBC Monitoring International Reports, 15 June 2005, in http://web.lexis-nexis.com/, accessed 23 August 2005. Abbas likewise observed that withdrawal must "be part of the road map." "Palestinian Leader Abbas, Italian Foreign Minister Discuss Gaza Pull-Out," 23 December 2004.

94. "PLO Executive Says New Government Needs 'Effective Guarantees'", Financial Times Information, Global News Wire- Asia Africa Intelligence Wire, BBC Monitoring/BBC, BBC Monitoring International Reports, 8 September 2003, in http://web.lexis-nexis.com/, accessed 23 August 2005; "PLO Official Says US Not Pressuring Israel Enough, Urges Greater EU Role," 1 September 2003; "Arafat's Adviser Says No Peace, Stability Without Agreement with PLO," 2 October 2003.

95. "Abbas Tells Israeli TV Palestinians to Call 'Truce', Urges Final Status Talks", Financial Times Information, Global News Wire- Asia Africa Intelligence Wire, BBC Monitoring/BBC, BBC Monitoring International Reports, 14 March 2005, in http://web.lexis-nexis.com/, accessed 23 August 2005; "New Palestinian President Underlines Commitment to Road Map," 15 January 2005. He insisted that "[p]eace can never be achieved through partial or temporary solutions." "New Palestinian President Underlines Commitment to Road Map," 15 January 2005. See as well "Abbas Calls on Bush to Protect Peace Process, 'Vision' of Palestinian State", Financial Times Information, Global News Wire- Asia Africa Intelligence Wire, BBC Monitoring/BBC, BBC Monitoring International Reports, 26 May 2005, in http://web.lexis-nexis.com/, accessed 23 August 2005.

96. "Palestinian Negotiator on Elections, Prospects of Road Map," 10 January 2005.

97. "Palestinian Minister Urayqat Hopes Israeli Withdrawal to Be Part of Road Map," 16 May 2004; "Palestinian Negotiator on Elections, Prospects of Road Map," 10 January 2005. Ahmad Quray similarly observed, "The situation will not improve and none will enjoy peace without addressing the final-status issues related to the peace process." "Palestinian Premier Says No Peace Without Final-Status Talks," 22 May 2005.

98. "Sharon Makes Case for Pull-Out Plan, Says 'Stalemate Cannot Continue Forever'", Financial Times Information, Global News Wire- Asia Africa Intelligence Wire, BBC Monitoring/BBC, BBC Monitoring International Reports, 31 March 2004, in http://web.lexis-nexis.com/, accessed 23 August 2005.

99. "Israel Cautiously Accepts Peace 'Road Map'", News Max Wires, 24 May 2003, in http://www.newsmax.com/, accessed 23 August 2005; "Israeli Cabinet Statement on Road Map and 14 Reservations", Jewish Virtual Library, 25 May 2003, in http://www.jewishvirtuallibrary.org/, accessed 23 August 2005. Indeed, Sharon stressed that Israel would participate in negotiations "based on the principles of President Bush's

speech—I repeat, President Bush's speech and not the *road map*." "Sharon Agrees to Talks Based on Bush Speech 'Not' Road Map", Financial Times Information, Global News Wire-Asia Africa Intelligence Wire, BBC Monitoring/BBC, BBC Monitoring International Reports, 30 May 2003, in http://web.lexis-nexis.com/, accessed 23 August 2005. The reservations included provisions calling for the *Road Map*'s "[m]onitoring mechanism . . . [to] be under American management." "Israeli Cabinet Statement on Road Map and 14 Reservations," 25 May 2003.

100. "Sharon Makes Case for Pull-Out Plan, Says 'Stalemate Cannot Continue Forever'", 31 March 2004.

101. "Israeli Cabinet Statement on Road Map and 14 Reservations", 25 May 2003; "Israel Opposes UN Involvement in Road Map Plan- Sharon", Financial Times Information, Global News Wire- Asia Africa Intelligence Wire, BBC Monitoring/BBC, BBC Monitoring International Reports, 5 November 2003, in http://web.lexis-nexis.com/, accessed 23 August 2005. See as well "Israel Formally Protests Russian Road Map Initiative", Financial Times Information, Global News Wire- Asia Africa Intelligence Wire, BBC Monitoring/BBC, BBC Monitoring International Reports, 25 November 2003, in http://web.lexis-nexis.com/, accessed 23 August 2005; "Israel PM Rejects Quartet's Aid 'For Now', Says Disengagement Leads to Road Map", Financial Times Information, Global News Wire- Asia Africa Intelligence Wire, BBC Monitoring/BBC, BBC Monitoring International Reports, 23 November 2004, in http://web.lexis- nexis.com/, accessed 23 August 2005.

102. "Israeli PM Booed During Speech on Settlement Removal, Adherence to Road Map", Financial Times Information, Global News Wire- Asia Africa Intelligence Wire, BBC Monitoring/BBC, BBC Monitoring International Reports, 5 January 2004, in http://web.lexis-nexis.com/, accessed 23 August 2005. See as well "Israel Ready to Make 'Brave Decisions' at Talks with Palestinians-Mufaz", Financial Times Information, Global News Wire- Asia Africa Intelligence Wire, BBC Monitoring/BBC, BBC Monitoring International Reports, 16 December 2003, in http://web.lexis-nexis.com/, accessed 23 August 2005, in which Israeli Defense Minister Shaul Mufaz, referring to the possibility of unilateral Israeli disengagement from Gaza, emphasized the importance of "US backing and support for every such step."

103. "Israeli Anger Grows at Arafat", Paul Reynolds, BBC News, 17 September 2003, in http://newsvote.bbc.co.uk/, accessed 23 August 2005. The *Jerusalem Post* declared, "we must kill Yasser Arafat, because the world leaves us no alternative. . . . The current jihad against us is being fuelled by the perception that Israel is blocked from taking decisive action to defend itself. . . . Killing Arafat, more than any other act, would demonstrate that the tool of terror is unacceptable . . . Arafat does not just stand for terror; he stands for the refusal to make peace with Israel under any circumstances and within any borders." "Israeli Anger Grows at Arafat," 17 September 2003.

104. "Israeli Anger Grows at Arafat," 17 September 2003. See as well "Road Map Disarray over Arafat Decision", Financial Times Information, Global News Wire- Europe Intelligence Wire, Sunday Business Post, 14 September 2003, in http://web.lexis-nexis.com/, accessed 23 August 2005. Bush feared that Arafat's expulsion or assassination would preclude *any* possibility of negotiations.

105. "Sharon Seeks U.S. Approval for Disengagement Plan," Financial Times Information, Global News Wire-Asia Africa Intelligence Wire, China News, Taiwan News, 14 April 2004, in http://web.lexis-nexis.com/, accessed 23 August 2005; "'Road Map' Put on Ice as Sharon Says Troops Stay in West Bank", Financial Times Information, Global News Wire- Europe Intelligence Wire, Independent Newspapers (UK) Limited, *The Independent*, 16 September 2004, in http://web.lexis-nexis.com/, accessed 23 August

2005. Sharon acknowledged his unilateralist impulses, declaring, "We acted when it was possible to do so, at a time when it was convenient for us. The same principle is also valid for Arafat. Arafat will be expelled. We will treat him the way we treated other murderers." "'Road Map' Put on Ice as Sharon Says Troops Stay in West Bank," 16 September 2004.

106. "Israeli Premier's Aide Confirms Road Map Commitment after Freeze Remarks", Financial Times Information, Global News Wire- Asia Africa Intelligence Wire, BBC Monitoring/BBC, BBC Monitoring International Reports, 6 October 2004, in http://web.lexis-nexis.com/, accessed 23 August 2005.

107. "Israeli Premier Outlines 'Disengagement Plan' in Herzliyya Speech", Financial Times Information, Global News Wire- Asia Africa Intelligence Wire, BBC Monitoring/BBC, BBC Monitoring International Reports, 18 December 2003, in http://web.lexis-nexis.com/, accessed 23 August 2005.

108. "Sharon's Vow is a Road Block on Path to Peace", Nationwide News Pty Limited, *Daily Telegraph* (Sydney, Australia), 13 April 2005, in http://web.lexis-nexis.com/, accessed 23 August 2005. He observed, "We have not, nor will we conduct political negotiations under fire. We will not reward terrorism." "Israeli PM Booed During Speech on Settlement Removal, Adherence to Road Map," 5 January 2004.

109. "Sharon to Ignore Warning by Bush", Financial Times Information, Global News Wire- Europe Intelligence Wire, Newsletter, 13 April 2005, in http://web.lexis-nexis.com/, accessed 23 August 2005. Emphasis added. See as well "After Israeli Disengagement", Martin Asser, BBC News, 21 August 2005, in http://newsvote.bbc.co.uk/, accessed 23 August 2005; "Israel's Sharon Tells Annan Disengagement Plan will be Implemented on Time", Financial Times Information, Global News Wire- Asia Africa Intelligence Wire, BBC Monitoring/BBC, BBC Monitoring Intelligence Reports, 14 March 2005, in http://web.lexis-nexis.com/, accessed 23 August 2005.

110. "Israeli Premier's Aide Confirms Road Map Commitment after Freeze Remarks," 6 October 2004. Defense Minister Shaul Mufaz likewise observed, "Israel has made it clear that under no circumstances will it tolerate the equation of terrorism waged concurrently with the continued implementation of the road map. The Palestinian government has to abide by its commitment to disband the terrorist organizations, making no concessions." "Palestinian Government Must Act to Retain Standing- Israeli Defence Minister", Financial Times Information, Global News Wire-Asia Africa Intelligence Wire, BBC Monitoring/BBC, BBC Monitoring International Reports, 4 September 2003, in http://web.lexis-nexis.com/, accessed 23 August 2005. See "Israelis Wary in Backing Road Map", Nationwide News Pty Limited, *The Australian*, 27 May 2003, in http://web.lexis-nexis.com/, accessed 23 August 2005, on the rejection of parallel obligations. See "Road Map for Palestine", Nationwide News Pty Limited, *Herald Sun* (Melbourne, Australia), 6 December 2002, in http://web.lexis-nexis.com/, accessed 23 August 2005, and "Sharon Talks Statehood", Nationwide News Pty Limited, *Hobart Mercury* (Australia), 6 December 2002, in http://web.lexis-nexis.com/, accessed 23 August 2005, for discussion of specific preconditions for negotiations.

111. "Israeli Cabinet Statement on Road Map and 14 Reservations," 25 May 2003. Emphasis added. Indeed, the Cabinet insisted that Israel was relieved of its Phase I commitments to a settlement freeze and redeployment of IDF forces absent "absolute quiet" by the Palestinians. "Israeli Cabinet Statement on Road Map and 14 Reservations," 25 May 2003.

112. "Israeli PM Booed During Speech on Settlement Removal, Adherence to Road Map," 5 January 2004. Ehud Olmert went even further, arguing that while a "PNA crackdown on terror is a prerequisite for restarting negotiations," it was "in no way a basis for

agreement on final-status peace negotiations." "Israeli Minister Says West Bank Withdrawal Needed after Gaza Pull-Out", Financial Times Information, Global News Wire-Asia Africa Intelligence Wire, BBC Monitoring/BBC, BBC Monitoring International Reports, 30 December 2004, in http://web.lexis-nexis.com/, accessed 23 August 2005.

113. "Israeli Premier Outlines 'Disengagement Plan' in Herzliyya Speech," 18 December 2003 (Emphasis added.); "Israeli Premier's Aide Confirms Road Map Commitment after Freeze Remarks," 6 October 2004. Emphasis added. Weissglas's candid assessment belied Sharon's publicly stated desire "to implement all stages of the road map, together with the 14 reservations, as fast as possible." "Israeli PM Booed During Speech on Settlement Removal, Adherence to Road Map," 5 January 2004.

114. "President Bush, Jordanian King Discuss Iraq, Middle East", Office of the Press Secretary, 6 May 2004, in http://www.whitehouse.gov/, accessed 17 August 2005; "Letter from President Bush to Prime Minister Sharon", Office of the Press Secretary, 14 April 2004, in http://www.whitehouse.gov/, accessed 17 August 2005. See as well "The German-American Alliance for the 21st Century: Joint Statement by President George W. Bush and Chancellor Gerhard Schroder", Office of the Press Secretary, 27 February 2004, in http://www.whitehouse.gov/, accessed 17 August 2005.

115. "President Meets with Leaders of Jordan, Israel, and Palestinian Authority", Office of the Press Secretary, 4 June 2003, in http://www.whitehouse.gov/, accessed 17 August 2005; "President Bush and Chancellor Schroder Discuss Partnership", Office of the Press Secretary, 23 February 2005, in http://www.whitehouse.gov/, accessed 17 August 2005; "President and King Abdullah of Jordan Discuss Middle East Peace, Trade", Office of the Press Secretary, 15 March 2005, in http://www.whitehouse.gov/, accessed 17 August 2005.

116. "President and King Abdullah of Jordan Discuss Middle East Peace, Trade," 15 March 2005; "President and Prime Minister Sharon Discuss Economy, Middle East", Office of the Press Secretary, 11 April 2005, in http://www.whitehouse.gov/, accessed 17 August 2005; "State of the Union Address", Office of the Press Secretary, 2 February 2005, in http://www.whitehouse.gov/, accessed 17 August 2005; "President Bush Welcomes Prime Minister Abbas to White House", Office of the Press Secretary, 25 July 2003, in http://www.whitehouse.gov/, accessed 17 August 2005. He supported multilateral efforts to help Abbas "set up a democracy in the Palestinian territories, so that Israel will have a democratic partner in peace," and promised Palestinians "help in consolidating security forces and training security forces to defeat the terrorists who would like to stop the march of freedom." "President Meets with E.U. Leaders", Office of the Press Secretary, 22 February 2005, in http://www.whitehouse.gov/, accessed 17 August 2005; "President and King Abdullah of Jordan Discuss Middle East Peace, Trade," 15 March 2005.

117. "Dr. Condoleezza Rice Discusses Iraq and the Middle East", Office of the Press Secretary, 4 May 2004, in http://www.whitehouse.gov/, accessed 17 August 2005; "Statement by the President", Office of the Press Secretary, 14 April 2004, in http://www.whitehouse.gov/, accessed 17 August 2005.

118. "Powell, Rice Discuss Road Map for Peace in the Middle East", Office of the Press Secretary, 4 June 2003, in http://www.whitehouse.gov/, accessed 17 August 2005; "Statement by the President," 14 April 2004; "Letter from President Bush to Prime Minister Sharon," 14 April 2004; "Bush, Blair Discuss Sharon Plan, Future of Iraq in Press Conference", Office of the Press Secretary, 16 April 2004, in http://www.whitehouse.gov/, accessed 17 August 2005; "President Bush, Jordanian King Discuss Iraq, Middle East," 6 May 2004.

119. "Dr. Condoleezza Rice Discusses Iraq and the Middle East," 4 May 2004.

120. "President Discusses Middle East Peace with Prime Minister Sharon", Office of the Press Secretary, 29 July 2003, in http://www.whitehouse.gov/, accessed 17 August 2005; "Letter from President Bush to Prime Minister Sharon," 14 April 2004.

121. "President and Prime Minister Sharon Discuss Economy, Middle East," 11 April 2005; "President Discusses Middle East Peace with Prime Minister Sharon", 29 July 2003.

122. See *Road Map*. Responding to Israel's extensive "reservations" to the *Road Map*, Bush pledged to "address any concerns," while Condoleezza Rice and Colin Powell indicated that the US "shares the view of the government of Israel that these are real concerns, and will address them fully and seriously in the implementation of the road map." "Israel Cautiously Accepts Peace 'Road Map'", 24 May 2003.

123. "President Discusses Middle East Peace with Prime Minister Sharon," 29 July 2003; "President Bush, Egyptian President Mubarak Meet with Reporters", Office of Press Secretary, 12 April 2004, in http://www.whitehouse.gov/, accessed 17 August 2005 (Emphasis added); "President Bush, Prime Minister Sabah of Kuwait Discuss Middle East", Office of the Press Secretary, 10 September 2003, in http://www.whitehouse.gov/, accessed 17 August 2005; "President Bush, European Leaders Act to Fight Global Terror: Remarks by President Bush, Prime Minister Simitis and President Prodi in Press Availability", Office of the Press Secretary, 25 June 2003, in http://www.whitehouse.gov/, accessed 17 August 2005.

124. "President Bush Presses for Peace in the Middle East," 9 May 2003; "President Bush Welcomes Prime Minister Abbas to White House," 25 July 2003; "President's Radio Address", Office of the Press Secretary, 5 March 2005, in http://www.whitehouse.gov/, accessed 17 August 2005. Emphasis added.

125. "President Bush Presses for Peace in the Middle East," 9 May 2003. Emphasis added. "Bush on Gaza Withdrawal", BBC News, 14 April 2004, in http://newsvote.bbc.co.uk/, accessed 23 August 2005. See as well "President Speaks to the American Israel Public Affairs Committee", Office of the Press Secretary, 18 May 2004, in http://www.whitehouse.gov/, accessed 17 August 2005; "President Bush Addresses United Nations General Assembly", Office of the Press Secretary, 23 September 2003, in http://www.whitehouse.gov/, accessed 17 August 2005.

126. "Israel, Palestinians Would Fall off 'Cliff' if Roadmap Abandoned: Powell", Xinhua News Agency, Xinhua General News Service, 21 August 2003, in http://web.lexis-nexis.com/, accessed 23 August 2005.

127. "President Bush Presses for Peace in the Middle East," 9 May 2003. See as well "President Bush Troubled with Israeli Helicopter Gunship Attacks: Remarks by the President and Ugandan President Museveni in Photo Opportunity", Office of the Press Secretary, 10 June 2003, in http://www.whitehouse.gov/, accessed 17 August 2005; "President's Statement on Palestinian Elections", Office of the Press Secretary, 9 January 2005, in http://www.whitehouse.gov/, accessed 17 August 2005.

128. "President Bush Discusses Top Priorities for the U.S.", Office of the Press Secretary, 30 July 2003, in http://www.whitehouse.gov/, accessed 17 August 2005; "Statement on the Middle East," 30 April 2003.

129. "President and Prime Minister Sharon Discuss Economy, Middle East," 11 April 2005. See as well "President Bush, Jordanian King Discuss Iraq, Middle East," 6 May 2004.

130. "Bush, Blair Discuss Sharon Plan, Future of Iraq in Press Conference," 16 April 2004; "Secretary-General and Quartet Members at Press Conference Following Quartet Meeting (unofficial transcript)", Secretary-General Office of the Spokesman, 26 September 2003, in http://www.un.org/, accessed 9 August 2005, 6.

131. "President Bush and Chancellor Schroder Discuss Partnership," 23 February 2005; "Secretary-General and Quartet Members at Press Conference Following Quartet Meeting (unofficial transcript)", Secretary-General Office of the Spokesman, 26 September 2003, in http://www.un.org/, accessed 9 August 2005; "Situation in the Middle East: Speech by the Rt. Hon. Chris Patten," Europa, 18 June 2003, in http://www.europa.eu.int/, accessed 16 August 2005.

132. Christopher Patten, "A road map paid for in euros," *The Financial Times*, 17 July 2003, in http://www.europa.eu.int/, accessed 16 August 2005; "Situation in the Middle East: Speech by the Rt. Hon. Chris Patten," Europa, 18 June 2003, in http://www.europa.eu.int/, accessed 16 August 2005. See as well "European Commission takes action with EUR 100 million to improve conditions in Gaza and the West Bank, and accelerate relaunch of the Palestinian economy," Europa, 17 July 2003, in http://www.europa.eu.int/, accessed 16 August 2005.

133. "Speech to the London Meeting on Supporting the Palestinian Authority: Speech by Dr. Benita Ferrero-Waldner," Europa, 1 March 2005, in http://www.europa.eu.int/, accessed 9 August 2005.

134. "Situation in the Middle East, Chris Patten," 18 June 2003; "Secretary-General and Quartet Members", 26 September 2003. Such monitoring was to include enlisting Arab support in developing mechanisms to "channel" aid to Palestinians that would "cut off public and private funding for the groups engaged in violence and terror." "Situation in the Middle East, Chris Patten," 18 June 2003.

135. "The EU, the Mediterranean and the Middle East—A longstanding partnership," Europa, 10 December 2004, in http://www.europa.eu.int/, accessed 16 August 2005; "Statement of the Quartet Task Force on Palestinian Reform", 11 December 2003, in http://www.europa.eu.int/, accessed 16 August 2005; "The EU's relations with West Bank and Gaza Strip," Europa, in http://www.europa.eu.int/, accessed 16 August 2005; "European Commission takes action with EUR 100 million," 17 July 2003.

136. "Commissioner Ferrero-Waldner attends London Meeting on the Palestinian Authority, Quartet," Europa, 28 February 2005, in http://www.europa.eu.int/, accessed 16 August 2005.

137. "Alternatives to Mideast Road Map May Help Settlement- Russian Minister", Financial Times Information, Global News Wire- Asia Africa Intelligence Wire, BBC Monitoring/BBC, BBC Monitoring International Reports, 20 November 2003, in http://web.lexis-nexis.com/, accessed 23 August 2005; "Russian Official Visits Lebanon, says 'No Alternative' to Road Map", Financial Times Information, Global News Wire- Asia Africa Intelligence Wire, BBC Monitoring/BBC, BBC Monitoring International Reports, 18 January 2004, in http://web.lexis-nexis.com/, accessed 23 August 2005. See as well "Russian, Palestinian Ministers See Road Map as Only Means to Israeli Settlement", Financial Times Information, Global News Wire- Asia Africa Intelligence Wire, BBC Monitoring/BBC, BBC Monitoring International Reports, 16 April 2004, in http://web.lexis-nexis.com/, accessed 23 August 2005; "Russian Foreign Minister Poised to Attend Quartet Meeting on Middle East", Financial Times Information, Global News Wire- Asia Africa Intelligence Wire, BBC Monitoring/BBC, BBC Monitoring International Reports, 22 September 2004, in http://web.lexis-nexis.com/, accessed 23 August 2005. Indeed, Russia went so far as to argue that "there is no other reasonable way out of the crisis at present except for the fulfilment of the Road Map." "Russia Ready to Assist in Implementation of Road Map Peace Plan", Financial Times Information, Global News Wire, NTIS, U.S. Dept of Commerce, World News Connection, 9 September 2003, in http://web.lexis-nexis.com/, accessed 23 August 2005. See as well "'Road Map' Remains the Only Way Out Russian Envoy says", Financial Times Information, Global News

Wire- Asia Africa Intelligence Wire, BBC Monitoring/BBC, BBC Monitoring International Reports, 17 October 2003, in http://web.lexis-nexis.com/, accessed 23 August 2005.

138. "Russia Calls for Urgent Measures in Middle East", Financial Times Information, Global News Wire, NTIS, U.S. Dept of Commerce, World News Connection, 16 September 2003, in http://web.lexis-nexis.com/, accessed 23 August 2005; "Russian Diplomat Says Israel's Step Should Be Welcomed", Financial Times Information, Global News Wire- Asia Africa Intelligence Wire, BBC Monitoring/BBC, BBC Monitoring International Reports, 2 April 2004, in http://web.lexis-nexis.com/, accessed 23 August 2005; "Russia, US to Set Up Monitoring Mechanism on Middle East", Xinhua News Agency, Xinhua General News Service, 11 July 2003, in http://web.lexis-nexis.com/, accessed 23 August 2005; "Russian, Palestinian Leaders Adopt Joint Statement", Financial Times Information, Global News Wire- Asia Africa Intelligence Wire, BBC Monitoring/BBC, BBC Monitoring International Reports, 31 January 2005, in http://web.lexis-nexis.com/, accessed 23 August 2005.

139. "Russian Official Visits Lebanon, says 'No Alternative' to Road Map," 18 January 2004; "Spokesman Says Russia's Mideast Role to Be Discussed By Abbas, Putin", Financial Times Information, Global News Wire- Asia Africa Intelligence Wire, BBC Monitoring/BBC, BBC Monitoring International Reports, 28 April 2005, in http://web.lexis-nexis.com/, accessed 23 August 2005.

140. "Russian Official at UN says 'Road Map is Not Dead'", Financial Times Information, Global News Wire, NTIS, U.S. Dept of Commerce, World News Connection, 13 September 2003, in http://web.lexis-nexis.com/, accessed 23 August 2005; "Russian Foreign Minister Advocates 'International Presence' in Middle East", Financial Times Information, Global News Wire- Asia Africa Intelligence Wire, BBC Monitoring/BBC, BBC Monitoring International Reports, 10 September 2003, in http://web.lexis-nexis.com/, accessed 23 August 2005.

141. "Russia Calls for Urgent Measures in Middle East," 16 September 2003; "Alternatives to Mideast Road Map May Help Settlement- Russian Minister," 20 November 2003.

142. "Russia Calls for Urgent Measures in Middle East," 16 September 2003; "Roundup: Sharon Fails to Dissuade Russia From New UN Mideast Resolution", Xinhua News Agency, Xinhua General News Service, 5 November 2003, in http://web.lexis-nexis.com/, accessed 23 August 2005. See as well "Terrorism 'Feeds On' Arab-Israeli Conflict- Russian Minister", Financial Times Information, Global News Wire- Asia Africa Intelligence Wire, BBC Monitoring/BBC, BBC Monitoring International Reports, 10 May 2005, in http://web.lexis-nexis.com/, accessed 23 August 2005; "Russian Diplomat Says Israel's Step Should Be Welcomed," 2 April 2004; "Russia Calls for Quartet Discussion of Israeli Disengagement Plan", Financial Times Information, Global News Wire- Asia Africa Intelligence Wire, BBC Monitoring/BBC, BBC Monitoring International Reports, 15 April 2004, in http://web.lexis-nexis.com/, accessed 23 August 2005; "Russian, Israeli Foreign Ministers Denounce Terrorism at Moscow Talks", Financial Times Information, Global News Wire, NTIS, U.S. Dept of Commerce, World News Connection, 9 June 2003, in http://web.lexis-nexis.com/, accessed 23 August 2005.

143. "Russian, Israeli FMs Discuss Middle East Peace Process", Financial Times Information, Global News Wire, NTIS, U.S. Dept of Commerce, World News Connection, 23 September 2003, in http://web.lexis-nexis.com/, accessed 23 August 2005. See as well "Russian President Putin Comments on Upcoming Sharon Visit", Financial Times Information, Global News Wire, NTIS, U.S. Dept of Commerce, World News Connection, 29 July 2003, in http://web.lexis-nexis.com/, accessed 23 August 2005; "Russian Envoy

Calls for Mideast Settlement Through Road Map", Financial Times Information, Global News Wire, NTIS, U.S. Dept of Commerce, World News Connection, 1 September 2003, in http://web.lexis-nexis.com/, accessed 23 August 2005; "PA Representatives Discuss Commitment to Fulfill Road Map with Russian Official", Financial Times Information, Global News Wire, NTIS, U.S. Dept of Commerce, World News Connection, 8 September 2003, in http://web.lexis-nexis.com/, accessed 23 August 2005; "Egyptian Foreign Minister, Russian Envoy Discuss Palestinian Situation", Financial Times Information, Global News Wire, NTIS, U.S. Dept of Commerce, World News Connection, 15 June 2003, in http://web.lexis-nexis.com/, accessed 23 August 2005; "Russian Minister, 'Quartet' Mediator Discuss Palestinian-Israeli Settlement", Financial Times Information, Global News Wire- Asia Africa Intelligence Wire, BBC Monitoring/BBC, BBC Monitoring International Reports, 15 June 2005, in http://web.lexis-nexis.com/, accessed 23 August 2005; "Russian Diplomat says Head-On Confrontation in Middle East Should be Prevented", Financial Times Information, Global News Wire, NTIS, U.S. Dept of Commerce, World News Connection, 11 June 2003, in http://web.lexis-nexis.com/, accessed 23 August 2005; "Russian Diplomat Says Israel's Step Should Be Welcomed," 2 April 2004.

144. "Russian Foreign Minister's ME Trip First 'Fully-Fledged' Visit in Three Years", Financial Times Information, Global News Wire, NTIS, U.S. Dept of Commerce, World News Connection, 10 July 2003, in http://web.lexis-nexis.com/, accessed 23 August 2005; "Russian Minister Calls for Settlement Plans to Help Overcome Mideast Crisis", Financial Times Information, Global News Wire- Asia Africa Intelligence Wire, BBC Monitoring/BBC, BBC Monitoring International Reports, 10 July 2003, in http://web.lexis-nexis.com/, accessed 23 August 2005; "Russia says Mideast Peace Should Not Depend on 'Terrorists and Extremists'", Financial Times Information, Global News Wire- Asia Africa Intelligence Wire, BBC Monitoring/BBC, BBC Monitoring International Reports, 27 August 2003, in http://web.lexis-nexis.com/, accessed 23 August 2005. In April 2005, Vladimir Putin became the first Russian President to visit Palestine. "Spokesman Says Russia's Mideast Role to Be Discussed By Abbas, Putin," 28 April 2005.

145. "Spokesman Says Russia's Mideast Role to Be Discussed By Abbas, Putin," 28 April 2005; "Quartet will Support Palestinian Elections- Russian Foreign Minister", Financial Times Information, Global News Wire- Asia Africa Intelligence Wire, BBC Monitoring/BBC, BBC Monitoring International Reports, 23 November 2004, in http://web.lexis-nexis.com/, accessed 23 August 2005; "Russia Delivers Humanitarian Aid for Palestinians", Financial Times Information, Global News Wire- Asia Africa Intelligence Wire, BBC Monitoring/BBC, BBC Monitoring International Reports, 20 July 2004, in http://web.lexis-nexis.com/, accessed 23 August 2005; "Russia Helped Resolve Rift Between Arafat and Abbas, says Ministry Spokesman", Financial Times Information, Global News Wire- Asia Africa Intelligence Wire, BBC Monitoring/BBC, BBC Monitoring International Reports, 15 July 2003, in http://web.lexis-nexis.com/, accessed 23 August 2005; "Russian Diplomat Affirms Importance of Complying with Mideast Road Map", Financial Times Information, Global News Wire, NTIS, U.S. Dept of Commerce, World News Connection, 28 August 2003, in http://web.lexis-nexis.com/, accessed 23 August 2005.

146. "Israeli Premier's Threats Against Arafat 'Unacceptable', Moscow Says", Financial Times Information, Global News Wire- Asia Africa Intelligence Wire, BBC Monitoring/BBC, BBC Monitoring International Reports, 24 April 2004, in http://web.lexis-nexis.com/, accessed 23 August 2005; "Russia Criticizes Israeli Stance on UN Road Map Resolution", Financial Times Information, Global News Wire- Asia

Africa Intelligence Wire, BBC Monitoring/BBC, BBC Monitoring International Reports, 29 November 2003, in http://web.lexis-nexis.com/, accessed 23 August 2005; "Russia Hopes for Restart of Middle East Road Map", Financial Times Information, Global News Wire- Asia Africa Intelligence Wire, BBC Monitoring/BBC, BBC Monitoring International Reports, 26 April 2005, in http://web.lexis-nexis.com/, accessed 23 August 2005.

147. "Secretary-General and Quartet Members", 26 September 2003, 2, 4. He noted, the "fact that the United States may have a greater influence does not mean that the others have none at all." "Secretary-General and Quartet Members", 26 September 2003.

148. "Secretary-General and Quartet Members", 26 September 2003, 4. Annan did express hope that "Israel and the United Nations have rediscovered each other." "Annan ends Middle East trip encouraged by Israeli-Palestinian peace moves", UN News Centre, 16 March 2005, in http://www.un.org/, accessed 9 August 2005. He also noted, "we [the Quartet] pool our efforts to make things happen." "Secretary-General and Quartet Members", 26 September 2003.

149. "Citing 'promise and potential,' Annan pledges support for Middle East peace moves," UN News Centre, 1 March 2005, in http://www.un.org/, accessed 9 August 2005; "International community must help Israel, Palestinians seal peace—Annan," UN News Centre, 7 February 2005, in http://www.un.org/, accessed 9 August 2005. The Quartet likewise called on "the international community to play a vital role in providing additional financial support to the Palestinians, which is essential in order to support needed reforms." "Quartet Statement", Jerusalem Media and Communication Centre, 1 March 2005, in http://www.jmcc.org/, accessed 17 September 2007. See as well the Quartet's commitment to enhancing security and addressing humanitarian and economic issues in, "Full Text of Middle East Quartet Communiqué", UN News Centre, 4 May 2004, in http://www.un.org/, accessed 9 August 2005.

150. "General Affairs & External Relations Council (GAERC): Extracts from successive General Affairs & External Relations Councils," Europa, in http://www.europa.eu.int/, accessed 16 August 2005; "The EU and the Middle East Peace Process," Europa, in http://www.europa.eu.int/, accessed 16 August 2005. See as well "Commissioner Ferrero-Waldner," 28 February 2005.

151. "Russian, Palestinian Ministers See Road Map as Only Means to Israeli Settlement," 16 April 2004; "'Road Map' Remains the Only Way Out Russian Envoy says," 17 October 2003. See as well "Russia Calls on Israel, Palestine Not to Deviate From Road Map", Financial Times Information, Global News Wire- Asia Africa Intelligence Wire, BBC Monitoring/BBC, BBC Monitoring International Reports, 9 September 2003, in http://web.lexis-nexis.com/, accessed 23 August 2005; "Russian, Palestinian Leaders Adopt Joint Statement," 31 January 2005.

152. "Russia Condemns Blasts in Israel and West Bank", Financial Times Information, Global News Wire- Asia Africa Intelligence Wire, BBC Monitoring/BBC, BBC Monitoring International Reports, 12 August 2003, in http://web.lexis-nexis.com/, accessed 23 August 2005; "Russian Envoy to UN Calls on Palestine and Israel to Adhere to 'Road Map'", Financial Times Information, Global News Wire- Asia Africa Intelligence Wire, BBC Monitoring/BBC, BBC Monitoring International Reports, 3 December 2003, in http://web.lexis-nexis.com/, accessed 23 August 2005; "'Road Map' Remains the Only Way Out Russian Envoy says," 17 October 2003.

153. "Russian Envoy to UN Calls on Palestine and Israel to Adhere to 'Road Map'", 3 December 2003.

154. "Quartet Urge Mid-East Peace Efforts", BBC News, 26 September 2003, in http://newsvote.bbc.co.uk/, accessed 23 August 2005. Emphasis added.

155. "Israeli-Palestinian Relations Bedevilled by Lack of Framework, UN Envoy Says", UN News Centre, 21 July 2005, in http://www.un.org/, accessed 9 August 2005. The Quartet adopted a similar position. See "Full Text of Middle East Quartet Communiqué", 4 May 2004; "Statement by Middle East Quartet", UN News Centre, Press Release SG/2091, 23 September 2004, in http://www.un.org/, accessed 9 August 2005.

156. "Remarks of Javier Solana, EU High Representative for the CFSP, on the occasion of a meeting with Palestinian Prime Minister Ahmed Qurei", 13 July 2005, in http://ue.eu.int/, accessed 18 September 2007. See as well the joint US-EU statement in "Joint Statement by the United States and the European Union Working Together to Promote Peace, Prosperity and Progress in the Middle East", Office of the Press Secretary, 20 June 2005, in http://www.whitehouse.gov/, accessed 17 August 2005; "Israel's Gaza Disengagement Plan 'A Moment Pregnant with Hope, but Also Fraught with Peril', Middle East Peace Envoy Tells Security Council", Press Release SC/8455, 21 July 2005, in http://www.un.org/, accessed 9 August 2005.

157. "General Affairs & External Relations Council," Europa. See as well "Press Release: Council of the European Union: 2656th Council meeting," Europa, 25 April 2005, in http://ec.europa.eu/, accessed 18 September 2007; "Remarks of Javier Solana," 13 July 2005.

158. "General Affairs & External Relations Council," Europa, 10. It also urged Israel to refrain from such unilateral measures as "the practice of extra-judicial killings which are contrary to international law" and any effort "to remove the elected President of the Palestinian Authority (Arafat)." "General Affairs & External Relations Council," Europa, 10.

159. "Situation in the Middle East: Speech by the Rt. Hon Chris Patten," Europa, 2 October 2004, in http://www.europa.eu.int/, accessed 16 August 2005. See as well "General Affairs & External Relations Council," Europa, 4, 8.

160. "Russian Foreign Minister, Palestinian Leader Discuss Mideast Settlement", Financial Times Information, Global News Wire- Asia Africa Intelligence Wire, BBC Monitoring/BBC, BBC Monitoring International Reports, 22 June 2005, in http://web.lexis-nexis.com/, accessed 23 August 2005.

161. "Putin Urges Further Efforts in Implementing Mideast Road Map", Xinhua News Agency, Xinhua General News Service, 22 May 2004, in http://web.lexis-nexis.com/, accessed 23 August 2005; "Russian Foreign Ministry Condemns New Israeli Settlements, Barrier", Financial Times Information, Global News Wire- Asia Africa Intelligence Wire, BBC Monitoring/BBC, BBC Monitoring International Reports, 3 October 2003, in http://web.lexis-nexis.com/, accessed 23 August 2005. See as well "Russia Calls for Quartet Discussion of Israeli Disengagement Plan," 15 April 2004; "Russian Foreign Minister Against Sharon's Disengagement Initiative", Financial Times Information, Global News Wire- Asia Africa Intelligence Wire, BBC Monitoring/BBC, BBC Monitoring International Reports, 19 December 2003, in http://web.lexis-nexis.com/, accessed 23 August 2005; "Russian Foreign Minister Speaks Against Israel's 'Separating Wall'", Financial Times Information, Global News Wire- Asia Africa Intelligence Wire, BBC Monitoring/BBC, BBC Monitoring International Reports, 21 January 2004, in http://web.lexis-nexis.com/, accessed 23 August 2005; "Russian Minister Sums Up Outcomes of Latest Middle East Quartet Meeting", Financial Times Information, Global News Wire- Asia Africa Intelligence Wire, BBC Monitoring/BBC, BBC Monitoring International Reports, 23 September 2004, in http://web.lexis-nexis.com/, accessed 23 August 2005.

162. "Russian, Palestinian Leaders Adopt Joint Statement," 31 January 2005; "Russian, Palestinian Ministers See Road Map as Only Means to Israeli Settlement," 16 April

2004; "Russian Diplomat Urges Resumption of Middle East 'Road Map' Talks", Financial Times Information, Global News Wire- Asia Africa Intelligence Wire, BBC Monitoring/BBC, BBC Monitoring International Reports, 20 April 2004, in http://web.lexis-nexis.com/, accessed 23 August 2005; "Russia Fears Israel's 'Expansion of Settlements in West Bank'- Envoy", Financial Times Information, Global News Wire- Asia Africa Intelligence Wire, BBC Monitoring/BBC, BBC Monitoring International Reports, 16 September 2004, in http://web.lexis-nexis.com/, accessed 23 August 2005.

163. "Road Map Remains 'Most Practical Way' to Achieve Aspirations of Israelis, Palestinians, Secretary-General Tells Palestinian Rights Committee", UN Press Release SG/SM/9194; "GA/PAL/946, 3 December 2004", in http://www.un.org/, accessed 9 August 2005.

164. "Israelis and Palestinians Should Not Let Extremists 'Hijack' Peace Process, Annan Says", UN News Centre, 13 May 2003, in http://www.un.org/, accessed 9 August 2005; "Annan Vows to Work to Turn Dream of Middle East Peace into Reality", UN News Centre, 8 March 2005, in http://www.un.org/, accessed 9 August 2005. The Quartet adopted a similar position on avoiding actions that could jeopardize the resolution of final status issues. See "Quartet Statement", U.S. Department of State, 9 May 2005, in http://www.state.gov/, accessed 17 September 2007.

165. "Israel Not Complying with General Assembly Demand to Halt Barrier-Annan", UN News Centre, 28 November 2003, in http://www0.un.org/, accessed 9 August 2005; "Global Partners and Responsible Media Can Enhance Mid-East Peace Process-Annan", UN News Centre, 13 June 2005, in http://www.un.org/, accessed 9 August 2005; "Road Map Remains 'Most Practical Way' to Achieve," 3 December 2004; "Secretary-General's Press Conference with Other Members of the Middle East 'Quartet'", Secretary-General Office of the Spokesman, 9 May 2005, in http://www.un.org/, accessed 9 August 2005. The UN General Assembly overwhelmingly adopted a resolution calling upon Israel to dismantle the barrier. "Russian Foreign Minister Urges Israelis, Palestinians to Follow Road Map", Financial Times Information, Global News Wire-Asia Africa Intelligence Wire, BBC Monitoring/BBC, BBC Monitoring International Reports, 21 July 2004, in http://web.lexis-nexis.com/, accessed 23 August 2005. The Quartet insisted that Israel work directly with the PA on Gaza disengagement. See "Quartet Statement", 9 May 2005.

166. "Israeli-Palestinian Relations Bedevilled," 21 July 2005.

167. "General Affairs & External Relations Council," Europa, 12; "Situation in the Middle East, Chris Patten," 2 October 2004.

168. "General Affairs & External Relations Council," Europa, 7; "The EU and the Middle East Peace Process," Europa.

169. "Russian, Palestinian Ministers See Road Map as Only Means to Israeli Settlement," 16 April 2004; "Russia, US to Set Up Monitoring Mechanism on Middle East," 11 July 2003.

170. "Russian Foreign Minister Welcomes Formation of Palestinian Government", Financial Times Information, Global News Wire- Asia Africa Intelligence Wire, BBC Monitoring/BBC, BBC Monitoring International Reports, 20 June 2003, in http://web.lexis-nexis.com/, accessed 23 August 2005; "Russian Envoy says Middle East 'Road Map' Should Include Syria, Lebanon", Financial Times Information, Global News Wire- Asia Africa Intelligence Wire, BBC Monitoring/BBC, BBC Monitoring International Reports, 18 June 2003, in http://web.lexis-nexis.com/, accessed 23 August 2005.

171. "Putin Calls for Arab League Action in Mideast", Financial Times Information, Global News Wire- Asia Africa Intelligence Wire, BBC Monitoring/BBC, BBC Monitoring International Reports, 22 May 2004, in http://web.lexis-nexis.com/, accessed 23

August 2005; "Russia Concerned About Saving Mideast Road Map", Financial Times Information, Global News Wire- Asia Africa Intelligence Wire, BBC Monitoring/BBC, BBC Monitoring International Reports, 1 September 2003, in http://web.lexis-nexis.com/, accessed 23 August 2005.

172. "Secretary-General and Quartet Members", 26 September 2003, 2; "Secretary-General's Message to the UN International Conference of Civil Society in Support of the Palestinian People [Delivered by Mr. Kieran Prendergast, Under-Secretary-General for Political Affairs]", Secretary-General Office of the Spokesman, 13 September 2004, in http://www.un.org/, accessed 9 August 2005; "Quartet Reaffirms Commitment to Two-State Middle East Solution, Annan Says", UN News Centre, 9 May 2005, in http://www.un.org/, accessed 9 August 2005.

173. "Palestinian Minister Insists Road Map Must be Implemented 'As it is'", 28 May 2003; "Palestinians Urge US to Withdraw Promises to Sharon on Gaza Plan", Financial Times Information, Global News Wire- Asia Africa Intelligence Wire, BBC Monitoring/BBC, BBC Monitoring International Reports, 3 May 2004, in http://web.lexis-nexis.com/, accessed 23 August 2005.

174. "President Bush Welcomes Prime Minister Abbas to White House," 25 July 2003, 3.

175. Eric Silver, "New Settlements Will Close Door to Peace, Warn Palestinians", Financial Times Information, Global News Wire- Europe Intelligence Wire, Independent Newspapers (UK) Limited, *The Independent*, 22 March 2005, in http://web.lexis-nexis.com/, accessed 23 August 2005. See as well "Palestinians Ask for US Clarification of Policy on Israeli Settlements," 23 August 2004, where Urayqat noted, "what is taking place squanders the opportunities of implementing the two-state solution." The Wall particularly was criticized as an attempt to "confiscate 58 percent of the West Bank land, control our groundwater and divide tens of Palestinian cities and villages to pave the way for expelling more than 200,000 Palestinian citizens from their homes." "Arafat Urges Implementation of Road Map in Message to Moroccan King", Financial Times Information, Global News Wire- Asia Africa Intelligence Wire, BBC Monitoring/BBC, BBC Monitoring International Reports, 21 August 2003, in http://web.lexis-nexis.com/, accessed 23 August 2005. See as well "Arafat Stresses Commitment to Implementing Hague Court Ruling on Barrier", Financial Times Information, Global News Wire- Asia Africa Intelligence Wire, BBC Monitoring/BBC, BBC Monitoring International Reports, 9 July 2004, in http://web.lexis-nexis.com/, accessed 23 August 2005; "Palestinian Minister Urayqat Hopes Israeli Withdrawal to Be Part of Road Map," 16 May 2004; "Palestinian Official Says Israeli Settlement Plans Will 'Bury' Road Map", Financial Times Information, Global News Wire- Asia Africa Intelligence Wire, BBC Monitoring International Reports, 26 October 2003, in http://web.lexis-nexis.com/, accessed 23 August 2005; "Palestinian Leadership Rejects 'So-Called Gaza Administration'", Financial Times Information, Global News Wire- Asia Africa Intelligence Wire, BBC Monitoring International Reports, 30 August 2004, in http://web.lexis-nexis.com/, accessed 23 August 2005.

176. "Palestinian Official Says Israeli Settlement Plans Will 'Bury' Road Map," 26 October 2003; "Palestinian Minister says Israel Must Choose Between 'Peace and Settlements'", Financial Times Information, Global News Wire- Asia Africa Intelligence Wire, BBC Monitoring/BBC, BBC Monitoring International Reports, 27 November 2003, in http://web.lexis-nexis.com/, accessed 23 August 2005. Officials stressed that settlement expansion would "close the door to peace." Silver, "New Settlements Will Close Door to Peace," 22 March 2005.

177. Silver, "New Settlements Will Close Door to Peace," 22 March 2005; "Palestinian Official Discusses Developments with UN, US, Russian Envoys," 10 November 2003; "Palestinian Official Says Israeli Settlement Plans Will 'Bury' Road Map," 26 October 2003; "Palestinian Premier Says No Peace Without Final-Status Talks," 22 May 2005. They accused Sharon of having "chosen the road of settlements and dictates." "Palestinian Minister says Israel Must Choose Between 'Peace and Settlements'", 27 November 2003. See as well "Palestinian Minister Says US, Quartet Need to Fulfil Road Map Responsibilities," 20 February 2004.

178. "Palestinian Negotiator on Elections, Prospects of Road Map," 10 January 2005. See as well Rupert Cornwell, "Time is Short for a Deal with Israel, Abbas Tells Bush in Symbolic Meeting", Financial Times Information, Global News Wire- Europe Intelligence Wire, Independent Newspapers (UK) Limited, *The Independent*, 27 May 2005, in http://web.lexis-nexis.com/, accessed 23 August 2005; "Arafat Calls for Palestinian Commitment to Road Map," 12 November 2003; "New Palestinian President Underlines Commitment to Road Map," 15 January 2005, 3; "Palestinian Minister says Israel Must Choose Between 'Peace and Settlements'", 27 November 2003.

179. "Arafat Speech Urges Quartet to Implement Road Map", Financial Times Information, Global News Wire- Asia Africa Intelligence Wire, BBC Monitoring/BBC, BBC Monitoring International Reports, 29 November 2003, in http://web.lexis-nexis.com/, accessed 23 August 2005.

180. "Palestinian Premier Briefs US Congress Delegation on Israeli Policies, Urges Aid", Financial Times Information, Global News Wire- Asia Africa Intelligence Wire, BBC Monitoring/BBC, BBC Monitoring International Reports, 19 March 2005, in http://web.lexis-nexis.com/, accessed 23 August 2005. See as well "Palestinian Premier Asks US for 'Clear Position' on Israeli Settlement Blocs", Financial Times Information, Global News Wire- Asia Africa Intelligence Wire, BBC Monitoring/BBC, BBC Monitoring International Reports, 3 April 2005, in http://web.lexis-nexis.com/, accessed 23 August 2005.

181. "Palestinian Premier Briefs US Congress Delegation on Israeli Policies, Urges Aid," 19 March 2005; "Arafat Urges Implementation of Road Map in Message to Moroccan King," 21 August 2003. See as well "Proceedings of Palestinian Cabinet's 22 December Session Reported", Financial Times Information, Global News Wire- Asia Africa Intelligence Wire, BBC Monitoring/BBC, BBC Monitoring International Reports, 23 December 2003, in http://web.lexis-nexis.com/, accessed 23 August 2005; "Palestinian Premier Warns of 'Explosion of the Situation' in Territories," 5 June 2005.

182. "Abbas Tells Israeli TV Palestinians to Call 'Truce', Urges Final Status Talks," 14 March 2005, 5; "New Palestinian President Underlines Commitment to Road Map," 15 January 2005, 3, 5; "Palestinian Foreign Minister: Return of Refugees to Israel 'Certain'", Financial Times Information, Global News Wire- Asia Africa Intelligence Wire, BBC Monitoring/BBC, BBC Monitoring International Reports, 15 August 2003, in http://web.lexis-nexis.com/, accessed 23 August 2005.

183. See, for example, "Commission provides a further EUR 1.35 million in aid for victims of house demolitions in Rafah (Gaza Strip)," Europa, 11 August 2004, in http://www.europa.eu.int/, accessed 16 August 2005. See as well the *Seville Declaration* of 22 June 2002 which declared, "A settlement can be achieved through negotiation, and only through negotiation. The objective is an end to the occupation and the early establishment of a democratic, viable, peaceful and sovereign State of Palestine, on the basis of the 1967 borders, if necessary with minor adjustments agreed by the parties." "The EU and the Middle East Peace Process," Europa, 2.

184. "Situation in the Middle East, Chris Patten," 18 June 2003; "Press Release: Council of the European Union: 2656th Council meeting," 25 April 2005. See as well "General Affairs & External Relations Council," Europa, 13.

185. "General Affairs & External Relations Council," Europa, 6; "Remarks of Javier Solana," 13 July 2005; "The EU and the Middle East Peace Process," Europa, 3.

186. "Russian Foreign Ministry Condemns New Israeli Settlements, Barrier," 3 October 2003; "Russia Fears Israel's 'Expansion of Settlements in West Bank'- Envoy," 16 September 2004; "Russian Envoy to UN Calls on Palestine and Israel to Adhere to 'Road Map'", 3 December 2003.

187. "Russia Calls for Quartet Discussion of Israeli Disengagement Plan," 15 April 2004; "Russian, Palestinian Leaders Adopt Joint Statement," 31 January 2005. Emphasis added.

188. "Israel's Separation Wall 'Obstacle' to two-State Solution-Annan", UN News Centre, 2 October 2003, in http://www.un.org/, accessed 9 August 2005; "Israel Not Complying with General Assembly Demand to Halt Barrier-Annan", UN News Centre, 28 November 2003, in http://www0.un.org/, accessed 9 August 2005.

189. "Israel's Separation Wall 'Obstacle' to two-State Solution-Annan", 2 October 2003; "Secretary-General's Message to the UN International Conference of Civil Society in Support of the Palestinian People," 13 September 2004; "Israel Not Complying with General Assembly Demand to Halt Barrier-Annan", 28 November 2003. Annan noted, "[S]ome 975 square kilometres, or 16.6 percent of the entire West bank, including the homes of some 220,000 Palestinians in East Jerusalem and 17,000 elsewhere, would lie between the barrier and the Green Line [the pre-1967 boundary], while a further 160,000 would live in almost completely encircled enclaves. The planned route also places 320,000 Israelis between the barrier and the Green Line, including some 178,000 in occupied East Jerusalem." "Israel Not Complying with General Assembly Demand to Halt Barrier-Annan", 28 November 2003.

190. "Sharon Attacked from All Sides over Plan for Peace Summit", Financial Times Information, Global News Wire- Europe Intelligence Wire, Independent Newspapers (UK) Limited, *The Independent*, 28 May 2003, in http://web.lexis-nexis.com/, accessed 23 August 2005; "Israeli PM Booed During Speech on Settlement Removal, Adherence to Road Map," 5 January 2004; "President and Prime Minister Sharon Discuss Economy, Middle East," 11 April 2005, 3. Sharon abandoned previous Israeli governments' insistence on describing Israel's presence in the West Bank and Gaza as one of "administration" rather than "occupation." See as well the comments of Shimon Peres in "Israel Puts Positive Spin on Bush-Abbas Meeting", Financial Times Information, Global News Wire- Asia Africa Intelligence Wire, *Turkish Daily News*, 28 May 2005, in http://web.lexis-nexis.com/, accessed 23 August 2005.

191. "Israeli Premier Outlines 'Disengagement Plan' in Herzliyya Speech," 18 December 2003, 3; "Sharon Renews Calls for Cooperation with the Palestinians", Financial Times Information, Global News Wire- Asia Africa Intelligence Wire, *Turkish Daily News*, 25 May 2005, in http://web.lexis-nexis.com/, accessed 23 August 2005; "Sharon Seeks U.S. Approval for Disengagement Plan," 14 April 2004. See as well Jonathan Marcus, "Israeli PM Faces West Bank Gamble", BBC News, 23 August 2005, in http://newsvote.bbc.co.uk/, accessed 23 August 2005; "Sharon Rips Up 'Road Map' With Plan for 1,001 New Settler Homes", Financial Times Information, Global News Wire- Europe Intelligence Wire, Independent Newspapers (UK) Limited, *The Independent*, 18 August 2004, in http://web.lexis-nexis.com/, accessed 23 August 2005; "Israel 'Ready' to Adopt Peace Plan", BBC News, 23 May 2003, in http://newsvote.bbc.co.uk/, accessed 23 August 2005; "Israel: Outpost Issue to Derail Sharon-Quray Summit, Says Palestinian

Official", Financial Times Information, Global News Wire- Asia Africa Intelligence Wire, BBC Monitoring/BBC, BBC Monitoring International Reports, 28 November 2003, in http://web.lexis-nexis.com/, accessed 23 August 2005. Those blocs included approximately 92,500 of the 220,000 West Bank Jewish settlers. "Sharon Seeks U.S. Approval for Disengagement Plan," 14 April 2004. See as well "Sharon's Vow is a Road Block on Path to Peace," 13 April 2005.

192. "President and Prime Minister Sharon Discuss Economy, Middle East," 11 April 2005, 7; "Sharon's Vow is a Road Block on Path to Peace," 13 April 2005; Marcus, "Israeli PM Faces West Bank Gamble," 23 August 2005; Silver, "New Settlements Will Close Door to Peace, Warn Palestinians," 22 March 2005.

193. Silver, "New Settlements Will Close Door to Peace," 22 March 2005.

194. "President and Prime Minister Sharon Discuss Economy, Middle East," 11 April 2005, 2–3. See as well "President Meets with Leaders of Jordan, Israel, and Palestinian Authority: Remarks by President Bush, His Majesty King Abdullah of Jordan, Prime Minister Sharon of Israel, and Prime Minister Abbas of the Palestinian Authority", Office of the Press Secretary, 4 June 2003, in http://www.whitehouse.gov/, accessed 17 August 2005, 3. Indeed, Sharon declared, "it is not in our interest to govern over the Palestinians." "President and Prime Minister Sharon Discuss Economy, Middle East," 11 April 2005, 2.

195. "Israeli PM's Statements Block Road Map Implementation- Palestinian Official", Financial Times Information, Global News Wire- Asia Africa Intelligence Wire, BBC Monitoring/BBC, BBC Monitoring International Reports, 3 August 2003, in http://web.lexis-nexis.com/, accessed 23 August 2005.

196. "Road Map for Palestine," 6 December 2002; James Reynolds, "Analysis: Israel's 'Road Map' Manoeuvres", BBC News, 31 March 2003, in http://newsvote.bbc.co.uk/, accessed 23 August 2005; "Israeli Premier Outlines 'Disengagement Plan' in Herzliyya Speech," 18 December 2003, 3–4. See as well "Sharon Makes Case for Pull-Out Plan, Says 'Stalemate Cannot Continue Forever'", 31 March 2004. Sharon declared, "Settlements to be relocated are those that under any possible format of a future and final arrangement will not be included within the territory of the State of Israel." Palestinians thus found it difficult to accept assurances that Gaza disengagement and the security barrier were intended not to establish Israel's "permanent border" but rather to reduce "friction" and "pave the way for the implementation of the road map." "Israeli Premier Outlines 'Disengagement Plan' in Herzliyya Speech," 18 December 2003; "President and Prime Minister Sharon Discuss Economy, Middle East," 11 April 2005, 3. See also "Israeli PM Booed During Speech on Settlement Removal, Adherence to Road Map," 5 January 2004. Their skepticism was heightened further by indications that concerns about a future Palestinian state's "territorial contiguity" and "viability" were to be addressed by a series of special roads and tunnels linking the state's fragments and bypassing those settlements retained by Israel. See "Israel May 'Bypass' Peace Plan", Financial Times Information, Global News Wire- Asia Africa Intelligence Wire, Kasturi & Sons Ltd (KSL), *The Hindu*, 6 December 2004, in http://web.lexis-nexis.com/, accessed 23 August 2005.

197. "Israeli Cabinet Statement on Road Map and 14 Reservations," 25 May 2003, 1, 3. See as well "Israel Approves Plan for Palestinian State by 2005", Financial Times Information, Global News Wire-Asia Africa Intelligence Wire, Kasturi & Sons Ltd (KSL), *The Hindu*, 26 May 2003, in http://web.lexis-nexis.com/, accessed 23 August 2005.

198. "Israeli Cabinet Statement on Road Map and 14 Reservations," 25 May 2003. One of the few exceptions to this intransigent posture was comments by Ehud Olmert,

Industry, Trade and Labour Minister, that Israel might consider ceding six outlying Arab neighborhoods in Jerusalem to the PA in a final settlement. Such comments ultimately presaged no change in policy. See "Israeli Minister Says West Bank Withdrawal Needed after Gaza Pull-Out," 30 December 2004.

199. "President Discusses American and European Alliance in Belgium", Office of the Press Secretary, 21 February 2005, in http://www.whitehouse.gov/, accessed 17 August 2005; "President and Prime Minister Sharon Discuss Economy, Middle East," 11 April 2005; "Statement by the President," 14 April 2004. See also "Israel: Outpost Issue," 28 November 2003; "Sharon's Vow is a Road Block on Path to Peace," 13 April 2005; "Sharon to Ignore Warning by Bush," 13 April 2005.

200. "President Bush Commends Israeli Prime Minister Sharon's Plan: Remarks by the President and Israeli Prime Minister Ariel Sharon", Office of the Press Secretary, 14 April 2004, in http://www.whitehouse.gov/, accessed 17 August 2005, 2; "President Discusses American and European Alliance in Belgium," 21 February 2005, 2; "President and Prime Minister Sharon Discuss Economy, Middle East," 11 April 2005, 2.

201. "Statement by the President," 14 April 2004. See also "Bush on Gaza Withdrawal," 14 April 2004; "Letter from President Bush to Prime Minister Sharon," 14 April 2004; "President Bush Commends Israeli Prime Minister Sharon's Plan," 14 April 2004. He also implored Sharon "to make sure that the fence sends the right signal that not only is security important, but the ability for the Palestinians to live a normal life is important as well." "President Discusses Middle East Peace with Prime Minister Sharon," 29 July 2003, 4.

202. "Statement by the President," 14 April 2004.

203. "Israeli PM Booed During Speech on Settlement Removal, Adherence to Road Map," 5 January 2004, 3; "Israeli Cabinet Statement on Road Map and 14 Reservations," 25 May 2003, 2–3. See as well "Israeli Premier's Aide Confirms Road Map Commitment after Freeze Remarks," 6 October 2004.

204. "Sharon's Cabinet Backs US Road Map", Nationwide News Pty Limited, *The Australian*, 26 May 2003, in http://web.lexis-nexis.com/, accessed 23 August 2005; "Israeli Cabinet Statement on Road Map and 14 Reservations," 25 May 2003.

205. "Press Release: Majority Support among Palestinians and Israelis for the Road Map and for Mutual Recognition of Israel as the State of the Jewish People and Palestine as the State of the Palestinian People- But Each Public Misperceives the Position of the Other", The Harry S. Truman Research Institute for the Advancement of Peace, 30 June 2003, in http://truman.huji.ac.il/, accessed 14 November 2005, 4; "Press Release: Israelis and Palestinians are Lukewarm and Far Apart on the Major Components of the Geneva Document", The Harry S. Truman Research Institute for the Advancement of Peace, 15 December 2003, in http://truman.huji.ac.il/, accessed 14 November 2005, 3; "Israeli PM Booed During Speech on Settlement Removal; Adherence to Road Map," 5 January 2004, 2.

206. "Israeli Premier Outlines 'Disengagement Plan' in Herzliyya Speech," 18 December 2003, 3.

207. "Road Map Disarray over Arafat Decision," 14 September 2003.

208. "Sharon Makes Case for Pull-Out Plan, Says 'Stalemate Cannot Continue Forever'", 31 March 2004; "Israeli Premier's Aide Confirms Road Map Commitment after Freeze Remarks," 6 October 2004, 3, 4.

209. See "Press Release: Israelis and Palestinians Support the Egyptian Initiative and the Deployment of International Presence in the Gaza Strip After Israel's Withdrawal as Part of Sharon's Disengagement Plan", The Harry S. Truman Research Institute for the Advancement of Peace, 5 July 2004, in http://truman.huji.ac.il/, accessed 14 November

2005; "Press Release: First Serious Signs of Optimism Since the Start of the Intifada", The Harry S. Truman Research Institute for the Advancement of Peace, 12 December 2004, in http://truman.huji.ac.il/, accessed 14 November 2005, 4; "Press Release: Palestinians and Israelis Disagree on How to Proceed with the Peace Process", The Harry S. Truman Research Institute for the Advancement of Peace, 16 March 2005, in http://truman.huji.ac.il/, accessed 14 November 2005, 2.

210. "Israel Rejects 'Meaningless' UN Resolution on Arafat- Radio," 20 September 2003; "Israeli Premier Outlines 'Disengagement Plan' in Herzliyya Speech," 18 December 2003, 2; "Israeli Anger Grows at Arafat," 17 September 2003; "Israel to Fight Hamas to 'Bitter End' Unless Palestinians Act- Israeli Minister", Financial Times Information, Global News Wire-Asia Africa Intelligence Wire, BBC Monitoring/BBC, BBC Monitoring International Reports, 21 April 2003, in http://web.lexis-nexis.com/, accessed 23 August 2005; "'Road Map' Put on Ice as Sharon Says Troops Stay in West Bank," 16 September 2004.

211. "Press Release: First Serious Signs," 12 December 2004, 3; "Press Release: Palestinians and Israelis Disagree," 16 March 2005, 2–3; "Press Release: Two Thirds Among Palestinians, Israeli Jews and Israeli Arabs Support the Mutual Recognition of Israel as the State of the Jewish People and Palestine as the State of the Palestinian People", The Harry S. Truman Research Institute for the Advancement of Peace, 25 September 2005, in http://truman.huji.ac.il/, accessed 14 November 2005, 5. A commentator in *Maariv* noted such domestic developments, observing, "Something has changed. Mainly, Arafat's disappearance and the great weariness of both peoples of the bloodbath of the last four years." "Press Split over Sharm al-Sheikh Summit", BBC News, 9 February 2005, in http://newsvote.bbc.co.uk/, accessed 23 August 2005, 3.

212. "Sharon Sees 'Encouraging Signs' From Palestinians", Financial Times Information, Global News Wire- Asia Africa Intelligence Wire, BBC Monitoring/BBC, BBC Monitoring International Reports, 27 January 2005, in http://web.lexis-nexis.com/, accessed 23 August 2005; "Sharon and Abbas Said Ready to Meet", Financial Times Information, Global News Wire- Asia Africa Intelligence Wire, *Turkish Daily News*, 29 November 2004, in http://web.lexis-nexis.com/, accessed 23 August 2005.

213. "Sharon to Ignore Warning by Bush," 13 April 2005; "Sharon Sees 'Encouraging Signs' From Palestinians," 27 January 2005; "After Israeli Disengagement," 21 August 2005, 2.

214. "Israeli Defence Minister Discusses Pullout Benefits Following Protests", Financial Times Information, Global News Wire- Asia Africa Intelligence Wire, BBC Monitoring/BBC, BBC Monitoring International Reports, 22 July 2005, in http://web.lexis-nexis.com/, accessed 23 August 2005, 3–4; "Israeli Minister Says West Bank Withdrawal Needed After Gaza Pull-Out," 30 December 2004. Indeed, Olmert stressed the Sharon government's readiness to "continue to progress by carrying out unilateral moves, including the possibility of further withdrawals that are in the interest of the state." "Israeli Minister Says West Bank Withdrawal Needed After Gaza Pull-Out," 30 December 2004.

215. "Arafat Calls for Palestinian Commitment to Road Map," 12 November 2003; "New Palestinian President Underlines Commitment to Road Map," 15 January 2005, 3. See as well comments by Negotiation Affairs Minister Sa'ib Urayqat in "Palestinian Minister says Israel Must Choose Between 'Peace and Settlements'", 27 November 2003, and by Foreign Affairs Minister Nabil Sha'th in "Palestinian Foreign Minister: Return of Refugees to Israel 'Certain'", 15 August 2003.

216. Rupert Cornwell, "Time is Short for a Deal with Israel, Abbas Tells Bush in Symbolic Meeting," 27 May 2005.

217. "Arafat Speech Urges Quartet to Implement Road Map," 29 November 2003, 2–3. See as well statements by the Revolutionary Council of the Fatah Movement that specifically criticize suicide attacks in, "Palestinian Fatah Issues 'Binding' Decision Not to Target Israeli Civilians", Financial Times Information, Global News Wire- Asia Africa Intelligence Wire, BBC Monitoring/BBC, BBC Monitoring International Reports, 6 February 2005, in http://web.lexis-nexis.com/, accessed 23 August 2005, and, "We Have an Opportunity and It Would be Irresponsible if We, the Israelis, or the World Allow It to Slip Away", Financial Times Information, Global News Wire- Asia Africa Intelligence Wire, BBC Monitoring/BBC, BBC Monitoring International Reports, 28 February 2005, in http://web.lexis-nexis.com/, accessed 23 August 2005.

218. "Palestinian Negotiator on Elections, Prospects of Road Map," 10 January 2005, 1–2.

219. "Palestinians Say Road Map Progress Depends on Active Quartet Role," 7 January 2004; "Palestinian Officials React to Quartet Recommendations," 26 September 2003; "Palestinian Minister Urayqat Hopes Israeli Withdrawal to Be Part of Road Map," 16 May 2004, 2; "PLO Executive Says New Government Needs 'Effective Guarantees'", 8 September 2003; "Arafat's Adviser Says No Peace, Stability Without Agreement with PLO," 2 October 2003; "Palestinian Premier Stresses Need for International Forces in Gaza," 8 March 2004, 2.

220. "Public Opinion Poll #6: While Indicating Important Shifts in Palestinian Public Attitudes Toward the Intifada and the Peace Process, PSR Poll Shows Significant Support for the Appointment of a Prime Minister and Refusal to Give Confidence in the New Palestinian Government", PSR-Survey Research Unit, 14-22 November 2002, in http://www.pcpsr.org/, accessed 14 November 2005, 7–8; "Press Release: Stable Majorities of the Israeli and Palestinian Publics Support the Quartet's Road Map; Abu Mazin's Nomination as Prime Minister Increases Optimism about Return to Negotiations", The Harry S. Truman Research Institute for the Advancement of Peace, 14 April 2003, in http://truman.huji.ac.il/, accessed 14 November 2005, 5–6.

221. See, for example, "Public Opinion Poll #2: The Mitchell Report, Cease Fire, and Return to Negotiations; Intifada and Armed Confrontations; Chances for Reconciliation; and, Internal Palestinian Conditions", PSR-Survey Research Unit, 5-9 July 2001, in http://www.pcpsr.org/, accessed 14 November 2005, 3; "Public Opinion Poll #6: While Indicating," 14-22 November 2002, 3; "Press Release: Israelis and Palestinians Support," 5 July 2004, 2.

222. "Public Opinion Poll #4: Palestinians Give Less Support for Bombings Inside Israel While Two Thirds Support the Saudi Plan and 91% Support Reforming the PA, but a Majority Opposes Arrests and Opposes the Agreements that Led to Ending the Siege on Arafat's Headquarter, Nativity Church, and Preventive Security Headquarter", PSR-Survey Research Unit, 15-19 May 2002, in http://www.pcpsr.org/, accessed 14 November 2005, 3; "Public Opinion Poll #5: While Sharply Divided Over the Ceasefire and Bombing Attacks Against Civilians, an Overwhelming Majority Supports Political Reform but Have Doubts About the PA's Intentions to Implement", PSR-Survey Research Unit, 18-21 August 2002, in http://www.pcpsr.org/, accessed 14 November 2005, 2; "Public Opinion Poll #6: While Indicating," 14-22 November 2002, 2; "Public Opinion Poll #2: The Mitchell Report," 5-9 July 2001, 3.

223. "Public Opinion Poll #4: Palestinians Give," 15-19 May 2002, 3; "Public Opinion Poll #6: While Indicating," 14-22 November 2002, 2; "Public Opinion Poll #2: The Mitchell Report," 5-9 July 2001, 3; "Press Release: Two Thirds Among Palestinians," 25 September 2005, 3.

224. "Public Opinion Poll #6: While Indicating," 14-22 November 2002, 2; "Press Release: Majority Support," 30 June 2003, 4.

225. "Public Opinion Poll #3: Palestinians Support the Ceasefire, Negotiations, and Reconciliation Between the Two Peoples but a Majority Opposes Arrests and Believe that Armed Confrontations have Helped Achieve National Rights," PSR-Survey Research Unit, 19-24 December 2001, in http://www.pcpsr.org/, accessed 14 November 2005, 3.

226. Confronted by Israeli intransigence, Arafat emphasized Palestinians' legitimate right of self-defense against what he characterized as Israel's increasingly brutal occupation. Such a position resonated with a public that overwhelmingly perceived "any violent act aimed at ending Israeli occupation, regardless of the means," as justifiable—approximately 90% of Palestinians rejected applying the label *terrorism* to Palestinian attacks against Israeli civilians or politicians, while nearly 60% supported "continued suicide bombings inside Israel if an opportunity arises"—and which characterized "all violent acts of the Israeli occupier" as *terrorism*. "Public Opinion Poll #3: Palestinians Support," 19-24 December 2001, 5–7; "Press Release: Israelis and Palestinians Support," 5 July 2004.

227. "Press Release: First Serious Signs," 12 December 2004, 3: "Press Release: Palestinians and Israelis Disagree," 16 March 2005, 2–3.

228. "Palestinian Leader Addresses London Meeting, Demands Adherence to Road Map," 1 March 2005, 2; "New Palestinian President Underlines Commitment to Road Map," 15 January 2005, 4.

229. "Press Release: Two Thirds Among Palestinians," 25 September 2005, 5, 2; "Press Release: Israeli Support for Disengagement Drops," 14 June 2005, 2; "Press Release: First Serious Signs," 12 December 2004, 4; "Press Release: Palestinians and Israelis Disagree," 16 March 2005, 2–3.

230. "Palestinian Leader Addresses London Meeting, Demands Adherence to Road Map," 1 March 2005, 2; "New Palestinian President Underlines Commitment to Road Map," 15 January 2005, 4.

231. "Palestinian Negotiator on Elections, Prospects of Road Map," 10 January 2005, 1, 3.

232. "President Discusses American and European Alliance in Belgium," 21 February 2005, 5, 2.

233. "President Bush Presses for Peace in the Middle East," 9 May 2003, 1; "President Bush Addresses United Nations General Assembly," 23 September 2003, 3. On the importance of Iraq to "the stability of the Middle East," see "President Bush Discusses Top Priorities for the U.S.," 30 July 2003, 1.

234. "President Bush Addresses United Nations General Assembly," 23 September 2003, 3; "President Believes Peace in Middle East is Achievable: Remarks by the President to the Travel Pool", Office of the Press Secretary, 15 June 2003, in http://www.whitehouse.gov/, accessed 17 August 2005, 2; "President Bush, Prime Minister Sabah of Kuwait Discuss Middle East," 10 September 2003, 1.

235. "President Bush, Egyptian President Mubarak Meet with Reporters," 12 April 2004, 5; "President Meets with E.U. Leaders," 22 February 2005, 4; "President Bush Discusses Top Priorities for the U.S.," 30 July 2003, 9.

236. "Statement by the President," 14 April 2004, 1.

237. "President Believes Peace in Middle East is Achievable," 15 June 2003, 1; "President Bush Discusses Top Priorities for the U.S.," 30 July 2003, 9.

238. "Public Opinion Toward Terrorism", American-Israeli Cooperative Enterprise, 2005, in http://www. jewishvirtuallibrary.org/, accessed 14 November 2005; "American

Attitudes Toward the Middle East," The American–Israeli Cooperative Enterprise, in http://jewishvirtuallibrary.org/, accessed 14 November 2005, 12–13.

239. See "American Attitudes Toward the Middle East," The American–Israeli Cooperative Enterprise, 33–34.

240. "Palestinian Homeland Polls", The American-Israeli Cooperative Enterprise, 14, 27, 3, 12.

241. "American Attitudes Toward the Middle East," The American–Israeli Cooperative Enterprise, 11, 13–15; "Public Opinion Toward Terrorism", The American-Israeli Cooperative Enterprise, 9, 2, 3. It also is important to recognize Americans' historic empathy toward Israel. Indeed, throughout the 2003–2005 *Road Map* period, the public consistently expressed greater sympathy for Israelis than for Palestinians (and Arabs), at times by margins approaching six to one. "American Sympathy toward Israel and the Arabs/Palestinians", The American-Israeli Cooperative Enterprise, 2005, in http://jewishvirtuallibrary.org/, accessed 14 November 2005, 6; "Gallup Polls on American Sympathy Toward Israel and the Arabs/Palestinians," The American-Israeli Cooperative Enterprise, in http://jewishvirtuallibrary.org/, accessed 14 November 2005, 3; "American Attitudes Toward the Middle East," The American–Israeli Cooperative Enterprise, 1–3. Americans expressed few concerns that US support for Israel was likely to increase future attacks on the US. See "American Attitudes Toward the Middle East," 30, 17; "Public Opinion Toward Terrorism," 1, 25, 28.

Conclusion

1. Buchanan, *Peace with Justice*, 3, 14–15, 11.

2. "Public Opinion Poll #4: Palestinians Give," 15-19 May 2002, 2; Buchanan, *Peace with Justice*, 25. See also "Public Opinion Poll #1: Camp David Summit, Chances for Reconciliation and Lasting Peace, Violence and Confrontations, Hierarchies of Priorities, and Domestic Politics", PSR-Survey Research Unit, 27-29 July 2000, in http://www.pcpsr.org/, accessed 14 November 2005, 4; "Public Opinion Poll #6: While Indicating," 14-22 November 2002, 4–5.

3. "Palestinian-Israeli Public Opinion Poll: Summary of Results", The Harry S. Truman Research Institute for the Advancement of Peace, July 2001, in http://truman.huji.ac.il/, accessed 14 August 2005; "Public Opinion Poll #1: Camp David Summit," 27-29 July 2000, 3; "Results of Surveys among Palestinian Refugees (and Non-Refugees) in the West Bank/Gaza Strip, Jordan and Lebanon", PSR-Survey Research Unit, January–June 2003, in http://www.pcpsr.org/, accessed 14 November 2005, 8. See as well "Public Opinion Poll #3: Palestinians Support," 19-24 December 2001, 4; "Public Opinion Poll #6: While Indicating," 14-22 November 2002, 5; "Public Opinion Poll #5: While Sharply Divided," 18-21 August 2002, 3.

4. "Press Release: Stable Majorities," 14 April 2003, 2; "Press Release: Israelis and Palestinians Support Return to Negotiations While Beliefs in the Success of the Armed Intifada Drop", The Harry S. Truman Research Institute for the Advancement of Peace, 29 November–16 December 2001 and 19-24 December 2001, in http://truman.huji.ac.il/, accessed 14 November 2005, 2. See also "Israeli Public Opinion", PSR-Survey Research Unit, 5-11 July 2001, in http://www.pcpsr.org/, accessed 14 November 2005, 7; "Press Release: Israelis and Palestinians Support the Peace Process and Reconciliation but are Less Willing to Pay the Price than Their Leaders", PSR-Survey Research Unit, 27-31 July 2000, in http://www.pcpsr.org/, accessed 14 November 2005, 4.

5. "Israeli Public Opinion Poll #1", PSR-Survey Research Unit, 27-31 July 2000, in http://www.pcpsr.org/, accessed 14 November 2005, 1–3, 7; "Press Release: Israelis and Palestinians Support," 27-31 July 2000, 2–5.

6. "Public Opinion Poll #3: Palestinians Support," 19-24 December 2001, 4; "Public Opinion Poll #5: While Sharply Divided," 18-21 August 2002, 3; "Public Opinion Poll #6: While Indicating," 14-22 November 2002, 5.

7. "Press Release: Israelis and Palestinians Support Return," 29 November–16 December 2001 and 19-24 December 2001, 3; "Public Opinion Poll #1: Camp David Summit," 27-29 July 2000, 4, 6.

8. "Israeli Public Opinion", 5-11 July 2001, 1, 4, 7; "Palestinian-Israeli Public Opinion Poll: Summary of Results," July 2001; "Press Release: 'Pessimism' Underscores Findings of New Israeli-Palestinian Public Opinion Poll", PSR-Survey Research Unit, 5-11 July 2001, in http://www.pcpsr.org/, accessed 14 November 2005; "Israeli Public Opinion Poll #1," 27-31 July 2000, 5.

9. "Joint Press Release: Important but Fragile Pragmatic Shifts in Palestinian and Israeli Public Opinion toward the Intifada and the Peace Process", PSR-Survey Research Unit, 28 November 2002, in http://www.pcpsr.org/, accessed 14 November 2005, 2; "Press Release: Stable Majorities," 14 April 2003, 2; "Public Opinion Poll #6: While Indicating," 14-22 November 2002, 2, 5. Belief in the efficacy of violence was coupled with continued support for "armed attacks against soldiers and settlers." "Press Release: Majority Support," 30 June 2003, 6; "Joint Press Release: Important but Fragile," 28 November 2002, 3; "Press Release: Stable Majorities," 14 April 2003, 2; "Public Opinion Poll #4: Palestinians Give," 15-19 May 2002, 3; "Public Opinion Poll #5: While Sharply Divided," 18-21 August 2002, 2.

10. Although deeply skeptical of US impartiality ("Public Opinion Poll #3: Palestinians Support," 19-24 December 2001, 2) and opposed to American-only efforts on behalf of the *Road Map*, (See "Press Release: Stable Majorities," 14 April 2003, 3) Palestinians recognized the importance of the US in operationalizing UNSCR 242's "land for peace" principle. Fully 79% of Palestinians endorsed increased US "involvement in trying to solve the Israeli-Palestinian conflict," while only 15% advocated a "decrease" in "involvement." "Press Release: Palestinians and Israelis Disagree," 16 March 2005, 3.

11. His support had fallen from 71% in 1996 to 46% in 2000 to the mid-35% range from 2001 through 2002. "Public Opinion Poll #3: Palestinians Support," 19-24 December 2001, 9; "Public Opinion Poll #4: Palestinians Give," 15-19 May 2002, 6; "Public Opinion Poll #5: While Sharply Divided," 18-21 August 2002, 7; "Public Opinion Poll #6: While Indicating," 14-22 November 2002, 10.

12. Fatah's support had deteriorated from 55% in 1996 to 37% in 2000 to 26–27% by the end of 2002, while Islamist groups, led by Hamas and Islamic Jihad, received 25–27% support in 2002, up from 17% in 2000. "Public Opinion Poll #3: Palestinians Support," 19-24 December 2001, 9; "Public Opinion Poll #4: Palestinians Give," 15-19 May 2002, 6; "Public Opinion Poll #5: While Sharply Divided," 18-21 August 2002, 7; "Public Opinion Poll #6: While Indicating," 14-22 November 2002, 10.

13. See "Public Opinion Poll #6: While Indicating," 14-22 November 2002, 3, for indications of public willingness to support a crackdown against extremists after a mutual cessation of violence.

14. "Public Opinion Poll #4: Palestinians Give," 15-19 May 2002, 4; "Public Opinion Poll #5: While Sharply Divided," 18-21 August 2002, 5–6; "Public Opinion Poll #6: While Indicating," 14-22 November 2002, 6–7.

15. Justin Huggler, "Palestinian Cabinet Approval Clears Way for Peace Plan", Financial Times Information, Global News Wire- Europe Intelligence Wire, Independent

Newspapers (UK) Limited, *The Independent*, 30 April 2003, in http://web.lexis-nexis.com/, accessed 23 August 2005. Arafat likewise pledged to implement the *Road Map* "immediately." "Israel, Palestinians End Meeting on Positive Note", Media Corporation of Singapore Pte Ltd., Channel News Asia, 29 May 2003, in http://web.lexis-nexis.com/, accessed 23 August 2005.

    16. The Islamist organizations characterized the *Road Map* as a "conspiracy" by which Israel sought to be delivered from the "quagmire of the Palestinian intifadah and the heroic resistance." "Hamas Leader says Road Map 'Conspiracy'; No Decision on Truce", Financial Times Information, Global News Wire- Asia Africa Intelligence Wire, BBC Monitoring/BBC, BBC Monitoring International Reports, 31 May 2003, in http://web.lexis-nexis.com/, accessed 23 August 2005. See as well "Abbas Denounces Terrorism, Says No Military Solution to Conflict", Deutsche Presse-Agentur, 29 April 2003, in http://web.lexis-nexis.com/, accessed 23 August 2005. Sheik Ahmed Yassin, leader of Hamas, noted, "The road map aims to assure security for Israel at the expense of the security of our people. It is a plan to liquidate the Palestinian cause (for independence). It is rejected by us," while an Islamic Jihad representative observed, "Any Palestinian government worth its weight should assert the right of our people to resistance and self-defence and it should protect them from aggression and blockades." "Palestinian PM Abbas Takes Office in Key Step to US-Led Peace Plan", Media Corporation of Singapore Pte Ltd., Channel News Asia, 20 April 2003, in http://web.lexis-nexis.com/, accessed 23 August 2005; Ramit Plushnick-Masti, "Palestine Appeal to Salvage Peace Plan", Nationwide News Pty Limited, *The Advertiser*, 10 September 2003, in http://web.lexis-nexis.com/, accessed 23 August 2005. It should be noted that 70% of Hamas supporters advocated bombing within Israel, compared to 47% of Fatah sympathizers, while only 36% supported a ceasefire, compared to 79% for Fatah. "Public Opinion Poll #4: Palestinians Give," 15-19 May 2002, 4; "Public Opinion Poll #3: Palestinians Support," 19-24 December 2001, 3.

    17. Huggler, "Palestinian Cabinet Approval Clears Way for Peace Plan", 30 April 2003.

    18. "Abbas Tells Israeli TV Palestinians to Call 'Truce', Urges Final Status Talks", Financial Times Information, Global News Wire- Asia Africa Intelligence Wire, BBC Monitoring/BBC, BBC Monitoring International Reports, 14 March 2005, in http://web.lexis-nexis.com/, accessed 23 August 2005, 2. Abbas rejected efforts to disarm or otherwise coerce Fatah's political rivals. "Palestinians Release Hamas Militant; Israel demands that Hamas Disarm Before Election", Financial Times Information, Global News Wire- Asia Africa Intelligence Wire, *Turkish Daily News*, 4 May 2005, in http://web.lexis-nexis.com/, accessed 23 August 2005; Atul Aneja, "Abbas Calls for Truce; Israel Snaps Contact", Financial Times Information, Global News Wire- Asia Africa Intelligence Wire, Kasturi and Sons Ltd. (KSL), *The Hindu*, 16 January 2005, in http://web.lexis-nexis.com/, accessed 23 August 2005.

    19. Huggler, "Palestinian Cabinet Approval Clears Way for Peace Plan", 30 April 2003.

    20. See Craig and George, *Force and Statecraft*, 165, for a description of normalization, innovation, and redistribution agreements.

    21. Israelis mentioned "security" as being Israel's "most important national interest" more than twice as frequently as "peace," three times as often as maintaining a "Jewish state," and nearly ten times more frequently than "economic prosperity." "Israeli Public Opinion Poll #2", 5-11 July 2001, 5. See also "Israeli Public Opinion Poll #1", 27-31 July 2000, 10. More than 96% of Israelis supported the *Road Map*'s call for "a mutual cessa-

tion of violence by both sides." "Joint Press Release: Important but Fragile," 28 November 2002, 2.

22. Less than half of the public supported increased spending on national security, while 93% wanted additional resources devoted to job creation, 81% to healthcare, and 75% to education. "Press Release: Stable Majorities," 14 April 2003, 5.

23. "Press Release: Stable Majorities," 14 April 2003, 5. See also "Press Release: Israelis and Palestinians Support Return," 29 November–16 December 2001 and 19-24 December 2001, 2, on Israeli support for a resumption of negotiations.

24. Buchanan, *Peace with Justice*, 141.

25. "Israel Cautiously Accepts Peace 'Road Map'", 24 May 2003; "Israeli Cabinet Statement on Road Map and 14 Reservations," 25 May 2003. Washington appeared amenable to such an approach. See "Israel Cautiously Accepts Peace 'Road Map'", 24 May 2003, 2.

26. Buchanan, *Peace with Justice*, 9.

27. He felt that such negotiations empowered extremists, those actors least amenable to accepting those compromises necessary for progress.

28. See *Road Map*.

29. *Road Map*; Buchanan, *Peace with Justice*, 65.

30. Buchanan, *Peace with Justice*, 55–58, 45.

31. See, for example, "Public Opinion Poll #1: Camp David Summit," 27-29 July 2000, 2.

32. Such a calculating, interest-based perspective demonstrated little change from the period immediately following Camp David in July 2000 to the end of the *Road Map* period in 2005. See "Public Opinion Poll #1: Camp David Summit," 27-29 July 2000; "Public Opinion Poll #5: While Sharply Divided," 18-21 August 2002, 2; "Public Opinion Poll #3: Palestinians Support," 19-24 December 2001, 4; "Public Opinion Poll #6: While Indicating," 14-22 November 2002, 5; "Press Release: Palestinians and Israelis Disagree," 16 March 2005, 3.

33. "Palestinian-Israeli Public Opinion Poll: Summary of Results," July 2001, 2. See "Public Opinion Poll #1: Camp David Summit," 27-29 July 2000; "Public Opinion Poll #5: While Sharply Divided," 18-21 August 2002, 2; "Public Opinion Poll #3: Palestinians Support," 19-24 December 2001, 4; "Public Opinion Poll #6: While Indicating," 14-22 November 2002, 5; "Press Release: Palestinians and Israelis Disagree," 16 March 2005, 3.

34. "Public Opinion Poll #6: While Indicating," 14-22 November 2002, 2; "Press Release: Palestinians and Israelis Disagree," 16 March 2005, 2; "Public Opinion Poll #3: Palestinians Support," 19-24 December 2001, 2; "Press Release: Israelis and Palestinians Support the Egyptian," 5 July 2004, 2; "Press Release: Israelis and Palestinians are Lukewarm", 15 December 2003, 2; "Public Opinion Poll #1: Camp David Summit," 27-29 July 2000, 7–8.

35. See "Palestinians and Israelis Disagree", 16 March 2005, 2; "Public Opinion Poll #6: While Indicating," 14-22 November 2002, 2–4; "Press Release: Majority Support," 30 June 2003, 4; "Press Release: Israeli Support for Disengagement Drops," 14 June 2005, 4. The public also supported Hamas's participation in administering Gaza after Israeli withdrawal. "Press Release: Israelis and Palestinians Support the Egyptian," 5 July 2004, 2.

36. "Abbas Tells Israeli TV Palestinians to Call 'Truce', Urges Final Status Talks," 14 March 2005, 2. His inability to convince Hamas that "a political party should not be a military party as well" was reflected in Hamas's refusal to forswear violence or surrender weapons. "Abbas Tells Israeli TV Palestinians to Call 'Truce', Urges Final Status Talks,"

14 March 2005, 2; Plushnick-Masti, "Palestine Appeal to Salvage Peace Plan", 10 September 2003; "Palestinian Hamas Rejects Road Map, Vows to Continue Operations", Financial Times Information, Global News Wire- Asia Africa Intelligence Wire, BBC Monitoring/BBC, BBC Monitoring International Reports, 20 June 2003, in http://web.lexis-nexis.com/, accessed 23 August 2005; "Mideast: Hamas Founder Calls Israeli Acceptance of Road Map 'Trick'", 28 May 2003.

37. For indications of Israelis' skepticism that a settlement could be reached within the next decade with a Palestinian leadership of uncertain intentions and capabilities, see "Joint Press Release: Important but Fragile," 28 November 2002, 2; "Press Release: Two Thirds Among Palestinians," 25 September 2005, 5; "Press Release: First Serious Signs," 12 December 2004, 3.

38. "Joint Press Release: Important but Fragile," 28 November 2002, 3; "Press Release: First Serious Signs," 12 December 2004, 3.

39. "Press Release: Palestinians and Israelis Disagree," 16 March 2005, 2; "Press Release: Israelis and Palestinians Support the Egyptian," 5 July 2004, 2; "Press Release: First Serious Signs," 12 December 2004, 4. Forty percent of the public perceived the Plan as a Palestinian victory. See "Press Release: First Serious Signs," 12 December 2004, 4.

40. "Press Release: Israeli Support for Disengagement Drops," 14 June 2005, 2. Sixty percent of settlers indicated they would resist evacuation by "legal means," including attempting "to bring down the government." "Press Release: Majority Support," 30 June 2003, 6–7.

41. See, for example, Kissinger's discussion of Ford's 1975 "reassessment" tactic in Hulme, *Palestinian Terrorism*, 125–129.

42. Hulme, *Palestinian Terrorism*, 12, 216.

43. Rupert Cornwell, "Time is Short for a Deal with Israel, Abbas Tells Bush in Symbolic Meeting", Financial Times Information, Global News Wire- Europe Intelligence Wire, Independent Newspapers (UK) Limited, *The Independent*, 27 May 2005, in http://web.lexis-nexis.com/, accessed 23 August 2005.

44. *Road Map*. Emphasis added.

SELECTED BIBLIOGRAPHY

"Abbas Calls on Bush to Protect Peace Process, 'Vision' of Palestinian State." *Financial Times Information* (26 May 2005). http://web.lexis-nexis.com/. 23 August 2005.

"Abbas Denounces Terrorism, Says No Military Solution to Conflict." *Deutsche Presse-Agentur* (29 April 2003). http://web.lexis-nexis.com/. 23 August 2005.

"Abbas Tells Israeli TV Palestinians to Call 'Truce', Urges Final Status Talks." *Financial Times Information* (14 March 2005). http://web.lexis-nexis.com/. 23 August 2005.

Abd al-Aziz, Fahd ibn. "The Fahd Plan (August 7, 1981)." In *The Israel-Arab Reader: A Documentary History of the Middle East Conflict*, edited by Walter Laqueur and Barry Rubin. New York: Penguin Books, 2001.

Abu-Sharif, Bassam. "PLO View: Prospects of a Palestinian-Israeli Settlement (18 June 1988)." In *The Israeli- Palestinian Conflict: a documentary record, 1967–1990*, edited by Yehuda Lukacs. Cambridge: Cambridge University Press, 1992.

Abu-Zayidah, Sufyan. "Interview (January 27, 1995)." In *The Israel-Arab Reader: A Documentary History of the Middle East Conflict*, edited by Walter Laqueur and Barry Rubin. New York: Penguin Books, 2001.

Allon, Yigal. "The Allon Plan, Article Reiterating his Plan for Peace (October 1976)." In *The Israeli-Palestinian Conflict: a documentary record, 1967–1990*, edited by Yehuda Lukacs. Cambridge: Cambridge University Press, 1992.

"Alternatives to Mideast Road Map May Help Settlement- Russian Minister." *Financial Times Information* (20 November 2003). http://web.lexis-nexis.com/. 23 August 2005.

"American Attitudes Toward the Middle East." *The American–Israeli Cooperative Enterprise* (2005). http://jewishvirtuallibrary.org/. 14 November 2005.

"American Sympathy toward Israel and the Arabs/Palestinians." *The American-Israeli Cooperative Enterprise* (2005). http://jewishvirtuallibrary.org/. 14 November 2005.

Aneja, Atul. "Abbas Calls for Truce; Israel Snaps Contact." *Financial Times Information* (16 January 2005). http://web.lexis-nexis.com/. 23 August 2005.

"Annan ends Middle East trip encouraged by Israeli-Palestinian peace moves." *UN News Centre* (16 March 2005). http://www.un.org/. 9 August 2005.

"Annan Vows to Work to Turn Dream of Middle East Peace into Reality." *UN News*

Bibliography

Centre (8 March 2005). http://www.un.org/. 9 August 2005.

Arab Democratic Party. "Platform (1988)." In *The Israeli-Palestinian Conflict: a documentary record, 1967–1990*, edited by Yehuda Lukacs. Cambridge: Cambridge University Press, 1992.

Arab League. "Baghdad Summit Conference Final Statement (5 November 1978)." In *The Israeli-Palestinian Conflict: a documentary record, 1967–1990*, edited by Yehuda Lukacs. Cambridge: Cambridge University Press, 1992.

———. "Baghdad Summit Conference Resolutions (31 March 1979)." In *The Israeli-Palestinian Conflict: a documentary record, 1967–1990*, edited by Yehuda Lukacs. Cambridge: Cambridge University Press, 1992.

———. "Rabat Summit Conference Communiqué (29 October 1974)." In *The Israeli-Palestinian Conflict: a documentary record, 1967–1990*, edited by Yehuda Lukacs. Cambridge: Cambridge University Press, 1992.

———. "Tripoli Summit Conference Declaration (5 December 1977)." In *The Israeli-Palestinian Conflict: a documentary record, 1967–1990*, edited by Yehuda Lukacs. Cambridge: Cambridge University Press, 1992.

"Arafat Asks Russia to Help Oversee Road Map Implementation." *Financial Times Information* (14 July 2003). http://web.lexis-nexis.com/. 23 August 2005.

"Arafat Calls for Palestinian Commitment to Road Map." *Financial Times Information* (12 November 2003). http://web.lexis-nexis.com/. 23 August 2005.

"Arafat's Adviser Says No Peace, Stability Without Agreement with PLO." *Financial Times Information* (2 October 2003). http://web.lexis-nexis.com/. 23 August 2005.

"Arafat Speech Urges Quartet to Implement Road Map." *Financial Times Information* (29 November 2003). http://web.lexis-nexis.com/. 23 August 2005.

"Arafat Stresses Commitment to Implementing Hague Court Ruling on Barrier." *Financial Times Information* (9 July 2004). http://web.lexis-nexis.com/. 23 August 2005.

"Arafat Thanks Russian President for Effort in Securing UN Road Map Resolution." *Financial Times Information* (21 November 2003). http://web.lexis-nexis.com/. 23 August 2005.

Arafat Urges Implementation of Road Map in Message to Moroccan King." *Financial Times Information* (21 August 2003). http://web.lexis-nexis.com/. 23 August 2005.

Arafat, Yasir. "Address to the European Parliament (13 September 1988)." In *The Israeli-Palestinian Conflict: a documentary record, 1967–1990*, edited by Yehuda Lukacs. Cambridge: Cambridge University Press, 1992.

———. "Address to the UN General Assembly (13 December 1988)." In *The Israeli-Palestinian Conflict: a documentary record, 1967–1990*, edited by Yehuda Lukacs. Cambridge: Cambridge University Press, 1992.

———. "Declaration on Terrorism (7 November 1985)." In *The Israeli-Palestinian Conflict: a documentary record, 1967–1990*, edited by Yehuda Lukacs. Cambridge: Cambridge University Press, 1992.

———. "Geneva Press Statement (15 December 1988)." In *The Israeli-Palestinian Conflict: a documentary record, 1967–1990*, edited by Yehuda Lukacs. Cambridge: Cambridge University Press, 1992.

———. "An Interview (August 1969)." In *The Israel-Arab Reader: A Documentary History of the Middle East Conflict*, edited by Walter Laqueur and Barry Rubin. New York: Penguin Books, 2001.

———. "Interview on Camp David (November 19, 1979)." In *The Israel-Arab Reader: A Documentary History of the Middle East Conflict*, edited by Walter Laqueur and Barry Rubin. New York: Penguin Books, 2001.

Bibliography

———. "Letter to the Emergency World Jewish Leadership Peace Conference Organized by the International Center for Peace in the Middle East (17 February 1990)." In *The Israeli-Palestinian Conflict: a documentary record, 1967–1990*, edited by Yehuda Lukacs. Cambridge: Cambridge University Press, 1992.

———. "Speech for Fatah's Anniversary (December 31, 1992)." In *The Israel-Arab Reader: A Documentary History of the Middle East Conflict*, edited by Walter Laqueur and Barry Rubin. New York: Penguin Books, 2001.

———. "Speech on the Intifada (September 1989)." In *The Israel-Arab Reader: A Documentary History of the Middle East Conflict*, edited by Walter Laqueur and Barry Rubin. New York: Penguin Books, 2001.

———. "Speech to Palestine National Council (February 14, 1983)." In *The Israel-Arab Reader: A Documentary History of the Middle East Conflict*, edited by Walter Laqueur and Barry Rubin. New York: Penguin Books, 2001.

———. "Speech to the UN General Assembly (13 November 1974)." In *The Israeli-Palestinian Conflict: a documentary record, 1967–1990*, edited by Yehuda Lukacs. Cambridge: Cambridge University Press, 1992.

al-Asad, Hafiz. "Reaction to Israel-PLO Agreement (October 1, 1993)." In *The Israel-Arab Reader: A Documentary History of the Middle East Conflict*, edited by Walter Laqueur and Barry Rubin. New York: Penguin Books, 2001.

———. "Speech (March 8, 1980)." In *The Israel-Arab Reader: A Documentary History of the Middle East Conflict*, edited by Walter Laqueur and Barry Rubin. New York: Penguin Books, 2001.

al-Asad, Hafiz, and Bill Clinton. "Statement on Their Meeting (January 16, 1994)." In *The Israel-Arab Reader: A Documentary History of the Middle East Conflict*, edited by Walter Laqueur and Barry Rubin. New York: Penguin Books, 2001.

Asfour, Hasan, and Mahmud Abbas (Abu Mazin). "Reflections on the Oslo Agreements 5th Anniversary (September 11, 1998)." In *The Israel-Arab Reader: A Documentary History of the Middle East Conflict*, edited by Walter Laqueur and Barry Rubin. New York: Penguin Books, 2001.

Asser, Martin. "After Israeli Disengagement." *BBC News* (21 August 2005). http://newsvote.bbc.co.uk/. 23 August 2005.

Baker, James. "Address Before the American-Israel Public Affairs Committee (22 May 1989)." In *The Israeli- Palestinian Conflict: a documentary record, 1967–1990*, edited by Yehuda Lukacs. Cambridge: Cambridge University Press, 1992.

Barak, Ehud. "Leaving for the Camp David Talks (July 10, 2000)." In *The Israel-Arab Reader: A Documentary History of the Middle East Conflict*, edited by Walter Laqueur and Barry Rubin. New York: Penguin Books, 2001.

———. "Presentation of the Government to the Knesset (July 6, 1999)." In *The Israel-Arab Reader: A Documentary History of the Middle East Conflict*, edited by Walter Laqueur and Barry Rubin. New York: Penguin Books, 2001.

———. "Statement after the Camp David Talks (July 25, 2000)." In *The Israel-Arab Reader: A Documentary History of the Middle East Conflict*, edited by Walter Laqueur and Barry Rubin. New York: Penguin Books, 2001.

Barghuti, Marwan. "The Israelis Must Leave the Territories (October 26, 2000)." In *The Israel-Arab Reader: A Documentary History of the Middle East Conflict*, edited by Walter Laqueur and Barry Rubin. New York: Penguin Books, 2001.

Begin, Menachem. "Autonomy Plan for the West Bank and Gaza Strip (December 28, 1977)." In *The Israel-Arab Reader: A Documentary History of the Middle East Conflict*, edited by Walter Laqueur and Barry Rubin. NewYork: Penguin Books, 2001.

———. "The Wars of No Alternative and Operation Peace for the Galilee (August 8, 1982)." In *The Israel-Arab Reader: A Documentary History of the Middle East Conflict*, edited by Walter Laqueur and Barry Rubin. New York: Penguin Books, 2001.

Brezhnev, Leonid I. "Position on Arab-Israeli Peace (23 February 1981)." In *The Israeli-Palestinian Conflict: a documentary record, 1967–1990*, edited by Yehuda Lukacs. Cambridge: Cambridge University Press, 1992.

———. "Position on the 1973 War (October 9, 1973)." In *The Israel-Arab Reader: A Documentary History of the Middle East Conflict*, edited by Walter Laqueur and Barry Rubin. New York: Penguin Books, 2001.

Brookings Institution. "Toward Peace in the Middle East (December 1975)." In *The Israeli-Palestinian Conflict: a documentary record, 1967–1990*, edited by Yehuda Lukacs. Cambridge: Cambridge University Press, 1992.

Buchanan, Andrew S. *Peace with Justice: A History of the Israeli-Palestinian Declaration of Principles on Interim Self-Government Arrangements*. New York: St. Martin's Press, 2000.

Bush, George H.W. "Statement Following Meeting with President Hosni Mubarak (3 April 1989)." In *The Israeli-Palestinian Conflict: a documentary record, 1967–1990*, edited by Yehuda Lukacs. Cambridge: Cambridge University Press, 1992.

———. "Statement Following Meeting with Prime Minister Yitzhak Shamir (6 April 1989)." In *The Israeli- Palestinian Conflict: a documentary record, 1967–1990*, edited by Yehuda Lukacs. Cambridge: Cambridge University Press, 1992.

———. "Statement on Jewish Settlements in the West Bank and East Jerusalem (3 March 1990)." In *The Israeli- Palestinian Conflict: a documentary record, 1967–1990*, edited by Yehuda Lukacs. Cambridge: Cambridge University Press, 1992.

———. "Statement on Suspension of the Dialogue Between the US and the PLO (20 June 1990)." In *The Israeli- Palestinian Conflict: a documentary record, 1967–1990*, edited by Yehuda Lukacs. Cambridge: Cambridge University Press, 1992.

"Bush on Gaza Withdrawal." *BBC News* (14 April 2004). http://newsvote.bbc.co.uk/. 23 August 2005.

"Camp David Summit Meeting: Frameworks for Peace (September 17, 1978)." In *The Israel-Arab Reader: A Documentary History of the Middle East Conflict*, edited by Walter Laqueur and Barry Rubin. New York: Penguin Books, 2001.

Carothers, Thomas. "Choosing a Strategy." In *Uncharted Journey: Promoting Democracy in the Middle East*, edited by Thomas Carothers and Marina Ottaway. Washington: Carnegie Endowment for International Peace, 2005.

Carothers, Thomas, and Marina Ottaway. "The New Democracy Imperative." In *Uncharted Journey: Promoting Democracy in the Middle East*, edited by Thomas Carothers and Marina Ottaway. Washington: Carnegie Endowment for International Peace, 2005.

Carter, Jimmy. "Middle East Peace (16 March 1977)." In *The Israeli-Palestinian Conflict: a documentary record, 1967–1990*, edited by Yehuda Lukacs. Cambridge: Cambridge University Press, 1992.

———. "Statement on Recognition of Palestinians (4 January 1978)." In *The Israeli-Palestinian Conflict: a documentary record, 1967–1990*, edited by Yehuda Lukacs. Cambridge: Cambridge University Press, 1992.

Bibliography

"Chris Patten Commissioner for External Relations Welcomes Statement from President Bush on the Middle East." *Europa* (5 April 2002). http://www.europa.eu.int/. 16 August 2005.

Christopher, Warren. "Letter to Israeli Prime Minister Benjamin Netanyahu (January 15, 1997)." In *The Israel-Arab Reader: A Documentary History of the Middle East Conflict*, edited by Walter Laqueur and Barry Rubin. New York: Penguin Books, 2001.

"Citing 'promise and potential,' Annan pledges support for Middle East peace moves." *UN News Centre* (1 March 2005). http://www.un.org/apps/. 9 August 2005.

Clinton, Bill. "The Clinton Plan (December 23, 2000)." In *The Israel-Arab Reader: A Documentary History of the Middle East Conflict*, edited by Walter Laqueur and Barry Rubin. New York: Penguin Books, 2001.

———. "Speech to the Palestinian Leadership (December 14, 1998)." In *The Israel-Arab Reader: A Documentary History of the Middle East Conflict*, edited by Walter Laqueur and Barry Rubin. New York: Penguin Books, 2001.

———. "Summarizing His Experience with the Peace Process (January 7, 2001)." In *The Israel-Arab Reader: A Documentary History of the Middle East Conflict*, edited by Walter Laqueur and Barry Rubin. New York: Penguin Books, 2001.

Clinton, Bill, Ehud Barak, and Faruk al-Shara. "Speeches at the Renewal of Syrian-Israeli Negotiations (December 15, 1999)." In *The Israel-Arab Reader: A Documentary History of the Middle East Conflict*, edited by Walter Laqueur and Barry Rubin. New York: Penguin Books, 2001.

Clinton, Bill, Yitzhak Rabin, and Yasir Arafat. "Speeches at the Signing of the Israeli-PLO Declaration of Principles (September 13, 1993)." In *The Israel-Arab Reader: A Documentary History of the Middle East Conflict*, edited by Walter Laqueur and Barry Rubin. New York: Penguin Books, 2001.

"Comments on the situation in the Middle East: Interview with Rt. Hon. Christopher Patten, External Relations Commissioner." *Europa* (10 April 2002). http://www.europa.eu.int/. 16 August 2005.

"Commission approves EUR 29 million in support of Palestinian reform efforts and in response to the deteriorating situation on the ground." *Europa* (28 October 2002). http://www.europa.eu.int/. 16 August 2005.

"Commission decides on emergency rehabilitation of administrative infrastructure of Palestinian Authority." *Europa* (27 June 2002). http://www.europa.eu.int/. 16 August 2005.

"Commissioner Ferrero-Waldner attends London Meeting on the Palestinian Authority, Quartet." *Europa* (28 February 2005). http://www.europa.eu.int/. 16 August 2005.

"Commission provides a further EUR 1.35 million in aid for victims of house demolitions in Rafah (Gaza Strip)." *Europa* (11 August 2004). http://www.europa.eu.int/. 16 August 2005.

"Communiqué Issued by the Quartet." *UN News Centre* (17 September 2002). http://www.un.org/news/. 9 August 2005.

"Communiqué of the Intifadah No. 1 (8 January 1988)." In *The Israeli-Palestinian Conflict: a documentary record, 1967–1990*, edited by Yehuda Lukacs. Cambridge: Cambridge University Press, 1992.

Cornwell, Rupert. "Time is Short for a Deal with Israel, Abbas Tells Bush in Symbolic Meeting." *Financial Times Information* (27 May 2005). http://web.lexis-nexis.com/. 23 August 2005.

Craig, Gordon A., and Alexander L. George. *Force and Statecraft: Diplomatic Problems of Our Time, third edition*. New York: Oxford University Press, 1995.

Darwish, Mahmoud. "Resigning from the PLO Executive Committee (August 1993)." In *The Israel-Arab Reader: A Documentary History of the Middle East Conflict*, edited by Walter Laqueur and Barry Rubin. New York: Penguin Books, 2001.

Dunne, Michele. "Integrating Democracy into the U.S. Policy Agenda." In *Uncharted Journey: Promoting Democracy in the Middle East*, edited by Thomas Carothers and Marina Ottaway. Washington: Carnegie Endowment for International Peace, 2005.

Eban, Abba. "Knesset Statement on Occupied Territories (13 May 1969)." In *The Israeli-Palestinian Conflict: a documentary record, 1967–1990*, edited by Yehuda Lukacs. Cambridge: Cambridge University Press, 1992.

———. "The Nine-Point Peace Plan (8 October 1968)." In *The Israeli-Palestinian Conflict: a documentary record, 1967–1990*, edited by Yehuda Lukacs. Cambridge: Cambridge University Press, 1992.

"Egypt and Israel: Peace Treaty (March 26, 1979)." In *The Israel-Arab Reader: A Documentary History of the Middle East Conflict*, edited by Walter Laqueur and Barry Rubin. New York: Penguin Books, 2001.

"Egyptian Foreign Minister, Russian Envoy Discuss Palestinian Situation." *Financial Times Information* (15 June 2003). http://web.lexis-nexis.com/. 23 August 2005.

"Egyptian-Israeli Accord on Sinai (September 1, 1975)." In *The Israel-Arab Reader: A Documentary History of the Middle East Conflict*, edited by Walter Laqueur and Barry Rubin. New York: Penguin Books, 2001.

Eisenberg, Laura Zittrain, and Neil Caplan. "The Israeli-Palestinian Peace Process in *Perspectives*, edited by Ilan Peleg. Albany, New York: State University of New York Press, 1998.

Eshkol, Levi. "Principles Guiding Israel's Policy in the Aftermath of the June 1967 War (9 August 1967)." In *The Israeli-Palestinian Conflict: a documentary record, 1967–1990*, edited by Yehuda Lukacs. Cambridge: Cambridge University Press, 1992.

Esposito, Michele K. "Quarterly Update on Conflict and Diplomacy." *Journal of Palestine Studies* XXXII, no. 2 (Winter 2003): 120–141.

"The EU and the Middle East Peace Process." *Europa*. http://www.europa.eu.int/. 16 August 2005.

"European Commission approves EUR 5.45 million to support Palestinian reform, plus EUR 2.5 million for election observation mission." *Europa* (17 December 2002). http://www.europa.eu.int/. 16 August 2005.

"European Commission takes action with EUR 100 million to improve conditions in Gaza and the West Bank, and accelerate relaunch of the Palestinian economy." *Europa* (17 July 2003). http://www.europa.eu.int/. 16 August 2005.

"European Commission welcomes Arafat announcement of elections and reforms and signature of Law on Independence of the Judiciary." *Europa* (16 May 2002). http://www.europa.eu.int/. 16 August 2005.

"European Commission welcomes Quartet's presentation of the Middle East Road Map." *Europa* (30 April 2003). http://www.europa.eu.int/. 16 August 2005.

European Community. "Brussels Declaration (23 February 1987)." In *The Israeli-Palestinian Conflict: a documentary record, 1967–1990*, edited by Yehuda Lukacs. Cambridge: Cambridge University Press, 1992.

———. "The Madrid Declaration (27 June 1989)." In *The Israeli-Palestinian Conflict: a documentary record, 1967–1990*, edited by Yehuda Lukacs. Cambridge: Cambridge University Press, 1992.

European Community Foreign Ministers. "Statement (6 November 1973)." In *The Israeli-Palestinian Conflict: a documentary record, 1967–1990*, edited by Yehuda Lukacs. Cambridge: Cambridge University Press, 1992.

European Council. "Venice Declaration (June 13, 1980)." In *The Israel-Arab Reader: A Documentary History of the Middle East Conflict*, edited by Walter Laqueur and Barry Rubin. New York: Penguin Books, 2001.

"E.U. says pressing ahead with Quartet Mideast peace plan." *Deutsche Presse-Agentur* (19 November 2002). http://web.lexis-nexis.com/. 23 August 2005.

"The EU's relations with West Bank and Gaza Strip." *Europa* (May 2004). http://www.europa.eu.int/. 16 August 2005.

"The EU, the Mediterranean and the Middle East—A longstanding partnership." *Europa* (10 December 2004). http://www.europa.eu.int/. 16 August 2005.

Fatah. "Fifth General Conference, Political Program (8 August 1989)." In *The Israeli-Palestinian Conflict: a documentary record, 1967–1990*, edited by Yehuda Lukacs. Cambridge: Cambridge University Press, 1992.

———. "Fourth General Conference, Political Program (31 May 1980)." In *The Israeli-Palestinian Conflict: a documentary record, 1967–1990*, edited by Yehuda Lukacs. Cambridge: Cambridge University Press, 1992.

———. "The Seven Points (January 1969)." In *The Israel-Arab Reader: A Documentary History of the Middle East Conflict*, edited by Walter Laqueur and Barry Rubin. New York: Penguin Books, 2001.

"1st Lead: Bush Announces Mideast Peace Road Map to be Delivered." *Deutsche Presse-Agentur* (14 March 2003). http://web.lexis-nexis.com/. 23 August 2005.

"Full Text of Middle East Quartet Communiqué." *UN News Centre* (4 May 2004). http://www.un.org/news/. 9 August 2005.

"'The Galili Plan, the'— Statement by Government Ministers of the Israeli Labor Party on Proposed Policy in the Occupied Territories (August 1973)." In *The Israeli-Palestinian Conflict: a documentary record, 1967–1990*, edited by Yehuda Lukacs. Cambridge: Cambridge University Press, 1992.

"Gallup Polls on American Sympathy Toward Israel and the Arabs/Palestinians." *The American–Israeli Cooperative Enterprise*. http://jewishvirtuallibrary.org/. 14 November 2005.

"General Affairs & External Relations Council (GAERC): Extracts from successive General Affairs & External Relations Councils." *Europa*. http://www.europa.eu.int/. 16 August 2005.

"Global Partners and Responsible Media Can Enhance Mid-East Peace Process-Annan." *UN News Centre* (13 June 2005). http://www.un.org/. 9 August 2005.

Gorbachev, Mikhail. "Speech on Relations with Israel (24 April 1987)." In *The Israeli-Palestinian Conflict: a documentary record, 1967–1990*, edited by Yehuda Lukacs. Cambridge: Cambridge University Press, 1992.

Gromyko, Andrei. "On the Camp David Agreement (September 25, 1979)." In *The Israel-Arab Reader: A Documentary History of the Middle East Conflict*, edited by Walter Laqueur and Barry Rubin. New York: Penguin Books, 2001.

———. "Statement on the Problem in the Middle East (25 September 1979)." In *The Israeli-Palestinian Conflict: a documentary record, 1967–1990*, edited by Yehuda Lukacs. Cambridge: Cambridge University Press, 1992.

Habash, George. "Interview (August 3, 1974." In *The Israel-Arab Reader: A Documentary History of the Middle East Conflict*, edited by Walter Laqueur and Barry Rubin. New York: Penguin Books, 2001.

Hadash Party. "Platform (1988)." In *The Israeli-Palestinian Conflict: a documentary record, 1967–1990*, edited by Yehuda Lukacs. Cambridge: Cambridge University Press, 1992.

Hamas. "Covenant (18 August 1988)." In *The Israeli-Palestinian Conflict: a documentary record, 1967–1990*, edited by Yehuda Lukacs. Cambridge: Cambridge University Press, 1992.

"Hamas Leader says Road Map 'Conspiracy'; No Decision on Truce." *Financial Times Information* (31 May 2003). http://web.lexis-nexis.com/. 23 August 2005.

Harkabi, Y. "Fatah's Doctrine (December 1968)." In *The Israel-Arab Reader: A Documentary History of the Middle East Conflict*, edited by Walter Laqueur and Barry Rubin. New York: Penguin Books, 2001.

al-Hasan, Hani. "Opposition to the Israel-PLO Accord (October 9, 1993)." In *The Israel-Arab Reader: A Documentary History of the Middle East Conflict*, edited by Walter Laqueur and Barry Rubin. New York: Penguin Books, 2001.

Hawatmah, Naif. "Statements Defending the Establishment of a Palestinian National Authority in Territories Liberated from Israeli Occupation (24 February 1974)." In *The Israeli-Palestinian Conflict: a documentary record, 1967–1990*, edited by Yehuda Lukacs. Cambridge: Cambridge University Press, 1992.

Huggler, Justin. "Palestinian Cabinet Approval Clears Way for Peace Plan." *Financial Times Information* (30 April 2003). http://web.lexis-nexis.com/. 23 August 2005.

Hussein, bin Talal (King), and Yitzhak Rabin. "Speeches on Signing the Washington Agreement (July 26, 1994)." In *The Israel-Arab Reader: A Documentary History of the Middle East Conflict*, edited by Walter Laqueur and Barry Rubin. New York: Penguin Books, 2001.

"International community must help Israel, Palestinians seal peace—Annan." *UN News Centre* (7 February 2005). http://www.un.org/. 9 August 2005.

"Israel Against UN Resolution on 'Road Map'- Israeli PM Tells Putin." *Financial Times Information* (3 November 2003). http://web.lexis-nexis.com/. 23 August 2005.

"Israel Agrees on Planned Exodus." *Financial Times Information* (16 November 2004). http://web.lexis-nexis.com/. 23 August 2005.

"Israel and Jordan: The Washington Agreement (July 26, 1994)." In *The Israel-Arab Reader: A Documentary History of the Middle East Conflict*, edited by Walter Laqueur and Barry Rubin. New York: Penguin Books, 2001.

"Israel and Palestinian Authority: Hebron Accords (January 15, 1997)." In *The Israel-Arab Reader: A Documentary History of the Middle East Conflict*, edited by Walter Laqueur and Barry Rubin. New York: Penguin Books, 2001.

"Israel and Palestinian Authority: Interim Agreement on the West Bank and Gaza Strip (September 28, 1995)." In *The Israel-Arab Reader: A Documentary History of the Middle East Conflict*, edited by Walter Laqueur and Barry Rubin. New York: Penguin Books, 2001.

"Israel and Palestinian Authority: The Wye River Memorandum (October 23, 1998)." In *The Israel-Arab Reader: A Documentary History of the Middle East Conflict*, edited by Walter Laqueur and Barry Rubin. New York: Penguin Books, 2001.

"Israel and PLO: Agreed Minutes to the Declaration of Principles on Interim Self-Government Arrangements (September 13, 1993)." In *The Israel-Arab Reader: A Documentary History of the Middle East Conflict*, edited by Walter Laqueur and Barry Rubin. New York: Penguin Books, 2001.

"Israel and PLO: Cairo Agreement (March 4, 1994)." In *The Israel-Arab Reader: A Documentary History of the Middle East Conflict*, edited by Walter Laqueur and Barry Rubin. New York: Penguin Books, 2001.

"Israel and PLO: Declaration of Principles on Interim Self-Government Arrangements ['The Oslo Agreement'] (September 13, 1993)." In *The Israel-Arab Reader: A Documentary History of the Middle East Conflict*, edited by Walter Laqueur and Barry Rubin. New York: Penguin Books, 2001.

"Israel Approves Plan for Palestinian State by 2005." *Financial Times Information* (26 May 2003). http://web.lexis-nexis.com/. 23 August 2005.

"Israel Cautiously Accepts Peace 'Road Map.'" *News Max Wires* (24 May 2003). http://www.newsmax.com/archives/. 23 August 2005.

"Israel Criticizes London Conference for Failure in Targeting Terror." *Xinhua News Agency* (2 March 2005). http://web.lexis-nexis.com/. 23 August 2005.

"Israel Formally Protests Russian Road Map Initiative." *Financial Times Information* (25 November 2003). http://web.lexis-nexis.com/. 23 August 2005.

"Israel Hopes Bush's New Anti-Oslo Appointee Will Improve Peace 'Road Map.'" *The Jerusalem Report* (30 December 2002). http://web.lexis-nexis.com/. 23 August 2005.

Israeli Cabinet. "Statement Insisting that Jordan Represents the Palestinians in Negotiations (21 July 1974)." In *The Israeli-Palestinian Conflict: a documentary record, 1967–1990*, edited by Yehuda Lukacs. Cambridge: Cambridge University Press, 1992.

"Israeli Cabinet Statement on Road Map and 14 Reservations." *Jewish Virtual Library* (25 May 2003). http://www.jewishvirtuallibrary.org/. 23 August 2005.

"Israeli Defence Minister Discusses Pullout Benefits Following Protests." *Financial Times Information* (22 July 2005). http://web.lexis-nexis.com/. 23 August 2005.

Israeli Foreign Ministry. "Statement on the Decisions of the 19th Palestine National Council (15 November 1988). In *The Israeli-Palestinian Conflict: a documentary record, 1967–1990*, edited by Yehuda Lukacs. Cambridge: Cambridge University Press, 1992.

Israeli Government. "Basic Guidelines (July 1999)." In *The Israel-Arab Reader: A Documentary History of the Middle East Conflict*, edited by Walter Laqueur and Barry Rubin. New York: Penguin Books, 2001.

———. "Basic Policy Guidelines (13 September 1984)." In *The Israeli-Palestinian Conflict: a documentary record, 1967–1990*, edited by Yehuda Lukacs. Cambridge: Cambridge University Press, 1992.

———. "Basic Policy Guidelines (23 December 1988)." In *The Israeli-Palestinian Conflict: a documentary record, 1967–1990*, edited by Yehuda Lukacs. Cambridge: Cambridge University Press, 1992.

———. "Basic Policy Guidelines (10 June 1990)." In *The Israeli-Palestinian Conflict: a documentary record, 1967–1990*, edited by Yehuda Lukacs. Cambridge: Cambridge University Press, 1992.

———. "Fundamental Policy Guidelines (August 5, 1981)." In *The Israel-Arab Reader: A Documentary History of the Middle East Conflict*, edited by Walter Laqueur and Barry Rubin. New York: Penguin Books, 2001.

———. "A Peace Initiative (14 May 1989)." In *The Israeli-Palestinian Conflict: a documentary record, 1967–1990*, edited by Yehuda Lukacs. Cambridge: Cambridge University Press, 1992.

———. "Statement Responding to the US-USSR Joint Declaration on the Middle East (1 October 1977)." In *The Israeli-Palestinian Conflict: a documentary record, 1967–1990*, edited by Yehuda Lukacs. Cambridge: Cambridge University Press, 1992.

"Israeli Minister Proposes Four Palestinian Cantons in West Bank." *Financial Times Information* (16 February 2004). http://web.lexis-nexis.com/. 23 August 2005.

"Israeli Minister Says West Bank Withdrawal Needed after Gaza Pull-Out." *Financial Times Information* (30 December 2004). http://web.lexis-nexis.com/. 23 August 2005.

"Israeli-Palestinian Relations Bedevilled by Lack of Framework, UN Envoy Says." *UN News Centre* (21 July 2005). http://www.un.org/. 9 August 2005.

"Israeli-Palestinian Road Map Plan is 'Historic Window of Opportunity'-Annan." *UN News Centre* (8 May 2003). http://www.un.org/. 9 August 2005.

"Israeli PM Booed During Speech on Settlement Removal; Adherence to Road Map." *Financial Times Information* (5 January 2004). http://web.lexis-nexis.com/. 23 August 2005.

"Israeli PM's Statements Block Road Map Implementation- Palestinian Official." *Financial Times Information* (3 August 2003). http://web.lexis-nexis.com/. 23 August 2005.

"Israeli Premier Outlines 'Disengagement Plan' in Herzliyya Speech." *Financial Times Information* (18 December 2003). http://web.lexis-nexis.com/. 23 August 2005.

"Israeli Premier's Aide Confirms Road Map Commitment after Freeze Remarks." *Financial Times Information* (6 October 2004). http://web.lexis-nexis.com/. 23 August 2005.

"Israeli Premier's Threats Against Arafat 'Unacceptable', Moscow Says." *Financial Times Information* (24 April 2004). http://web.lexis-nexis.com/. 23 August 2005.

"Israeli Prime Minister to Present 'Disengagement' Plan as Part of Road Map." *Financial Times Information* (18 February 2004). http://web.lexis-nexis.com/. 23 August 2005.

"Israeli Public Opinion." *PSR-Survey Research Unit* (5–11 July 2001). http://www.pcpsr.org/. 14 November 2005.

"Israeli Public Opinion Poll #1." *PSR-Survey Research Unit* (27–31 July 2000). http://www.pcpsr.org/. 14 November 2005.

"Israelis and Palestinians Should Not Let Extremists 'Hijack' Peace Process, Annan Says." *UN News Centre* (13 May 2003). http://www.un.org/. 9 August 2005.

"Israelis Wary in Backing Road Map." *Nationwide News Pty Limited* (27 May 2003). http://web.lexis-nexis.com/. 23 August 2005.

"Israel: Law on the Golan Heights (December 14, 1981)." In *The Israel-Arab Reader: A Documentary History of the Middle East Conflict*, edited by Walter Laqueur and Barry Rubin. New York: Penguin Books, 2001.

"Israel May 'Bypass' Peace Plan." *Financial Times Information* (6 December 2004). http://web.lexis-nexis.com/. 23 August 2005.

"Israel Not Complying with General Assembly Demand to Halt Barrier-Annan." *UN News Centre* (28 November 2003). http://www0.un.org/. 9 August 2005.

"Israel Opposes UN Involvement in Road Map Plan- Sharon." *Financial Times Information* (5 November 2003). http://web.lexis-nexis.com/. 23 August 2005.

"Israel: Outpost Issue to Derail Sharon-Quray Summit, Says Palestinian Official." *Financial Times Information* (28 November 2003). http://web.lexis-nexis.com/. 23 August 2005.

"Israel Out to Change 'Road Map.'" *Nationwide News Pty Limited* (13 April 2003). http://web.lexis-nexis.com/. 23 August 2005.

"Israel, Palestinians End Meeting on Positive Note." *Media Corporation of Singapore Pte Ltd.* (29 May 2003). http://web.lexis-nexis.com/. 23 August 2005.

"Israel, Palestinians Would Fall off 'Cliff' if Roadmap Abandoned: Powell." *Xinhua News Agency* (21 August 2003). http://web.lexis-nexis.com/. 23 August 2005.

"Israel PM Rejects Quartet's Aid 'For Now', Says Disengagement Leads to Road Map." *Financial Times Information* (23 November 2004). http://web.lexis-nexis.com/. 23 August 2005.

"Israel Postpones Troop Withdrawal from West Bank Towns." *MCN International Pte Ltd.* (18 August 2003). http://web.lexis-nexis.com/. 23 August 2005.

"Israel Puts Positive Spin on Bush-Abbas Meeting." *Financial Times Information* (28 May 2005). http://web.lexis-nexis.com/. 23 August 2005.

"Israel 'Ready' to Adopt Peace Plan." *BBC News* (23 May 2003). http://newsvote.bbc.co.uk/. 23 August 2005.

"Israel Ready to Make 'Brave Decisions' at Talks with Palestinians-Mufaz." *Financial Times Information* (16 December 2003). http://web.lexis-nexis.com/. 23 August 2005.

"Israel Rejects 'Meaningless' UN Resolution on Arafat- Radio." *Financial Times Information* (20 September 2003). http://web.lexis-nexis.com/. August 2005.

"Israel's Gaza Disengagement Plan 'A Moment Pregnant with Hope, but Also Fraught with Peril', Middle East Peace Envoy Tells Security Council." *Press Release SC/8455* (21 July 2005). http://www.un.org/. 9 August 2005.

"Israel's Separation Wall 'Obstacle' to two-State Solution-Annan." *UN News Centre* (2 October 2003). http://www.un.org/. 9 August 2005.

"Israel's Sharon Tells Annan Disengagement Plan will be Implemented on Time." *Financial Times Information* (14 March 2005). http://web.lexis-nexis.com/. 23 August 2005.

"Israel to Fight Hamas to 'Bitter End' Unless Palestinians Act- Israeli Minister." *Financial Times Information* (21 April 2003). http://web.lexis-nexis.com/. 23 August 2005.

"Israel to Leave Occupied Areas Road Map Agreement." *Nationwide News Pty Limited* (31 May 2003). http://web.lexis-nexis.com/. 23 August 2005.

"Israel to Withdraw from Four Towns." *Financial Times Information* (17 April 2003). http://web.lexis-nexis.com/. 23 August 2005.

Jaffee Center for Strategic Studies. "Israel, the West Bank and Gaza: Toward a Solution (1989)." In *The Israeli-Palestinian Conflict: a documentary record, 1967–1990*, edited by Yehuda Lukacs. Cambridge: Cambridge University Press, 1992.

Johnson, Lyndon. "Statement on Principles for Peace (19 June 1967)." In *The Israeli-Palestinian Conflict: a documentary record, 1967–1990*, edited by Yehuda Lukacs. Cambridge: Cambridge University Press, 1992.

"Joint Statement by the Governments of the US and the USSR (1 October 1977)." In *The Israeli-Palestinian Conflict: a documentary record, 1967–1990*, edited by Yehuda Lukacs. Cambridge: Cambridge University Press, 1992.

"Joint Statement by the Quartet." *UN News Centre* (20 December 2002). http://www.un.org/. 9 August 2005.

"Joint Statement on the Middle East: 10th EU-Russia Summit." *Europa* (11 November 2002). http://www.europa.eu.int/. 16 August 2005.

Jordanian Government. "Refusal to Join the Reagan Peace Initiative (April 10, 1983)." In *The Israel-Arab Reader: A Documentary History of the Middle East Conflict*, edited by Walter Laqueur and Barry Rubin. New York: Penguin Books, 2001.

Kalb, Bernard. "Statement on the Legitimate Rights of the Palestinian People (15 February 1985)." In *The Israeli-Palestinian Conflict: a documentary record, 1967–1990*, edited by Yehuda Lukacs. Cambridge: Cambridge University Press, 1992.

Kissinger, Henry. *Years of Upheaval*. Boston: Little, Brown and Company, 1982.

"Law Enacted by Israel's Knesset Proclaiming Jerusalem the Capital of Israel (29 July 1980)." In *The Israeli-Palestinian Conflict: a documentary record, 1967–1990*, edited by Yehuda Lukacs. Cambridge: Cambridge University Press, 1992.

Likud Party. "Platform (March 1977)." In *The Israel-Arab Reader: A Documentary History of the Middle East Conflict*, edited by Walter Laqueur and Barry Rubin. New York: Penguin Books, 2001.

"London Agreement Between Foreign Minister Shimon Peres and King Hussein (11 April 1987)." In *The Israeli-Palestinian Conflict: a documentary record, 1967–1990*, edited by Yehuda Lukacs. Cambridge: Cambridge University Press, 1992.

Marcus, Jonathan. "Israeli PM Faces West Bank Gamble." *BBC News* (23 August 2005). http://newsvote.bbc.co.uk/. 23 August 2005.

Marcus, Yoel. "'If They Want It, They'll Take It' (December 26, 2000)." In *The Israel-Arab Reader: A Documentary History of the Middle East Conflict*, edited by Walter Laqueur and Barry Rubin. New York: Penguin Books, 2001.

Meir, Golda. "Statement in the Knesset (October 23, 1973)." In *The Israel-Arab Reader: A Documentary History of the Middle East Conflict*, edited by Walter Laqueur and Barry Rubin. New York: Penguin Books, 2001.

"Memorandum of Agreement between the Governments of Israel and the United States (September 1975)." In *The Israeli-Palestinian Conflict: a documentary record, 1967–1990*, edited by Yehuda Lukacs. Cambridge: Cambridge University Press, 1992.

"Mideast: Hamas Founder Calls Israeli Acceptance of Road Map 'Trick.'" *Financial Times Information* (28 May 2003). http://web.lexis-nexis.com/. 23 August 2005.

Mubarak, Hosni. "Egypt and Israel (October 14, 1981)." In *The Israel-Arab Reader: A Documentary History of the Middle East Conflict*, edited by Walter Laqueur and Barry Rubin. New York: Penguin Books, 2001.

"Netanyahu Reaffirms Israeli Peace Course." *Deutsche Presse-Agentur* (23 December 2002). http://web.lexis-nexis.com/. 23 August 2005.

"New Palestinian President Underlines Commitment to Road Map." *Financial Times Information* (15 January 2005). http://web.lexis-nexis.com/. 23 August 2005.

Office of the Press Secretary. "Bush, Blair Discuss Sharon Plan; Future of Iraq in Press Conference: Remarks by the President and United Kingdom Prime Minister Tony Blair in Press Availability." 16 April 2004. http://www.whitehouse.gov/. 17 August 2005.

———. "Dr. Condoleezza Rice Discusses Iraq and the Middle East." 4 May 2004. http://www.whitehouse.gov/. 17 August 2005.

———. "The German-American Alliance for the 21st Century Joint Statement by President George W. Bush and Chancellor Gerhard Schroder." 27 February 2004. http://www.whitehouse.gov/. 17 August 2005.

———. "Joint Statement by the United States and the European Union Working Together to Promote Peace, Prosperity and Progress in the Middle East." 20 June 2005. http://www.whitehouse.gov/. 17 August 2005.

———. "Letter from President Bush to Prime Minister Sharon." 14 April 2004. http://www.whitehouse.gov/. 17 August 2005.

———. "Powell, Rice Discuss Road Map for Peace in the Middle East: Remarks by Secretary of State Colin Powell and National Security Advisor Condoleezza Rice to the Press Pool." 4 June 2003. http://www.whitehouse.gov/. 17 August 2005.

———. "President and King Abdullah of Jordan Discuss Middle East Peace, Trade." 15 March 2005. http://www.whitehouse.gov/. 17 August 2005.

———. "President and Prime Minister Sharon Discuss Economy, Middle East." 11 April 2005. http://www.whitehouse.gov/. 17 August 2005.

———. "President Believes Peace in Middle East is Achievable: Remarks by the President to the Travel Pool." 15 June 2003. http://www.whitehouse.gov/. 17 August 2005.

———. "President Bush Addresses United Nations General Assembly." 23 September 2003. http://www.whitehouse.gov/. 17 August 2005.

———. "President Bush and Chancellor Schroder Discuss Partnership." 23 February 2005. http://www.whitehouse.gov/. 17 August 2005.

———. "President Bush Calls for New Palestinian Leadership." 24 June 2002. http://www.whitehouse.gov/. 17 August 2005.

———. "President Bush Commends Israeli Prime Minister Sharon's Plan: Remarks by the President and Israeli Prime Minister Ariel Sharon in Press Availability." 14 April 2004. http://www.whitehouse.gov/. 17 August 2005.

———. "President Bush Discusses Top Priorities for the U.S." 30 July 2003. http://www.whitehouse.gov/. 17 August 2005.

———. "President Bush, Egyptian President Mubarak Meet with Reporters: Remarks by President Bush and President Hosni Mubarak of Egypt in Press Availability." 12 April 2004. http://www.whitehouse.gov/. 17 August 2005.

———. "President Bush, European Leaders Act to Fight Global Terror: Remarks by President Bush, Prime Minister Simitis and President Prodi in Press Availability." 25 June 2003. http://www.whitehouse.gov/. 17 August 2005.

———. "President Bush, Jordanian King Discuss Iraq, Middle East: Remarks by President Bush and His Majesty King Abdullah II of the Hashemite Kingdom of Jordan in a Press Availability." 6 May 2004. http://www.whitehouse.gov/. 17 August 2005.

———. "President Bush, King Abdullah Discuss Middle East Peace: Remarks by the President and His Majesty King Abdullah of the Hashemite Kingdom of Jordan in Photo Opportunity." 1 August 2002. http://www.whitehouse.gov/. 17 August 2005.

———. "President Bush Meets with Egyptian President Mubarak: Remarks by President Bush and President Mubarak in Press Availability." 8 June 2002. http://www.whitehouse.gov/. 17 August 2005.

———. "President Bush Meets with European Leaders." 2 May 2002. http://www.whitehouse.gov/. 17 August 2005.

———. "President Bush Meets with German Chancellor Schroder: Remarks by President Bush and Chancellor Schroder of Germany in Press Availability." 23 May 2002. http://www.whitehouse.gov/. 17 August 2005.

———. "President Bush, President Putin Release Joint Statement on Middle East: Joint Statement by President George W. Bush and President Vladimir V. Putin on the Situation in the Middle East." 24 May 2002. http://www.whitehouse.gov/. 17 August 2005.

———. "President Bush Presses for Peace in the Middle East: Remarks by the President in Commencement Address at the University of South Carolina." 9 May 2003. http://www.whitehouse.gov/. 17 August 2005.

———. "President Bush, Prime Minister Sabah of Kuwait Discuss Middle East: Remarks by the President and Prime Minister Sabah of Kuwait in a Photo Opportunity." 10 September 2003. http://www.whitehouse.gov/. 17 August 2005.

———. "President Bush, Secretary Powell Discuss Middle East: Remarks by the President and Secretary of State Colin Powell in Photo Opportunity." 18 April 2002. http://www.whitehouse.gov/. 17 August 2005.

———. "President Bush Troubled with Israeli Helicopter Gunship Attacks: Remarks by the President and Ugandan President Museveni in Photo Opportunity." 10 June 2003. http://www.whitehouse.gov/. 17 August 2005.

———. "President Bush Welcomes Prime Minister Abbas to White House: Remarks by President Bush and Prime Minister Abbas." 25 July 2003. http://www.whitehouse.gov/. 17 August 2005.

———. "President Bush Welcomes Prime Minister Sharon to White House." 16 October 2002. http://www.whitehouse.gov/. 17 August 2005.
———. "President Condemns Terrorist Attack in Israel: Statement by the President." 5 January 2003. http://www.whitehouse.gov/. 17 August 2005.
———. "President Discusses American and European Alliance in Belgium." 21 February 2005. http://www.whitehouse.gov/. 17 August 2005.
———. "President Discusses Economy, Middle East Following Cabinet Meeting: Remarks by the President in Photo Opportunity with the Cabinet." 31 July 2002. http://www.whitehouse.gov/. 17 August 2005.
———. "President Discusses Middle East Peace with Prime Minister Sharon." 29 July 2003. http://www.whitehouse.gov/. 17 August 2005.
———. "President Discusses Missile Tests in Pakistan and Middle East: Remarks by the President Following Tour of Choral Synagogue." 26 May 2002. http://www.whitehouse.gov/. 17 August 2005.
———. "President Discusses Roadmap for Peace in the Middle East: Remarks by the President on the Middle East." 14 March 2003. http://www.whitehouse.gov/. 17 August 2005.
———. "President Meets with E.U. Leaders." 22 February 2005. http://www.whitehouse.gov/. 17 August 2005.
———. "President Meets with Foreign Ministers of Egypt, Jordan, and Saudi Arabia." 18 July 2002. http://www.whitehouse.gov/. 17 August 2005.
———. "President Meets with Leaders of Jordan, Israel, and Palestinian Authority: Remarks by President Bush, His Majesty King Abdullah of Jordan, Prime Minister Sharon of Israel, and Prime Minister Abbas of the Palestinian Authority." 4 June 2003. http://www.whitehouse.gov/. 17 August 2005.
———. "President Meets with Muslim Leaders: Remarks by the President in Meeting with Muslim Community Leaders." 26 September 2001. http://www.whitehouse.gov/. 14 June 2005.
———. "President Reiterates Path for Peace in Middle East: Remarks by the President and Prime Minister Blair in Photo Opportunity." 26 June 2002. http://www.whitehouse.gov/. 17 August 2005.
———. "President Speaks to the American Israel Public Affairs Committee: Remarks by the President to the American Israel Public Affairs Committee." 18 May 2004. http://www.whitehouse.gov/. 17 August 2005.
———. "President's Radio Address." 5 March 2005. http://www.whitehouse.gov/. 17 August 2005.
———. "President's Statement on Palestinian Elections." 9 January 2005. http://www.whitehouse.gov/. 17 August 2005.
———. "President to Meet With Israeli Prime Minister Sunday: Remarks by the President Upon Return from Camp David." 2 December 2001. http://www.whitehouse.gov/. 14 June 2005.
———. "President Welcomes Quartet Principals to White House: Remarks by President Bush, Secretary General Kofi Annan, Danish Foreign Minister Per Stig Moeller, and Russian Foreign Minister Igor Ivanov in Photo Opportunity with the Quartet Principals." 20 December 2002. http://www.whitehouse.gov/. 17 August 2005.
———. "Press Conference by the President." 29 March 2001. http://www.whitehouse.gov/. 14 June 2005.
———. "Statement by the President." 14 April 2004. http://www.whitehouse.gov/. 17 August 2005.
———. "Statement by the President on the Middle East." 28 April 2002. http://www.whitehouse.gov/. 17 August 2005.

———. "Statement by the President: Terrorist Bombing in Jerusalem." 9 August 2001. http://www.whitehouse.gov/. 14 June 2005.

———. "Statement by the Press Secretary: Election of Ariel Sharon as Prime Minister of Israel." 6 February 2001. http://www.whitehouse.gov/. 14 June 2005.

———. "Statement on the Middle East: Statement by the President on the Middle East." 30 April 2003. http://www.whitehouse.gov/. 17 August 2005.

———. "State of the Union Address." 2 February 2005. http://www.whitehouse.gov/. 17 August 2005.

———. "Text of U.S. - E.U. Declaration Supporting Peace, Progress, and Reform in the Broader Middle East and in the Mediterranean." 26 June 2004. http://www.whitehouse.gov/. 17 August 2005.

Ottaway, Marina. "The Problem of Credibility." In *Uncharted Journey: Promoting Democracy in the Middle East*, edited by Thomas Carothers and Marina Ottaway. Washington: Carnegie Endowment for International Peace, 2005.

Palestine Liberation Organization. "Statement Rejecting UN Resolution 242 (23 November 1967)." In *The Israeli-Palestinian Conflict: a documentary record, 1967–1990*, edited by Yehuda Lukacs. Cambridge: Cambridge University Press, 1992.

Palestine Liberation Organization Central Committee. "Statement (9 January 1988)." In *The Israeli-Palestinian Conflict: a documentary record, 1967–1990*, edited by Yehuda Lukacs. Cambridge: Cambridge University Press, 1992.

Palestine Liberation Organization Central Council. "Statement (16 October 1989)." In *The Israeli-Palestinian Conflict: a documentary record, 1967–1990*, edited by Yehuda Lukacs. Cambridge: Cambridge University Press, 1992.

Palestine Liberation Organization Executive Committee. "Letter to Delegate Walter Fauntroy (5 October 1979)." In *The Israeli-Palestinian Conflict: a documentary record, 1967–1990*, edited by Yehuda Lukacs. Cambridge: Cambridge University Press, 1992.

———. "On the Intifada (December 1987)." In *The Israel-Arab Reader: A Documentary History of the Middle East Conflict*, edited by Walter Laqueur and Barry Rubin. New York: Penguin Books, 2001.

———. "Statement (7 March 1986)." In *The Israeli-Palestinian Conflict: a documentary record, 1967–1990*, edited by Yehuda Lukacs. Cambridge: Cambridge University Press, 1992.

———. "Statement on the Amman Accord (19 February 1985)." In *The Israeli-Palestinian Conflict: a documentary record, 1967–1990*, edited by Yehuda Lukacs. Cambridge: Cambridge University Press, 1992.

———. "Statement on the Intifada (April 1988)." In *The Israel-Arab Reader: A Documentary History of the Middle East Conflict*, edited by Walter Laqueur and Barry Rubin. New York: Penguin Books, 2001.

Palestine National Assembly. "Political Resolutions (17 July 1968)." In *The Israeli-Palestinian Conflict: a documentary record, 1967–1990*, edited by Yehuda Lukacs. Cambridge: Cambridge University Press, 1992.

Palestine National Council. "Declaration of Independence (November 15, 1988)." In *The Israel-Arab Reader: A Documentary History of the Middle East Conflict*, edited by Walter Laqueur and Barry Rubin. New York: Penguin Books, 2001.

———. "Political and Organizational Program (23 January 1979)." In *The Israeli-Palestinian Conflict: a documentary record, 1967–1990*, edited by Yehuda Lukacs. Cambridge: Cambridge University Press, 1992.

———. "Political Communiqué (15 November 1988)." In *The Israeli-Palestinian Conflict: a documentary record, 1967–1990*, edited by Yehuda Lukacs. Cambridge: Cambridge University Press, 1992.

———. "Political Communiqué (September 28, 1991)." In *The Israel-Arab Reader: A Documentary History of the Middle East Conflict*, edited by Walter Laqueur and Barry Rubin. New York: Penguin Books, 2001.

———. "Political Program (12 January 1973)." In *The Israeli-Palestinian Conflict: a documentary record, 1967–1990*, edited by Yehuda Lukacs. Cambridge: Cambridge University Press, 1992.

———. "Political Program (8 June 1974)." In *The Israeli-Palestinian Conflict: a documentary record, 1967–1990*, edited by Yehuda Lukacs. Cambridge: Cambridge University Press, 1992.

———. "Political Resolutions (22 February 1983)." In *The Israeli-Palestinian Conflict: a documentary record, 1967–1990*, edited by Yehuda Lukacs. Cambridge: Cambridge University Press, 1992.

———. "Political Statement (21 April 1981)." In *The Israeli-Palestinian Conflict: a documentary record, 1967–1990*, edited by Yehuda Lukacs. Cambridge: Cambridge University Press, 1992.

———. "Political Statement (29 November 1984)." In *The Israeli-Palestinian Conflict: a documentary record, 1967–1990*, edited by Yehuda Lukacs. Cambridge: Cambridge University Press, 1992.

———. "Resolutions of the Political Committee (26 April 1987)." In *The Israeli-Palestinian Conflict: a documentary record, 1967–1990*, edited by Yehuda Lukacs. Cambridge: Cambridge University Press, 1992.

"Palestine National Covenant (1968)." In *The Israeli-Palestinian Conflict: a documentary record, 1967–1990*, edited by Yehuda Lukacs. Cambridge: Cambridge University Press, 1992.

"Palestinian Authority Welcomes UN Resolution on Road Map." *Financial Times Information* (20 November 2003). http://web.lexis-nexis.com/. 23 August 2005.

"Palestinian Dahlan 'Not Surprised' by Israeli Pullout Delay Decision." *Financial Times Information* (10 May 2005). http://web.lexis-nexis.com/. 23 August 2005.

"Palestinian Declaration of Independence (15 November 1988)." In *The Israeli-Palestinian Conflict: a documentary record, 1967–1990*, edited by Yehuda Lukacs. Cambridge: Cambridge University Press, 1992.

"Palestinian Fatah Issues 'Binding' Decision Not to target Israeli Civilians." *Financial Times Information* (6 February 2005). http://web.lexis-nexis.com/. 23 August 2005.

"Palestinian Foreign Minister: Return of Refugees to Israel 'Certain.'" *Financial Times Information* (15 August 2003). http://web.lexis-nexis.com/. 23 August 2005.

"Palestinian Government Must Act to Retain Standing- Israeli Defence Minister." *Financial Times Information* (4 September 2003). http://web.lexis-nexis.com/. 23 August 2005.

"Palestinian Hamas Rejects Road Map, Vows to Continue Operations." *Financial Times Information* (20 June 2003). http://web.lexis-nexis.com/. 23 August 2005.

"Palestinian Homeland Polls." *The American-Israeli Cooperative Enterprise* (2005). http://www.jewishvirtuallibrary.org/. 14 November 2005.

"Palestinian-Israeli Public Opinion Poll: Summary of Results." *The Harry S. Truman Research Institute for the Advancement of Peace* (July 2001). http://truman.huji.ac.il/. 14 August 2005.

"Palestinian Leader Abbas, Italian Foreign Minister Discuss Gaza Pull-Out." *Financial Times Information* (23 December 2004). http://web.lexis-nexis.com/. 23 August 2005.

"Palestinian Leader Addresses London Meeting, Demands Adherence to Road Map." *Financial Times Information* (1 March 2005). http://web.lexis-nexis.com/. 23 August 2005.

"Palestinian Leadership Rejects 'So-Called Gaza Administration.'" *Financial Times Information* (30 August 2004). http://web.lexis-nexis.com/. 23 August 2005.
"Palestinian Minister Insists Road Map Must be Implemented 'As it is.'" *Financial Times Information* (28 May 2003). http://web.lexis-nexis.com/. 23 August 2005.
"Palestinian Minister: Israel Replacing Road Map Steps With 'Formalities.'" *Financial Times Information* (30 May 2003). http://web.lexis-nexis.com/. 23 August 2005.
"Palestinian Minister Notes Need for UK Pressure on US Over Sharon Plan." *Financial Times Information* (4 May 2004). http://web.lexis-nexis.com/. 23 August 2005.
"Palestinian Minister says Israel Must Choose Between 'Peace and Settlements.'" *Financial Times Information* (27 November 2003). http://web.lexis-nexis.com/. 23 August 2005.
"Palestinian Minister says No Israeli Plan to Withdraw from Gaza." *Financial Times Information* (13 March 2004). http://web.lexis-nexis.com/. 23 August 2005.
"Palestinian Minister Says US, Quartet Need to Fulfil Road Map Responsibilities." *Financial Times Information* (20 February 2004). http://web.lexis-nexis.com/.23 August 2005.
"Palestinian Minister Urayqat Hopes Israeli Withdrawal to Be Part of Road Map." *Financial Times Information* (16 May 2004). http://web.lexis-nexis.com/. 23 August 2005.
"Palestinian Minister Urges Quartet to Stop Israeli Settlement Activity." *Financial Times Information* (27 January 2005). http://web.lexis-nexis.com/. 23 August 2005.
Palestinian Negotiating Team. "Remarks and Questions Regarding the Clinton Plan (January 2, 2001)." In *The Israel-Arab Reader: A Documentary History of the Middle East Conflict*, edited by Walter Laqueur and Barry Rubin. New York: Penguin Books, 2001.
"Palestinian Negotiator on Elections, Prospects of Road Map." *Financial Times Information* (10 January 2005). http://web.lexis-nexis.com/. 23 August 2005.
"Palestinian Official Discusses Developments with UN, US, Russian Envoys." *Financial Times Information* (10 November 2003). http://web.lexis-nexis.com/. 23 August 2005.
"Palestinian Official Says Israeli Settlement Plans Will 'Bury' Road Map." *Financial Times Information* (26 October 2003). http://web.lexis-nexis.com/. 23 August 2005.
"Palestinian Officials React to Quartet Recommendations." *Financial Times Information* (26 September 2003). http://web.lexis-nexis.com/. 23 August 2005.
"Palestinian PM Abbas Takes Office in Key Step to US-Led Peace Plan." *Media Corporation of Singapore Pte Ltd.* (20 April 2003). http://web.lexis-nexis.com/. 23 August 2005.
"Palestinian PM Tells Russian TV We Must Deal with Sharon." *Financial Times Information* (8 July 2003). http://web.lexis-nexis.com/. 23 August 2005.
"Palestinian Premier Asks US for 'Clear Position' on Israeli Settlement Blocs." *Financial Times Information* (3 April 2005). http://web.lexis-nexis.com/. 23 August 2005.
"Palestinian Premier Briefs US Congress Delegation on Israeli Policies, Urges Aid." *Financial Times Information* (19 March 2005). http://web.lexis-nexis.com/. 23 August 2005.
"Palestinian Premier Says No Peace Without Final-Status Talks." *Financial Times Information* (22 May 2005). http://web.lexis-nexis.com/. 23 August 2005.
"Palestinian Premier Stresses Need for International Forces in Gaza." *Financial Times Information* (8 March 2004). http://web.lexis-nexis.com/. 23 August 2005.
"Palestinian Premier Warns of 'Explosion of the Situation', in Territories." *Financial Times Information* (5 June 2005). http://web.lexis-nexis.com/. 23 August 2005.

"Palestinians Ask for US Clarification of Policy on Israeli Settlements." *Financial Times Information* (23 August 2004). http://web.lexis-nexis.com/. 23 August 2005.
"Palestinians, Egyptians Envoy Discuss Mideast Peace Ahead of Abbas-Sharon Meeting." *Financial Times Information* (15 June 2005). http://web.lexis-nexis.com/. 23 August 2005.
"Palestinians Release Hamas Militant; Israel demands that Hamas Disarm Before Election." *Financial Times Information* (4 May 2005). http://web.lexis-nexis.com/. 23 August 2005.
"Palestinians Say Road Map Progress Depends on Active Quartet Role." *Financial Times Information* (7 January 2004). http://web.lexis-nexis.com/. 23 August 2005.
"Palestinians Urge US to Withdraw Promises to Sharon on Gaza Plan." *Financial Times Information* (3 May 2004). http://web.lexis-nexis.com/. 23 August 2005.
"PA Representatives Discuss Commitment to Fulfill Road Map with Russian Official." *Financial Times Information* (8 September 2003). http://web.lexis-nexis.com/. 23 August 2005.
Patten, Christopher. "A road map paid for in euros." *The Financial Times* (17 July 2003). http://www.europa.eu.int/. 16 August 2005.
Peres, Shimon. "Address Proposing a Non-Confidence Motion to the Knesset (15 March 1990)." In *The Israeli-Palestinian Conflict: a documentary record, 1967–1990*, edited by Yehuda Lukacs. Cambridge: Cambridge University Press, 1992.
"Pledging UN Support for Road Map, Annan Appeals for All to 'Stay the Course.'" *UN News Centre* (30 April 2003). http://www0.un.org/. 9 August 2005.
"PLO Executive Says New Government Needs 'Effective Guarantees.'" *Financial Times Information* (8 September 2003). http://web.lexis-nexis.com/. 23 August 2005.
"PLO Official Says US Not Pressuring Israel Enough, Urges Greater EU Role." *Financial Times Information* (1 September 2003). http://web.lexis-nexis.com/. 23 August 2005.
Plushnick-Masti, Ramit. "Palestine Appeal to Salvage Peace Plan." *Nationwide News Pty Limited* (10 September 2003). http://web.lexis-nexis.com/. 23 August 2005.
Popular Front for the Liberation of Palestine. "Statement Announcing Withdrawal from the Executive Committee of the PLO (26 September 1974)." In *The Israeli-Palestinian Conflict: a documentary record, 1967–1990*, edited by Yehuda Lukacs. Cambridge: Cambridge University Press, 1992.
"Powell Acknowledges No Movement Likely Until Israeli Elections." *Deutsche Presse-Agentur* (18 December 2002). http://web.lexis-nexis.com/. 23 August 2005.
"Powell Says US Ready for Mideast Peace." *Xinhua News Agency* (3 April 2003). http://web.lexis-nexis.com/. 23 August 2005.
"President Prodi and Commissioner Patten Receive Emissary of Israeli PM Elect Sharon." *Europa* (16 February 2001). http://www.europa.eu.int/. 16 August 2005.
"Press Release: Council of the European Union: 2656th Council meeting." *Europa* (25 April 2005). http://ec.europa.eu/. 18 September 2007.
"Press Release: First Serious Signs of Optimism Since the Start of the Intifada." *The Harry S. Truman Research Institute for the Advancement of Peace* (12 December 2004). http://truman.huji.ac.il/. 14 November 2005.
"Press Release: Israelis and Palestinians are Lukewarm and Far Apart on the Major Components of the Geneva Document." *The Harry S. Truman Research Institute for the Advancement of Peace* (15 December 2003). http://truman.huji.ac.il/. 14 November 2005.
"Press Release: Israelis and Palestinians Support Return to Negotiations While Beliefs in the Success of the Armed Intifada Drop." *The Harry S. Truman Research In-*

stitute for the Advancement of Peace (29 November–16 December 2001 and 19–24 December 2001). http://truman.huji.ac.il/. 14 November 2005.
"Press Release: Israelis and Palestinians Support the Egyptian Initiative and the Deployment of International Presence in the Gaza Strip After Israel's Withdrawal as Part of Sharon's Disengagement Plan." *The Harry S. Truman Research Institute for the Advancement of Peace* (5 July 2004). http://truman.huji.ac.il/. 14 November 2005.
"Press Release: Israelis and Palestinians Support the Peace Process and Reconciliation but are Less Willing to Pay the Price than Their Leaders." *PSR-Survey Research Unit* (27–31 July 2000). http://www.pcpsr.org/. 14 November 2005.
"Press Release: Israeli Support for Disengagement Drops, Israelis See Declining Prospects for the Settlement Project in the West Bank, Whereas Palestinians Expect it to Grow." *The Harry S. Truman Research Institute for the Advancement of Peace* (14 June 2005). http://truman.huji.ac.il/. 14 November 2005.
"Press Release: Majority Support among Palestinians and Israelis for the Road Map and for Mutual Recognition of Israel as the State of the Jewish People and Palestine as the State of the Palestinian People- But Each Public Misperceives the Position of the Other." *The Harry S. Truman Research Institute for the Advancement of Peace* (30 June 2003). http://truman.huji.ac.il/. 14 November 2005.
"Press Release: Palestinians and Israelis Disagree on How to Proceed with the Peace Process." *The Harry S. Truman Research Institute for the Advancement of Peace* (16 March 2005). http://truman.huji.ac.il/. 14 November 2005.
"Press Release: 'Pessimism' Underscores Findings of New Israeli-Palestinian Public Opinion Poll." *PSR-Survey Research Unit* (5–11 July 2001). http://www.pcpsr.org/. 14 November 2005.
"Press Release: Stable Majorities of the Israeli and Palestinian Publics Support the Quartet's Road Map; Abu Mazin's Nomination as Prime Minister Increases Optimism about Return to Negotiations." *The Harry S. Truman Research Institute for the Advancement of Peace* (14 April 2003). http://truman.huji.ac.il/. 14 November 2005.
"Press Release: Two Thirds Among Palestinians, Israeli Jews and Israeli Arabs Support the Mutual Recognition of Israel as the State of the Jewish People and Palestine as the State of the Palestinian People." *The Harry S. Truman Research Institute for the Advancement of Peace* (25 September 2005). http://truman.huji.ac.il/. 14 November 2005.
"Press Split over Sharm al-Sheikh Summit." *BBC News* (9 February 2005). http://newsvote.bbc.co.uk/. 23 August 2005.
"Press Watches Gaza Finale." *BBC News* (22 August 2005). http://newsvote.bbc.co.uk/. 23 August 2005.
"Proceedings of Palestinian Cabinet's 22 December Session Reported." *Financial Times Information* (23 December 2003). http://web.lexis-nexis.com/. 23 August 2005.
"Public Opinion Poll #1: Camp David Summit, Chances for Reconciliation and Lasting Peace, Violence and Confrontations, Hierarchies of Priorities, and Domestic Politics." *PSR-Survey Research Unit* (27–29 July 2000). http://www.pcpsr.org/. 14 November 2005.
"Public Opinion Poll #2: The Mitchell Report, Cease Fire, and Return to Negotiations: Intifada and Armed Confrontations; Chances for Reconciliation; and, Internal Palestinian Conditions." *PSR-Survey Research Unit* (5–9 July 2001). http://www.pcpsr.org/. 14 November 2005.
"Public Opinion Poll #3: Palestinians Support the Ceasefire, Negotiations, and Reconciliation Between the Two Peoples but a Majority Opposes Arrests and Believe that Armed Confrontations have Helped Achieve National Rights." *PSR-Survey*

Research Unit (19–24 December 2001). http://www.pcpsr.org/. 14 November 2005.

"Public Opinion Poll #4: Palestinians Give Less Support for Bombings Inside Israel While Two Thirds Support the Saudi Plan and 91% Support Reforming the Pa, but a Majority Opposes Arrests and Opposes the Agreements that Led to Ending the Siege on Arafat's Headquarter, Nativity Church, and Preventive Security Headquarter." *PSR-Survey Research Unit* (15–19 May 2002). http://www.pcpsr.org/. 14 November 2005.

"Public Opinion Poll #5: While Sharply Divided Over the Ceasefire and Bombing Attacks Against Civilians, an Overwhelming Majority Supports Political Reform but Have Doubts About the PA's Intentions to Implement." *PSR-Survey Research Unit* (18–21 August 2002). http://www.pcpsr.org/. 14 November 2005.

"Public Opinion Poll #6: While Indicating Important Shifts in Palestinian Public Attitudes Toward the Intifada and the Peace Process, PSR Poll Shows Significant Support for the Appointment of a Prime Minister and Refusal to Give Confidence in the New Palestinian Government." *PSR-Survey Research Unit* (14–22 November 2002). http://www.pcpsr.org/. 14 November 2005.

"Putin Calls for Arab League Action in Mideast." *Financial Times Information* (22 May 2004). http://web.lexis-nexis.com/. 23 August 2005.

"Quartet Reaffirms Commitment to Two-State Middle East Solution, Annan Says." *UN News Centre* (9 May 2005). http://www.un.org/. 9 August 2005.

"Quartet Statement." *Jerusalem Media and Communication Centre* (1 March 2005). http://www.jmcc.org/. 17 September 2007.

"Quartet to Approve Israeli- Palestinian Peace Plan in February: Russia." *Xinhua News Agency* (23 December 2002). http://web.lexis-nexis.com/. 23 August 2005.

"Quartet Urge Mid-East Peace Efforts." *BBC News*. 26 September 2003. http://newsvote.bbc.co.uk/. 23 August 2005.

"Quartet will Support Palestinian Elections- Russian Foreign Minister." *Financial Times Information* (23 November 2004). http://web.lexis-nexis.com/. 23 August 2005.

Rabin, Yitzhak. "Accepting the UNESCO Peace Prize (July 6, 1994)." In *The Israel-Arab Reader: A Documentary History of the Middle East Conflict*, edited by Walter Laqueur and Barry Rubin. New York: Penguin Books, 2001.

———. "Inaugural Speech (July 13, 1992)." In *The Israel-Arab Reader: A Documentary History of the Middle East Conflict*, edited by Walter Laqueur and Barry Rubin. New York: Penguin Books, 2001.

———. "Speech at Peace Rally (November 4, 1995)." In *The Israel-Arab Reader: A Documentary History of the Middle East Conflict*, edited by Walter Laqueur and Barry Rubin. New York: Penguin Books, 2001.

———. "Speech to Knesset (September 21, 1993)." In *The Israel-Arab Reader: A Documentary History of the Middle East Conflict*, edited by Walter Laqueur and Barry Rubin. New York: Penguin Books, 2001.

———. "Speech to Knesset (April 18, 1994)." In *The Israel-Arab Reader: A Documentary History of the Middle East Conflict*, edited by Walter Laqueur and Barry Rubin. New York: Penguin Books, 2001.

———. "Statement Following the Rabat Conference (5 November 1974)." In *The Israeli-Palestinian Conflict: a documentary record, 1967–1990*, edited by Yehuda Lukacs. Cambridge: Cambridge University Press, 1992.

Rabin, Yitzhak, and Yasir Arafat. "Speeches at the Signing of the Cairo Agreement (March 4, 1994)." In *The Israel-Arab Reader: A Documentary History of the Middle East Conflict*, edited by Walter Laqueur and Barry Rubin. New York: Penguin Books, 2001.

Reagan, Ronald. "Reagan Peace Plan (1 September 1982)." In *The Israeli-Palestinian Conflict: a documentary record, 1967-1990*, edited by Yehuda Lukacs. Cambridge: Cambridge University Press, 1992.
———. "Statement on Relations with the PLO (14 December 1988)." In *The Israeli-Palestinian Conflict: a documentary record, 1967-1990*, edited by Yehuda Lukacs. Cambridge: Cambridge University Press, 1992.
———. "Statement on the Establishment of New Israeli Settlements (27 August 1983)." In *The Israeli-Palestinian Conflict: a documentary record, 1967-1990*, edited by Yehuda Lukacs. Cambridge: Cambridge University Press, 1992.
———. "Text of 'Talking Points' Sent to Prime Minister Menachem Begin by President Ronald Reagan (8 September 1982)." In *The Israeli-Palestinian Conflict: a documentary record, 1967-1990*, edited by Yehuda Lukacs. Cambridge: Cambridge University Press, 1992.
"Remarks of Javier Solana, EU High Representative for the CFSP, on the occasion of a meeting with Palestinian Prime Minister Ahmed Qurei." (13 July 2005). http://ue.eu.int/. 18 September 2007.
"Results of Surveys among Palestinian Refugees (and Non-Refugees) in the West Bank/Gaza Strip, Jordan and Lebanon." *PSR-Survey Research Unit* (January–June 2003). http://www.pcpsr.org/. 14 November 2005.
Reynolds, James. "Analysis: Israel's 'Road Map' Manoeuvres." *BBC News* (31 March 2003). http://newsvote.bbc.co.uk/. 23 August 2005.
Reynolds, Paul. "Israeli Anger Grows at Arafat." *BBC News* (17 September 2003). http://newsvote.bbc.co.uk/. 23 August 2005.
"Road Map Disarray over Arafat Decision." *Financial Times Information* (14 September 2003). http://web.lexis-nexis.com/. 23 August 2005.
"Road Map for Palestine." *Nationwide News Pty Limited* (6 December 2002). http://web.lexis-nexis.com/. 23 August 2005.
"Roadmap Peace Plan to be Released Soon: Israel Radio." *Xinhua News Agency* (12 April 2003). http://web.lexis-nexis.com/. 23 August 2005.
"'Road Map' Put on Ice as Sharon Says Troops Stay in West Bank." *Financial Times Information* (16 September 2004). http://web.lexis-nexis.com/. 23 August 2005.
"Road Map Remains 'Most Practical Way' to Achieve Aspirations of Israelis, Palestinians, Secretary-General Tells Palestinian Rights Committee." *UN Press Release SG/SM/9194; GA/PAL/946* (3 December 2004). http://www.un.org/. 9 August 2005.
"'Road Map' Remains the Only Way Out Russian Envoy says." *Financial Times Information* (17 October 2003). http://web.lexis-nexis.com/. 23 August 2005.
Rogers, William. "The Rogers Plan (9 December 1969)." In *The Israeli-Palestinian Conflict: a documentary record, 1967-1990*, edited by Yehuda Lukacs. Cambridge: Cambridge University Press, 1992.
"Romano Prodi Congratulates Ariel Sharon." *Europa* (29 January 2003). http://www.europa.eu.int/. 16 August 2005.
"Roundup: Israel Wants 15 Changes to International Peace Plan." *Deutsche Presse-Agentur* (4 April 2003). http://web.lexis-nexis.com/. 23 August 2005.
"Roundup: Sharon Fails to Dissuade Russia From New UN Mideast Resolution." *Xinhua News Agency* (5 November 2003). http://web.lexis-nexis.com/. 23 August 2005.
Rubin, Barry. "United it Stalls, the PLO (March 21, 1983)." In *The Israel-Arab Reader: A Documentary History of the Middle East Conflict*, edited by Walter Laqueur and Barry Rubin. New York: Penguin Books, 2001.
"Russia Calls for Quartet Discussion of Israeli Disengagement Plan." *Financial Times Information* (15 April 2004). http://web.lexis-nexis.com/. 23 August 2005.

"Russia Calls for Urgent Measures in Middle East." *Financial Times Information* (16 September 2003). http://web.lexis-nexis.com/. 23 August 2005.

"Russia Calls for Urgent Meeting of Mideast Mediators." *Deutsche Presse-Agentur* (28 January 2003). http://web.lexis-nexis.com/. 23 August 2005.

"Russia Calls on Israel, Palestine Not to Deviate From Road Map." *Financial Times Information* (9 September 2003). http://web.lexis-nexis.com/. 23 August 2005.

"Russia Concerned About Saving Mideast Road Map." *Financial Times Information* (1 September 2003). http://web.lexis-nexis.com/. 23 August 2005.

"Russia Condemns Blasts in Israel and West Bank." *Financial Times Information* (12 August 2003). http://web.lexis-nexis.com/. 23 August 2005.

"Russia Condemns Jerusalem Suicide Bombing." *Xinhua News Agency* (20 August 2003). http://web.lexis-nexis.com/. 23 August 2005.

"Russia Criticizes Israeli Stance on UN Road Map Resolution." *Financial Times Information* (29 November 2003). http://web.lexis-nexis.com/. 23 August 2005.

"Russia Delivers Humanitarian Aid for Palestinians." *Financial Times Information* (20 July 2004). http://web.lexis-nexis.com/. 23 August 2005.

"Russia Fears Israel's 'Expansion of Settlements in West Bank'- Envoy." *Financial Times Information* (16 September 2004). http://web.lexis-nexis.com/. 23 August 2005.

"Russia Helped Resolve Rift Between Arafat and Abbas, says Ministry Spokesman." *Financial Times Information* (15 July 2003). http://web.lexis-nexis.com/. 23 August 2005.

"Russia Hopes for Restart of Middle East Road Map." *Financial Times Information* (26 April 2005). http://web.lexis-nexis.com/. 23 August 2005.

"Russian Diplomat Affirms Importance of Complying with Mideast Road Map." *Financial Times Information* (28 August 2003). http://web.lexis-nexis.com/. 23 August 2005.

"Russian Diplomat says Head-On Confrontation in Middle East Should be Prevented." *Financial Times Information* (11 June 2003). http://web.lexis-nexis.com/. 23 August 2005.

"Russian Diplomat Says Israel's Step Should Be Welcomed." *Financial Times Information* (2 April 2004). http://web.lexis-nexis.com/. 23 August 2005.

"Russian Diplomat Urges Resumption of Middle East 'Road Map' Talks." *Financial Times Information* (20 April 2004). http://web.lexis-nexis.com/. 23 August 2005.

"Russian Envoy Calls for Mideast Settlement Through Road Map." *Financial Times Information* (1 September 2003). http://web.lexis-nexis.com/. 23 August 2005.

"Russian Envoy says Middle East 'Road Map' Should Include Syria, Lebanon." *Financial Times Information* (18 June 2003). http://web.lexis-nexis.com/. 23 August 2005.

"Russian Envoy to UN Calls on Palestine and Israel to Adhere to 'Road Map.'" *Financial Times Information* (3 December 2003). http://web.lexis-nexis.com/. 23 August 2005.

"Russian Foreign Minister Advocates 'International Presence" in Middle East." *Financial Times Information* (10 September 2003). http://web.lexis-nexis.com/. 23 August 2005.

"Russian Foreign Minister Against Sharon's Disengagement Initiative." *Financial Times Information* (19 December 2003). http://web.lexis-nexis.com/. 23 August 2005.

"Russian Foreign Minister Denies Mideast-For-Iraq Deal With Washington." *Financial Times Information* (21 May 2003). http://web.lexis-nexis.com/. 23 August 2005.

"Russian Foreign Minister, Palestinian Leader Discuss Mideast Settlement." *Financial Times Information* (22 June 2005). http://web.lexis-nexis.com/. 23 August 2005.
"Russian Foreign Minister Poised to Attend Quartet Meeting on Middle East." *Financial Times Information* (22 September 2004). http://web.lexis-nexis.com/. 23 August 2005.
"Russian Foreign Minister's ME Trip First 'Fully-Fledged' Visit in Three Years." *Financial Times Information* (10 July 2003). http://web.lexis-nexis.com/. 23 August 2005.
"Russian Foreign Minister Speaks Against Israel's 'Separating Wall.'" *Financial Times Information* (21 January 2004). http://web.lexis-nexis.com/. 23 August 2005.
"Russian Foreign Minister Urges Israelis, Palestinians to Follow Road Map." *Financial Times Information* (21 July 2004). http://web.lexis-nexis.com/universe/printdoc. 23 August 2005.
"Russian Foreign Minister Welcomes Formation of Palestinian Government." *Financial Times Information* (20 June 2003). http://web.lexis-nexis.com/. 23 August 2005.
"Russian Foreign Ministry Condemns New Israeli Settlements, Barrier." *Financial Times Information* (3 October 2003). http://web.lexis-nexis.com/. 23 August 2005.
"Russian, Israeli FMs Discuss Middle East Peace Process." *Financial Times Information* (23 September 2003). http://web.lexis-nexis.com/. 23 August 2005.
"Russian, Israeli Foreign Ministers Denounce Terrorism at Moscow Talks." *Financial Times Information* (9 June 2003). http://web.lexis-nexis.com/. 23 August 2005.
"Russian Minister Calls for Settlement Plans to Help Overcome Mideast Crisis." *Financial Times Information* (10 July 2003). http://web.lexis-nexis.com/. 23 August 2005.
"Russian Minister, 'Quartet' Mediator Discuss Palestinian-Israeli Settlement." *Financial Times Information* (15 June 2005). http://web.lexis-nexis.com/. 23 August 2005.
"Russian Minister Sums Up Outcomes of Latest Middle East Quartet Meeting." *Financial Times Information* (23 September 2004). http://web.lexis-nexis.com/. 23 August 2005.
"Russian Official at UN says 'Road Map is Not Dead.'" *Financial Times Information* (13 September 2003). http://web.lexis-nexis.com/. 23 August 2005.
"Russian Official Visits Lebanon, says 'No Alternative' to Road Map." *Financial Times Information* (18 January 2004). http://web.lexis-nexis.com/. 23 August 2005.
"Russian, Palestinian Leaders Adopt Joint Statement." *Financial Times Information* (31 January 2005). http://web.lexis-nexis.com/. 23 August 2005.
"Russian, Palestinian Ministers See Road Map as Only Means to Israeli Settlement." *Financial Times Information* (16 April 2004). http://web.lexis-nexis.com/. 23 August 2005.
"Russian President Putin Comments on Upcoming Sharon Visit." *Financial Times Information* (29 July 2003). http://web.lexis-nexis.com/. 23 August 2005.
"Russia Ready to Assist in Implementation of Road Map Peace Plan." *Financial Times Information* (9 September 2003). http://web.lexis-nexis.com/. 23 August 2005.
"Russia says Mideast Peace Should Not Depend on 'Terrorists and Extremists.'" *Financial Times Information* (27 August 2003). http://web.lexis-nexis.com/. 23 August 2005.
"Russia Tells Palestinians Get a Government or Suffer More." *Deutsche Presse-Agentur* (22 April 2003). http://web.lexis-nexis.com/. 23 August 2005.
"Russia, US to Set Up Monitoring Mechanism on Middle East." *Xinhua News Agency* (11 July 2003). http://web.lexis-nexis.com/. 23 August 2005.

Sadat, Anwar. "Statement to the Israeli Knesset (20 November 1977)." In *The Israeli-Palestinian Conflict: a documentary record, 1967–1990*, edited by Yehuda Lukacs. Cambridge: Cambridge University Press, 1992.

Saunders, Harold H. "Statement on the Palestinians (12 November 1975)." In *The Israeli-Palestinian Conflict: a documentary record, 1967–1990*, edited by Yehuda Lukacs. Cambridge: Cambridge University Press, 1992.

———. "U.S. Foreign Policy and Peace in the Middle East (November 12, 1975)." In *The Israel-Arab Reader: A Documentary History of the Middle East Conflict*, edited by Walter Laqueur and Barry Rubin. New York: Penguin Books, 2001.

Scranton, William W. "Statements on Occupied Territories (23 March 1976)." In *The Israeli-Palestinian Conflict: a documentary record, 1967–1990*, edited by Yehuda Lukacs. Cambridge: Cambridge University Press, 1992.

Secretary-General Office of the Spokesman. "Secretary-General and Quartet Members at Press Conference Following Quartet Meeting (unofficial transcript)." 26 September 2003. http://www.un.org/. 9 August 2005.

———. "Secretary-General's Message to the UN International Conference of Civil Society in Support of the Palestinian People [Delivered by Mr. Kieran Prendergast, Under-Secretary-General for Political Affairs]." 13 September 2004. http://www.un.org/. 9 August 2005.

———. "Secretary-General's Press Conference with Other Members of the Middle East 'Quartet.'" 9 May 2005. http://www.un.org/. 9 August 2005.

———. "Secretary-General's Remarks to a Delegation of Visiting Palestinian Journalists (unofficial transcript)." 31 March 2003. http://www0.un.org/. 9 August 2005.

Shamir, Yitzhak. "Address at the Knesset in Response to the Non-Confidence Motion (15 March 1990)." In *The Israeli-Palestinian Conflict: a documentary record, 1967-1990*, edited by Yehuda Lukacs. Cambridge: Cambridge University Press, 1992.

———. "Address to the Knesset (23 December 1988)." In *The Israeli-Palestinian Conflict: a documentary record, 1967–1990*, edited by Yehuda Lukacs. Cambridge: Cambridge University Press, 1992.

———. "Address to the Likud Party's Central Committee (5 July 1989)." In *The Israeli-Palestinian Conflict: a documentary record, 1967–1990*, edited by Yehuda Lukacs. Cambridge: Cambridge University Press, 1992.

———. "Israel's Role in a Changing Middle East (Spring 1982)." In *The Israel-Arab Reader: A Documentary History of the Middle East Conflict*, edited by Walter Laqueur and Barry Rubin. New York: Penguin Books, 2001.

———. "Statement on the Israeli Peace Initiative (17 May 1989)." In *The Israeli-Palestinian Conflict: a documentary record, 1967–1990*, edited by Yehuda Lukacs. Cambridge: Cambridge University Press, 1992.

———. "Statement on Yasser Arafat's Speech to the UN (13 December 1988)." In *The Israeli-Palestinian Conflict: a documentary record, 1967–1990*, edited by Yehuda Lukacs. Cambridge: Cambridge University Press, 1992.

Shamir, Yitzhak, and Haydar Abd al-Shafi. "Speeches at the Madrid Peace Conference (October 21, 1991)." In *The Israel-Arab Reader: A Documentary History of the Middle East Conflict*, edited by Walter Laqueur and Barry Rubin. New York: Penguin Books, 2001.

"Sharon Agrees to Talks Based on Bush Speech 'Not' Road Map." *Financial Times Information* (30 May 2003). http://web.lexis-nexis.com/. 23 August 2005.

"Sharon and Abbas Said Ready to Meet." *Financial Times Information* (29 November 2004). http://web.lexis-nexis.com/. 23 August 2005.

Sharon, Ariel. "Israel's Security (December 15, 1981)." In *The Israel-Arab Reader: A Documentary History of the Middle East Conflict*, edited by Walter Laqueur and Barry Rubin. New York: Penguin Books, 2001.

"Sharon Attacked from All Sides over Plan for Peace Summit." *Financial Times Information* (28 May 2003). http://web.lexis-nexis.com/. 23 August 2005.

"Sharon Calls for More Palestinian Pressure on Extremists." *Xinhua News Agency* (11 April 2005). http://web.lexis-nexis.com/. 23 August 2005.

"Sharon Makes Case for Pull-Out Plan, Says 'Stalemate Cannot Continue Forever.'" *Financial Times Information* (31 March 2004). http://web.lexis-nexis.com/. 23 August 2005.

"Sharon Promises to Help Palestinians with Their Election." *Financial Times Information* (23 November 2004). http://web.lexis-nexis.com/. 23 August 2005.

"Sharon Renews Calls for Cooperation with the Palestinians." *Financial Times Information* (25 May 2005). http://web.lexis-nexis.com/. 23 August 2005.

"Sharon Rips Up 'Road Map' With Plan for 1,001 New Settler Homes." *Financial Times Information* (18 August 2004). http://web.lexis-nexis.com/. 23 August 2005.

"Sharon Says Evacuation of Outposts Part of Roadmap Obligations." *Xinhua News Agency* (13 March 2005). http://web.lexis-nexis.com/. 23 August 2005.

"Sharon's Cabinet Backs US Road Map." *Nationwide News Pty Limited* (26 May 2003). http://web.lexis-nexis.com/. 23 August 2005.

"Sharon Seeks U.S. Approval for Disengagement Plan." *Financial Times Information* (14 April 2004). http://web.lexis-nexis.com/. 23 August 2005.

"Sharon Sees 'Encouraging Signs' From Palestinians." *Financial Times Information* (27 January 2005). http://web.lexis-nexis.com/. 23 August 2005.

"Sharon's Vow is a Road Block on Path to Peace." *Nationwide News Pty Limited* (13 April 2005). http://web.lexis-nexis.com/. 23 August 2005.

"Sharon Talks Statehood." *Nationwide News Pty Limited* (6 December 2002). http://web.lexis-nexis.com/. 23 August 2005.

"Sharon to Ignore Warning by Bush." *Financial Times Information* (13 April 2005). http://web.lexis-nexis.com/. 23 August 2005.

Shultz, George. "Address Before the Washington Institute for Near East Policy (16 September 1988)." In *The Israeli-Palestinian Conflict: a documentary record, 1967–1990*, edited by Yehuda Lukacs. Cambridge: Cambridge University Press, 1992.

———. "Arrival Statements during Visit to the Middle East (Cairo, 3 June 1988; Amman, 4 June 1988; Tel Aviv, 5 June 1988)." In *The Israeli-Palestinian Conflict: a documentary record, 1967–1990*, edited by Yehuda Lukacs. Cambridge: Cambridge University Press, 1992.

———. "Congressional Testimony (July 12, 1982)." In *The Israel-Arab Reader: A Documentary History of the Middle East Conflict*, edited by Walter Laqueur and Barry Rubin. New York: Penguin Books, 2001.

———. "Plan (March 6, 1988)." In *The Israel-Arab Reader: A Documentary History of the Middle East Conflict*, edited by Walter Laqueur and Barry Rubin. New York: Penguin Books, 2001.

———. "Speech before American-Israel Public Affairs Committee (17 May 1987)." In *The Israeli-Palestinian Conflict: a documentary record, 1967–1990*, edited by Yehuda Lukacs. Cambridge: Cambridge University Press, 1992.

———. "Statement on Dialogue with the PLO (14 December 1988)." In *The Israeli-Palestinian Conflict: a documentary record, 1967–1990*, edited by Yehuda Lukacs. Cambridge: Cambridge University Press, 1992.

———. "Statement on Jordan and the Peace Process (19 June 1985)." In *The Israeli-Palestinian Conflict: a documentary record, 1967–1990*, edited by Yehuda Lukacs. Cambridge: Cambridge University Press, 1992.

———. "This is the Plan (18 March 1988)." In *The Israeli-Palestinian Conflict: a documentary record, 1967–1990*, edited by Yehuda Lukacs. Cambridge: Cambridge University Press, 1992.

———. *Turmoil and Triumph: My Years as Secretary of State*. New York: Charles Scribner's Sons, 1993.

Silver, Eric. "New Settlements Will Close Door to Peace, Warn Palestinians." *Financial Times Information* (22 March 2005). http://web.lexis-nexis.com/. 23 August 2005.

"Situation in the Middle East: Speech by the Rt. Hon. Chris Patten." *Europa* (18 June 2003). http://www.europa.eu.int/. 16 August 2005.

"Situation in the Middle East: Speech by the Rt. Hon Chris Patten." *Europa* (2 October 2004). http://www.europa.eu.int/. 16 August 2005.

"Situation in the Middle East: Speech by the Rt. Hon. Christopher Patten, External Relations Commissioner." *Europa* (9 April 2002). http://www.europa.eu.int/. 16 August 2005.

"Six-Point Programme agreed to by the Various Palestinian Organizations Calling for the Formation of a 'Steadfastness and Confrontation Front' in Opposition to Sadat's Negotiations with Israel (4 December 1977)." In *The Israeli-Palestinian Conflict: a documentary record, 1967–1990*, edited by Yehuda Lukacs. Cambridge: Cambridge University Press, 1992.

"Speech to the London Meeting on Supporting the Palestinian Authority: Speech by Dr. Benita Ferrero-Waldner." *Europa* (1 March 2005). http://www.europa.eu.int/. 9 August 2005.

"Spokesman Says Russia's Mideast Role to Be Discussed By Abbas, Putin." *Financial Times Information* (28 April 2005). http://web.lexis-nexis.com/. 23 August 2005.

"Statement by Middle East Quartet." *UN News Centre* (23 September 2004). http://www.un.org/. 9 August 2005.

"Statement by the State Department on the Rejection of PLO Chairman Yasser Arafat's Visa Application to the US (26 November 1988)." In *The Israeli-Palestinian Conflict: a documentary record, 1967–1990*, edited by Yehuda Lukacs. Cambridge: Cambridge University Press, 1992.

"Statement of Chris Patten, Commissioner for External Relations, on partial release of tax revenues by Israel to the Palestinian Authority." *Europa* (25 July 2002). http://www.europa.eu.int/. 16 August 2005.

"Statement of the Middle East Quartet." *Europa* (16 July 2002). http://www.europa.eu.int/. 16 August 2005.

"Statement of the Quartet Task Force on Palestinian Reform." *Europa* (11 December 2003). http://www.europa.eu.int/. 16 August 2005.

"Statement of the Task Force on Palestinian Reform." *Europa* (14–15 November 2002). http://www.europa.eu.int/. 16 August 2005.

"Statements of the President of the Commission concerning the speech of President Bush 05/04/2002." *Europa* (3 April 2002; 29 March 2002). http://www.europa.eu.int/. 16 August 2005.

"Statement to the Foreign Affairs Committee on EU budgetary assistance to the Palestinian Authority: Statement by the Rt. Hon. Christopher Patten, External Relations Commissioner." *Europa* (19 June 2002). http://www.europa.eu.int/. 16 August 2005.

"Summit of Anti-Sadat 'Steadfastness and Confrontation Front' (23 September 1978)." In *The Israeli-Palestinian Conflict: a documentary record, 1967–1990*, edited by Yehuda Lukacs. Cambridge: Cambridge University Press, 1992.

"Terrorism 'Feeds On' Arab-Israeli Conflict- Russian Minister." *Financial Times Information* (10 May 2005). http://web.lexis-nexis.com/. 23 August 2005.

"Text of Israel's Communiqué on the Reagan Plan (2 September 1982)." In *The Israeli-Palestinian Conflict: a documentary record, 1967–1990*, edited by Yehuda Lukacs. Cambridge: Cambridge University Press, 1992.

UN General Assembly. "Resolution 194 (December 11, 1948)." In *The Israel-Arab Reader: A Documentary History of the Middle East Conflict*, edited by Walter Laqueur and Barry Rubin. New York: Penguin Books, 2001.

———. "Resolution 3236 (22 November 1974)." In *The Israeli-Palestinian Conflict: a documentary record, 1967–1990*, edited by Yehuda Lukacs. Cambridge: Cambridge University Press, 1992.

———. "Resolution 41/43D (2 December 1986)." In *The Israeli-Palestinian Conflict: a documentary record, 1967–1990*, edited by Yehuda Lukacs. Cambridge: Cambridge University Press, 1992.

———. "Resolution A/43/L.53 (14 December 1988)." In *The Israeli-Palestinian Conflict: a documentary record, 1967–1990*, edited by Yehuda Lukacs. Cambridge: Cambridge University Press, 1992.

Unified National Command of the Intifada. "Call No.6 (February 1988)." In *The Israel-Arab Reader: A Documentary History of the Middle East Conflict*, edited by Walter Laqueur and Barry Rubin. New York: Penguin Books, 2001.

Unified National Leadership of the Intifada. "Calls No. 12, 16, and 18 (April–May 1988)." In *The Israel-Arab Reader: A Documentary History of the Middle East Conflict*, edited by Walter Laqueur and Barry Rubin. New York: Penguin Books, 2001.

UN Security Council. "Israel's Withdrawal from Lebanon (June 19, 2000)." In *The Israel-Arab Reader: A Documentary History of the Middle East Conflict*, edited by Walter Laqueur and Barry Rubin. New York: Penguin Books, 2001.

———. "Resolution 242 (22 November 1967)." In *The Israeli-Palestinian Conflict: a documentary record, 1967–1990*, edited by Yehuda Lukacs. Cambridge: Cambridge University Press, 1992.

———. "Resolution 425, on Lebanon (March 19, 1978)." In *The Israel-Arab Reader: A Documentary History of the Middle East Conflict*, edited by Walter Laqueur and Barry Rubin. New York: Penguin Books, 2001.

———. "Resolution 605 (22 December 1987)." In *The Israeli-Palestinian Conflict: a documentary record, 1967–1990*, edited by Yehuda Lukacs. Cambridge: Cambridge University Press, 1992.

———. "Resolution 607 (5 January 1988)." In *The Israeli-Palestinian Conflict: a documentary record, 1967–1990*, edited by Yehuda Lukacs. Cambridge: Cambridge University Press, 1992.

"U.S. and Israel: Memorandum of Understanding (November 30, 1981)." In *The Israel-Arab Reader: A Documentary History of the Middle East Conflict*, edited by Walter Laqueur and Barry Rubin. New York: Penguin Books, 2001.

U.S. Department of State. "Quartet Statement." 9 May 2005. http://www.state.gov/. 17 September 2007.

"U.S. Envoy Says Only Mitchell Plan Can Stop Violence." *Deutsche Presse-Agentur* (9 August 2001). http://web.lexis-nexis.com/. 23 August 2005.

"U.S. Letter of Assurances to the Palestinians (October 18, 1991)." In *The Israel-Arab Reader: A Documentary History of the Middle East Conflict*, edited by Walter Laqueur and Barry Rubin. New York: Penguin Books, 2001.

"US Policy on an International Middle East Peace Conference (13 January 1984)." In *The Israeli-Palestinian Conflict: a documentary record, 1967–1990*, edited by Yehuda Lukacs. Cambridge: Cambridge University Press, 1992.

"US Pushing for Israel-Palestinian Talks: Rice." *AFX News Limited* (16 October 2001). http://web.lexis-nexis.com/. 23 August 2005.

"US Senators' Letter to Secretary of State George Shultz (3 March 1988)." In *The Israeli-Palestinian Conflict: a documentary record, 1967–1990*, edited by Yehuda Lukacs. Cambridge: Cambridge University Press, 1992.

"We Have an Opportunity and It Would be Irresponsible if We, the Israelis, or the World Allow It to Slip Away." *Financial Times Information* (28 February 2005). http://web.lexis-nexis.com/. 23 August 2005.

West Bank-Gaza Palestinian Leaders. "Fourteen Points (January 14, 1988)." In *The Israel-Arab Reader: A Documentary History of the Middle East Conflict*, edited by Walter Laqueur and Barry Rubin. New York: Penguin Books, 2001.

———. "Memorandum to Chairman Yasir Arafat (November 1993)." In *The Israel-Arab Reader: A Documentary History of the Middle East Conflict*, edited by Walter Laqueur and Barry Rubin. New York: Penguin Books, 2001.

West Bank National Conference. "Statement (1 October 1978)." In *The Israeli-Palestinian Conflict: a documentary record, 1967–1990*, edited by Yehuda Lukacs. Cambridge: Cambridge University Press, 1992.

Youngs, Richard. "Europe's Uncertain Pursuit of Middle East Reform." In *Uncharted Journey: Promoting Democracy in the Middle East*, edited by Thomas Carothers and Marina Ottaway. Washington: Carnegie Endowment for International Peace, 2005.

INDEX

Abbas, Mahmoud: and Arafat, 120; and Bush (George W.), 98, 121, 123; and final status issues, 106; and Hamas, 127, 128, 132, 190, n.18, 191-192, n.36; and Israel, 105, 106, 108, 116, 120-121, 122-123, 134, 135; and Jerusalem, 116, 121, 127; and negotiations, 122-123, 135; and Palestinian Authority, 122, 126-127, 128, 135; and Palestinian public opinion, 122, 123, 132, 135; and Palestinian state, 116, 121, 127; and Quartet, 105, 122; and refugees, 117, 121; and *Road Map*, 104, 105, 106, 121, 122-123, 127, 169, n.93; and Russia, 135; and separation barrier, 106, 116, 121; and settlements, 106, 116, 121, 127; and terrorism, 108, 121, 127, 133-135; and United Nations, 135; and United States, 105, 124, 135
Abd-Rabbuh, Yasir, 105-106
Abdullah, Crown Prince (Saudi Arabia), 131
ABM. *See* Anti-Ballistic Missile System
Abu-Sharif, Bassam, 40
Achille Lauro hijacking, 63, 80, 85
Afghanistan, 83
Africa, 21-22, 24, 92, 131, 145, n.123
Albright, Madeleine, 17
ALF. *See* Arab Liberation Front
Algeria, 19, 60, 92
Allon, Yigal, 43, 51
American Israel Public Affairs Committee, 27-28, 47
Amr, Nabil, 105
Annan, Kofi: and Israel, 117, 177, n.148; and Israeli-Palestinian conflict, 97, 115; and Palestinian Authority, 94-95, 103, 113; and Palestinians, 97, 103, 104, 113, 117; and Quartet, 97; and *Road* Map, 100, 101, 103, 114-118, 164, n.47; and separation barrier, 117, 182, n.189; and settlements, 117; and Syria, 100; and terror, 117; and United Nations, 7, 11, 103, 115; and United States, 177, n.147; and West Bank, 117. *See also* United Nations
Anti-Ballistic Missile System, 79
Anti-Terrorism Research and Development Committee, 79
al-Aqsa Intifada. *See* Intifada II
al-Aqsa Mosque, 23
Arab Democratic Party, 153, n.106
Arab-Israeli conflict: and Arafat, 34, 67; and Europeans, 7, 10; and Ford, 158, n.102; and Kissinger, 13-14, 16; and Nixon, 16, 73; and Rabin, 32-33, 49; and Rogers, 73-74; and Russia, 7, 113; and United Nations, 7, 10-11; and United States, 18, 74
Arab League, 19, 63, 95, 96, 130-131, 144, n. 94. *See also* Rabat Summit
Arab Liberation Front, 19, 32, 33, 40, 48, 60, 145, n.106
Arabs: and Arafat, 29, 68; and Ford, 78, 149-150, n.48; and Israel, 2, 4, 19, 20, 22, 23-24, 29, 37-38, 43-44, 63, 65, 74, 75-76, 78-79, 127, 149-150, n.48, 158, n.102; and Kissinger, 6, 14, 18, 79, 85; and oil embargo, 13-14, 15, 75; and Palestinians, 25, 30, 61, 75-77, 84, 129-130; and Reagan, 14, 47; and Steadfastness and Confrontation Front, 19; and terror, 30, 61, 74; and

Index

United Nations, 11; and United States, 4, 73, 74, 92-93, 131, 188, n.241

Arafat, Yasser: and Abbas, 120; and Arab-Israeli conflict, 34, 67; and Black September Organization, 29; and Bush (George W.), 4, 9, 28, 90, 95, 101, 123-124, 163-164, n.38; and Camp David negotiations (2000), 66, 88-89; and Camp David summit (1977), 19, 63, 69; and Carter, 19, 27, 69; and Clinton, 28, 82, 88; death of, 120, 122, 128, 185, n.211; and Egypt, 22, 63; and Europeans, 34, 94, 95, 96, 102, 166, n.67; and Fatah, 28-29, 31-33, 64, 126-127; and fedayeen, 30; and final status issues, 31, 126; and Ford, 77-78; and Gaza Strip, 46; and Hamas, 33, 64, 85-86, 88; and Hussein (Saddam), 86; and Intifada I, 22, 31-32, 53-54, 63, 70-71, 86-87; and Intifada II, 23, 31, 32, 34, 66-67, 72-73, 89, 122, 135, 144, n.88; and Islamist challenge, 86-87, 88, 122, 135; and Israel, 22-23, 25, 26, 28, 29-32, 34, 40, 46, 49, 62, 63, 66-73, 82, 84-86, 88-89, 105, 107, 116, 121, 122, 134-135; and Jerusalem, 53-54, 66, 68, 73, 88-89, 116; and *Jerusalem Post*, 170, n.103; and Kissinger, 22, 77; and Lebanon, 31, 68, 85; and Netanyahu, 26, 66, 72, 87-88; and *Oslo Accords*, 22-23, 31-34, 66-67, 82, 86-89, 122, 134-135; and Palestinian Authority, 34, 66, 86, 89-90, 126-127; and Palestinians, 22, 34, 40, 48-49, 53-54, 64, 68-73, 87, 88, 90, 126, 135, 187, n.226; and Palestinian state, 40, 46, 53-54, 64, 105, 121; and PFLP, 29, 64; and PLO, 22-23, 30-31, 32, 40, 64, 68, 69, 146, n.132; and PNC, 146, n.133; and public opinion, 122, 126, 135, 189, n.11; and Rabin, 61-62, 82, 87, 88; and Reagan, 87; and refugees, 48-49; and *Road Map*, 16, 105, 121, 122, 134-135, 189-190, n.15; and Russia, 94, 95, 102, 168, n.85; and Sadat, 22; and settlements, 46, 63, 68-69, 88; and Sharon, 9, 26, 28, 67, 89, 90, 120-121, 144, n.88; 160, n.145, 170-171, n.105; strategy of, 22-23, 29-32, 33, 34, 40, 46, 63, 64, 69, 86-89, 116, 146, n.132, 146, n.133, 157, n.52, 187, n.226; and terror, 22-23, 28, 30-32, 34, 53, 64, 66-71, 76, 78, 82, 85-90, 94-95, 101, 121, 122, 124, 133-135, 142, n.57, 144, n.88, 145, n.112; and United Nations, 40, 68, 94, 95, 102; and United Nations General Assembly, 8, 22, 25, 30-32, 34, 48-49, 64, 68, 71, 85, 86, 157, n.52; and United Nations Security Council Resolution 242, 28, 34, 66; and United States, 28, 34, 68, 82, 86-87, 102; and West Bank, 46, 66, 116

Ariel, 118
Army (US), 79
al-Asad, Hafez, 19-20
Asia, 21-22, 145, n.123
Assassination policy (Israel), 70-71, 78, 82, 83, 88, 89, 93, 97, 106, 115, 124, 135, 160, n.145, 170, n.104
Athens, 71
Atherton, Alfred, Jr., 76

Ba'ath, Iraqi, 33, 145, n.106
Baker, James, 14-15, 41, 44
al-Bana, Sabri. *See* Nidal, Abu
Barak, Ehud: and Arafat, 26, 66, 87; and Clinton, 83; and defeat by Sharon, 33, 39, 89; and final borders, 43; and Golan Heights, 43; and Israeli public opinion, 126; and Jerusalem, 52; and Lebanon, 156, n.41; and *Oslo*, 87; and Palestinian Authority, 88; and Palestinian negotiations, 26, 33, 38-39, 43, 66, 88, 89, 143, n.87; and Palestinians, 38-39, 87, 156, n.41; and refugees, 49-50, 126; settlements, 45-46, 125-126; and Syria, 20, 156, n.41; and terrorism, 66, 87-88, 156, n.41; and West Bank, 52, 126
Barghuti, Marwan, 67, 73
Begin, Menachem, 19, 24, 45, 62, 63, 84, 152, n.96, 153, n.102, 155, n.21
Belgium, 106
Bella, Ben, 29
Bin-Laden, Osama, 83, 93
Black September, 29, 31

Black September Organization, 21, 27, 29, 31, 73-74, 85
Brezhnev, Leonid, 7, 10, 17-18
Britain. *See* United Kingdom
Brussels Declaration, 8, 15-16
Buchanan, Andrew, 3-4, 26, 38, 45, 64, 78, 127, 128
Bush, George H.W.: and Arabs, 20; and Gaza, 41-42; and Intifada I, 82; and Israel, 28, 41, 44, 47, 50, 82, 87; and Jerusalem, 47, 55; and Jordan, 41-42; and Madrid Peace Conference, 14, 17, 28, 41-42, 82, 87; and Palestinians, 17, 20, 41-42, 50, 65, 82, 87; and Palestinian state, 42; and peace process, 16, 17, 20, 41-42, 44, 65; and PLO, 28, 87; and refugees, 50; and settlements, 47; and Shamir, 28; and terrorism, 87; and United States, 17, 28, 65, 87; and West Bank, 41-42, 47
Bush, George W.: and Abbas, 98, 121, 123; and Arab moderates, 9; and Arab states, 91-93, 98, 102; and Arafat, 4, 9, 28, 90, 101, 107, 123-124, 170, n.104; and Clinton, 95; and comprehensive negotiations, 9, 99; and European states, 7, 92, 93, 98, 123-124; and final status issues, 94, 99-101, 109, 118-119; and Gaza disengagement, 110, 111; and Hamas, 110, 123; and Hussein (Saddam), 96-97, 161, n.8; and incremental negotiations, 8-9, 99, 111; and Intifada II, 83, 96; and Iraq, 16, 92, 93, 96-97; and Israel, 3, 4, 9, 11, 28, 94-102, 104, 107, 109-111, 118-119, 123-124, 135; and Israeli-Palestinian conflict, 16, 91, 96-97, 161, n.7; and Jerusalem, 95, 102; and Lebanon, 97; and Middle East, 9, 91-92, 99-101, 104, 109-111, 123; and *Mitchell Report*, 94; and Occupied Territories, 83, 118-119; and Palestinian Authority, 28, 83, 95, 100, 101, 109-111, 123-124, 135-136; and Palestinian governance, 4, 98, 99, 101, 110, 111, 163-164, n.38; and Palestinians, 3-5, 9, 95-101, 104, 109-111, 123-124, 135, 184, n.201; and Palestinian state, 94, 97-101, 109-111, 118-119, 123; and peace process, 91-92, 93-94, 96-98, 100-102, 104, 109-111, 118, 121, 135-136, 162, n.16, 164, n.42; and Quartet, 6, 16, 93-94, 97-98; and refugees, 95, 102, 118-119; and *Road Map*, 4, 9, 16, 98, 99-102, 104, 110-111, 118, 123, 135, 173, n.122; and Russia, 5, 9, 93, 95, 98-99, 123-124; and separation barrier, 110, 119, 135, 184, n.201; and settlements, 94-95, 101-102, 109-111, 118-119, 135; and Sharon, 4-5, 9, 28, 83, 90, 95, 97, 102, 110, 111, 118-120, 123-124, 135, 184, n.201; and Syria, 97; and terror, 1, 4-5, 9, 28, 67, 83, 90, 91, 95, 98, 100-102, 104, 109-111, 123-124, 133, 135, 165, n.59, 165, n.60, 165, n.62, 172, n.116; and United Nations, 5, 9, 11, 83, 92, 93, 95, 97, 98-99, 123-124; and United Nations Security Council Resolution 242, 94, 102; and United States, 9, 93, 96-99, 109, 124; and "war on terror", 1, 9, 67, 90, 123-124; and West Bank, 9, 97, 118-119, 123-124

Cabinet Committee to Combat Terrorism, 74-75, 77, 79, 85
Cabinet Committee to Combat Terrorism Emergency Watch Group, 74
Cabinet Committee to Combat Terrorism Working Group, 74-75, 77, 79
Cairo Agreement, 15, 20, 23, 71, 88
Camp David *Frameworks*, 9, 19, 24, 27, 34, 48, 62-63, 85, 152, n.89
Camp David negotiations (2000), 15, 17, 20, 26, 28, 52, 54, 66, 88-89, 146-147, n.145
Camp David process (1977), 10, 14, 18-20, 37-38, 41, 47, 69, 147, n.9
Canada, 139, n.59
"Carlos the Jackal", 76
Carter, James Earl (Jimmy): and Arab states, 43-44; and Arafat, 19, 27, 69; and Camp David approach, 14, 19, 41, 47; and Camp David *Frameworks*, 27, 50; and Egypt, 18-19; and Israel, 18-19, 43-44, 47, 50;

and Jerusalem, 55; and Occupied Territories, 43-44; and Palestinians, 27, 41; and PLO, 27; and refugees, 41, 50; and Sadat, 18-19; and settlements, 47; and terrorism, 76
CENTO, 75
Central Intelligence Agency, 76, 79
Cheney, Dick, 97
China. *See* People's Republic of China
Christian Science Monitor, 76
CIA. *See* Central Intelligence Agency
Clinton Plan, 17, 48, 49, 54, 55
Clinton, William Jefferson: and Arafat, 28, 82, 88; and Barak, 83; and *Cairo Agreement,* 15, 20; and Camp David talks, 15, 17, 20, 28; and *Clinton Plan*, 17, 48, 55; and diplomatic approach, 15, 17-18, 42, 44, 55; and *Hebron Accords*, 15, 20; and *Interim Agreement on the West Bank and Gaza Strip*, 20; and Intifada II, 17, 42, 44, 82-83, 89-90; and Islam, 89; and Israel, 17, 20, 42, 47-48, 50-51, 55, 82-83, 90; and Israeli-Jordanian *Peace Treaty*, 15, 20; and Jerusalem, 17, 55; and Jordan, 20; and *Oslo Accords*, 15, 28, 44, 47-48, 50, 82, 89-90; and *Oslo II*, 15; and Palestinian Authority, 17, 20, 28, 83-83; and Palestinians, 28, 50-51, 82-83, 88, 89, 90; and Palestinian state, 42, 50-51; and peace process, 16; and PLO, 88; and refugees, 17, 50-51; and settlements, 42, 47-48; and Syria, 20; and terrorism, 82-83, 88-89, 90; and unilateral actions, 50, 55; and United States, 17-18, 20, 51, 89; and West Bank, 17, 42, 44, 48; and *Wye River Memorandum*, 15, 20
Collective punishment, 11, 31, 71, 83, 135
Committee on the Exercise of the Inalienable Rights of the Palestinian People, 8, 11
Communists (Palestinians), 64
Comprehensive negotiations, 2-3, 8-11, 13, 18-21, 91, 94, 99, 122-123, 129, 135
Congress, 18, 44, 74, 76, 77, 78, 81, 82
Craig, Gordon A., 137, n.11
Cyprus, 71

Darfur, 103
Darwish, Mahmoud, 34, 71-72
Dayan, Moshe, 61
Declaration of Principles. *See Oslo Accords*
Defense Department, 79, 81
Developing States. *See* Third World

East Jerusalem, 47, 51, 52, 55, 116-118, 126, 154, n.135, 182, n.189
Eban, Abba, 42, 49, 149, n.37
EC. *See* European Community
EEC. *See* European Economic Community
Egypt: and Arab League, 19; and Arafat, 22, 63; and Begin, 84; and Camp David negotiations, 19; and Carter, 18-19; and Egyptian-Israeli disengagement, 10, 14, 76; and Geneva Conference, 9; and Islamic Conference, 19; and Israel, 10, 18-19, 61, 62, 63, 73, 75-76, 84, 99-100, 129, 142, n.66; and Kissinger, 16, 18, 20-21, 75-76, 141, n.48; mentioned, 68; and Non-Aligned Movement, 19; and Organization of African Unity, 19; and Palestinian Authority, 130-131; and Palestinians, 18-19, 63; and Rabin, 61; and *Road Map*, 99-100; and Russia, 10, 23-24, 73, 112; and Sadat, 14, 18-20; and *Sinai II*, 16; and Syria, 19-20; and United States, 63, 73, 75, 93, 131
Egyptian-Israeli *Peace Treaty*, 10, 19, 23-24, 34-35, 62-63, 84
El Al airline, 80
England. *See* United Kingdom
Entebbe hijacking, 22, 60, 76-77, 145, n.108
Eshkol, Levi, 49, 149, n.37
Etzion, 118
EU. *See* European Union
Euro-Mediterranean Partnership, 92, 112
European Commission, 94, 160-161, n.1
European Community, 8, 10, 15-16, 80
European Economic Community, 8, 149, n.47
European Parliament, 30-31, 34, 70
European Union: and Arab-Israeli

conflict, 7; and Arafat, 94, 95-96, 102, 166, n.67; and Bush (George W.) 7, 92, 93, 98, 123-124; and diplomatic approach, 4, 5, 7, 8, 10, 16, 94-95, 97, 100, 101, 111, 129, 135, 140, n.11, 181, n.183; and Euro-Mediterranean Partnership, 92, 112; and final status issues, 94-95, 102-103, 113; and Gaza Strip, 97, 114, 124; and Israel, 3, 5, 9, 13, 21, 91, 94, 95-96, 100-103, 111, 113-117, 124, 129-130; and Israeli-Palestinian conflict, 5, 91, 129; and Jerusalem, 117; and Occupied Territories, 5-6, 9, 103, 163, n.36; and Palestinian Authority, 21, 94-96, 99, 102-103, 113, 130; and Palestinians, 5, 8, 10, 94, 95-96, 99, 101, 102, 103, 111-112, 113, 115, 116, 138, n.34; and procedural issues, 9, 10, 21, 113-114, 115; and Quartet, 3-4, 7, 13, 14, 97, 98-99, 101, 111-112, 115, 128, 133, 168, n.85; and refugees, 6, 117; and *Road Map*, 1, 3, 5, 7, 9, 13-14, 91, 99, 103, 104, 111-115, 129-130; and Russia, 21, 91, 94-95, 97, 101, 103, 112; and separation barrier, 114, 117; and settlements, 5-6, 95, 96, 100, 103, 113, 114, 117; and Sharon, 5, 96, 102, 166, n.67; and two-state solution, 95, 101, 102-103, 104, 112, 114, 115, 116, 117; and unilateral actions, 103, 113-114, 178, n.158; and United Nations, 5, 8, 10, 13, 21, 96, 116, 130; and United Nations Security Council Resolution 242, 5-6, 103; and United States, 6, 7, 9-10, 13, 16, 21, 91-95, 98, 100, 111-112, 115-116, 128; and terrorism, 21, 92, 94-97, 102, 113-114, 124, 174, n.134; and West Bank, 96, 97, 114, 117, 124

Fanon, Franz, 60
Fatah: and Algeria, 19; and Arab states, 19, 29, 60; and Arafat, 28-29, 31-33, 64, 126-127; and armed struggle, 21-22, 28, 60; and Black September, 29, 31; and Black September Organization, 29; and Gaza, 29; and Hamas, 67, 122, 123; and Intifada I, 22, 67; and Iraq, 19; and Israel, 29, 60, 64, 67, 122; and Libya, 19; and "mini-state" formula, 29-30, 39-40; and Nidal (Abu) 30; and *Oslo Accords*, 71; and Palestinian Authority, 128; and Palestinian movement, 32, 33, 122, 126, 134-135, 146, n.131, 189, n.12,190, n.16, 190, n.18; and Palestinian state, 39, 40; and PLO, 19, 71; and refugees, 48-49; and "Rejection Front", 29, 33; and *Road Map*, 126; and Sadat, 19, 32; and "Steadfastness and Confrontation Front," 19; and Syria, 19; and terror, 21-22, 25, 28-29, 31-32, 60; and "Unified Command of Palestine Resistance", 28-29; and West Bank, 29; and Yemen, 19; and Yom Kippur War, 29, 39; and Zionism, 19, 39
Fearey, Robert, 77
Fedayeen: and Arab states, 33; and Arafat, 30; and Camp David *Frameworks*, 63; and Fatah, 146, n.131; and Israel, 22-23, 60, 61-62, 84; strategy of, 21-23; and terror, 21-22, 30, 60, 74-78; and United States, 74-78, 142, n.66
Fedotov, Yuriy, 112, 113, 115
Ferrero-Waldner, Benita, 111-112
Final status issues: and Abbas, 106-107; and Arafat, 31, 126; and Bush (George W.), 94, 99-101, 109, 118-119; and European Union, 94-95, 102-103, 113; and Israel, 32-33; and *Oslo Accords*, 32-33; and Palestinian Authority, 102-103; and Palestinians, 106; and refugees, 152, n.96; and *Road Map*, 91, 126, 131, 132-133; and Russia, 94-95, 102-103, 113, 114; and United Nations, 94-95, 102-103, 113-115; and United States, 42, 94
Fischer, Joschka, 92
Ford, Gerald R.: and American Jewish community, 77; and Arab-Israeli conflict, 158, n.102; and Arabs, 78, 149-150, n.48; and Arafat, 77-78; and Israel, 26-27, 43, 47, 54, 77-79, 149-150, n.48, 160, n.133; and Jerusalem, 54; and Kissinger, 40-41; and *Memorandum of Agreement*

(US-Israeli, 1975), 27, 77-78; and Palestinians, 27, 77-79; and PLO, 26, 27, 77-79, 160, n.133; strategy of, 13-14, 26, 54, 77-79, 149-150, n.48, 160, n.133; and terror, 26-27, 77-79, 160, n.133; and United Nations, 78
Foreign Affairs, 25
France, 15, 60, 92, 139, n.59
Fulbright, J. William, 16, 140, n.20

Galilee, 45
Galili Plan, 44-45, 62
Gaza Disengagement Plan (Sharon), 106, 108-110, 114-116, 118, 120, 122, 123, 128, 132, 135, 170, n.102, 191, n.35
Gaza Strip: and Arafat, 46; and Barak, 45-46; and Bush (George H.W.), 41-42; and Bush (George W.), 9, 111, 123-124; and Camp David *Frameworks*, 27, 37-38, 41; and Carter, 19; and Clinton, 42; and European Union, 97, 114, 124; and Fatah, 29; and Israel, 5-6, 32-33, 34, 37-38, 41, 43-46, 52, 62, 106-107, 110, 113-115, 118, 120, 124, 125, 127, 128, 132, 142, n.66, 170, n.102, 191, n.35; and *Oslo Accords*, 32-33; and Palestinian Authority, 23, 106, 116; and Palestinians, 30, 53, 122, 125; and Palestinian state, 33, 34, 38, 41; and Quartet, 179, n.165; and Rabin, 26, 45, 88; and Reagan, 41, 44, 47; and Russia, 97, 112-113; and settlements, 6, 44-45; and Shamir, 43, 45; and Sharon, 9, 45, 89, 107-109, 118, 120, 123, 134, 182, n.190; and United Nations, 97, 115; and United Nations Security Council Resolution 242, 5-6; and United States, 110, 135
General Affairs and External Relations Council, 114
General Security Service (Israel), 24-25
Geneva Conference (1973), 9, 14, 16, 17, 76-78, 139, n.48, 140, n.5, 144, n.95
Geneva Convention (1949), 6, 47, 94, 117, 131, 151, n.71
George, Alexander L., 137, n.11
Germany, 92, 94, 139, n.59

Givat Zeev, 118
Global warming, 93
Golan Heights, 42, 43, 45, 68, 115
Goldberg, Arthur, 54
Gorbachev, Mikhail, 7, 10
Gromyko, Andrei, 7, 10

Ha'aretz, 66
Habash, George, 30
Hadash party (Israel), 153, n.106
Haddad, Wadi, 30
Hamas: and Abbas, 127, 128, 132, 190, n.18, 191-192, n.36; and Arafat, 33, 64, 85-86, 88; and Bush (George W.), 110, 123; *Covenant* of, 22, 33-34; and Fatah, 67, 122, 123; and Intifada I, 53, 63-64, 85-86; and Intifada II, 31, 34, 67; and Israel, 63, 65-66, 72, 85-86, 88, 120, 134, 190, n.16, 191, n.35; and Jerusalem, 53; and Jihad, 22, 63, 85-86; and Palestinian Authority, 34, 72, 87-88, 123, 128; and Palestinian state, 53; and PLO, 85; popular support for, 31, 64, 85-86, 87-88, 122, 132, 134, 189, n.12; religious focus of, 63, 85-86; and *Road Map*, 127, 132, 190, n.16; strategy of, 22, 33-34, 63, 85-86, 132, 191-192, n.36; and terror, 31, 64-66, 85-86, 110-111, 127
Haram Temple Mount, 17, 55
Harkabi, Yehoshafat, 60
al-Hasan, Hani, 30, 34, 72
Hassan, Khalad, 29
Hebron, 72
Hebron Accords, 15, 20, 23, 146-147, n.145
Holy of Holies, 17
House demolitions (Israel), 25, 70, 71, 78, 82, 83, 88, 90, 93, 97, 115, 124, 135
Hussein, King (Jordan), 29, 73
Hussein, Saddam, 16, 86-87, 93, 96-97, 161, n.8

Incremental negotiations, 5, 8-10, 13, 21, 91, 94, 99, 109, 111, 115, 129, 135. *See also* step-by-step diplomacy
Interest groups, 12, 58, 59, 82, 133
Interim Agreement on the West Bank and Gaza Strip, 20, 23, 71, 88, 146-

147, n.145
International Civil Aviation Organization, 75, 80
International Labour Organization, 21-22, 145, n.123
International Monetary Fund, 164, n.42
International Task Force on Palestinian Reform, 98-99, 102, 112, 164, n.42
Interpol, 75, 80
Intifada I: and Arafat, 22, 31-32, 53-54, 63, 70-71, 86-87; and Bush (George H.W.), 82; and Fatah, 22, 67; and Hamas, 53, 63, 64, 85-86; and Israel, 11, 24, 63, 64, 69-70, 85-86; and Jerusalem, 53; and Palestinians, 22, 53, 63, 142, n.59; and PLO, 20, 22, 63-64, 69-70; and Rabin, 24-25, 26, 64, 143, n.73; and terror, 63, 64, 69-70, 87; and United States, 4, 41, 64, 87
Intifada II: and Abbas, 121-122; and Arafat, 23, 31, 32, 34, 66-67, 72-73, 89, 122, 135, 144, n.88; and Barak, 89; and Bush (George W.), 83, 96; casualties of, 163, n.37; and Clinton, 17, 42, 44, 82-83, 89-90; and Hamas, 31, 34, 67; and Israel, 11, 23, 24-25, 32, 38, 66-67, 89, 90, 125; mentioned, 2, 34, 54, 65; and Palestinian Authority, 23, 34; and Palestinians, 23, 24-25, 38, 67, 72-73, 90, 121, 125-126; and PLO, 72; and Quartet, 103-104; and *Road Map*, 91, 99-100, 121; and Sharon, 23, 89, 127, 144, n.88; and terrorism, 24-25, 31, 88-90, 121; and United States, 42, 83, 88-90
Iran, 7, 26, 64, 65, 85-86, 93, 156, n.41
Iraq: and Arab states, 92, 98; and Canada, 139, n.59; and China, 139, n.59; and Egypt, 93; and European Union, 7; and France, 92, 139, n.59; and Germany, 92, 139, n.59; and Israel, 163, n.34; and Jordan, 92-93; and Palestinians, 19; and Quartet, 103; and *Road Map*, 98, 103-104; and Russia, 103; and United Nations, 92, 93, 103, 139, n.59; and United States, 1, 16, 92, 93, 96-97, 98, 103, 119, 128
Islam, 51, 89

Islamic Conference, 19
Islamic fundamentalism, 26, 65, 141, n.43
Islamic Jihad, 64, 67, 72, 88, 127, 189, n.12, 190, n.16
Israel: and Abbas, 105, 106, 116, 121, 122, 135; and Annan, 117, 177, n.148; and Arab-Israeli conflict, 10-11, 33, 49, 60; and Arab Israelis, 4; and Arab League, 19; and Arabs, 2, 4, 19, 20, 22, 23-24, 29, 37-38, 43-44, 63, 65, 74, 75-76, 78-79, 127, 149-150, n.48; and Arafat, 22-23, 25, 28, 29-32, 34, 40, 46, 49, 61-63, 66-67, 68-71, 73, 82, 84-86, 88-89, 105, 107, 116, 121-122, 134-135; assassination policy of, 70-71, 78, 82, 83, 88, 89, 93, 97, 106, 123-124, 135, 160, n.145, 170, n.104; and Bush (George H.W.), 28, 41, 44, 47, 50, 82, 87; and Bush (George W.), 3, 4, 9, 11, 28, 94-102, 104, 107, 109-111, 118-119, 123-124, 135; Cabinet of, 25, 107-109, 118, 119, 127-128; and Camp David *Frameworks*, 24, 37-38; and Camp David negotiations (2000), 52, 66; and Carter, 18-19, 43-44, 47, 50; and Clinton, 17, 20, 42, 47-48, 50-51, 55, 82-83, 90; and East Jerusalem, 47, 51; and Egypt, 10, 14, 18-20, 23-24, 34-35, 61, 62, 63, 73, 75-76, 84, 99-100, 129, 142, n.66; and European Union, 3, 5-6, 9, 13, 21, 91, 94-96, 100-103, 111, 113-117, 124, 129-130; and Fatah, 29, 60, 64, 67, 122; and fedayeen, 23, 60-62, 84; and final status issues, 32-33; and Ford, 26, 27, 43, 47, 54, 77-79, 149-150, n.48, 160, n.133; and Gaza, 5-6, 32-33, 34, 37-38, 41, 43, 44-46, 52, 62, 106-107, 110, 113-115, 118, 120, 124-125, 128, 132, 142, n.66, 170, n.102, 191, n.35; and Geneva Conference, 9; and Golan Heights, 42, 43; and Hamas, 63, 65-66, 72, 85-86, 88, 120, 134, 190, n.16, 191, n.35; and Intifada I, 11, 24, 63-64, 69-70, 85-86; and Intifada II, 11, 23, 24-25, 32, 39, 66-67, 89, 90, 125; and Iran, 26, 85-86; and Islamic

fundamentalism, 26, 64-65, 73, 86-88; and Jerusalem, 6, 42, 51-54, 55, 66, 107, 109, 118, 126, 153, n.106, 183-184, n.198; and Johnson, 54-55; and Jordan, 10, 15, 20, 28, 32-33, 34-35, 37-38, 42, 61, 75-76, 85, 92-93, 99-100, 129; and Kissinger, 6, 8-9, 13-18, 22, 40, 43, 75-79, 85, 142, n.66, 146, n.131, 149, n.46, 149, n.47, 149-150, n.48; and Lebanon, 2, 24, 32-33, 63, 69, 84, 97, 100, 115, 130, 156, n.41; and Likud, 45; and Madrid Peace Conference, 20, 26; and Nixon, 47, 50, 54, 75-76; and Occupied Territories, 5, 6, 9, 11, 22, 29-31, 33, 40, 42-43, 47, 55, 60, 72, 87-88, 125-127; and "Operation Peace for Galilee", 24, 63; and *Oslo Accords*, 11, 32-33, 45, 46, 49, 52, 65-67, 72, 86-89; and Palestinian Authority, 11, 17, 20, 21, 23, 34, 38-39, 49-50, 65-67, 82, 87-88, 90, 104-109, 116, 122, 124, 126, 128-130, 132, 135; and Palestinians, 4, 11, 13, 20, 23-26, 32-35, 37-40, 42-43, 46, 49, 51-54, 57, 60, 65, 68-71, 78, 81-82, 84-85, 92, 103-109, 116, 118, 120-123, 125-127, 129-130, 132, 134, 155, n.18, 156, n.41; and Palestinian state, 37-39, 126; and PDFLP, 22; and PFLP, 21, 30, 60, 85; and PFLP-GC, 22; and PLO, 19, 22-26, 28, 31-32, 34, 39-40, 45, 49, 61-66, 69, 72, 78, 84, 86, 89, 141, n.43, 144, n.102; and political institutions, 13, 32; and public opinion, 76, 119-121, 125-126, 132, 134-136, 191, n.22, 192, n.39, 192, n.40; and Quartet, 3, 4, 13-14, 93, 101, 103-104, 107, 125, 128, 130, 179, n.165; and Rabat summit, 61; and Rabin, 45, 52, 65, 87-88; and Reagan, 14, 27, 41, 44, 47, 50, 82; and refugees, 6, 49-51, 62, 84, 109, 118, 119, 125-126, 152, n.89; and *Road Map*, 1-5, 10, 12, 13, 14, 16, 32, 34-35, 37, 98, 100, 103-105, 107-111, 116, 118, 120, 125-133, 135, 190-191, n.21; and Russia, 3, 5-6, 9-10, 13, 21, 23-24, 38, 62, 65, 91, 95, 97, 100, 101-104, 112-116, 124, 129-130; and Sadat, 18, 32; and security, 2-5, 9, 11, 17-19, 23-25, 33, 38, 43-45, 47, 61-62, 66, 86, 89, 109, 128; and separation barrier, 103-104, 106, 110, 114, 116-119, 122, 128, 135; and settlements, 6, 44-48, 55, 62, 73, 88, 103, 107, 109, 113-114, 116-119, 132, 171, n.111; and Sharon, 9, 24, 33, 89, 102, 107, 109, 118, 120-121, 127, 134, 169-170, n.99; and Shultz, 27-28, 44; and Six Day War, 23, 61; and step-by-step diplomacy, 20; strategy of, 37, 38, 84, 129; and Syria, 2, 10, 14, 16, 19-20, 22, 32-33, 42, 61, 65, 75-76, 97, 100, 115, 130, 156, n.41; and terror, 4, 9, 11, 25-26, 57, 60-66, 68-72, 76, 79, 83-88, 91-92, 104, 107-111, 119-122, 124, 129, 142, n.66, 155, n.18, 158, n.100, 170, n.103, 171, n.110; and unilateral actions, 103, 104, 106, 107, 110, 128, 135, 170, n.102, 178, n.158; and United Nations, 3, 5-7, 9, 13, 21, 91, 95, 97, 100, 101, 104, 107, 113-118, 124, 129-131, 177, n.148; and United Nations Security Council Resolution 242, 6, 17, 42, 131; and United States, 3-6, 10, 11, 13, 14, 16-18, 20-21, 27, 41-42, 43, 46-47, 50-51, 55, 61, 63-65, 67, 72-74, 76, 78, 84-85, 90, 96, 107, 119, 126-133, 135; and West Bank, 5-6, 17, 32-33, 34, 37-38, 41, 44-46, 48, 66, 95-97, 110, 116-117, 124-128, 132; and Yom Kippur War, 23, 61

Israeli Defense Force, 5, 24-25, 63, 81-82, 89

Israeli-Palestinian conflict, 1-8, 12, 13, 16, 26, 34, 37, 44, 57, 65, 67, 91, 92, 93, 95-97, 103-104, 115, 119, 129-131

Ivanov, Igor, 103, 112, 113

Japan, 9, 164, n.42
Jarring, Gunnar, 15
Jericho, 23
Jerusalem: and Abbas, 116, 121, 127; and Arafat, 53-54, 66, 68, 73, 88-89, 116; and Barak, 52; and Bush (George H.W.), 47, 55; and Bush (George W.), 95, 102; and Clinton, 17, 55; and European Union, 117;

and Israel, 6, 42, 51-55, 66, 107, 109, 118, 126, 153, n.106, 183-184, n.198; and Johnson, 54-55; and Nixon, 54; and *Oslo* Accords, 52, 54; and Palestinian Authority, 54, 55, 183-184, n.198; and Palestinians, 51-54, 106, 116-117, 121; and Rabin, 45, 52, 153, n.110, 153, n.111; and Reagan, 17, 55; and *Road* Map, 2-3, 5, 37, 91, 116, 132; and Russia, 112, 117; and Sharon, 118; and United Nations, 103; and United States, 6, 47, 54-55, 154, n.135

Jerusalem Post, 107, 170, n.103

Jews: and Hamas, 22; and Israel, 4, 45, 52; and Palestinians, 39, 106; and *Road Map*, 2-3; and United States, 54-55

Jihad, 22, 33-34, 63, 85-86, 97, 170, n.103

Jihad, Abu, 70-71

Jiryis, Abbu, 155, n.18

Johnson, Lyndon B., 43, 54, 149, n.44

Joint Chiefs of Staff, 159, n.111

Jordan: and Bush (George H.W.), 41-42; and Clinton, 20; and Israel, 9, 15, 20, 28, 32-33, 34-35, 37-38, 42, 61-62, 75-76, 84, 92-93, 99-100, 129; and Kissinger, 18, 20-21, 40-41, 73, 75; and Nixon, 40-41, 54, 73, 75; and Palestinians, 28-29, 37-38, 60- 61, 73, 92-93, 125, 130-131; and Reagan, 41, 44; and *Road Map*, 99-100; and Russia, 112; and United States, 41-42, 92-93, 144, n.94

Jordanian-Israeli *Peace Treaty*, 15, 34-35

Judea, 37-38, 43, 45-46, 52, 62, 88, 107, 118, 150, n.61

June War. *See* Six Day War

Kadima party, 134

Khalabje, 93

Khartoum attack, 25, 73, 74

Kiryat Arba, 118

Kiryat Shmona attack, 22, 60, 75-76

Kissinger, Henry: and Arab-Israeli conflict, 13-14, 16; and Arabs, 6, 14, 18, 75-77, 78, 85; and Arafat, 22, 77; and China, 75; and Egypt, 16, 18, 20-21, 75-76, 141, n.48; and Europeans, 8-9, 13-14, 15; and Geneva Conference, 9, 16, 76; and Israel, 6, 8, 9, 13-18, 22, 40, 43, 75-79, 85, 142, n.66, 146, n.131, 149, n.46, 149, n.47, 149-150, n.48; and Japan, 8-9; and Jordan, 18, 20-21, 40-41, 73, 75; and Middle East, 13-16, 18, 75; and Nixon, 75-76; and Occupied Territories, 151, n.71; and Palestinians, 8-9, 13-15, 18, 40, 73-77, 85; and PLO, 18, 26-27, 40-41, 75-79, 85, 146, n.131; and Rogers, 75, 158, n.86; strategy of, 8-9, 13-19, 40, 73, 75-76, 78, 129, 139, n.3, 140, n.5, 191, n.27; and Syria, 18, 20-21, 75-76; and terror, 26-27, 60, 75, 77-78, 142, n.66; and United Nations, 13-14, 15; and USSR, 6, 8-9, 13-16, 18, 75, 77, 78; and Vietnam War, 75; and West Bank, 40-41

Knesset, 25, 26, 37, 45, 51, 52, 53, 163, n.34

Kuwait, 97

Kyoto Protocol, 7

Labor party (Israel), 44-45, 51-52, 62, 65, 106, 150, n.65

Latin America, 21-22, 145, n.123

Lavrov, Sergei, 115

Lebanon: and Annan, 100; and Arafat, 31-32, 68, 85; and Begin, 24; and France, 92; and Israel, 2, 24, 32-33, 63, 69, 84, 97, 100, 115, 130, 156, n.41; and Palestinians, 24, 125; and PLO, 31-32, 63, 85; and *Road Map*, 2, 10, 100, 115; and Russia, 112, 115; and terror, 24, 68, 69; and United States, 80, 97

Libya, 19, 81, 85

Likud party (Israel): and Begin, 62-63, 155, n.21; and Israel, 45; and Netanyahu, 32-33, 66, 72; and Palestinians, 84; and PLO, 25; and settlements, 45, 62; and Shamir, 84; and Sharon, 39, 46, 89, 109, 120, 124, 128

Lod airport attack, 23, 25, 60

Maaleh Adumim, 118

Ma'alot attack, 22, 25, 60, 61

Maariv, 185, n.211

Madrid Declaration, 15-16
Madrid Peace Conference: and Arafat, 86; and Bush (George H.W.), 14-15, 17, 28, 41-42, 82, 87; and European Union, 103; and Geneva Conference, 14; and Israel, 20, 26; and Palestinians, 17, 26, 53-54, 71; and PLO, 20, 22-23, 71; and Reagan, 14; and Russia, 103; and Shamir, 20, 28, 43, 52
Marcus, Yoel, 66-67
Marine attack (1983), 80
Media, 12, 58-59, 76, 78, 82, 92-93, 133
Mediation, 10, 11, 17, 21, 94-95, 137, n.15. *See also* third party diplomacy
Mediterranean region, 10, 131
Meir, Golda, 23, 37, 42-43, 84, 159, n.124
Memorandum of Agreement (1975 US-Israeli), 17, 27, 77-78
Memorandum of Understanding on Strategic Cooperation (1981 US-Israeli), 47
Middle East: and Arafat, 22-23, 69; and Bush (George H.W.), 41; and Bush (George W.), 9, 91-92, 99-101, 104, 109-111, 123; and Europeans, 7, 15-16, 94-95, 97, 101, 103; and France, 92; and Germany, 94; and Israel, 23-24, 26, 38, 62, 89; and Kissinger, 13-16, 18, 75; and Nixon, 17-18; and Palestinians, 105; and Reagan, 41; and *Road Map*, 2, 131; and Russia, 7, 10, 94, 97, 101, 103, 112-113, 115, 139, n.48; and terror, 30; and United Nations, 7, 8, 10-11, 97, 114; and United Nations Security Council Resolution 242, 34-35, 137, n.18; and United States, 6, 47, 55, 65, 74, 77, 82, 96-97, 102-103, 131, 138, n.26, 139, n.48. *See also* Egypt; Iran; Iraq; Israel; Jordan; Lebanon; Saudi Arabia; Syria
Mitchell Report, 94-95, 99-100
Moeller, Per Stig, 101, 103
Montville, J.V., 4
Morocco, 92
Mossad, 23, 62, 81-82, 159, n.125
Mufaz, Shaul, 121, 170, n.102, 171, n.110
Munich Olympics hostage seizure, 21, 23, 25, 27, 60, 73-75, 85

Nablus, 72
NATO. *See* North Atlantic Treaty Organization
Negev, 45
Negotiation strategies. *See* comprehensive negotiations; incremental negotiations; step-by-step diplomacy; third party diplomacy
Netanyahu, Benjamin: and Arafat, 26, 66, 72, 87-88; and diplomacy, 88; and Likud, 32-33, 66, 72; and *Oslo*, 26, 32-33, 38, 87-88; and Palestinian Authority, 38, 66, 72, 87; and PLO, 26; and terrorism, 66, 87-89
Nidal, Abu, 25, 30
9/11. *See* September 11, 2001
1948 War, 11, 39, 48, 50, 68-69, 73, 121
1973 War. *See* Yom Kippur War
1967 War. *See* Six Day War
Nixon, Richard M.: and Arab-Israeli conflict, 16, 73; and Arabs, 73, 75-76; and Egypt, 75; and Geneva Conference, 9; and Israel, 26-27, 47, 50, 54, 75-76, 142, n.66; and Jerusalem, 54; and Jordan, 40-41, 54, 73, 75; and Kissinger, 75-76; mentioned, 82; and Palestinians, 40, 50, 85; and PLO, 26-27, 40, 85; and Rogers, 74, 75; and Russia, 9-10, 17-18; strategy of, 5, 13-14, 16-18, 85; and Syria, 75; and terror, 26-27, 73-76, 85; and United Nations, 15, 74
Non-Aligned Movement, 19
North Africa, 92, 131
North Atlantic Treaty Organization, 59, 75, 80, 83, 103
North Korea, 7, 93
Norway, 164, n.42

OAU. *See* Organization of African Unity
Occupied Territories: and Arafat, 22, 29, 32, 46, 70-71, 85, 87-89; and Bush (George H.W.), 41; and Bush (George W.), 83, 118-119; and Carter, 43-44; and Europeans, 5-6,

9, 103, 163, n.36; and Hamas, 85-86; and Israel, 5-6, 9, 11, 22, 29-31, 32-33, 40, 42-43, 47, 55, 60, 72, 87-88, 125-127; and Kissinger, 151, n.71; and Palestinians, 5, 34, 60, 63, 72, 84-85, 130-131; and PLO, 20; and Rabin, 38, 87; and Reagan, 47; and Russia, 5-6, 9, 103, 112-113; and Sharon, 33, 83; and United Nations, 5-6, 9; and United States, 5-6, 46-47, 55. *See also* Gaza Strip; Golan Heights; Jerusalem; West Bank
October War. *See* Yom Kippur War
Oil embargo, 13, 15, 75-76
Oil-for-food program, 103
Olmert, Ehud, 121, 171-172, n.112, 183-184, n.198, 185, n.214
OPEC. *See* Organization of Petroleum Exporting Countries
"Operation Peace for Galilee", 24, 63
Organization of African Unity, 19
Organization of American States, 59, 74-75
Organization of Petroleum Exporting Countries, 13-14, 22, 76-77
Oslo Accords: and Arafat, 22-23, 31-34, 46, 66-67, 82, 86-89, 122, 134-135; and Clinton, 15, 28, 44, 47-48, 50, 82, 89-90; and collapse of, 10, 11, 34, 46, 50, 89; and European Union, 95-96; and Fatah, 71; and final status issues, 32-33; incremental negotiations, 9, 10, 129; and Israel, 26, 32-33, 38-39, 45, 46, 49, 52, 65, 66-67, 72, 86-89; and Jerusalem, 52, 54; and Netanyahu, 26, 32-33, 38, 87-88; and Palestinian Authority, 40, 42, 54, 72, 82; and Palestinians, 34-35, 46, 54, 66, 71-72, 88, 89, 106, 129, 156, n.47; and Palestinian terror, 82; and PLO, 20, 34, 71-72, 82; and Rabin, 26, 38, 45, 65, 82, 86-88; and refugees, 50; and Sharon, 33, 89; and United Nations, 11; and United States, 82; and West Bank, 32-33, 46
Oslo II, 15

PA. *See* Palestinian Authority
Palestine Armed Struggle Command, 32
Palestine Economic Development Group, 109
Palestine Liberation Army, 28-29
Palestine Liberation Front, 19, 32, 40, 48
Palestine Liberation Organization: and Arabs, 61, 84, 144, n.94, 145, n.123, 158, n.97; and Arafat, 22-23, 30-31, 32, 40, 64, 68, 69, 146, n.132; and Bush (George H.W.), 28, 87; and Camp David *Frameworks*, 48, 63; and Carter, 27; and Clinton, 88; and Congress, 77; and Egypt, 19; and Europeans, 8; and Ford, 26, 27, 77-78, 160, n.133; and Hamas, 85; and Hussein (King), 73; international position of, 21-22, 25, 143, n.77, 145, n.123; and Intifada I, 20, 22, 63, 64, 69-70; and Israel, 19, 22-26, 27-28, 31-32, 34, 39, 40, 45, 49, 61-66, 69, 72, 78, 84, 86, 89, 141, n.43, 144, n.102; and Jordan, 29; Kissinger, 18, 26-27, 40-41, 75-79, 85, 146, n.131; and Lebanon, 31-32, 63, 85; and Madrid Peace Conference, 20, 22, 71; and media, 76; and Netanyahu, 26; and Nixon, 26, 40, 85; and Occupied Territories, 20; and *Oslo Accords*, 20, 34, 71-72, 82; and Palestinians, 34, 48, 69, 71-72, 86; and PFLP, 28-30, 40; and Rabin, 26, 65-66, 87, 88, 141, n.43; and Reagan, 27, 38, 64, 81-82, 85-87; and refugees, 48; and Russia, 7, 21-22, 62, 145, n.123; and Sharon, 24, 63, 89; strategy of, 22-23, 28-29, 31, 32, 39-40, 48, 64, 69, 86; and terror, 24-29, 30-32, 63-66, 76-78, 82-86, 89; and United Nations, 8, 10-11, 21-22, 48, 61, 143, n.77, 145, n.123, 158, n.97; and United States, 26-28, 49, 64-65, 76-78, 82, 86-87, 144, n.94, 144, n.102; and West Bank, 34
Palestine Liberation Organization Central Committee, 22
Palestine Liberation Organization Central Council, 39, 49
Palestine Liberation Organization Executive Committee, 19, 22, 32-34, 40, 48, 53, 69-70, 71

Palestine National Assembly, 25, 39
Palestine National Council, 19, 22, 25-26, 29, 31, 38, 40, 46, 48, 53-54, 69-71, 84-85, 142, n.59, 146, n.133, 152, n.85
Palestine Popular Struggle Front, 33, 60, 64, 145, n.106
Palestinian Authority: and Abbas, 122, 126-127, 128, 135; and Arafat, 34, 86, 89-90, 126-127; and Bush (George W.), 28, 83, 95, 97, 98, 100-101, 109-111, 123-124, 135-136; and *Cairo Agreement*, 23; and Clinton, 17, 20, 28, 49, 82-83; and East Jerusalem, 116; and Egypt, 130-131; and European Union, 21, 94-96, 99, 102-103, 113, 130; and Gaza Strip, 23, 106, 116; and Hamas, 34, 72, 87-88, 123, 128; and Israel, 11, 17, 20-21, 23, 34, 38-39, 49-50, 65-67, 87-88, 90, 104-109, 116, 122, 124, 126, 128-130, 132, 135; and Jerusalem, 54, 55, 183-184, n.198; and Netanyahu, 38, 66, 72, 87; and *Oslo Accords*, 11, 40, 42, 54, 72, 82; and Palestinians, 34, 66, 72, 88, 105-107, 122, 126, 128, 135; and Quartet, 105, 114, 128, 130, 179, n.165; and refugees, 49-50, 117, 130-131; and *Road Map*, 1-2, 12, 21, 34, 91, 99-100, 104-108, 121-123, 126, 128-130, 135, 168, n.90; and Russia, 21, 94-95, 102-103, 112-114, 130; and Sharon, 23, 26, 33, 39, 67, 83, 89, 107-109, 120-121, 134; strategy of, 5, 20-21, 88, 89, 105-107, 116-117, 119, 130, 134-136; and terrorism, 21, 23, 66, 72, 82, 83, 89, 91, 94-95, 100-101, 109, 111, 113-114, 120-121, 129, 134-135, 171-172, n.112; and United Nations, 21, 94-95, 102-103, 113-115, 130; and United States, 21, 90, 104-105, 109-110, 124, 126; and West Bank, 106, 116; and *Wye River Memorandum*, 72
Palestinian Front, 64
Palestinian Legislative Council, 105
Palestinian National Covenant, 39, 52-53, 146, n.132
Palestinians: and Annan, 97, 103, 104, 113, 117; and Arabs, 19-20, 25, 30, 61, 75-77, 84, 129-130; and Arafat, 22, 34, 40, 48-49, 53-54, 64, 68-73, 88, 90, 122, 126, 135, 187, n.226; and Bush (George H.W.), 17, 20, 41-42, 50, 65, 82, 87; and Bush (George W.), 3-5, 9, 95-101, 104, 109-111, 123-124, 135, 184, n.201; and Carter, 19, 27, 41; and Clinton, 28, 50-51, 82-83, 89-90; and Egypt, 18, 63; and Europeans, 5, 8, 10, 94, 95-96, 99, 101, 102, 103, 111-112, 113, 115-116, 138, n.34; and Fatah, 29, 122; and Ford, 27, 77-79, 158, n.102; and Gaza Strip, 30, 53, 122, 125, 183, n.196; and Hamas, 122, 132; and Intifada II, 23, 24-25, 38, 67, 72-73, 90, 121, 125; and Israel, 4, 11, 13, 20, 23-26, 32-34, 37-40, 42-43, 46, 49, 51-54, 57, 60, 65, 68-71, 76, 82, 84-85, 103-109, 116, 118, 120-123, 125-127, 129-130, 132, 134, 155, n.18, 156, n.41; and Jerusalem, 51-54, 106, 116-117, 121; and Jordan, 28-29, 37-38, 60-61, 73, 92-93, 125; and Kissinger, 8-9, 13-15, 18, 40, 73-77, 85; and Lebanon, 24; and Madrid Conference, 17, 26, 54, 71; and Nixon, 40, 50, 85; and Occupied Territories, 5, 34, 60, 63, 72, 130-131; and *Oslo*, 34, 46, 54, 66, 71-72, 88, 89, 106, 129, 156, n.47; and Palestinian Authority, 34, 66, 72, 88, 105-107, 122, 126, 128, 135; and PLO, 34, 48, 69, 71-72, 87; and Quartet, 4, 13-14, 103, 104-105, 121-122, 125, 128, 130, 177, n.149, 179, n.165; and Rabin, 33, 38, 49, 65, 84; and Reagan, 14, 27, 41, 50, 81-82, 87; and refugees, 48-51, 116, 152, n.85; and *Road Map*, 1-4, 13, 34-35, 37, 103-109, 116, 121-123, 125-130, 132-133; and Russia, 3, 5, 7-9, 69, 100-103, 112-117; and separation barrier, 106, 116-117, 121, 180, n.175, 183, n.196; and settlements, 46, 54, 67, 71, 73, 85, 103, 106, 116-117, 121; and Sharon, 83, 106-108, 116, 118-120, 122, 123, 127, 134, 183, n.194; strategy of, 20, 39-40, 46, 60, 88, 107, 116, 121-123, 125-126, 129; and terror,

11, 21-32, 57, 60, 62-66, 68-71, 74-80, 82-89, 97, 102-104, 107, 109-110, 119-122, 123, 124, 158, n.100, 187, n.226; and unilateral actions, 106, 122; and United Nations, 5-6, 8, 10-11, 13, 15, 42, 68, 95, 100, 102, 113, 115-116; and United States, 5-6, 13-14, 25, 34, 41-42, 50, 65, 72-74, 76-77, 82, 85, 104-105, 107, 116, 188, n.241, 189, n.10; and West Bank, 30, 33-34, 46, 53, 72, 116, 125, 180, n.175

Patten, Christopher, 92, 94, 95-96, 99, 104, 111, 161, n.14, 162, n.15, 163, n.31, 163, n.36, 174, n.134

PDF. *See* Popular Democratic Front

PDFLP. *See* Popular Democratic Front for the Liberation of Palestine

Peled, Mattityahu, 155, n.18

People's Republic of China, 75, 93, 139, n.59

Peres, Shimon, 51-52, 150, n.65

Persian Gulf War (1991), 20, 26, 65, 86

PFLP. *See* Popular Front for the Liberation of Palestine

PFLP-GC. *See* Popular Front for the Liberation of Palestine— General Command

PLO. *See* Palestine Liberation Organization

Popular Democratic Front, 25, 60

Popular Democratic Front for the Liberation of Palestine, 19, 22, 32, 39-40, 48, 64

Popular Front for the Liberation of Palestine: and Arafat, 29, 64; and Israel, 21, 30, 60, 85; and Palestinian state, 40; and PLO, 28-29, 30, 40; and refugees, 48; and Rejection Front, 33, 145, n.106; and Sadat, 19; and Steadfastness and Confrontation Front, 19, 32; strategy of, 21, 25, 28-29, 85; and terror, 21-22, 25, 28-30, 60, 73, 85; and Unified Command of Palestine Resistance, 28-29; and United States, 21, 73; and Zionism, 19, 21

Popular Front for the Liberation of Palestine— General Command, 19, 22, 25, 29, 32, 33, 40, 48, 60, 145, n.106

Powell, Colin, 111, 162, n.24, 173, n.122

Prodi, Romano, 94-95, 96, 104, 160-161, n.1

Putin, Vladimir, 7, 10, 93, 94, 115, 168, n.85, 176, n.144

Qadhafi, Muammar, 81-82

al-Qaeda, 90, 91, 93, 124

Quartet: disagreements among members, 3-4, 6-8, 13, 91, 93-94, 97, 99, 104, 116, 128, 130, 132-133; and European Union, 3-4, 7, 13-14, 97-99, 101, 111-112, 115, 128, 133, 168, n.85; and Gaza Strip, 179, n.165; and Intifada II, 103-104; and Iraq, 103; and Israel, 3-4, 13-14, 93, 101, 103, 104, 107, 125, 128, 130, 179, n.165; mentioned, 102; and Palestinian Authority, 105, 114, 128, 130, 179, n.165; and Palestinians, 4, 13-14, 103, 104-105, 121-122, 125, 128, 130, 177, n.149, 179, n.165; perceptions of, 34-35; performance of, 128, 135; and *Road Map*, 1, 3-4, 9, 13-14, 34-35, 91, 99-100, 103, 104, 115-116, 119, 130; and Russia, 1, 3-4, 7, 13-14, 97-99, 101, 112, 128; and separation barrier, 104; and terrorism, 109, 119; and United Nations, 3, 7, 13-14, 97-99, 113-114, 128, 133; and United States, 3, 6-7, 13-14, 16, 93-94, 96-99, 109, 128, 135

Quneitra, 68

Quray, Ahmad, 116-117, 121, 168, n.85, 169, n.97

Rabat Summit, 7, 61, 84, 144, n.94

Rabin, Yitzhak: and Arab-Israeli conflict, 32-33, 49; and Arabs, 61, 64; and Arafat, 61-62, 82, 87, 88; assassination of, 32, 66, 72, 88; and Egypt, 61; and fedayeen, 62; and Gaza Strip, 26, 45, 88; and Hamas, 65-66; and Intifada I, 24-25, 26, 64, 143, n.73; and Iran, 64; and Israel, 45, 52, 65, 87-88; and Jerusalem, 45, 52, 153, n.110, 153, n.111; and Jordan, 61-62; and *Oslo Accords*, 26, 38, 45, 65, 82, 86-88; and Palestinian Authority, 65-66,

87-88; and Palestinians, 33, 38, 49, 65, 84; and peace process, 24-25, 26, 32-33, 65; and PLO, 26, 65-66, 87, 88, 141, n.43; and refugees, 49; and settlements, 45; strategy of, 38, 43, 49, 65-66, 84, 87, 141, n.43, 143, n.84, 156, n.44; and terror, 24-25, 61, 64, 65, 66, 84, 86, 87-88; and United Nations, 61

Ramallah, 97, 160, n.145

Reagan Plan, 41, 50, 144, n.98, 148, n.30, 152, n.89

Reagan, Ronald: and Arabs, 14, 47; and Arafat, 87; and Gaza Strip, 41, 44, 47; and Iran, 85; and Israel, 17, 27-28, 41, 44, 47, 50, 81-82; and Jerusalem, 17, 55; and Jordan, 41, 44; and Libya, 81, 85; and Palestinians, 14, 27, 41, 50, 81-82, 87; and PLO, 26-28, 38, 64, 81-82, 85-86, 87; and refugees, 17, 50, 152, n.96; and Russia, 14, 85; and settlements, 47; strategy of, 14, 16, 17, 26-28, 41, 47, 140, n.8; and Syria, 85; and terror, 80-82, 85-87, 160, n.134; and United Nations Security Council Resolution 242, 44; and West Bank, 41, 44, 47

"Reassessment" (1975), 192, n.41

Refugees: and Abbas, 117, 121; and Bush (George H.W.), 50; and Bush (George W.), 95, 102, 118-119; and Camp David *Frameworks*, 48, 50; and Carter, 41, 50; and Clinton, 17, 50-51; and Europeans, 5-6, 117; and Israel, 5-6, 49-51, 62, 84, 109, 118-119, 125-126, 152, n.89; and *Oslo Accords*, 50; and Palestinian Authority, 49-50, 117, 130-131; and Palestinians, 34, 48-51, 116, 152, n.85; perspective of, 125; and PLO, 48; and Reagan, 17, 50, 152, n.96; and *Road* Map, 2-3, 5, 37, 91, 116, 131-132; and Russia, 5-6, 112; and Sharon, 83, 116, 127; and United Nations, 5-6, 48, 103; and United States, 6, 50-51

Rejection Front, 29-30, 33, 145, n.106, 146, n.133

Rice, Condoleezza, 94, 110, 162, n.21, 173, n.122

Road Map: and Abbas, 104, 105, 106, 121, 122-123, 127, 169, n.93; and Annan, 100, 101, 103, 114-118, 164, n.47; and Arafat, 16, 105, 121, 122, 134-135, 189-190, n.15; and Bush (George W.), 4, 9, 16, 98, 99-102, 104, 110-111, 118, 124, 135, 173, n.122; and Egypt, 99-100; and European Union, 1, 3, 5, 7, 9, 13-14, 91, 99, 103, 104, 111-115, 129-130, 133; failure of, 1, 12, 91, 128, 131-133, 136; and final borders, 2-3, 5, 37, 132; and final status issues, 91, 126, 131, 132-133; and Hamas, 127, 132, 190, n.16; implementation of, 1, 3, 4, 6, 7, 9, 21, 105, 107, 112, 116, 119, 121, 128-130; and Intifada II, 91, 99-100, 121, 125; and Iraq, 98, 103-104; and Israel, 1-5, 10, 12, 13-14, 16, 32, 34-35, 37, 98, 100, 103-105, 107-111, 115-116, 118, 120, 125-133, 135, 190-191, n.21; and Jerusalem, 2-3, 5, 37, 91, 116, 132; and Jordan, 99-100; and Kissinger, 13-14; and Lebanon, 2, 10, 100, 115; mentioned, 28-29, 57; objectives of, 1-5, 8, 9, 34-35, 37, 100, 103-104, 111, 116, 119, 125-127, 129-132, 136; and Palestinian Authority, 1-2, 12, 21, 34, 91, 99-100, 104-108, 121-123, 126, 128-130, 135, 168, n.90; and Palestinians, 1-4, 13, 34, 37, 103-109, 116, 121-123, 125-130, 132-133; and Phase I, 1-2, 3, 9, 98, 99-102, 106, 108-111, 113, 127, 129-130; and Phase II, 2, 100, 108-109, 127, 130; and Phase III, 2, 3, 100, 109, 127, 130; and process, 3, 6, 9, 13, 21, 32, 91, 98, 99, 104, 108, 110, 119, 126, 129, 131; and al-Qaeda, 91; and Quartet, 1, 3-4, 9, 13-14, 34-35, 91, 99-100, 103, 104, 115-116, 119, 130; and refugees, 2-3, 5, 37, 91, 116, 131-132; release of, 1, 16, 91, 98, 99, 104, 111; and Russia, 1, 3, 7, 9, 13-14, 21, 91, 103, 107, 111-115, 129-130, 133, 164, n.47, 174-175, n.137; and security, 5; and settlements, 2-3, 5, 37, 44, 91, 99-102, 109, 111, 116-117, 132; and Sharon, 67, 107-109, 119-121, 127-130, 132-133, 169-170, n.99, 172, n.113; and substance, 3, 91, 132; and Syria, 2, 10, 100, 115, 129-130; and terrorism, 1, 3, 4, 8, 91, 108-111, 119, 120, 129; and United Nations, 1, 3, 7, 9, 13-14, 21, 91, 103, 107, 111, 113-116, 129-130, 133; and United Nations Security Council Resolution 242, 2-3, 5-6, 37, 131; and United States, 1, 3, 8, 13-14, 16, 21, 91, 101, 103, 104-105, 107, 110, 119-120, 126, 128-129, 131-133, 135-136, 173, n.122

Rogers Plan, 43

Rogers, William, 50, 73-74, 75, 152, n.92, 158, n.86

Rome airport attack, 60, 80

Russia: and Abbas, 135; and Arab-Israeli conflict, 7, 113; and Arabs, 7, 9, 14, 113, 117; and Arafat, 94, 95, 102, 168, n.85; and Bush (George W.), 5, 9, 93, 95, 98-99, 123-124; and Egypt, 10, 23-24, 73, 112; and European Union, 21, 91, 94-95, 97, 101, 103, 112; and final status issues, 94-95, 102-103, 113, 114; and Gaza Strip, 97, 112-113; international position of, 7, 10, 20, 65, 93; and Iraq, 103; and Israel, 3, 5, 9-10, 13, 21, 23-24, 38, 62, 65, 91, 95, 97, 100-104, 112-116, 124, 129-130; and Israeli-Palestinian conflict, 4-5, 91, 95, 97, 103, 104, 112, 129-130, 174-175, n.137; and Jerusalem, 112, 117; and Jordan, 112; and Kissinger, 6, 9, 13-16, 18, 75, 77, 78; and Lebanon, 112, 115; and Middle East, 7, 10, 94, 97, 101, 103, 112-113, 115, 139, n.48; and Nixon, 9, 10, 17; and Occupied Territories, 5-6, 9, 103, 112-113; and Palestinian Authority, 21, 94-95, 102-103, 112-114, 130; and Palestinians, 3, 5, 7-9, 69, 100-103, 112-117; and PLO, 7, 21-22, 62, 145, n.123; and Putin, 7, 10, 93, 115; and Quartet, 1, 3-4, 7, 13-14, 97-99, 101, 112, 128; and Reagan, 14, 85; and refugees, 5-6, 112; and *Road Map*, 1, 3, 7, 9, 13-14, 21, 91, 103, 107, 111-115, 129-130, 133, 164, n.47, 174-175, n.137; and separation barrier, 114, 117; and settlements, 5, 100, 103, 113-114; and Sharon, 5, 24, 107; strategy of, 7, 9-10, 24, 94-95, 97, 100, 101, 103, 111-115, 117, 129-130, 139, n.48; and Syria, 20, 112, 115; and terror, 21, 79, 85, 94-95, 102, 112-114, 124; and unilateral actions, 103, 113-114; and United Nations, 21, 91, 112; and United Nations General Assembly, 5, 130; and United Nations Security Council, 5, 7, 107, 112, 113, 130; and United Nations Security Council Resolution 242, 5-6, 103; and United States, 6-7, 9-10, 13-16, 18, 21, 73, 91, 93, 94-95, 98, 100, 102, 107, 112, 115-116, 128, 139, n.48; and West Bank, 97, 114, 124

Sadat, Anwar, 14, 18-20, 22, 32, 69, 139, n.48

Sa'iqa, 19, 25, 28-29, 32, 39-40, 48, 60

Saltanov, Aleksandr, 112

Samaria, 37-38, 43, 45-46, 52, 62, 88, 107, 118, 150, n.61

Sanchez, Ilich Ramirez. *See* "Carlos the Jackal"

Sartawi, Issam, 155, n.18

Satterfield, David, 94

Saudi Arabia, 93, 130-131, 165, n.55

Saunders, Harold, 18, 144, n.94, 158, n.100

Schroder, Gerhard, 94, 111

Scranton, William, 47, 54-55, 151, n.71

SEATO, 75

Security fence. *See* separation barrier

Separation barrier: and Abbas, 106, 116, 121; and Annan, 117, 182, n.189; and Bush (George W.), 110, 119, 135, 184, n.201; and European Union, 114, 117; and Intifada II, 121; and Israel, 104, 106, 110, 114, 116-119, 122, 128, 135; and Palestinians, 106, 116-117, 121, 180, n.175, 183, n.196; and Quartet, 103-104; and Russia, 114, 117; and Sharon, 119, 134, 184, n.201; and United Nations, 114-115, 118; and United States, 110; and West Bank, 110, 117-118, 128, 134, 180, n.175, 182, n.189

September 11, 2001, 1, 11, 67, 83, 90, 92, 123, 124, 135
Settlements: and Abbas, 106, 116, 121, 127; and Annan, 117; and Arafat, 46, 63, 68-69, 88; and Barak, 45-46, 125-126; and Bush (George H.W.), 47; and Bush (George W.), 94-95, 101-102, 109-111, 118-119, 135; and Carter, 47; and Clinton, 42, 47-48; and Europeans, 5-6, 95-96, 100, 103, 113-114, 117; and Ford, 47, 78; and Gaza Strip, 6, 44-45; and Intifada II, 121; and Israel, 6, 44-48, 55, 62, 73, 88, 103, 107, 109, 113-114, 116-119, 132, 171, n.111; and Jerusalem, 52, 54, 55, 116, 118; and *Oslo Accords*, 46; and Palestinian Authority, 88; and Palestinians, 46, 54, 67, 71, 73, 85, 103, 106, 116-117, 121; and Rabin, 45; and Reagan, 47; and *Road Map*, 2-3, 37, 44, 91, 99-102, 109, 111, 116-117, 132; and Russia, 5, 100, 103, 113-114; and Shamir, 45; and Sharon, 45, 46, 107, 116, 118-119, 134, 183, n.196; and United Nations, 5-6, 100, 103, 114-115, 117-118; and United States, 3, 6, 46-47, 55, 110,151, n.71; and West Bank, 6, 44, 46-47, 95-96, 106, 110, 114, 116-119, 132, 182-183, n.191
Seville Declaration, 181, n.183
Shamir, Yitzhak, 20, 25, 28, 38, 43, 45, 51-52, 64-65, 84, 144, n.102, 147, n.9, 150, n.61
al-Shara, Faruk, 20
Sharansky, Natan, 163, n.34
Sharm el-Sheikh, 42
Sharon, Ariel: and Abbas, 108, 120-121, 122, 134, 135; and Arabs, 24; and Arafat, 9, 26, 28, 67, 89, 90, 120-121, 144, n.88, 160, n.145, 166, n.67, 170-171, n.105; and Barak, 33, 39, 89; and borders, 116; and Bush (George W.), 4, 9, 28, 83, 90, 95, 97, 102, 110, 111, 118-120, 123-124, 135, 169-170, n.99, 184, n.201; and Camp David *Frameworks*, 24; and Europeans, 5, 96, 102, 166, n.67; and Gaza, 9, 45, 89, 107-109, 118, 120, 123, 134, 182, n.190; and Intifada II, 23, 89, 127, 144, n.88;

and Israel, 9, 24, 33, 89, 102, 107-109, 118, 120-121, 127, 134, 169-170, n.99; and Jerusalem, 116, 118; and Kadima party, 134; and Likud, 38-39, 46, 89, 109, 120, 124, 128; mentioned, 92-93; and Occupied Territories, 33, 83; and *Oslo Accords*, 33, 89; and Palestinian Authority, 23, 26, 33, 39, 67, 83, 89, 107-109, 120-121, 134; and Palestinians, 83, 106-108, 116, 118-120, 122, 123, 127, 134, 183, n.194; and PLO, 24, 63, 89; and Quartet, 130; and refugees, 83, 116, 127; and *Road Map*, 67, 107-109, 119-121, 127-130, 132-133, 169-170, n.99, 172, n.113; and Russia, 5, 24, 107; and separation barrier, 119, 134, 184, n.201; and September 11, 67; and settlements, 45-46, 107, 116, 118-119, 134, 183, n.196; and stroke, 134; and terrorism, 9, 24, 28, 67, 83, 89-90, 107-109, 119-121, 133, 144, n.88, 171, n.108; and unilateral actions, 107-108, 109, 119-120, 132, 134, 170-171, n.105, 185, n.214; and United Nations, 5, 107; and United States, 67, 107, 110, 120, 124, 127-128, 134; and West Bank, 9, 89, 97, 116, 118, 182, n.190
Sha'th, Nabil, 117
Shevardnadze, Eduard, 7-8
Shirabi, Hisham, 21
Shultz, George P., 6, 27-28, 41, 44, 47, 57, 80-82, 159, n.111, 159, n.114, 160, n.134
Shultz Plan, 144, n.98
Sinai Peninsula, 18-19, 22, 68
Sinai II, 14, 16
Sisco, Joseph, 50, 74
Six Day War, 6, 10, 21, 23, 39-40, 43-44, 48, 50, 54, 61, 68-69, 73, 84-85, 149, n.37
Solana, Javier, 117, 166, n.67
de Soto, Alvaro, 114, 115
Soviet Union. *See* Russia
State Department, 75, 79-80, 98
Steadfastness and Confrontation Front, 19-20, 32
Step-by-step diplomacy, 8-10, 13, 18-20, 75-76, 77-79, 85, 94, 100, 129,

149, n.47. *See also* incremental negotiations; Kissinger
Suicide attacks, 11, 23, 28, 67, 83, 89, 97, 104, 124. *See also* terrorism
Syria; and Annan, 100; and Asad, 19-20; and Bush (George W.), 97; and Clinton, 20; and Geneva Conference, 9; and Israel, 2, 10, 14, 16, 19-20, 22, 32-33, 42, 61, 65, 75-76, 97, 100, 115, 130, 142, n.66, 156, n.41; and Kissinger, 18, 20-21, 75-76; and Nixon, 75; and Palestinians, 19-20; and Reagan, 85; and *Road Map*, 2, 10, 100, 115, 129-130; and Russia, 112, 115; and Sadat, 19; strategy of, 20-21; and terror, 85; and United States, 20-21

Taliban, 83
Terrorism: and Abbas, 108, 121, 124, 127, 133-135; and Annan, 117; and Arabs, 30, 61, 74; and Arafat, 22-23, 28-32, 34, 53, 64, 66-71, 76, 78, 82, 85, 86-90, 94-95, 101, 121-122, 124, 133-135, 142, n.57, 144, n.88, 145, n.112, 160, n.134, 170, n.103; and Barak, 66, 87-88, 156, n.41; and Begin, 24, 63, 84; and Bush (George H.W.), 87; and Bush (George W.), 1, 4-5, 9, 28, 67, 83, 90-91, 95, 98, 100-102, 104, 109-111, 123-124, 133, 135, 165, n.59, 165, n.60, 165, n.62, 172, n.116; and Carter, 77; and Clinton, 82-83, 88, 89, 90; and Europeans, 21, 92, 94-97, 102, 113-114, 124, 174, n.134; and Fatah, 21-22, 25, 29, 31-32, 60; and fedayeen, 21-22, 30, 60, 74-78; and Ford, 26-27, 77-79, 160, n.133; and Hamas, 31, 64-66, 85-86, 110-111, 127; impact of, 11-12, 13, 21-22, 25, 32, 57-61, 63, 67, 69, 74, 77-79, 83-90, 133-134; and Intifada I, 63, 64, 69-70, 87; and Intifada II, 24-25, 31, 88-90, 121; and Iran, 85; and Israel, 4, 9, 11, 21-28, 30-31, 57, 60-66, 68-72, 76, 79, 83-88, 91-92, 107-111, 119-122, 124, 129, 142, n.66, 155, n.18, 158, n.100, 170, n.103, 171, n.110; and Jordan, 20, 29; and Kissinger, 26-27, 75, 77-78, 85, 142, n.66; and Lebanon, 24, 68, 69; and Libya, 85; and Netanyahu, 66, 87-88; and Nixon, 26-27, 73-76, 85; and Olmert, 121, 171-172, n.112; and Palestinian Authority, 21, 23, 66, 72, 82, 83, 89-91, 94-95, 100-101, 109, 111, 113-114, 120-121, 129, 134-135, 171-172, n.112; and Palestinians, 11, 21-32, 57, 60, 62-66, 68-72, 74-80, 82-89, 97, 102-104, 107, 109-110, 119-122, 124, 156, n.41, 158, n.100, 162, n.24, 187, n.226; and PFLP, 21-22, 25, 28-30, 60, 73, 85; and al-Qaeda, 91, 124; and Quartet, 102, 109, 119; and Rabin, 24-25, 61, 64-66, 84, 86-88; and Reagan, 80-82, 85-87, 160, n.134; and *Road Map*, 1, 3, 4, 8, 91, 108-109, 111, 119, 120, 129; and Russia, 21, 79, 85, 94-95, 102, 112-114, 124; and September 11 (2001), 92, 123, 124; and Shamir, 25, 37-38, 64-65; and Sharon, 9, 24, 28, 67, 83, 89, 90, 107-109, 119-121, 124, 133, 144, n.88, 171, n.108; and Syria, 85; and United Nations, 21, 94, 97, 102, 114, 117-118, 124; and United States, 4, 8, 21, 25, 61, 64-65, 68-69, 72-85, 87, 88-90, 91, 96, 123, 124, 128, 129, 134, 158, n.81, 158, n.100, 162, n.24
Terrorism Special Action Group, 79
Third party diplomacy, 1, 13, 17, 21. *See also* mediation
Third World, 13-14, 15, 139, n.59
Tunisia, 92
TWA hijackings, 63, 80-81, 85

Uganda, 22, 60, 145, n.108. *See also* Entebbe hijacking
Unified Command of Palestine Resistance, 28-29, 32
Unified National Command of the Intifada, 24, 48, 53, 70
Unilateral actions: and Clinton, 50, 55; European Union, 103, 113-114, 178, n.158; and Israel, 103, 104, 106, 107, 110, 128, 135, 170, n.102, 178, n.158; and Palestinians, 106, 122; and Russia, 103, 113-114; and Sharon, 107-108, 109, 119-120, 132, 134, 170-171, n.105, 185, n.214; and United Nations, 113-115; and

238   Index

United States, 41, 47, 54-55, 104,
    110, 151, n.71, 170, n.102
United Kingdom, 92-93, 168,
    n.85
United Nations: and Abbas, 135; and
    Arab-Israeli conflict, 7, 10-11; and
    Arabs, 11; and Arafat, 40, 49, 68;
    and Bush (George W.), 5, 9, 11, 83,
    92, 93, 95, 98-99, 123-124; and
    Europeans, 5, 8, 10, 13, 21, 116; and
    final status issues, 94-95, 102-103,
    113-115; and Gaza Strip, 97, 115;
    and Iran, 93; and Iraq, 92, 93, 103;
    and Israel, 3, 5-7, 9, 13, 21, 91, 95,
    97, 100, 101, 104, 114-118, 124,
    129-131, 177, n.148; and Israeli-
    Palestinian conflict, 4-5, 91-92, 97,
    130; and Jerusalem, 103; and
    Kissinger, 13, 15; and Middle East,
    7, 8, 10-11, 97, 114; and Nixon, 15;
    and North Korea, 93; and Occupied
    Territories, 5-6, 9; and Palestinian
    Authority, 21, 94, 102-103, 113-
    115, 130; and Palestinians, 5-6, 8,
    13, 42, 68, 95, 100, 102, 113, 114,
    116, 152, n.85; and PLO, 8, 11, 21-
    22, 48, 61, 143, n.77, 145, n.123,
    158, n.97; and Quartet, 3, 7, 13-14,
    97-99, 113-114, 128, 133; and
    Rabin, 61; and refugees, 5-6, 48,
    103; and *Road Map*, 1, 3, 7, 9, 13-
    14, 21, 91, 103, 107, 111, 113-116,
    129-130, 133; and Russia, 21, 91,
    112; and separation barrier, 114-
    115, 118; and settlements, 5-6, 100,
    103, 114-115, 117-118; and Sharon,
    5, 107; strategy of, 9, 10-11, 13, 94,
    111, 113-116; and terror, 21, 94, 97,
    102, 114, 117-118, 124; and
    unilateral actions, 113-115; and
    United Nations Resolutions, 5-6, 31,
    40, 48, 49, 115, 130, 152, n.85; and
    United States, 5-7, 9, 13, 15, 21, 80,
    91, 92, 94-95, 98, 100, 113, 115-
    116, 128, 131, 138, n.26; and West
    Bank, 117-118, 182, n.189. *See also*
    Annan; United Nations General
    Assembly; United Nations General
    Assembly Resolution 179; United
    Nations General Assembly
    Resolution 194; United Nations
    Security Council; United Nations

Security Council Resolution 242;
    United Nations Security Council
    Resolution 338
United Nations General Assembly: and
    Arafat, 8, 22, 25, 30-32, 34, 48, 64,
    68, 71, 85, 86, 157, n.52; and
    Committee on the Exercise of the
    Inalienable Rights of the Palestinian
    People, 8, 11; and Europeans, 5,
    130; and Israel, 131, 179, n.165; and
    Kissinger, 13-14, 15; and Nixon, 74;
    and Palestinian Authority, 103, 130;
    and Palestinians, 8, 10-11, 15; and
    PLO, 8, 10-11, 21-22, 61, 143, n.77,
    145, n.123, 158, n.97; and Rabat
    Summit, 61; and Rabin, 61;
    resolutions of, 5, 103, 130, 179,
    n.165; and Russia, 5, 130; and
    Shamir, 25; and Third World, 13;
    and United Nations, 5, 130; and
    United States, 131
United Nations General Assembly
    Resolution 181, 40
United Nations General Assembly
    Resolution 194, 5-6, 48-51, 116,
    117, 119, 131, 152, n.85
United Nations Relief and Works
    Agency, 152, n.92
United Nations Security Council; and
    Bush (George W.), 97; and
    European Union, 5, 96, 130; and
    Iraq, 139, n.59; and Israel, 107, 113,
    131; and Palestinian Authority, 103,
    130; resolutions of, 2-3, 5, 103, 130;
    and *Road Map*, 2-3, 107, 113; and
    Russia, 5, 7, 107, 112, 113, 130; and
    United Nations, 5, 8, 103, 130; and
    United States, 15, 17, 47, 54-55, 77-
    78, 107, 131, 139, n.59
United Nations Security Council
    Resolution 242: and Arafat, 28, 34,
    66; and Bush (George W.), 94, 102;
    and European Union, 5-6, 103;
    failure of, 34; and Israel, 6, 17, 42,
    131; and Middle East, 34-35, 137,
    n.18; and Palestinian Authority,
    130-131; and Palestinians, 48, 189,
    n.10; and PLO, 27, 48; and *Road
    Map*, 2-3, 5-6, 37, 131; and Russia,
    5-6, 103; and United Nations, 5-6, 8;
    and United States, 6, 17, 27, 43, 44,
    75, 77-78, 146, n.131, 189, n.10

United Nations Security Council
Resolution 338, 2-3, 8, 17, 27,
34, 44, 66, 77-78, 94, 102-103, 131
United Nations Security Council
Resolution 1397, 2, 3, 103
United States: and Abbas, 105, 124,
135; and Arab-Israeli conflict, 18,
73-74; and Arabs, 4, 73, 74, 92-93,
131, 188, n.241; and Arafat, 28, 34,
68, 82, 86-87, 102; and Bush
(George H.W.), 17, 28, 65; and
Bush (George W.), 9, 87, 93, 96-99,
109, 124; and Clinton, 17, 20, 51,
89; and Egypt, 63, 73, 93, 131; and
Europeans, 6, 7, 9-10, 13, 15-16, 21,
91-95, 98, 100, 111-112, 115-116,
128; and fedayeen, 74-78, 142, n.66;
and final border, 43-44; and Gaza
Strip, 110, 135; and Intifada I, 4, 41,
64, 87; and Intifada II, 42, 83, 88-
90; and Iraq, 1, 16, 92, 93, 96-98,
103, 119, 128, 139, n.59; and Israel,
3-6, 10-11, 13, 14, 16-18, 20-21, 27-
28, 41-43, 46-47, 50, 51, 55, 61, 63-
65, 72-74, 76, 78, 84-85, 96, 105,
107, 113, 119, 126-133, 135, 140,
n.20, 144, n.95, 173, n.122; and
Israeli-Palestinian conflict, 4, 6, 12,
91-92, 96, 119, 129, 131; and
Jerusalem, 6, 47, 54-55; and Jordan,
41-42, 144, n.94; and Kissinger, 9,
13, 16-18, 26-27, 73, 75, 85, 129,
151, n.71; and Lebanon, 80, 97; and
Libya, 81; and Middle East, 6, 47,
55, 65, 74, 77, 82, 96-97, 102-103,
131, 138, n.26, 139, n.48; and
Nixon, 26-27, 85; and Occupied
Territories, 5-6, 46-47, 55; and
Palestinian Authority, 21, 104-105,
109-110, 126; and Palestinians, 5, 6,
13-14, 16, 21, 25, 34, 40, 42, 50, 65,
72-74, 76-77, 82, 85, 104-105, 107,
116, 139, n.48, 188, n.241; and
PLO, 26-28, 49, 64-65, 76-78, 82,
86-87, 144, n.94, 144, n.102; and
Quartet, 3, 7, 13-14, 16, 96-99, 109,
128, 135; and Reagan, 26-27, 47,
81; and refugees, 6, 50-51; and
Road Map, 1, 3, 8, 13-14, 16, 21,
91, 101, 103-105, 107, 110, 119-
120, 126, 128-129, 131-133, 135-
136, 173, n.122; and Russia, 6, 7, 9-
10, 13-16, 18, 21, 73, 91, 93, 94-95,
98, 100, 102, 107, 112, 115-116,
128, 139, n.48; and separation
barrier, 110; and settlements, 3, 6,
46-47, 55, 110, 151, n.71; and
Sharon, 67, 107, 110, 120, 124, 127-
128, 134; strategy of, 6, 10, 13, 17,
25, 44, 65, 98, 109-110, 115, 129-
130, 135; and Syria, 20-21; and
terror, 4, 8, 21, 25, 61, 68-69, 72-85,
87, 88-90, 91, 96, 123, 124, 128-
129, 134, 158, n.81, 162, n.24; and
unilateral actions, 41, 47, 54-55,
104, 110, 151, n.71, 170, n.102; and
United Nations, 5-7, 9, 13-14, 21,
80, 91, 92, 94-95, 98, 100, 113, 115-
116, 128, 131, 138, n.26; and United
Nations Security Council, 15, 17,
47, 55, 78, 107, 131, 139, n.59; and
United Nations Security Council
Resolution 242, 6, 17, 27, 43, 44,
75, 77, 146, n.131, 189, n.10; and
West Bank, 41, 46, 110
United States, House of
Representatives, Committee on
International Relations, 77
United States, Senate, Foreign
Relations Committee, 16
United States, Senate, Judiciary
Committee, 77
UNRWA. *See* United Nations Relief
and Works Agency
Urayqat, Sa'ib, 105-107, 116, 121-123,
180, n.175
USSR. *See* Russia

Venice Declaration, 8, 15
Vidovin, Andre, 104
Vienna attack, 80
Vietnamese, 29
"Vietnam Syndrome", 81
Vietnam War, 75

Wall (Israeli). *See* separation barrier
Walters, Vernon, 76, 152, n.95
Weinberger, Caspar, 81, 159, n.111
Weissglas, Dov, 108, 109, 120
West Bank: and Annan, 117; and
Arafat, 46, 66, 116; and Barak, 52,
126; and Bush (George H.W.), 41-
42, 47; and Bush (George W.), 9,
97, 118-119, 123-124; and Camp

David *Frameworks*, 27, 41; and
Camp David negotiations (2000),
66; and Carter, 19; and Clinton, 17,
42, 44, 48; and Europeans, 96, 97,
114, 117, 124; and Fatah, 29-30; and
Interim Agreement, 20, 71, 88; and
Israel, 5-6, 17, 32-33, 34, 37-38, 44-
46, 66, 95-97, 106-107, 110, 116-
117, 124-128, 132; and Kissinger,
40-41; and *Oslo Accords*, 32-33, 46;
and Palestinian Authority, 106, 116;
and Palestinians, 30, 33-34, 46, 53,
72, 116, 125, 180, n.175; and PLO,
34; and Reagan, 41, 44, 47; and
refugees, 125; and Russia, 97, 114,
124; and separation barrier, 110,
117-118, 128, 134, 180, n.175, 182,
n.189; and settlements, 6, 44, 46-47,
95-96, 106, 110, 114, 116-119, 132,
182-183, n.191; and Sharon, 9, 89,
97, 116, 118, 182, n.190; and United
Nations, 117-118, 182, n.189; and
United States, 41, 46, 110
West Berlin attack, 80
Western Europe, 21-22, 69, 145, n.123
Western Wall, 17, 55
Wicker, Tom, 76-77
World Bank, 164, n.42
World Health Organization, 21-22,
145, n.123
Wye River Memorandum, 15, 20, 23,
72, 146-147, n.145

Yakovenko, Alexander, 115
Yassin, Ahmed, 190, n.16
Yediot Ahronot, 107-108
Yemen, 19, 92
Yom Kippur War, 7, 8, 9, 11, 14, 22-
24, 29, 39, 61, 75, 84, 98
Yost, Charles W., 54

Zionism, 19, 21, 30, 39, 45, 53, 60, 63,
68-70, 84-85, 127, 147, n.13, 157,
n.52

About the Author

Derick L. Hulme, Jr. is Professor of Political Science at Alma College in Alma, Michigan. He is the author of *The Political Olympics: Moscow, Afghanistan, and the 1980 U.S. Boycott* (Praeger, 1990) and *Palestinian Terrorism and U.S. Foreign Policy, 1969-1977: Dynamics of Response* (Edwin Mellen Press, 2004).